15 22/2

FREUD IN GERMANY

FREUD IN GERMANY

REVOLUTION AND REACTION
IN SCIENCE, 1893-1907

HANNAH S. DECKER

Psychological Issues
Monograph 41

INTERNATIONAL UNIVERSITIES PRESS, INC.
New York

Library of Congress Cataloging in Publication Data

Decker, Hannah S
    Freud in Germany.

    (Psychological Issues : Monograph ; 41)
    Bibliography: p.
    Includes index.
    1. Psychoanalysis — Germany — History. 2. Freud,
Sigmund, 1856-1939. I. Title. II. Series.
RC503.D4   150'.19'52   77-20062
ISBN 0-8236-2023-9
ISBN 0-8236-2022-0 pbk.

Manufactured in the United States of America

To Norman

CONTENTS

ILLUSTRATIONS

ACKNOWLEDGMENTS

Now that I have completed my first book, I have come to understand the pleasure an author derives from recording what may appear to others to be platitudes of acknowledgment. In actuality, these sentiments are expressions of the author's unique odyssey and, therefore, symbols which matter very much. It is in this special mood of discovery that I would like first to thank my teachers and friends: Fritz Stern for his unparalleled insight, guidance, and instruction; Eric T. Carlson for his unique knowledge and unfailing encouragement; Marc Raeff for the wide-ranging suggestions that have enhanced this book throughout. Sadly, I cannot thank the late Lionel Trilling. But I can record my debt and my remembrance.

I am glad, however, to have the opportunity to tender public thanks to various people for whose advice or help I remain grateful: Hans Kleinschmidt, David Joravsky, Jeffry Adelman, Karl Webb, Loren Graham, William McGuire, and the members of the Section on the History of Psychiatry and the Behavioral Sciences of the Department of Psychiatry, Cornell University Medical College. I cannot mention all the members by name, but I thank everyone, particularly Oskar Diethelm.

Librarians and libraries deserve a separate mention, especially Erich Meyerhoff of the Cornell University Medical Library and his staff, and Mary Andresen of the Payne-Whitney Psychiatric Library. I wish also to acknowledge the aid of numerous persons at the following institutions: Columbia University Library, the New York Academy of Medicine Library, the A. A. Brill Library of the New York Psychoanalytic Institute, the New York Public Library, and the Jesse H. Jones Library of the Texas Medical Center in Houston.

Many persons kindly consented to be interviewed or wrote me informative letters. Their names are listed at the end of this volume, and I wish to thank them once again.

I received generous financial support for this study from the Josiah Macy, Jr. Foundation in the form of a three-year fellowship. This aid was truly invaluable. The University of Houston awarded me a summer research grant which enabled me to put this book into its final form, and for that I am most grateful. Dean John Guilds deserves special thanks for providing funds for typing.

The original typist of this manuscript was Shirley Lerman, a woman of wide talents. Lanette Joubert was a dedicated research assistant during many weeks of revision. The final typing was done by Marilyn Rhinehart and members of the secretarial staff of the history department at the University of Houston.

Suzette H. Annin has been a superb editor.

By convention, acknowledgment of family members is relegated to the final paragraph. Perhaps this is unjust since they have borne heavy burdens. In my case, my husband in no way belongs last since he has shared so much of his knowledge with me and has consistently buoyed me up at critical moments. I wish also to thank my children for their understanding over the years.

The author wishes to thank the following:

The New York Academy of Medicine Library for their courtesy in allowing the reproduction of the photographs of Emil Kraepelin, Wilhelm Weygandt, William Stern, Willy Hellpach, Ludolf Krehl, Paul Julius Moebius, Iwan Bloch, Albert Moll, Paul Eugen Bleuler, Robert Eugen Gaupp, and Ernst Adolf von Strümpell.

The University of Oklahoma Press for permission to reprint the photograph of Christian von Ehrenfels from *The Austrian Philosophy of Values* by Howard O. Eaton (Copyright 1930).

Charles C Thomas, Publisher for permission to use the photograph of Hermann Oppenheim from Haymaker, Webb, THE FOUNDERS OF NEUROLOGY, 1953

Clark University Press for permission to reprint the photograph of Theodor Ziehen from *A History of Psychology in Autobiography*, Vol. 1, edited by Carl Murchison, 1930, p. xvii.

American Psychiatric Association for use of the photograph of Gustav Aschaffenburg which appeared in the *American Journal of Psychiatry*, vol. 101, p. 427, November, 1944.

The Clinical Psychology Publishing Co., Inc. for permission to use material previously published in "*The Interpretation of Dreams*: Early Reception by the Educated German Public," *Journal of the History of the Behavioral Sciences*, Vol. 11, April, 1975.

The Johns Hopkins University Press for permission to use material previously published in "The Medical Reception of Psychoanalysis in Germany, 1894-1907," *Bulletin of the History of Medicine*, Vol. XLV, Sept.-Oct., 1971.

Photograph of C. G. Jung, 1912, in New York (Campbell Studios) from *The Freud/Jung Letters: The Correspondence between Sigmund Freud and C. G. Jung*, ed. William McGuire, trans. Ralph Mannheim and R. F. C. Hull. Bollingen Series XCIV. © 1974 by Princeton University Press. Reproduced by permission of Mr. Franz Jung and the publisher.

Photograph of Karl Abraham about 1904 from *A Psycho-Analytical Dialogue: The Letter of Sigmund Freud and Karl Abraham, 1907-1926*, ed. Hilda C. Abraham and Ernst L. Freud, trans. Bernard Marsh and Hilda C. Abraham. New York: Basic Books, 1965. Reproduced by permission of Sigmund Freud Copyrights Ltd.

INTRODUCTION

PSYCHOANALYSIS AND GERMAN CULTURE AND SOCIETY

Very early in his psychoanalytic career, Sigmund Freud began to write to friends and associates that his work was being ignored, and that if any attention was paid to it, it was all unrelentingly hostile. Freud's later historical accounts of the psychoanalytic movement as well as autobiographical essays told a similar story. This was the view unquestioningly adopted by most psychoanalysts and eventually given the respectability of footnotes by Ernest Jones (1955) in the second volume of his three-volume life of Freud. Jones did not originate the view, but he gave it its most comprehensive coverage in recent times.

As far as early reception in Germany is concerned, however, I have found much evidence that Freud was by no means totally ignored or rejected. To present this material—some of it either unknown or overlooked by previous historians—is one of the major goals of this book. In so doing, I have taken issue with some of the earlier interpretations. Since Ernest Jones was, in a way, the official codifier of these beliefs, I have found it convenient to quote him when I wished to refute a particular interpretation. Some readers may therefore think that I have conferred on Jones the exclusive responsibility for these views, or that I have singled him out for special attack. I do attack Jones, but I have concentrated on his remarks only because of the clarity and emphasis with which he presents the traditional psychoanalytic viewpoint of the reaction to Freud. Jones is but a representative of a widely shared outlook.

Jones is also the representative of an interpretation which lays extraordinarily heavy weight on Victorian sexual morality as the main factor in explaining the resistance Freud's work

1

encountered. But the German medical and psychological hostility or indifference to psychoanalysis was not a simple matter of disgust at Freud's sexual theories. I do not wish to underestimate the importance of sexual matters for the German reaction. Below I discuss some features of Wilhelmine sexual attitudes that were certainly important for the response to psychoanalysis. But the reasons why psychoanalysis ultimately failed to make a significant impression in German professional circles are manifold and extend beyond the usually repeated trio of sexual prejudice, anti-Semitism, and the critic's personal neurosis.

RECEPTION OF PSYCHOANALYSIS IN GERMANY AND IN THE WESTERN WORLD

When studies of the reception of ideas are limited to one country, a special difficulty arises. Authors of such studies run the risk of imparting a false quality of uniqueness to their causal connections. Discouragingly enough, the more scrupulously these writers try to ensure that their interpretations and conclusions correspond only to the evidence they have gathered, the greater is the likelihood that they may seem to be saying: "What happened in country X only happened there."

This book is about events in Germany seventy-five years ago. Similar events took place in other Western countries at the same time. Even more important, some of the reasons for those occurrences lay in Western and not peculiarly German circumstances. The wave of materialism and positivism that swept over Germany in the second half of the nineteenth century also engulfed England, France, and the United States. At the turn of the century, medicine everywhere in the West had a strongly organic basis. "Science" was enshrined at many institutions and not only in the laboratories of German physicians and psychologists. The history of psychiatry in nineteenth-century Germany has certain parallels in other countries. Industrialism and its effects were obviously not confined to Germany.[1]

---

[1] The future will no doubt enable some scholar to compare the reactions to psychoanalysis in several Western countries and write a synthetic work. Well-docu-

Still, the role of this study is limited to what happened in Germany. I only rarely stray into comparative remarks or general comments about Western culture. Some German reactions were unique or appeared more strikingly than they did elsewhere. Other reactions had roots in both particular and Western circumstances; often it is not possible to determine precisely which was the preponderant influence. Still others were obviously shared with every Western country and were prompted by the same factors in each instance. Except in isolated instances, where I am sure of my material and its interpretation, it is not my intent to plead for or against a unique German response to Freud's ideas. I am presenting the German reaction to psychoanalysis, aware that some of the same things could be said of the reaction of physicians, psychologists, and educated laymen in other Western nations.

Still, some readers may wonder if certain findings about Germany apply also to Vienna, Freud's own city. I am in no position to comment on the Viennese reaction, except to say that two works that deal with Viennese reception support some of my conclusions. These studies are Bry and Rifkin's (1962) investigation of early reviews of Freud's works and Ellenberger's (1970, Chapters 7 and 10) extensive overview of dynamic psychiatry.

THE ZEITGEIST AND THE INNOVATOR

The examination of the reception of psychoanalysis is also the study of a challenge to the established order. As such, the perennially ticklish question of the *Zeitgeist* arises. Just what was Freud's relationship to his times? Was he a radical innovator, breaking with everything around him? Or were his preoccupations anticipated or simultaneously shared by the avantgarde in other fields? Such questions can be asked in various ways (see Ross, 1969, p. 256, fn. 2). The study of the reception of psychoanalysis supports the view that neither the individual nor the *Zeitgeist* is supreme. The historical issue is best

---

mented studies about the United States by Burham (1967) and Hale (1971) have already appeared, and other historians are currently studying the response in Spain, the Netherlands, and France.

phrased: *To what extent* is the challenger radical, and *to what extent* is he responding to contemporaneous events?

On the one hand, psychoanalysis can be seen as a body of ideas for which the times were ready, if one examines the preoccupations of avant-garde philosophical, literary, and artistic figures whose work was contemporaneous with Freud's. Recognition of "subconscious" or "unconscious" elements in the mind formed an intrinsic part of the philosophy and psychology of Bergson, Croce, Dilthey, James, and Nietzsche. The stories, novels, and poetry of Hofmannsthal, Proust, Rilke, Schnitzler, and Zweig clearly displayed the complex and often unknown motivations that underlie most actions and thoughts. Impressionist composers showed a decreased interest in the order and form that had previously characterized Western music in order to admit less disciplined tonal patterns. Debussy—and Strauss, too—wished to express the strong surges of feeling that continually broke the surface of "ordinary" life. So did the post-Impressionist painters who were impelled to use bolder and novel color combinations and to move away from representational art.

It is true that the European middle classes found much of this incomprehensible, and often reacted with outrage to what they considered an assault on their sensibilities. What is sometimes forgotten, however, is that there were large segments of the European upper classes who rapidly accepted many of the avant-garde artists, and not merely for social reasons. Proust painted excellent portraits of representatives of these elite groups.

But there are other way to assess Freud's relationship to his world. One must examine Victorian attitudes toward sexuality, toward childhood, and toward that explosive combination of the two—infantile sexuality. There is no doubt that the Wilhelmine middle classes were trained to consider any open display or acknowledgment of sexuality disgraceful. There was a great amount of unconscious sexual repression and of conscious suppression. Broaching the topic of sexuality aroused anxiety, guilt, shame, or disgust. Freud's open concern with sexuality, his emphasis on its significance in all human life, and his broadening of the concept inevitably aroused resistance. Freud's first German pupil to open a medical practice in Berlin soon found that "it is the tendency of our time to conceal as much as possible anything having to do with sex. Sordid or calculating motives are attributed to the person who dares to speak freely and openly about sexual life" (Gattel, 1898, p. 68).

But the story does not end there. Societal demands for sexual repression were of a peculiar kind. The Victorian middle classes were not what we have become accustomed to call "Puritanical."[2] The hallmarks of Wilhelmine sexual attitudes were not only repression but also hypocrisy.

The widely traveled Stefan Zweig recalled that in his youth sexuality was looked upon "as an anarchical and therefore disturbing element . . . which was not allowed to see the light of day." Instead a "remarkable compromise" was invented. A sexual life was not forbidden, at least to men. "If it was not feasible to do away with sexuality, then at least it must not be visible in the world of morality. A silent pact was therefore reached, by which the entire bothersome affair was not mentioned in school, in the family, or in public . . ." (Zweig, 1945, p. 68). The most popular way of satisfying sexual desires outside of marriage was through prostitutes, and prostitutes were seen everywhere on city streets before World War I. Thus, "in addition to the social pressure, which constantly enforced precaution and secrecy, there was at that time another element that overshadowed the happiest moments: the fear of infection." In doctors' neighborhoods, one could read on every sixth or seventh door: "Specialist for Skin and Venereal Diseases."

The dual nature of the sexual mores of middle-class Victorians—repression and hypocrisy—created resistance to investigation of sexuality and to wide dissemination of its findings and, at the same time, assured the inevitability of such re-

---

[2] Since the appearance of John Demos's (1970, pp. 131-154) book on Plymouth Colony, there has been some question about the extent of sexual repression among the seventeenth-century Puritans. Actually, it is worth pondering if any Western *society* (as opposed to sect) was ever truly "Puritanical." The French *Annales* school has also produced evidence that "forbidden" sexual practices have frequently found expression throughout Western history.

search and its application. Hypocrisy, even more than repression, invited attack, so that, at the turn of the century, psychoanalysis did not stand alone in its pursuit of sexual knowledge. Freud lived in an era in which several movements and individuals explicitly sought changes in sexual customs, an endeavor which psychoanalysis only implicitly supported.

At the turn of the century, public attitudes about sexuality were being slowly changed as more and more sexual subjects were dealt with openly: the laws regarding homosexuality and sexual offenses; venereal diseases; illegitimacy; prostitution; contraception; sex education. The German Association to Fight Venereal Diseases was founded in 1902. Whatever its stated aims, it was a powerful force for the sex education of children, adolescents, and adults. The remarkable sales of Iwan Bloch's (1907b) *The Sexual Life of Our Time* (*Sexualleben unserer Zeit*) showed that the subject of sexuality could not indefinitely continue to be avoided publicly (see Chapter 12). A tremendous debate raged in medical and lay periodicals before the war over whether sex education was good or bad. More privately, among doctors and a good many patients, there was great concern with contraception. The birth-control movement had gathered momentun in the nineteenth century. Now that contraception was more highly regarded, the limited methods of achieving it were taxed to their utmost. Regular reliance on coitus interruptus and masturbation was regarded by many doctors, including Freud, as dangerous to health. The problem of finding safe and effective contraception was becoming so widespread that it was soon to be discussed openly. In 1911 there was an international birth-control conference in Dresden.

Organizations concerned with various aspects of sexuality were founded. Sometimes, as with the League for the Protection of Maternal Rights (*Bund für Mutterschutz*), organized in 1905, their aims extended in several directions and their membership was interested in a variety of other than purely sexual reforms (see Chapter 12). It became apparent that sexuality and sex education were not isolated subjects, but intricately connected with many important areas of modern life. The 1911 Dresden International Congress for Maternal Rights and

Sexual Reform dealt with a broad spectrum of issues. In 1913 there appeared the Medical Society for the Study and Research of Sexuality and Constitution (*Ärztliche Gesellschaft für Sexualwissenschaft und Konstitutionsforschung*) as well as the International Society for Sexual Research (*Internationale Gesellschaft für Sexualforschung*). All the organizations mentioned generated a variety of popular and scientific publications.

Concurrent with growing concern for sexual reform — and significant for seeing the relationship of psychoanalysis to its time — was the burgeoning interest in child study and early personality development. Like sexual reform, this interest was, of course, a Western phenomena; and as with the former, its manifestation in German life was clear. In 1899 both the German Association for Child Research (*Allgemeiner deutscher Verein für Kinderforschung*) and the Berlin Association for Child Psychology (*Verein für Kinderpsychologie in Berlin*) were founded. In rapid succession there came new periodicals: *Childhood Disorders, A Journal Devoted to Pathology and Therapy in Education* (*Die Kinderfehler*), first published in 1896; *Children's Minds: Journal for Educational Psychology and Pathology* (*Die Kinderseele*), which appeared in 1900; the *International Archives for School Hygiene* (*Internationales Archiv für Schulhygiene*) of 1905.

These movements and their journals devoted themselves to all areas of childhood, but particularly to educational reform. Their members and readers remembered their own numbing and often degrading years in school. Now, as school physicians and teachers, they had professional contact with the traditional school system. Thomas Mann in *Buddenbrooks* provided a harrowing picture of German school life. A highly regarded physician for nervous diseases, Willy Hellpach, blamed secondary education for much of the nervous disturbance to be seen in adolescents and young adults (see below, pp. 305-307). He gave a clinical picture of secondary school which matched Zweig's own recollection of Gymnasium as

compulsion, ennui, dreariness, a place where we had to assimilate the "science of the not-worth-knowing" in exactly measured portions . . . that learning mill. . . . For eight years no teacher asked us even once what we personally wished to learn . . . .[Our teachers were] poor devils who were slavishly bound to the schedule, the officially designated curriculum. . . . They did not love us, they did not hate us, and why should they, for they knew nothing about us. . . . They had nothing to do but to determine how many mistakes we had made in our last lesson. They sat up at their desks and we sat below, they questioned us and we had to reply, and there was no other relation between us. . . . A pause of ten minutes in the cold, narrow halls was thought sufficient in a period of four or five hours of motionless squatting [Zweig, 1945, pp. 29-31].[3]

From about 1890 on, educational reformers, together with leaders of the youth movement, women's movement, and workers' movement, worked to ease the rigidity common in both primary and secondary education. Educational reformers wished education to proceed "from the child outward." That meant a "total education," not one limited to the traditional subjects. A Movement for Education in the Arts was organized early in the century and sponsored "Artistic Education" festivals in Weimar, Dresden, and Hamburg, trying to awaken in the public a receptiveness to artistic and musical training for children in the schools. Some reformers stressed the importance of working with one's hands. This, together with demands for vocational training suitable to a technological era, led to the concept of the technical high school. Communal country boarding schools were advocated as a means of promoting the health and physical development of the young; there arose open-air schools and country boarding schools. Prominent among the innovations were Otto's Experimental School (tutorial schools of 1901); Wyneken's Free Elementary School of 1906; Steiner's Free Open Air School; the League for Public Elementary Schools, founded in 1909; and the League for School Reform, founded in 1910.

The need for flexibility in education was recognized in some of the reforms of the secondary school system. After 1900, entrance to almost all faculties of the universities was opened to

[3] See also pp. 32-39. Accurate as far as it went, this was, of course, a one-sided perception. A more balanced account would have made some mention of the long-term advantages of the traditional classical education.

the graduates of the "modern" (*Real*) schools, whereas before it had been limited to the graduates of the classical schools (Gymnasium). A small amount of experimentation in the state-designed classical curricula had been allowed since 1892. Latin could be postponed to the lower fourth term and French could be substituted as the first foreign language. Students were not immediately "tracked" upon entrance; that was postponed until about the age of twelve. Moreover, some schools were allowed to vary the course of study in the last two grades in preparation for the freedom of choice that was to come in the university.

Educational reform was but one practical application of the greater concern with childhood that arose in Western society at the end of the last century. Freud's own psychoanalytic contributions underscored the extreme importance of childhood for later development. In particular, Freud's theory of the libidinal stages of development (oral, anal, phallic, and genital) in children emphasized the significance of sexuality in the years before seven and again at adolescence.

The *Three Essays on the Theory of Sexuality* which appeared in 1905 was original and profound, but it did not stand alone in its avowal of the importance of sexuality. One of the most telling indications that the concerns of psychoanalysis were a part of the European *Zeitgeist*, and not just Freud's personal preoccupation, was the simultaneous appearance of Expressionist drama (c. 1912-1924). Some of Freud's famous case histories, particularly those of "Dora," the "Rat Man," and the "Wolf Man," could easily have provided the core (plus a great many details) for the plays of the Expressionists and their predecessors, Wedekind and Strindberg. Freud's case histories, of course, were not meant to be judgmental. Only rarely, and then in other contexts, did Freud explicitly express his feelings about the familial and social consequences of individual neuroses and about the part played by social mores in producing the neuroses that shattered individual lives. Only occasionally and tentatively did Freud ally himself with reformers who wanted to establish a new sexual order.

In their dramas, the Expressionists described the same phenomena that Freud had observed clinically. But the Expressionists were social crusaders who directly attacked both the repression and the hypocrisy of the times. Expressionism savagely exposed the sham in the relations between all human beings, unambiguously depicting the resulting horrors. No one and nothing was left out: parents and teachers ruined the lives of children and students; wives destroyed the sanity of their husbands; men and women, friend and friend, were disloyal, capricious, vengeful.

The plays of Frank Wedekind (1864-1918) announced the movement well before it had any coherence or definition. In 1891, Wedekind's *Spring's Awakening* portrayed parental insensitivity to adolescent sexuality and the abysmal failure of sex education. To the dramatist the result was inevitable: suicide. Other plays of Wedekind dealt with bizarre sado-masochistic relationships; murders; murders that appeared as suicides; prostitution; grotesque marital relationships. Rationality seemed to have vanished, as brutal and horrible ideas were matter-of-factly expressed by one character and quickly adopted by another. Human sexuality, in all its forms, was never hidden. In bourgeois society, Wedekind felt, people were always hiding their desires. In his plays, all the characters acted on their desires.

Expressionist drama began to blossom in the years immediately preceding World War I. The first "pure" representative of the genre is probably R. J. Sorge's *The Beggar* of 1912. In place of the individual persons of the Naturalists' drama, the Expressionists used human "types": the father, the son, the woman, the mother, the beggar. The Expressionists' speech had a loosened form. Purely logical words — articles, conjunctions — were eliminated; strict grammar was ignored. Scenes followed upon one another in a dazzlingly quick array. Emotions were never controlled, but expressed vividly, sharply, ecstatically. The stage sets were not realistic but symbolic. Always the world of the father, with its hypocritical morality and order, was under attack. The recurrent father-son conflict was emphasized.

The independent but simultaneous appearance of Expressionism and psychoanalysis is significant. They stressed similar themes. Human sexuality is ubiquitous. People (unconsciously or consciously) feel one thing, but say or do another. In all of us there are savage, primitive forces. Deep, keenly felt emotions govern our acts. The son always tries to overthrow the father; the daughter always tries to replace her mother. Symbols are constantly employed in human expression, both in the waking state and in dreams. There is a "primary process," an irrational thought patterning that eschews logical transitions and reasoned steps. Each human being shares a common psychic development: what is true for one "son" is true for all sons.

Freud's relationship to his times supports the view that change always occurs *both* as a result of the individual's unique contribution and of corresponding developments that are simultaneous and independent. The revolutionary individual is both separate from and a part of his era. To some extent Freud was a radical innovator, breaking with his immediate time. Clearly, psychoanalysis was not in the mainstream of late nineteenth- and early twentieth-century German medicine and psychology; it was basically antithetical to the concerns and beliefs of many physicians and most psychologists (see Chapters 1 and 7). Moreover, many nonprofessional segments of German society were unprepared for the open and explicit discussion of sexuality and unconscious motivation.

Yet, to some extent, Freud's preoccupations had been anticipated or were being simultaneously shared by the avant-garde in other fields. The positivism and materialism of the nineteenth century were crumbling. Sexual concerns were attracting serious public attention. The issue of sex education particularly was a common subject in both professional journals and lay magazines and literary supplements. Educators and physicians were coming to realize that the early years were truly significant, and they founded organizations and periodicals to investigate various aspects of childhood. Actual changes in educational methods were taking place. Themes dealing with unknown or dimly comprehended aspects of the mind began to dominate artistic, literary, and philosophical works. In the broad cultural sense, Freud was not in "splendid isolation."

REACTION TO NEW SCIENTIFIC IDEAS:
THE SPECIAL CASE OF THE BEHAVIORAL SCIENCES

Can one draw any general conclusions about the reception of new scientific ideas, using the example of the early reception of psychoanalysis in Germany? To do so in a sophisticated manner requires some knowledge of the reception other behavioral sciences have encountered. Unfortunately, historians and sociologists of science have devoted little time specifically to the reactions aroused by the behavioral sciences. They have concentrated their energies on the physical and biological sciences. Most notable here are the works of Thomas Huxley, Thomas Kuhn, Bernard Barber, Gunther Stent, and the papers resulting from a week-long symposium on scientific change held at Oxford in 1961 (Crombie, 1963). These works contain some conclusions, however, that do seem to be borne out by my investigations. Huxley (Bibby, 1959) and Barber (1961), for example, have described the recurrent opposition to scientific change that has its stronghold in already-established "schools" and among academic "authorities." Freud clearly faced opposition from such groups or individuals (see Chapters 1, 6, and 7). Max Planck (Kuhn, 1963) concluded that scientific progress occurs as the opponents of a new scientific hypothesis die off and the next generation learns the new theory from the start. There is certainly nothing in my study to contradict this obvious but useful observation.

Kuhn (1970) argues that the very dogmatism of scientists that inhibits their acceptance of new ideas also serves a useful function in the long-term development of a particular discipline. It is unsafe to discard tradition completely. Some of the criticisms of the past eighty years which have been leveled at certain innovations of psychoanalysis have been proved justified (see pp. 101-102, 137, 188).

The molecular geneticist Gunther Stent (1972) has proposed that a scientific discovery can truly be "premature if its implications cannot be connected . . . with canonical knowledge." This was somewhat the case of the relationship of psychoanalysis with medicine, and even more so of psychoanalysis with psychology. Perhaps Stent's observation is most accurate regarding Freud's work on dream interpretation, which did not go unnoticed and was considered important, but had virtually no effect on the study of human psychology for twenty years.

Two sociologists (Ben-David, 1960; Ben-David and Collins, 1966) have discussed social factors in the origins of new sciences, including the behavioral. In doing so, they have touched tangentially on some of the issues affecting the reception of experimental psychology and psychoanalysis. Ben-David, in particular, has called needed attention to the importance of purely scientific objections to the new theories of psychoanalysis. But it has not been the intention of the two men to deal primarily with problems of reception. They are concerned with the formation of new scientific disciplines, particularly with the part played by the factors of professional roles and status. Thus their work has but limited applicability to the history of the reception of psychoanalysis.

Perhaps some of Lewis Feuer's conclusions are more applicable. In differentiating "scientific revolutions" from social revolutions, Feuer (1974, pp. 252-272), a philosopher and sociologist, has developed two generalizations which can be applied to psychoanalysis—even though Feuer himself mistakenly believes one of them can not. Feuer states that "the scientific community, on the eve of revolution, has generally been placid, confident, and content with itself." This was the case with a large group of German clinical psychiatrists and neurologists (see Chapter 1). Feuer's second generalization is that modern scientific revolutions have never had to undergo "the ordeal of closed publication." Uncritically accepting Freud's own dour remarks about the reception of his writings, Feuer has excluded the case of psychoanalysis from his generalization. In fact, Freud and other psychoanalysts had no trouble getting their papers and books published before they founded their own journals (see Chapter 3 ff.). Freud wanted to found a uniquely psychoanalytic periodical not because he was having difficulties in getting his work published, but in order to obtain increased recognition for psychoanalysis (McGuire, 1974, pp. 59, 154).

Feuer's conclusions are useful. Yet his thoughts about

psychoanalysis are basically passing observations contained in a larger study of the genesis of scientific creativity. Thus there remains an urgent need for historical and sociological investigations of the special circumstances which influenced the reception of each of the behavioral sciences. One such contribution has already been made by Bry and Rifkin (1962), who point out that Freud's works faced a unique difficulty in securing reviews in the professional journals. Because of the wide scope of Freud's subject matter, as well as its novel combinations, it properly belonged in very few journals of the day. Though interdisciplinary journals had already appeared at the turn of the century, they were still few. Psychoanalysis was a pioneering discipline, and Freud was the founder of one of the new behavioral sciences. Accordingly, Freud's works received less publicity than they would have if there had been adequate vehicles for their review.

Bry and Rifkin believe that, particularly with *The Interpretation of Dreams,* Freud

> unwittingly experienced early significant clashes between the evolving behavioral sciences and the tradition-bound structure available in the organization of science. . . . *The Interpretation of Dreams* was reviewed in nonmedical journals because the topic was not suitable for the medical review literature. The essay *On Dreams,* however, was reviewed in medical and psychiatric journals because it appeared in a series with the word "nervous" in its title [1962, pp. 22-23].

The limited notice of *The Psychopathology of Everyday Life* (Freud, 1901b) is another instance of how the reception of psychoanalysis was affected by the traditional organization of disciplines. Strictly speaking, when this work was published in book form in 1904, it had no place in the conventional scholarly structure. Because it had the word "Psychopathology" in the title, it attracted a few reviews in the medical literature. But such notice was grossly inadequate for the scope of the book.

The special circumstances affecting the reviews of psychoanalytic literature are just one illustration of the complexities that are relevant to the reception of new scientific ideas. Such complexities include scientific factors, personal idiosyncrasies, and broad historical and philosophical factors, the latter often overlooked.

One somewhat underinvestigated area in the study of the reception of new scientific ideas is the personal role played by the discoverer in advancing or retarding knowledge of his discoveries. The innovator's role has received only peripheral attention because it is often difficult to determine if the way he chose to promulgate his theories did, in fact, have any effect on the way they were received. I, too, have found it difficult to assess definitively this personal factor. Freud had no inclinations to any sort of wild or unorthodox behavior. He completely shared traditional ideas about proper scientific attitudes and conduct. Nevertheless, certain aspects of his presentation of his ideas did affect the reception of psychoanalysis.

Freud's style of writing was always important. It was unusual for scientific literature of the day to be written as vividly and compellingly as Freud's often was. Moreover, his habit of arguing by analogy was very suspect in certain scientific circles. The extraordinary occurrence of Freud's receiving the Goethe Prize for literature in 1930 shows that his literary style was indeed a prominent part of his work. This style always affected his readers, either positively or negatively (see Chapters 6, 10, and 12; also Schönau, 1968).

Another factor was Freud's attitude about public discussion of his work. The impact of this attitude on the reception of psychoanalysis is less clear than Freud's writing style. But Freud's very definite feelings about publicizing his work seem to have acted as a deterrent to its dissemination.

Freud himself never attended a general medical or psychiatric congress and repeatedly urged his followers not to do so. He always believed it was useless to engage in public scientific debate because such debate would have no effect whatsoever in making physicians more receptive to psychoanalysis. When followers reported negative reactions at congresses, his response invariably was: "What did you expect? I warned you." Freud was also against the popularization of his ideas, believing they would inevitably be distorted or watered down. He always viewed the more favorable reception of psychoanalysis in the United States with dissatisfaction.

I do not wish to make too much of this point and therefore am confining most of my remarks about it to this Introduction. The reader can bear it in mind in the chapters ahead, allowing it to assume whatever weight he wishes. What I wish to make clear is that Freud's attitude about public discussion and popularization of psychoanalysis was certainly not decisive for the reception of psychoanalysis in Germany. A very different attitude could not have made a serious dent in the medical and scientific commitments of Freud's contemporaries (see Chapter 1).

Still, Freud's emotional reaction to criticism and to hostility, both overt and covert, did play its part in retarding the dissemination of accurate information about psychoanalysis and may have lost the movement some early converts. First, before 1904, Freud did not publish any detailed papers on his method. And then that one paper—published as a chapter in another doctor's book—stood alone. Specific information about psychoanalytic techniques and treatment could have been spread at regional and national medical meetings if Freud had so desired. There are any number of reports of physicians who tried to use psychoanalysis but gave it up after a couple of cases because they got nowhere. Their failure was inevitable, based on the meager information at their disposal—in turn the result of Freud's own reticence.

Second, Freud was convinced that it would do no good, or even tarnish his scientific image, to engage in public debate. If he did so, he once wrote, he would appear no better than his critics. So Freud publicly defended his ideas only twice in his psychoanalytic career. Yet one time, in 1895, it did have the effect of making his critic, Leopold Löwenfeld, reconsider his own criticisms (see Chapter 4).

Freud's reputation is that of a strong-minded and sometimes authoritarian leader of the psychoanalytic movement—a person of great inner strength and intense single-mindedness. Yet it seems clear from Jones's biography that Freud was a person easily hurt in relationships with significant men in his life. Twice Freud convinced Jung to abandon a particular position and soon afterward fainted. Freud interpreted these spells as having to do with unconscious death wishes toward Jung.[4] Freud's way of dealing with hostility seems to have been to dismiss his critic or withdraw from attack rather than risk another entanglement. This is seen, for example, in the incident with the *Neue Rundschau* (see Chapter 10). Sometimes Freud's defensive maneuvers were quite realistic and justified, but sometimes he unnecessarily gave up the chance to publicize his findings, believing that a specific rebuff indicated inevitable future rebuffs.

Third, disciples' reports about their reception at medical meetings were not all negative. Privately, doctors approached Freud's followers to tell them of their interest. This sort of recognition was systematically ignored by Freud. Obviously (and not unnaturally) he was more affected by the public attacks of some of the leaders of German psychiatry and neurology. Freud may have felt that the handful of lesser lights who might be attracted was not worth the effort to be expended and the public ignominy to be suffered.

Finally, Freud had vacillating and self-defeating views about attracting followers. His complaints about his "splendid isolation" are well known. But in 1899 he wrote to Fliess:

> I have given up my lectures this year in spite of numerous enrollments, and do not propose to resume them in the immediate future. I have the same horror of the uncritical adulation of the very young that I used to have for the hostility of their elders. Also the whole thing is not ripe yet — *nonum prematur in annum!* Pupils *a la Gattl* [*sic*: he meant Felix Gattel] are to be had for the asking; as a rule they end by asking to become patients themselves [1887-1902, p. 280].

RELIGION AND ANTI-SEMITISM

There are two areas about which little is said in this study: the impact of religious beliefs and of anti-Semitic prejudice on the reception of psychoanalysis. This is not because I am unaware of their significance but rather because there is very little evidence to use as a basis for meaningful remarks. One can speculate about the importance of strong Protestant and

---

[4] This is but one of the many meanings — both psychological and physiological — of these fainting spells, which were no doubt overdetermined (Schur, 1972, pp. 264-272).

Catholic traditions in the response to psychoanalysis. Catholicism in the South and Protestantism in the North affected in different ways sexual attitudes and behavior, views about mental illness and its treatment, family structure, theological-philosophical beliefs, and traditions of pastoral care. But there is almost no material before the First World War which one can use to evaluate the role religious differences played in the reaction to psychoanalysis. In a study of psychoanalysis in the Weimar years and after 1945 the religious issue can be considered effectively. (See Birk [1970] for a springboard to such a study.)

Similarly, I have said little about anti-Semitism, though it has been frequently cited as a major reason for hostility to psychoanalysis. There is no doubt that anti-Semitism in new racial dress was on the increase after 1890. Anti-Semitism did retard the careers of Jewish psychoanalysts, mainly because they were Jewish—not primarily because they were psychoanalysts. Karl Abraham's attempt to secure a university appointment is a good case in point. But to prove Freud was attacked before World War I in *Germany* (I am not talking about Vienna) because he was Jewish is an exceedingly difficult task. Almost no documentation exists. The natural processes of aging have affected either the recall or the coherence of almost all of the few persons still alive who were connected with the analytic movement before 1914. The same problems, fortunately, do not exist for the years after 1920. A study of that period could do justice to the relationship between psychoanalysis and anti-Semitism.

ORGANIZATION AND SOURCES

The largest portion of this book deals with the medical reception of psychoanalysis. This is a reflection of several facts: (1) Freud was a physician, an exceptionally well-trained and bright neurologist; (2) from 1893 to 1905, all of Freud's psychoanalytic papers were published in medical journals; (3) Freud at first desired (and expected) medical, not lay acceptance; (4) psychoanalysis and its predecessor, the cathartic method, were initially developed in response to deeply puzzling medical problems of the late nineteenth century; (5)

physicians, particularly psychiatrists and neurologists, did pay more attention to psychoanalysis than did any other group before World War I.

I have carried the story of medical reaction through 1907 for two reasons. The unexpectedly large amount of pre-1914 medical material spurred my search for a logical date as a cut-off. I found that Freud himself considered the first stage of reception to have ended around 1907. In 1925, he wrote in his autobiography that "the history of psychoanalysis falls . . . into two phases. In the first of these I stood alone and had to do all the work myself: this was from 1895-6 until 1906 or 1907" (1925, p. 55). Moreover, 1907 is an important date for the history of psychoanalysis in Germany. Before that year Freud had a small number of supporters, admirers, and imitators in Germany, but he had no disciple who had received his official approval. In December, 1907, Karl Abraham, a young German psychiatrist with a two-year interest in psychoanalysis, returned from a visit to Vienna and established a psychiatric practice in Berlin. Abraham and Freud had already been corresponding since June, 1907, and after the Vienna visit they quickly developed a close scientific friendship (H. C. Abraham and Freud, 1965). Within the year Abraham embarked upon several propagandizing and proselytizing ventures and thus introduced a new variable into the course of psychoanalysis in Germany. Therefore, the period after 1907 must be treated separately.

The early medical reception of psychoanalysis can be assessed through a wide variety of sources, but two kinds of material are peripheral to the period before 1908. First, interviews with individuals who have pertinent reminiscences generally yield information pertaining only to the 1920's. Nevertheless, some material from interviews is relevant and appears sporadically in this study. Second, there is no immediate evidence that information about psychoanalysis was included in the teaching of psychiatry in Germany before 1908. One of Freud's greatest problems was his failure to gain official academic backing at a German university before 1928, when a seminar on psychoanalysis was made available to students at the Institute for Social Research at the University of Frankfurt. Such official acceptance was necessary for any organized presentation of psychoanalysis. This does not mean that medical students and residents were not exposed to informal comments on and brief references to psychoanalysis. There is evidence that this occurred. Students were also introduced to psychoanalysis in textbooks. We know that a doctor who was also a psychologist gave a series of lectures c. 1900 on psychopathology at the University of Leipzig, in which some of Freud's ideas were closely examined (see Chapter 8). But there is no way at present to ascertain who attended these lectures.

The second portion of this study investigates the early interaction of experimental psychology and psychoanalysis. I have kept to the same time limits as in the medical reception in order to facilitate comparison between physicians' and psychologists' response to Freud. When compared to the medical reaction to psychoanalysis, the response of the physiological psychologists appears quite limited. This is initially puzzling. Freud's works were consistently reviewed in the leading experimental psychology journal, but his ideas were not—with but few exceptions—discussed in psychological texts, monographs, or at meetings. This is in sharp contrast to the medical reception of psychoanalysis, in which physicians' *response* to psychoanalysis matched their *exposure* to it. Psychologists were aware of the existence of psychoanalysis, but they did not accord it any extensive consideration. Why? The answer lies in the vast differences in the theoretical concerns and dominant interests of the psychologists and the early psychoanalysts (see Chapter 7). It is significant that the revolutionary discoveries by the "Würzburg" psychologists about higher thought processes brought them very close to sharing psychoanalytic views about the operation of unconscious processes. Yet such concordance was an impossibility for experimental psychologists in 1905. Chapter 8 evaluates the actual response of psychologists to psychoanalysis.

The appearance of *The Interpretation of Dreams* in November, 1899, made psychoanalysis for the first time the direct concern of the intellectual who was neither a physician nor a psychologist. The book dealt with a topic of universal concern and was written in Freud's usual elegant style. Except for Chapter VII, a difficult theoretical section, it could be easily understood by any educated person. Thus the response of the educated German public to psychoanalysis began in 1900.

The study of the lay reception of psychoanalysis would no doubt have benefited if it had been extended to 1914. More so than for the reactions in medicine and psychology, the war years were an obvious watershed in the lay reaction to psychoanalysis. Before 1914, psychoanalysis found gradually increasing acceptance in lay circles. But in the Weimar period, lay appreciation and understanding of psychoanalysis blossomed dramatically. The history of the lay reception of psychoanalysis is, therefore, most logically bisected at 1914. But to have discussed the lay response up to 1914 in this study would have created the anomaly of a work in which two thirds of the material dealt with 1893-1907 and one third with 1900-1914. Thus caught, I chose the expedient of also concluding Part III with 1907.

The book ends with an assessment of certain nineteenth-century intellectual trends which I consider vital to the reception of psychoanalysis in Germany.

PART I

GERMAN MEDICINE AND PSYCHOANALYSIS

1

GERMAN PSYCHIATRY IN THE NINETEENTH CENTURY

> *To be sure there are still many de-*
> *fects to be remedied and improve-*
> *ments to be made, but we are not*
> *presumptuous in stating that we*
> *have discovered the approach to*
> *be followed henceforth in psy-*
> *chiatry.*
> —Kraepelin, *One Hundred*
> *Years of Psychiatry*

ROMANTIC TO SCIENTIFIC: AN OVERVIEW

In 1845, eleven years before Sigmund Freud was born, two significantly different psychiatric textbooks appeared in Germany. One
was Ernst von Feuchtersleben's *Principles of Medical Psychology*;
the other was Wilhelm Griesinger's *Mental Pathology and Therapeutics*. Feuchtersleben's *Medical Psychology* stressed the relationship between psychological and physiological phenomena and
advanced the theory of the biological unity of the human organism.
He differentiated between what we now call psychoses and neuroses
and spoke of all mental aberrations as transitory stages between
health and disease. Many of his ideas were no novelty to the
educated world conversant with the views of certain physicians of
the Romantic period. But by 1845 Feuchtersleben's belief that there
was no sharp line between sickness and health was fast disappearing.

Although Feuchtersleben's textbook was so in demand that the
publisher, in order to supply booksellers, had to recall those copies
that had been distributed gratis to the trade (Veith, 1965, p. 185), it
is not his work, but rather Griesinger's, which acquired the more
lasting fame. There is no German doctor who has not heard Griesinger's renowned phrase: *"Geisteskrankheiten sind Gehirnkrank-*

25

heiten" — mental diseases are diseases of the brain. Griesinger is remembered as one of the fathers of brain psychiatry, and not for his comment that the largest and most important part of mental events is unconscious. Griesinger's belief in unconscious ideation had its roots in early nineteenth-century philosophical conceptions. These conceptions were fast losing their popularity at mid-century. New materialistic and positivistic concerns in the second half of the century drastically lessened interest in ideas about an unconscious.

German physical and biological sciences succeeded in charting hitherto unknown areas of human anatomy and physiology, providing not only keener understanding for scientists but more effective medicine and surgery for the treatment of human disease and malfunction. It appeared to many that control of large segments of nature was within reach. Darwin's evolutionary theories seemed to explain finally the origins and development of all living things. The theory of natural selection, whose processes could be observed, appeared to deny the existence of any intangible forces. The popularity of this point of view was demonstrated by the large sales of Ernst Haeckel's *History of Creation*, which appeared in 1868 and was in its tenth edition by 1902.

Industrialization and the successes of German applied science fostered the belief that the late nineteenth century was the greatest period in the history of civilization. The theme of Emil du Bois-Reymond's 1877 lecture, "The History of Civilization and Its Study," was that technology was providing Western (and German) civilization with a stable and lasting foundation.

In the political sphere, too, a new mood was abroad. In 1848, German unification on a voluntary basis had failed. The established powers had made a shambles of many intellectuals' long-cherished ideas of federation. Despair among these patriots was widespread. Then the martial and diplomatic events of the decade 1860-1870 convinced many a disillusioned person that only through the bold use of force would union result. Prussian power had its vigorous and persuasive advocates in respected scholars like Droysen, Haeusser, Mommsen, Sybel, and Treitschke. First the attention and then often the pride of much of German society was focused on the successes of policies and politics that stressed "reality." Action and not introspection appeared to be the path to national fulfillment.

These scientific, economic, social, and political events became the determinants of a drastically revised *Weltanschauung* which affected all areas of thought, including late nineteenth-century psychiatry. In turn, the character of this psychiatry determined not only the fate of Griesinger's and Feuchtersleben's books, but the medical reception of psychoanalysis as well.

To understand the substance and vitality of late nineteenth-century psychiatry, it is necessary to be acquainted with the psychiatry that preceded it. This has been called "Romantic psychiatry" because it coincided temporally with and was influenced by the Romantic era in German thought: 1780-1840.

Romantic psychiatry had two salient features. The first was its close connection (and indeed the close connection of all medical thought c. 1780-1840) with philosophy. The repercussions of this tie are important in explaining the later rejection of Romantic psychiatry and anything reminiscent of it. The second feature of German Romantic psychiatry was its spectacular development and its growth to parity with psychiatry in France and England. This trend is significant because it accelerated after 1850 and was responsible for some important underlying attitudes of late nineteenth-century German psychiatrists. Both aspects of late nineteenth-century psychiatry—its violent reaction against Romantic psychiatry and its heady feeling of success—help to explain some of the responses to psychoanalysis.

ROMANTIC PSYCHIATRY: 1780-1840

The prevailing metaphysics in Romantic Germany was *Naturphilosophie*, the mystical, pantheistic monism of the philosopher Friedrich W. J. von Schelling (1775-1854). Schelling wished to bring a "higher recognition to the study of nature," nature being defined as a universal organism endowed with a world soul. Schelling thought that "blind and idealess research" had followed the "ruination of philosophy by Bacon, and of physics by Newton" (Marx, 1965, p. 752; Leibbrand, 1956, pp. 89ff.). Schelling and other Romantic philosophers and writers, captivated by a notion of the basic unity of all life, believed that "the whole of the universe and of being, human and all other, is bound together in an all-prevading, all-meaningful relatedness, and only in this relatedness is any portion of the total to be comprehended" (Galdston, 1956, pp. 498-499).

Influenced by this philosophy, many German doctors became preoccupied with the irrational, emotional, and hidden forces of the human personality (Leibbrand, 1956; Leibbrand and Wettley, 1961, pp. 387-402, 465-508). Many were also poets and philosophers, concerned with the "passions." These early psychiatrists were keenly interested in the subjective state of the mentally ill, in the actual thoughts and feelings of their patients. Many saw that they could learn about mental health by studying mental illness and believed that mental disease was a result of the individual's psychological development. They held beliefs now considered quite sophisticated: the notion of inner conflict; the idea of the human being as a psychobiological entity; that if intense and ungratified "passions" could not find an outlet, the result might be a breakdown of personality function; that ideas can become symbolized and expressed in physical reactions; the belief in an "unconscious."[1]

These beliefs were those of the *Psychiker* — "mentalists," as one historian (Marx, 1965, p. 752) has called them. But they were opposed by the views of the *Somatiker*, the somaticists. In truth, in the first half of the nineteenth century, a tremendous theoretical debate raged between those physicians espousing a somatic explanation and those favoring a psychic explanation of mental disease. The mentalists, however, by virtue of their close ties with the literary and philosophic Romanticism of the era, were more representative of Romantic psychiatry.

The ideas of *Naturphilosophie* inspired Romantic psychiatrists to recognize some of the attributes of the human psyche and to comprehend its complexity and vast influence. The very same philosophy, however, led them astray. According to the *Naturphilosophiker*, the relationships of all living organisms could be subjectively divined and did not need experimental confirmation. Thus, most Romantic psychiatrists, some of whom were philosophers in their own right (e.g., Friedrich Groos [1768-1852] and August Eschenmayer [1768-1852]) came to rely on a priori constructions and often neglected clinical experience. This was in spite of the fact that some of these same men were administrators of mental hospitals and had ready access to abundant clinical material. But these psychiatrists believed their theoretical approach was in

---

[1] See Kirchhoff (1921, pp. 28-240) for short biographical essays about many Romantic psychiatrists. See also Birnbaum (1928, pp. 22-34). The three standard German histories of psychiatry (Kornfeld, 1905; Kirchhoff, 1912; Birnbaum, 1928) are dated, and are primarily useful for what they inadvertently reveal about psychiatric attitudes in the early twentieth century. Leibbrand and Wettley's book (1961) is essentially a long essay with commentaries on quotations from various authors, but it does supplement the biographical information on Kirchhoff (1921, 1924) and Kolle (1956, 1959, 1963).

part sanctioned by Schelling's designation of his work as "speculative physics." One Romantic physician, D. G. Kieser (1779-1862), concluded that "medicine in the higher sense [is] but the application of philosophy to the explanation of the phenomena of human life in health and disease" (Marx, 1965, p. 752).

The philosophy of nature had as corollaries a variety of theological and mystical beliefs. Some Romantic psychiatrists —including the highly acknowledged J. C. Heinroth (1773-1843)—believed every illness to be the result of sin. In mental illness God had punished the sinner by depriving him of his freedom of will. J. Kerner (1786-1862) and Eschenmayer revived the concept of possession and once more recommended exorcism. Vitalism was resurrected to a position of respectability in a mystical way that acted as a deterrent to further scientific progress.[2] The result of all these trends was the production of a psychiatric literature at once speculative, moralistic, and theological. Metaphysical observations accounted for visionary insights. Diffuse terminology was matched by stylistic verbosity. Later psychiatrists heaped scorn on the Romantics' poor investigative methods and dizzy flights into abstract reasoning. Ernest Jones (1953, p. 43) characterized their undisciplined thought as "unbalanced megalomanic emotionalism."[3]

But the relationship between German philosophy and psychiatry in the early nineteenth century was more than just a simple case of prevailing philosophical ideas leaving their imprint on the science of an era. By virtue of their traditional concern with psychology, German philosophers did not consider psychology a medical subject, and they laid claim as

[2] The Romantics resuscitated the vitalist philosophy of G. A. Stahl (1660-1734), the German physician who taught that the soul was not a spirit but had a special force, a drive characteristic of every living organism. In Western history, this idea goes back to those Greeks who viewed life as the realization of a divine plan, and the life processes as a manifestation of a mystical, goal-directed force. Of course, not all vitalists eschewed observation and experimentation. Johannes Müller (1801-1858), the great physiologist and teacher of Virchow and Helmholtz, was a vitalist and a mystic.

[3] See also Garrison (1929, pp. 428-429) for a witty and insightful synopsis of German medicine in the first half of the nineteenth century.

well to the fields of psychopathology, psychotherapy, and even forensic psychiatry. The philosophers' assertiveness was complemented by the hesitancy of most medical men. Physicians were unable to claim a sure place for psychiatry in the medicine of the day because psychiatry had barely emerged from the mysticism and superstition of the preceding centuries. The early Romantic psychiatrists had just renounced dependence on magic and, in some cases, on theology, but they knew no more than they had before about the nature of emotions and the relationship of mind and body. In this state, they did not feel very self-reliant. The philosophers' claims and the psychiatrists' uncertainties neatly dovetailed.

Thus, when the eminent physician C. W. Hufeland (1762-1836) wrote a book on public health, he sent a copy to Immanuel Kant (1724-1804), soliciting the philosopher's opinions of the book's sections on mental hygiene. Hufeland considered Kant a psychiatric expert not only because Kant had written on human sense perceptions and their aberrations, but also because Kant had proposed his own classification of mental diseases (Veith, 1965, p. 188; Kraepelin, 1917, p. 18). On his side, Kant believed that a philosopher was more of an authority on mental disturbances than was a physician. Kant insisted that expert psychiatric witnesses in criminal cases, in which the question of insanity arose, should be invited from the faculty of philosophy and not from the medical faculty (Zilboorg, 1941, p. 289). Only a few *Psychiker* —Feuchtersleben the most prominent—challenged Kant on this matter.

A further illustration of the reliance of German Romantic psychiatry on philosophy is seen in the publishing career of Johann Christian Reil (1759-1813), who had an encyclopedic knowledge of medicine, neurology, and clinical psychiatry. Early in the century, Reil founded two periodicals dedicated to psychotherapeutic matters. Each time he called in a philosopher (A. A. A. Kayssler, then J. C. Hoffbauer) to aid him.

In their justifiable eagerness to condemn the Romantics' method and association with "metaphysicians," late nineteenth-century psychiatrists indiscriminately renounced the rich thought of their intellectual forebears. Psychiatrists after

1850 concentrated their energies in arranging data into classifications and in localizing the site of mental illness in the nervous system (Alexander and Selesnick, 1966, p. 146). Romantic psychobiology suddenly came "to a halt in the middle of the century; it disappeared as if by the touch of a magic wand." After the death of one of the last renowned *Psychiker*, C. W. Ideler (1795-1860), there was no trace of his influence. Although Ideler had been the chief psychiatrist at the University Hospital in Berlin, he was repudiated as an idealist, and the famous Kraepelin spoke of Ideler's writing as "pure play of thoughts" (Zilboorg, 1941, pp. 475-476). Most late nineteenth-century psychiatrists lacked any interest in notions of inner psychic conflict, the role of the "passions" in mental disease, symbolism, and the unconscious. The intensity with which psychiatrists had shifted their attention from these matters was significant for the reception of psychoanalysis.

The second salient characteristic of German psychiatry before 1850 was its spectacular growth, starting from a point of virtual nonexistence as a medical specialty. This burgeoning is quite marked when the pre-1800 contributions and achievements of German psychiatrists are compared with those in England and France. If Kirchhoff (1921) is correct, the first German doctoral dissertation on psychiatry came only in 1797, with Johann Gottfried Langermann's (1768-1832) "On the Method of Recognizing and Curing Lasting Mental Diseases." And for the first half of the nineteenth century it was French psychiatry that led the world. When a Bavarian count was tried for murder, the French psychiatrist Bénédict Augustin Morel (1809-1873) was invited to Munich to give his expert psychiatric opinion on the defendant. Indeed, Paris was the Mecca of Western medicine at that time. The French school of psychiatry was relatively free from the Romanticism which had swept over German psychiatry. French clinicians were careful to describe the psychological manifestations of mental disease rather than seek their ultimate psychological origin. Yet it was in this period of French supremacy that German psychiatry began the rapid growth that was to leave it the victor over France before the end of the nineteenth century. The Franco-Prussian War had its scientific parallels.

The development of German psychiatry in the early years of the last century was a part of the general renaissance of German science. At the end of the eighteenth century, German science was in a state of decline. It was rescued by the influence of Carl Friedrich Gauss (1777-1855), the great mathematician; by the example of the activity of the French universities; by the ferment associated with the nationalism aroused by the Napoleonic occupation; and by the stimulus to thought provided by the spread of *Naturphilosophie*. The University of Göttingen began to pay greater attention to the teaching of science and medicine, and the University of Berlin soon emulated this example with its new science syllabus of 1810. Other universities followed suit: in Prussia—Breslau, Königsberg, Halle, Bonn; in the other German states—Jena, Erlangen, Munich, Würzburg, and Tübingen. Further factors in Germany's scientific revival were the explorations and scholarship of Alexander von Humboldt (1769-1859) and the influential activities of the Society of German Scientists and Physicians (*Gesellschaft deutscher Naturforscher und Ärzte*), founded in 1822 by Lorenz Oken (1779-1851), an ardent liberal and enthusiastic philosopher of nature. The annual lectures and meetings the Society organized in different cities were extremely well attended and played an important part in the nineteenth-century German scientific renaissance.

Within the context of this general scientific blossoming, German psychiatrists made significant pioneering contributions. Heinroth became in 1811 the first professor of psychotherapy (*psychische Therapie*) in the German-speaking world. Believing that the body and the psyche are but two aspects of the same thing, he used the word "psychosomatic" for its first time in a discussion of the etiology of insomnia. Reil published the first systematic treatise of psychotherapy (*die psychische Curmethode*) in 1803, and in 1808 was the first to use the term "psychiatry" (from the Greek *psyche* [mind] and *iatros* [physician]). And in 1811 the first German textbook of mental diseases was published by Alexander Haindorf (1782-1862). Later, in 1845, Feuchtersleben introduced the term "psychosis" in its modern sense.

During the eighteenth century, insanity had come to be recognized as a disease and, therefore, within the scope of medical practice. By 1805, the first two German medical journals dealing with mental illness had appeared; the third soon followed in 1808. These journals were always short-lived, but they were numerous. The years 1805-1838 saw about ten psychiatric periodicals make their appearances. Finally, in 1844, the *Allgemeine Zeitschrift für Psychiatrie* was founded, the first German psychiatric journal which still survives.[4] General interest in psychiatry became great enough in 1847 to warrant the formation of a separate section on anthropology and psychiatry of the Society of German Scientists and Physicians.

In attempting to catch up with psychiatry in France and England, German psychiatry was confronted by two major problems: first, the need to build hospitals and establish humane care of patients; second, the search for a system, for a means of sorting out the mass of psychological phenomena into an orderly arrangement. Although it was worked on continually, the latter problem was not satisfactorily solved until the end of the nineteenth century. But the Germans made quick progress in meeting the challenge of hospital organization in the first half of the nineteenth century.

For most of the eighteenth century in Germany there were no special institutions for the insane, only wards in poorhouses, prisons, orphanages, workhouses, and hospitals in which troublesome mental patients were confined. Those causing no trouble to society were allowed to eke out an existence as beggars or harmless lunatics. There were only seven hospitals for the insane in Germany and "these institutions were nothing more than dumping grounds for raging, incurable derelicts" (Kraepelin, 1917, pp. 10, 99-100).

But in 1811 the first modern institution was opened at Sonnenstein. A contemporary psychiatrist called it "the dawn of a new day in the treatment of mental disease in Germany. . . . The bright rays from the height brought light, warmth and

---

[4] For details of editors, titles, and dates see Ackerknecht (1959, p. 55); Amdur (1943, pp. 205-216); Bromberg (1954, pp. 103-104); Mora (1967, p. 27); Veith (1965, p. 184); Zilboorg (1941, p. 289).

life into other institutions where darkness prevailed . . ."
(Damerow, quoted in Kraepelin, 1917, p. 104). Influenced by
Pinel and Esquirol, the French advocates of "moral
treatment" (humane handling and conditions) for the insane,
German doctors flocked to study Sonnenstein. They drew in-
spiration from it and planned similar structures, some of
which came under the direction of the most outstanding psy-
chiatrists of the first half of the century: Siegburg under
Jacobi; Sachsenberg under Flemming; Winnenthal under
Zeller, who was Griesinger's teacher; Halle under Damerow;
Illenau under Roller (Ackerknecht, 1959, pp. 54-55).

By 1866 there were in Germany 103 public institutions for
the care of the insane, 69 private asylums, 29 so-called "open
asylums" for patients with nonpsychotic "nervous diseases,"
and 32 private institutions for the mentally retarded
(Letchworth, 1889, p. 203).

The Germans began the nineteenth century almost without
an institutional system, an education system, or a theoretical
system. They attacked all three deficiencies simultaneously
with great zeal.

> The German professor of psychiatry from the very beginning
> had to be administrative chief of a hospital or clinic as well as
> teacher, research worker, and doctor to his patients. It was
> necessary to build and to organize while the scientific work was
> being carried on. [Yet] the German hospital became an
> institution for treatment and research work almost within one
> generation. Nowhere in the world during the middle part of the
> century was so much research work done in psychiatry as in Ger-
> many. [The] number [of psychiatrists] increased more rapidly
> than in France or England [Zilboorg, 1941, p. 446].

Karl Jaspers has rightly called this early period of German
psychiatry the era of "institutional psychiatry," as opposed to
the period of "university psychiatry" which followed.[5]
Although many psychiatrists combined careers of speculative
writing with jobs as superintendents of the ever more numer-

[5] See Bromberg (1954, pp. 96-97) on the pioneering role of J. C. Reil in the
administrative organization of German mental institutions. For a short but useful
history of insane asylums and institutional treatment see Adam (1928). For more
contemporaneous descriptions see Pliny Earle (1854) and Kirchhoff (1890).

ous hospitals, the professional dominance of the philosophical psychiatrists began to wane after 1830. By mid-century the leading psychiatrists were the administrators of mental institutions. They were concerned with practical matters—the keeping of records, the care of patients, and the promotion of professional organizations and publications. It was three leading mental hospital administrators—Damerow, Flemming, and Roller—who founded the *Allgemeine Zeitschrift für Psychiatrie*. The administrators were interested in criminology and medicolegal problems involving the criminally insane. In scientific practice they tended to be eclectic. In matters of theory, though some remained convinced *Psychiker*, the majority were increasingly *Somatiker*, ascribing mental illness to organic defects, very often to brain pathology.

Institutional psychiatrists shared a remote rural life with their patients and were involved in the daily activities of the asylums. In their writings can be detected a "certain humanity . . . and at times a certain pastoral dignity" (Jaspers, 1964, pp. 846-847). When the psychiatrist Langermann was director of a mental hospital at Bayreuth from 1805 to 1810, he abolished the strait jacket and was against all restaints.[6] C. F. S. Hahnemann (1755-1843), the founder of homeopathy, treated psychotic patients with kindness and found that they improved.

In at least one instance, however, their practical humanity was countered by an obsession with theoretical considerations. Similarly, fifty years later, philosophical and emotional commitments to theory would affect reactions to psychoanalysis. One particular mid-nineteenth-century debate was whether the insane were as much a part of the human race as healthy people. The debate had its analogies in the disputations of the Spaniards in the sixteenth century about whether New World natives were as human as Europeans and possessed the same "souls." Indecision about the precise place of the insane in the genealogical tree of mankind did prevent some

---

[6] Kraepelin (1917, pp. 135-139) unaccountably claims that the first German doctor to remove restraints did so in 1862.

German psychiatrists from abolishing physical restraint of their patients. In 1861 Griesinger admitted that he had wished to institute nonrestraint but had been inhibited from doing so by the "adverse opinions of German psychologists" (Bromberg, 1954, p. 99).

Still, the period of institutional psychiatry helped usher in a new scientific era because of the untold opportunities the hospitals offered psychiatrists to study a great number of patients and to observe each patient for a long period of time. The discerning physician was given all the material he needed.

SCIENTIFIC PSYCHIATRY: AN OVERVIEW

With growing momentum, German psychiatry now passed into a new age. The second half of the nineteenth century was the time of a reaction against Romanticism, of a changed political and social climate, of the excitement generated by the Helmholtzian school of physics and physiology. Griesinger's textbook found a sympathetic audience, and brain psychiatry flourished. Clinical psychiatry moved haltingly though inexorably toward the production of a psychiatric classification whose appeal was enormous.

Slowly but unambiguously the Germans replaced the French as leaders in psychiatry. By the middle of the nineteenth century, the German universities and medical schools were assiduously cultivating such basic sciences as physics, chemistry, histology and cellular pathology, and bacteriology. All physicians had to be well grounded in these subjects. In Paris, clinical medicine still reigned supreme; for the French medical student, the laboratory sciences were only ancillary and often neglected. In the early nineteenth century, students from Europe and the United States had flocked to Paris to study the clinical and bedside techniques which the French had developed to an advanced state. After 1850, it was the German universities that attracted foreigners in great numbers. The French medical educational system was at "first a tremendous asset, later on a serious handicap" (Ackerknecht's [1966] "Introduction" to Puschmann, [1889]). (See also Garrison, 1929, pp. 755-765; Castiglione, 1958, pp. 763, 913.)

In Germany, psychiatry and neurology, united in the field of neuropsychiatry[7] began to benefit from the enormous technical progress

---

[7] "Neuropsychiatry" is a word of American origin, coined during World War I. But its current meaning accurately describes an already existing medical subspecialty in late nineteenth-century Germany.

and anatomic-physiologic discoveries of German medicine. The development of a scientific clinical psychiatry was also fostered by the German system of university psychiatric clinics, which rapidly expanded after 1860. It was primarily this particular feature of German medical life which gave German psychiatry leadership over that in England or the United States. In the English-speaking countries, the teaching hospitals were not university clinics but technical schools under the control of groups of nonacademic specialists, chiefly internists and general surgeons. There was no separate section of psychiatry in these schools (Fish, 1964, p. 301). Moreover, Griesinger's text came at a particularly fitting time in the evolution of German psychiatry and served at once as a focal point and as a catalyst for current and future developments. As part of a new, scientifically vigorous and creative Germany, German psychiatrists not only finally became a part of European medicine but also the leaders of Western psychiatry.

The new German psychiatry was characterized by an altered mood not out of character with the chastened liberal spirit and the great concentration on the purely practical applications of science that accompanied the unification of Germany in the 1860's and 1870's. In a revulsion against the speculations of the Romanticists, there was a search for and a cult of objectivity in all fields of human knowledge. The attempts of the *Psychiker* to understand the disordered mind not as a result of organic disease but as a result of individual psychic development seemed to the now dominant *Somatiker* to have been the last flickerings of unscientific thinking, best forgotten — at worst, painfully remembered. The psychodynamic orientation of the Romanticists was completely eclipsed as German psychiatry declared "the supremacy of the brain over any other structure" (Zilboorg, 1941, p. 435). Psychobiology was abandoned. Romantic psychiatry had "focused on the individual and on his unique response — on the basis of his personality — to an individual approach. [Now] organically oriented psychiatry focused on the common *Anlage* [hereditary predisposition] of each individual and on the common means geared to modify a pathological condition uniformly affecting each individual" (Mora, 1965, p. 47).[8]

---

[8] But German psychiatry of the second half of the nineteenth century should not be dismissed as "a sterile period of data-gathering" (Alexander and Selesnick, 1966, p. 146). Such a judgment disregards positive achievements of the era and the emotions they generated. For example, the discovery was made that the reflex kick of the leg could be used in the diagnosis of the dread general paralysis of the insane. In the 1870's and 1880's the most astute neurologists and psychiatrists were understandably excited and pleased as they sought to elicit a patient's "knee jerk," in order to decide whether a palsied leg had a hysterical or an organic etiology.

MID-CENTURY: THE HELMHOLTZIANS AND GRIESINGER

Organic psychiatry was decisively influenced by a generation of physiologists, physicists, pathologists, and embryologists, representative of whom were Emil du Bois-Reymond (1818-1896), Ernst Brücke (1819-1892), Hermann von Helmholtz (1821-1894), Rudolf von Kölliker (1817-1905), Carl Ludwig (1816-1895), and Rudolf Virchow (1821-1902). Their brilliance was instrumental in placing Germany in the forefront of science and medicine. With the exception of Kölliker's and Virchow's work, their preoccupations and outlook have often (if not entirely correctly) been subsumed under the term "the school of Helmholtz."[9] As a scientific and philosophical approach to the problems of medicine, the Helmholtzian school signified three things. Firstly, it was a belief in the materialism and tangibility of all matter. In 1842 du Bois-Reymond wrote:

> Brücke and I pledged a solemn oath to put into effect this truth: "No other forces than the common physical-chemical ones are active within the organism. In those cases which cannot at the time be explained by these forces one has either to find the specific way or form of their action by means of the physical-mathematical method or to assume new forces equal in dignity to the chemical-physical forces inherent in matter, reduceable to the force of attraction and repulsion" [quoted in Jones, 1953, pp. 40-41].

The way the scientist learned about these forces was through experimentation and observation; these methods were the only ones that could lead to acceptable explanations.

Building on these beliefs, the Helmholtzian school found no evidence of any teleology or ultimate goal in nature. In 1858 Virchow showed that disease develops when severe stimuli disturb the life processes of the cells. Any vitalist notion that invisible, ethereal substances were at work was ruled out; all cells came from other cells. When, a year after Virchow's book, Darwin published his theory of natural selection, the

---

[9] Cranefield (1966, pp. 35-39) has taken exception to this phrase, introduced by Siegfried Bernfeld (1944), and prefers the term the "biophysics movement of 1847." He believes the word "school" cannot be applied to "a small group of physiologists" and, at any rate, its leader was not Helmholtz but du Bois-Reymond.

issue appeared to be settled.[10] It was no longer necessary to explain the purposefulness of living organisms by a mystical vital force that pursues pre-established goals. It could now be shown that a causality completely intelligible to ordinary perception could explain nature's processes. Nothing seemed to stand in the way of solving all the mysteries of life, organic and psychological, by the new scientific methods. When Brücke published his *Lectures on Physiology* in 1874, he proclaimed that there were "no spirits, essences or entelechies, no superior plans or ultimate purposes" at work in the evolution of life. Physical energies alone caused effects—somehow (Jones, 1953, p. 42).

The third point to be made about the Helmholtzians is that their commitments to the use of observation and experiment, to the reduction of nature to physics and chemistry, and to antiteleological beliefs were also emotional commitments. Du Bois-Reymond had declared fervently: "Brücke and I pledged a solemn oath to put into effect this truth." Their scientific work was based on a repugnance for and violent reaction to the old *Naturphilosophie*, with its "speculative physics." Though the philosophy of nature was now disdained, the new physics and physiology nevertheless retained the quality of the Romantic era's science: its one-sided, whole-hearted dedication to its ideals. The new terms of physical physiology— "unity of science," "science," and "physical forces"—were not merely guidelines or hypotheses. Jones labels them "objects of worship." And they were more than methods of research; they were a *Weltanschauung*. In Berlin, with du Bois-Reymond, this temper remained high, intertwined with Prussian patriotism.[11]

It is no accident that Griesinger's psychiatric textbook appeared in the same year, 1845, that the Helmholtzians founded the Berlin Physics Society (*Berliner physikalische*

---

[10] Ironically, Virchow refused to accept Darwin's conclusions. Some other German scientists also balked, but not enough to prevent the general acceptance of Darwinian biology in educated circles.

[11] Cranefield (1966, p. 36) believes that the initial fervor of the "biophysics movement" had already begun to wane in the 1850's and that by the mid 1870's "the self-confident mechanism of the 1847 movement had nearly died."

Gesellschaft). The somaticists' rise to dominance over German psychiatry took place in the intensely stimulating scientific atmosphere that was being created by Virchow and Helmholtz.

> The experimental laboratory entered the field of medicine. It soon became the adjunct, the integral part of medicine—the very legs of the patient's bed, the doctor's right hand at the bedside. Everywhere this great change was felt. . . . The great ambition cherished by all [psychiatrists from the start of the nineteenth century], the ambition not only to capture psychiatry but to make it a legitimate branch of general medicine or neorology seemed . . . to have entered the phase of actual fulfillment [Zilboorg, 1941, p. 400].

Thus German psychiatry tried to become modern and scientific by explaining disordered emotional behavior in terms of the anatomic concept of disease: the first step toward a knowledge of symptoms is their "locality," i.e., their dependence on a given organ. This materialistic concept of mental disease found expression in Wilhelm Griesinger's *Mental Pathology and Therapeutics*. Griesinger (1817-1868) tried to establish the principle of cerebral localization of mental diseases and symptoms. He was sure that the brain is the seat of mental diseases, although he acknowledged that it had not yet been possible to discover specific brain damage corresponding to individual mental disorders. The clinician was advised that once a diagnosis of mental disease had been made, he should always ask himself which part of the brain has been affected. "The impression was given that the solution of the problems involved in insanity was reached as soon as they could be expressed in terms of anatomy and physiology" (Riese, 1967, p. 114).[12] Psychiatry received the alternate title of "study of cerebral disease."

Griesinger's discussions of the role of the unconscious, ego structure, frustration, and wish fulfillment in mental symptoms and dreams got lost in his other teachings and were quickly and completely forgotten.

---

[12] See also Bodamer (1953, pp. 511-535), R. Kuhn (1957, pp. 41-67), Leibbrand and Wettley (1961, pp. 509-518).

The enthusiastic reception given Griesinger's book is partly explained by the *Zeitgeist*. Griesinger believed his mission was to free German psychiatry from Romantic conceptions. He thought that by proving that mental derangements had organic causes he could move away from poetic speculations about insanity. Griesinger severed his ties with philosophy. In 1845 he wrote that since insanity was a disease of the brain, it could only be studied from the medical point of view. All nonmedical, "particularly all poetical and ideal conceptions of insanity [are] of the smallest value" (Griesinger, 1845, pp. 9-10). This was not Feuchtersleben's belief. In the same year he declared that "all branches of human research and knowledge are naturally blended with each other." He could not give "a complete view" of any science without discussing what "other departments" had to say about it. His lectures on medical psychology had the goal of effecting a union between philosophers and physicians, and to this end he first entered into "some philosophical discussions." Feuchtersleben considered what mind (*Geist*) was, leaning heavily on Spinoza, Kant, Fichte, Schelling, and Hegel. He decided that "the notion, *mental disease*, must therefore be deduced, neither from the mind, nor from the body, but from the relation of each to the other" (Feuchtersleben, 1845, pp. 3-4, 8, 13, 75). Feuchtersleben's conclusion was far more sophisticated than Griesinger's, but his philosophical preoccupations discredited him. "To students of psychiatry, Griesinger represented science, Feuchtersleben literature. The former was diligently read; the latter was scanned for enjoyment and perhaps was not taken quite seriously. Griesinger was the embodiment of the new German science . . ." (Veith, 1965, p. 193).[13]

But the universal impact of Griesinger's work demands additional explanation. Griesinger was not only representative of the new science, but his career exemplified the life sought after by the new psychiatrist. He was not an institutional

[13] See Leibbrand and Wettley (1961, p. 507) on Feuchtersleben's career as a poet and his literary interests and connections. It should not be thought, however, that Feuchtersleben's medical life was insignificant. He was Dean of the Medical Faculty at the University of Vienna, and his psychiatric textbook was published in England by the Sydenham Society only two years after it appeared in Germany.

psychiatrist, but one of the novel breed of "university psychiatrists," and he spent almost his entire professional career as a
"professor." When in 1865 he was appointed to the newly
created Chair of Psychiatry and Neurology at the University of
Berlin, his position became still more authoritative. Though
Griesinger had been a professor of internal medicine, he had
always treated psychiatric patients in his medical clinics.
When he arrived at the Charité (university hospital) in Berlin,
he created psychiatric wards where the mentally ill could be
treated by physicians and studied by the students, just as were
the physically ill on the other wards. Griesinger's insistence
that psychiatry become an independent medical speciality
increased his standing with other German psychiatrists. His
"deeply felt conviction [that] psychiatry and neurology . . . are
but one field in which only one language is spoken and the
same laws rule" (quoted in Zilboorg, 1941, p. 436) attested to
his modernity. In promulgating these ideas, Griesinger had
the assistance of a good literary style and a forceful
personality, and as a reformer exerted much influence on the
practical treatment of the mentally ill.[14]

Griesinger expressed himself concisely and concentrated on
description. His scheme of mental disease was compact
because he jettisoned the idea that in emotional illnesses the
psychiatrist is really dealing with a variety of diseases. Rather,
quite simply, mental disease is brain disease; various emotional aberrations are but signs of one disease: brain disease. This
view, well-stated and backed by an academic authority,
became enormously popular because it offered an attractive
alternative to the Romantic tradition of considering every
mental symptom a new disease. "Psychiatry before Griesinger
had been saturated with nomenclature and . . . Latin and
Greek etymology . . . Heinroth's forty-eight diseases were
offered in place of Plater's twenty-three. There was a host of
melancholias . . . and manias" (Zilboorg, 1941, p. 438).
German psychiatrists longed for clarity and simplification and

---

[14] For an excellent short account of Griesinger's life and work see Ackerknecht
(1959, pp. 55-65). See also Kirchhoff (1924, pp. 1-15) and Kolle (1956, pp. 115-
127).

for an end to the etymological whim of every new observer. They gladly accepted Griesinger even at the cost of oversimplification and of accepting on faith his "deeply felt conviction" about the unity of psychiatry and neuropathology.[15]

BRAIN PSYCHIATRY AND THE LABORATORY

Griesinger's influence quickened the metamorphosis of German psychiatry from an institutional into a university psychiatry. His demand for an alliance between psychiatry and neurology could only be achieved in university laboratories. After 1860 more and more university neuropsychiatric clinics were established and the leadership of German psychiatry shifted to the professors who were the heads of these clinics (see Kolle, 1956, pp. 267-276). German psychiatry took on a new coloration from this change.

> Now it was carried on by people who no longer shared their whole life from morning to night with their patients. It found its way into the laboratories for brain anatomy or for experimental psychopathology; it became more coldblooded, detailed, impersonal and less humane. It lost itself in endless particulars, measurements, statistics and findings. It lost imagination and design [Jaspers, 1964, p. 847].

The new psychiatry fit securely into a Germany where technological expansion and political consolidation left little room for Romantic trends of thought and preoccupations with the individual and the individual's mind. It was this new Germany which Nietzsche found so uncongenial and which he denounced at every turn. He condemned "that moral law which requires [that] the individual shall sacrifice himself . . . in spite of all individual counter desires and advantages" (1881, p. 16). He sought to awake all workers to "the essential

---

[15] Of course, there were sophisticated physicians who did not immediately fall prey to the materialistic trap. One was Friedrich Nasse (1778-1851), an expert physiologist and experienced clinician who was initially cautious. He founded a journal in an attempt to solve the mind-body riddle, but the answer eluded him. Finally Nasse turned to a purely organic orientation and decided that somnambulism and even character defects were caused by neurological changes (Kirchhoff, 1921, pp. 105-117). Nasse's assessment of somnambulism seems to have been proved correct by modern sleep research.

part of their misery, i.e., their impersonal enslavement. . . . Fie, that there should be a regular price at which a man should cease to be a personality and become a screw [in a machine] instead!" (p. 214). Nietzsche rebelled against "the tyranny of the majority" where institutions threatened the "wellbeing . . . and continued existence" of the individual and caused him to "suffer . . . atrophy or perish" (1879, pp. 154-155). The new age was one which demanded "absolute regularity, punctilious and unthinking obedience, a mode of life fixed once and for all, fully occupied time . . . indeed, training for 'impersonality,' for self-forgetfulness, for '*incuria sui*' [neglect of self] . . . " (1887, p. 570).

Modern man had become a "maggot . . . hopelessly mediocre and insipid." Because "the diminution and leveling of European man constitutes our greatest danger," Nietzsche cried out for a new "higher" individual, an *Übermensch* not mired in mass attitudes and concerns and free from the dominance of the new politicians and industrialists (1874, pp. 155-157). The "individual" was Nietzsche's leitmotiv and the theme around which so much of German youth rallied at the turn of the century.

The era of brain psychiatry inaugurated by Griesinger did little to advance a concern with the psychiatric patient as an individual. Brain psychiatry did contribute to the understanding of the structure and function of the brain and spinal cord and the sympathetic nervous system. As a result of the neuroanatomical orientation in psychiatry and of the advances made in the technique of microscopy, an enormous literature began to develop in anatomy and pathology. Medical men became hopeful that they had found the key to mental illness. Yet they expressed their hopes in a fashion which caused Nietzsche to speak of the "regression" of modern science. Franz Nissl (1860-1919), the outstanding neuropathologist and professor at Heidelberg, was sure that "as soon as we agree to see in all mental derangements the clinical expression of definite disease processes in the cortex, we remove the obstacle which makes impossible agreement among alienists" (quoted in Bromberg, 1937, p. 207). Another physician called the emotional phenomena which he saw on hospital wards "brain life" (*Hirnleben*) (Zilboorg, 1941, pp. 439-440). One of the leaders of the movement, Theodor Meynert (1833-1892), professor at Vienna and one of Freud's teachers, produced a text which had a powerful effect on his German contemporaries. He wrote in the preface: "The reader will find no other definition of 'Psychiatry' in this book but the one given on the title page: Clinical Treatise on Diseases of the Fore-Brain. The historical term psychiatry, i.e., 'treatment of the soul,' implies more than we can accomplish, and transcends the bounds of accurate scientific investigation" (Riese, 1967, p. 114). Meynert declared that one day psychiatry would merge into the study of the lesions of the frontal lobe and its connections. That hospital wards of "brain life" also housed human beings was not the primary concern.[16]

Thus the brain psychiatrists espoused a materialistic and mechanistic medicine. To these men the brain was the creator of all mind processes. In conformity with the doctrine of cerebral localization, the brain researchers turned over an ever-increasing number of faculties and functions to "cerebral centers." In many circles it was unthinkable to admit of any basic mental process not strictly correlated with a specific area of the brain. The brain psychiatrists lost sight of the sum of the parts. Hardly anyone questioned whether a human being might be something more than the physical total of his bodily organs.[17]

Such simplistic materialism often went hand in hand with single-minded devotion to a mechanistic explanation of mental processes, indeed, of all life processes. The human being functioned like a machine, and all his activities were capable of complete explanation by the laws of physics and chemistry. Though the failure of physiological research to yield anything clinically useful had turned many German psychiatrists into skeptics by the end of the nineteenth century, the mechanistic premises still retained their charm and were. taught to medical students. Theodor Puschmann, a psychiatrist who trained under Meynert and became a promi-

[16] Brain psychiatry is still a flourishing field in Germany today.

[17] However, concerns with cerebral localization had significant scientific meaning in the nineteenth century which cannot be overlooked (see Chapter 7).

nent historian of medicine, wrote as late as 1889: "The civilization of the present day has been established on the abundance of newly-discovered facts which have enriched the natural sciences during the nineteenth century, and in the knowledge of their mutual relationships and common laws, which has rendered possible a simplified view of the life of nature" (Puschmann, 1889, pp. 443-444).

An antiteleogical view of life processes was a concomitant of the mechanistic *Weltanschauung*. Two influential lectures given in 1872 and 1880 by the energetic and fiery Helmholtzian, du Bois-Reymond, were still famous among German psychiatrists at the turn of the century. In them, du Bois-Reymond had professed a rigid denial of final causes in regard to such problems as the nature of force and matter, the origin of motion, the origin of life, the purposeful character of natural phenomena, the origin of sensation, the origin of thought, and the freedom of the will. Du Bois-Reymond had summed up his philosophy with the words *ignoramus et ignorabimus* — we do not know and we shall never know — and this phrase was still much in vogue (Garrison, 1929, p. 535).[18]

At their most ambitious, but at the same time on insubstantial theoretical grounds, some of the brain psychiatrists tried to correlate their anatomical findings with mental disorders. Such men as Meynert, Karl Westphal (1833-1890), Wilhelm Erb (1840-1921), and Carl Wernicke (1848-1905) were driven to skillful speculative constructions.[19] Meynert became convinced that inadequate blood circulation of the brain led to states of excitement (manias) and that overflow of blood

[18] Indeed, psychiatric familiarity with du Bois-Reymond's attitude still exists in Germany. Wolfgang Loch, a German psychoanalyst, quoted du Bois-Reymond's words in a letter to me, March 20, 1963.

Du Bois-Reymond's convictions — in some ways quite antiscientific — were not just an expression of the mechanism prevalent in many areas of nineteenth-century thinking. His views hold a place in the history of German thought at least from the time of Kant, who firmly declared that knowledge had its limits and that there were areas of life it was fruitless to investigate. Jaspers, first as a psychiatrist and then as a philosopher, agreed with Kant about the limits of scientific investigation (see below, pp. 324-325).

[19] See Birnbaum (1928, pp. 34-42); Kirchhoff (1924) on Nissl (pp. 288-296), on Meynert (pp. 121-135), on Wernicke (pp. 238-251), and on Westphal (pp. 110-121); Kolle (1959) on Nissl (pp. 13-31) and on Wernicke (pp. 106-128); and Leibbrand and Wettley (1961, pp. 546-557).

into the cerebral vessels produced depressions. He then proposed a systematic classification of mental illness based on his histopathological studies.

Their view of mental disease provided the brain psychiatrists with great certitude. In the tradition of Helmholtzian science, they were convinced that only material changes could produce mental changes. Blinded by the emotionalism of the Helmholtzians, they seemed to demand little factual confirmation; their beliefs sustained them.[20] However, even contemporaries derided the classification of mental diseases based on the theory of localization. Hans Gruhle (1880-1958) called it the school of "brain mythology" and Emil Kraepelin (1856-1926) "speculative anatomy" (Zilboorg, 1941, p. 441; Ackerknecht, 1959, p. 66). The organicists did, of course, have a few discoveries which sustained their hopes. The main ones centered on the connection between syphilis and the general paresis of the insane. Also, it was shown that the electrical stimulation of certain areas of the cortex produced movements in the limbs on the opposite side of the body. Furthermore, it was known that destruction of certain other areas would lead to aphasia. Finally, the enunciation of the concept of the neuron (structural and functional unit of nervous tissue) was encouraging.

It is true that brain psychiatry was a stimulus to further study of general paresis, various febrile exhaustive states, alcoholic mental disorders, and senile psychoses due to severe vascular changes in the brain. Yet it did not lead to an understanding of mental aberrations. Though intensive brain research vaulted many a physician into a professorship, it yielded few practical results for psychiatry and was largely worthless to clinicians.

CLINICAL PSYCHIATRY: CLASSIFICATION AND KRAEPELIN

The psychiatrists who were more interested in clinical than in laboratory work began to cast about for another approach. In spite of the enthusiastic claims of their brethren in re-

---

[20] Freud himself remained convinced that brain physiology would ultimately bring the answers to the problems of mental processes. But he saw that psychological explanations and treatments were intermediate and necessary stopgaps until that far-off day arrived.

search, the clinicians clearly saw that there was a large group of patients with severe mental disorders in which no positive post-mortem findings occurred. The clinicians began to feel that the most useful method was a strict empiricism which refrained from causal speculations, limited itself to minute observation of the patient, and followed each stage of the disease carefully until recovery or death. This medical empiricism took happy advantage of the vogue of asylum-building that had continued throughout the nineteenth century. By 1911, for a population of almost 65 million, there were 187 public asylums, 16 university clinics, 5 psychiatric wards in military hospitals, 11 wards in penal institutions, 225 private institutions, and 85 sanatoria for alcoholics and patients suffering from nervous disorders (Kraepelin, 1917, p. 106). Large numbers of mental patients had been brought together under the same roof, and much clinical material had been amassed. There were 143,410 psychiatric in-patients in Germany in 1911. This meant that since 1850, the percentage of such patients out of Germany's total population had increased between two and three times (Kraepelin, 1917; Jaspers, 1964, p. 740). It was conveniently possible to verify old observations and also to make new ones.

At the same time, psychiatrists were attracted by what was being done in neurology.

> Neurologists were grouping neurological symptoms into syndromes and finally into diseases; neuropathologists were localizing the lesions to explain these clinical phenomena; and duly impressed neuropsychiatrists began to apply similar principles to behavior. Some neurological diseases could be differentiated by clinical observation alone, even without the benefit of pathological investigation. Why should it not be possible, then, to systematize mental symptoms on a clinical basis in a similar manner? . . . later, neuropathological confirmation of disease entities would be forthcoming [Alexander and Selesnick, 1966, p. 161].

Clinicians began to use the welter of clinical material that had accumulated. Realizing, however, that classifying mental illnesses according to symptoms was a futile exercise, some psychiatrists began to delineate disease pictures by observing mental illnesses throughout their total course. These men were exposed to an ideal model for such an observation. Up to 30 percent of all admissions in mental hospitals were of patients suffering from the paresis of syphilis. A group of gifted observers of clinical phenomena arose, among whom Karl Kahlbaum (1828-1899) was the most eminent (De Boor, 1954, Part I, Kirchhoff, 1924, pp. 87-97; Leibbrand and Wettley, 1961, pp. 560-566).

As a result of some highly creative contributions in the early 1870's, it seemed as if German psychiatry was on the verge of solving the problems of classification that had vexed and retarded it throughout the century. But for the next twenty years, until the appearance of the fifth edition of Kraepelin's text, a satisfactory nosology was not forthcoming. That is not to say that there was any lack of new classifications. Continually searching for a way to order the piles of clinical data, German psychiatrists proffered one short-lived classification after another. These attempts succeeded only in adding to the already vast psychiatric terminology.

> To give a comprehensive nosology . . . almost seems to have become the unspoken ambition of every psychiatrist of industry and promise, as it is the ambition of a good tenor to strike a high C. This classificatory ambition was so conspicuous that the composer Berlioz was prompted to remark that after their studies have been completed a rhetorician writes a tragedy and a psychiatrist a classification [Zilboorg, 1941, p. 450. See also Havens, 1965, p. 17; Lewis, 1941, p. 128]

The busy classifiers and energetic brain researchers were characteristic of German psychiatry in the closing decades of the nineteenth century. It was on this confusing scene of great industry and few results that Kraepelin's classification descended in 1896, one year after Breuer and Freud's *Studies on Hysteria*. Kraepelin's proposals were contained in the fifth edition (1896) of a textbook that he had been steadily expanding since 1883. Kraepelin had tried and abandoned brain research, and by 1896 already had a ten-year professorial career behind him. Although all Kraepelin's students remember him as a great teacher, they are not unanimous about the nature of his personality. Eugen Kahn (1956, 1959) remembers him fondly. Edith Jacobson (personal interview,

1963) recalls strongly Kraepelin's ready use of sarcasm. His writings do reveal a sarcastic bent, but obviously many of his residents were not affected by it. He had a talent for organization, both of ideas and people. Zilboorg (1941, p. 452) cites his "tactful ability in bringing people to work as an organized group." Alexander and Selesnick (1966, p. 163) consider Kraepelin's "tact" a veneer which covered a forceful personality. "After he assumed the directorship of a hospital and clinic there was never a question of who was the man in charge. 'Imperial German psychiatry' was said to have gained its prominence under the 'chancellorship' of Kraepelin, one of Bismarck's admirers."[21]

Kraepelin was a tireless and meticulous observer of clinical phenomena. He collected and studied thousands of case histories, covering not only the story of each illness, but the history of each patient's life before the illness and a follow-up of his life after he had left the hospital. Through this vast factual knowledge, Kraepelin was able to impose a long-a-waited order on psychiatry everywhere. When Kraepelin adopted Kahlbaum's concept that a disease is a group of illnesses with common symptoms and a common course, psychiatry finally ceased to be the fine art of defining symptoms. Since previously described *démence précoce* (Morel in 1860), hebephrenia (Hecker in 1871), and catatonia (Kahlbaum in 1874) all had symptoms in common and all ended in personality deterioration, Kraepelin grouped them together as a disease entity which he called "dementia praecox." He delineated two more psychotic entities, paranoia and manic-depressive psychosis, as well as making other groupings. This approach received much acknowledgment from many clinicians, and Kraepelin's system of descriptive psychiatry is still used to classify patients on the basis of their manifest symptoms and disease history (De Boor, 1954, Part II; Kolle, 1957; Wyrsch, 1956).

With Kraepelin's classification to support them, German psychiatrists ceased to feel like the stepchildren of German

---

[21] For biographies of Kraepelin see Kahn (1959), Kolle (1956, pp. 175-185), and Leibbrand and Wettley (1961, pp. 577-586). Birnbaum (1928, pp. 43-45) briefly discusses Kahlbaum and Kraepelin.

medicine. At last there was a demonstrable process of disease in the mentally ill. A mental disease was like a physical disease with regular attacks, of increasing severity, and with decreasing times between each attack. Just as a physician studies the life history of a patient with heart disease or typhoid fever, so now the psychiatrist could study the natural course of a "mental case": a youth who developed a mania at 18, had a second attack at 28 and a third at 36 and then progressed to a final state of mental deterioration (dementia). To believe conclusively that such disease processes existed gave many psychiatrists great confidence in their professional abilities.

Kraepelin's textbook came to exercise a decisive influence on the future development of German psychiatry. Kraepelin's authority, though challenged, was vast at the turn of the century and the following two decades, and his *Lehrbuch* became the bible of modern psychiatry. Jaspers (1964, p. 852) flatly stated: "Kraepelin's Textbook has been the best read of all psychiatric texts." There were four more editions after the famous fifth, culminating in a massive work of 2,425 pages issued in cooperation with Johannes Lange.

Kraepelin was also influential as a teacher. Three times a week he held clinical lectures for 1¾ hours each, twice for beginners, once for advanced students (Kahn, 1956, p. 294). Several German psychoanalysts who attended Kraepelin's lectures or worked under him have testified to the impact he had on those around him (personal conversations).

It is still an exciting experience to read Kraepelin's case presentations. One then sees that Kraepelin's method is not easily summed up by the traditional phrase "observation and classification." The word "observation" scarcely conveys Kraepelin's Holmesian talent for noting every detail of a patient's actions. One must also read Kraepelin's lectures to be aware of the mystique with which he endowed each observation, so that it could be indicative of only one particular type of illness in his nosology. In turn, the word "classification" barely imparts the iron certainty of the process by which a diagnosis was nailed to a patient.

Under the influence of Wilhelm Wundt (see Chapter 7 below), Kraepelin introduced physiological psychology into

German psychiatry. This meant that Kraepelin was a pioneer in the use of "objective" tests to determine the psychological deficits of his patients as well as an originator in evaluating the effects of drugs on human behavior in the laboratory. It also meant that as a clinician Kraepelin believed that the scientific study of psychiatry belonged in the laboratory. In keeping with this orientation, Kraepelin was ever vigilant not to stray from "facts." Thus, although his colleagues found him personally responsive, Kraepelin kept his distance from the inner life of his patients. (He wrote in a brief autobiographical statement: "I never read poems although I composed some myself occasionally. I had the feeling that a poem is only for the writer himself in order to keep a valuable mood in his memory.") He discussed the relevance of psychological ideas in the general sections of his text but left these behind when he got down to clinical work. It is quite obvious in his *Lectures on Clinical Psychiatry* (1901) that his patients' complaints were secondary. Rather, he concentrated on what he could observe with no special concern for constructing a therapeutic or confidential relationship. There were no provisions in his clinic for doctors to have private conversations with their patients (Green, 1974, p. 65). Thus Kraepelinian psychiatry furthered the attitude, already fostered by brain psychiatry, of paying less attention to the patient as a person in favor of giving more attention to his disease.

To Kraepelin a mentally sick person was a collection of symptoms. Moreover, in dealing with the numerous life histories he had compiled, Kraepelin sorted out everything the many individuals had in common, leaving out of consideration the unique data and the specific order in which symptoms had emerged. In his textbook he used composite portraits, groupings of signs from many cases. He thus arrived at "clinical pictures," which exemplified a mental illness as a whole. The underlying disease process was assumed to come through fractionally in each individual case.

Kraepelin's approach also served to entrench more profoundly the pessimistic outlook prevalent among German psychiatrists. The failure of years of laboratory research to help the mentally ill had taken its emotional toll. Only the brain researchers held out the hope that soon a cure would be found. But the Kraepelinians saw nothing to be gained from entertaining such optimistic thoughts.

Kraepelin believed that the current state of psychiatric knowledge did not enable pathology or anatomy, etiology or symptoms, to be the basis for any systematic understanding of mental illness. All the psychiatrist could do was to know clinical disease patterns, and, along with a diagnosis, provide a prognosis. Once the prognosis was made, the future was sealed. With dementia praecox the patient was incurable, with a manic-depressive psychosis the patient would improve. Treatment, aside from environmental manipulation, was not usually discussed, and besides, it could not alter the inevitable progression of the illness. More often than not, the prognoses were gloomy, and an air of resigned pessimism enveloped German psychiatry. Additionally, this outlook often capriciously affected the actual outcome of a patient's illness. Those patients who were predicted to get better were automatically dealt with in an entirely different manner from those patients who were expected to deteriorate.

Though at first Kraepelin's nosological creations had a stimulating effect, in the end they rigidified psychiatric thought. Factors not recognized by Kraepelin in his system were rarely taken into account because the Kraepelinian structure became too sacred to touch. Though in his lifetime Kraepelin faced much professional criticism, it did little to diminish his acceptance. Psychiatrists were absorbed with diagnoses and prognoses as ends in themselves, and the system degenerated into pure formalism. Clinicians thought they had completed their duties after observing and classifying each case (Ackerknecht, 1959, pp. 70-71; Bromberg, 1942, p. 126; Schilpp, 1957, p. 440; Zilboorg, 1941, p. 457).

If the mood of German psychiatry at the turn of the century and the paths it was going to follow in the future can be seen in the work of one representative figure, that figure is Kraepelin. He had provided the long-awaited order that gave some sense to the multiplicity of psychiatric symptoms. As Kraepelin's classification received ever-increasing acceptance, something like a feeling of fulfillment after the completion of a confusing task settled over German psychiatry. The adaptability and the convenience of the Kraepelinian system, coming, as they did, after decades of fruitless efforts, were a welcome professional haven.

THE PSYCHOTHERAPIES

Smug in their steady progress, complacent about their patients' welfare, and secure in their world leadership, German psychiatrists paid scant attention to the one area in psychiatry that was still ruled by the French: hypnotism and suggestion therapies.

German suspicion of hypnotism at this time was a complex phenomenon. Partly, the distrust was a disavowal of the medical and general acceptance of mesmerism in the first decades of the nineteenth century, when mesmerism and *Naturphilosophie* were closely linked (Leibbrand, 1956, p. 174; von Gruenewaldt, 1927, pp. 55-64). In 1812 Frederick William III of Prussia, at the urging of his chief minister, had convened a special commission under Dr. Hufeland to investigate hypnosis, which Mesmer said worked by "animal magnetism," a fluid which supposedly emanated from the hypnotist's person. The psychiatrist Haindorf had called mesmerism "man's best weapon against disease" (quoted in Kraepelin, 1917, p. 68). Mesmerism acquired a foothold in several universities, and well-known philosophers hailed it as an epoch-making discovery (Ellenberger, 1967, pp. 169-170; 1970, pp. 74-83, 158-160, 162, 199-210). Schelling saw in "magnetic somnambulism" (as it was also called) a means for establishing a connection between man and the World Soul. J. G. Fichte (1762-1814) believed it demonstrated an aspect of the Ego, a key concept in his ethical writings. Arthur Schopenhauer (1788-1869) wrote that "from a philosophical point of view, Animal Magnetism is the most momentous discovery ever made." A group of Catholic mystical philosophers endeavored to synthesize mesmersim with the teachings of the Church. Hardly a German Romantic poet remained untouched by the influence of magnetism; the work of E. T. A. Hoffmann is permeated with it. Mesmerism was a favorite topic in popular literature as well, and was the theme of numerous best sellers which are forgotten today. In many localities mesmerism became almost a religion and profoundly affected social and medical life (Veith, 1965, p. 221).

The activity of the magnetizers in Germany during the first half of the nineteenth century was enormous. They worked in small local groups, but had journals, congresses, and celebrations. They organized teaching and published a great number of textbooks and monographs. Their work is especially notable in the history of German medicine for its attempt to focus on neurotic phenomena as opposed to preoccupation with psychoses (Ellenberger, 1967, pp. 167-168; 1970, pp. 77-81). Some of these men practiced quite effective psychotherapy based on their understanding of the special rapport that existed between patient and magnetizer. These therapists described almost all aspects of what we today call transference, including its erotic connotations and pitfalls.

Then in the 1840's and 1850's, organicist, positivistic, and mechanistic trends came to dominate German psychiatry. Hypnotism (so called since 1841) fell into disrepute, if not oblivion. This state of affairs was prevalent throughout Europe. What was unique in Germany was the almost complete contempt for hypnotism that continued after hypnotism became a legitimate field of study and treatment in the Western world. The new respectability of hypnotism was due to the demonstrations of the renowned French neurologist, Jean Charcot (1825-1893), and to the recognition by the French Academy of Science in 1881 of his work with hysterical patients. Charcot and his assistants hypnotized hysterical patients at the Salpêtrière in Paris, causing their hysterical symptoms to appear and disappear. The historical importance of his work was recognized by his younger contemporary Pierre Janet (1859-1947), the celebrated psychologist and neurologist, who remarked of Charcot's 1882 paper: "It broke a dam and let in a torrent which was ready to rush" (quoted in Zilboorg, 1941, p. 363).[22]

---

[22] Charcot's belief that only hysterics could by hypnotized was proved wrong by Hippolyte Bernheim, Professor of Medicine at Nancy.

Charcot's famous Tuesday morning clinics drew physicians (including Freud) from all over the world, and the scientific literature of the 1880's—except in Germany—was inundated with publications on hypnotism. German doctors also did not generally agree with the implications of Charcot's findings: that the numerous, apparently willfully misbehaving, disagreeable patients who flooded mental clinics and private offices, and who were suspected of malingering, were really sick people.

German psychiatrists and neurologists labeled Charcot's demonstrations "theatrical" and referred to them with disdain. Not only did the German physicians never see such cases in their clinics, but they could explain the reason why: Economically and politically the French had already given indications of decadence. Now it was clear that Frenchmen were growing decadent morally. The large number of hysterical patients reported by the French showed this. Griesinger had established the principle that different nations are variously predisposed to mental ill health (Rosen, 1968, p. 187), and the French experience with hysteria seemed to be bearing him out. Already in 1867, the famous French brain surgeon and anthropologist Paul Broca (1824-1880) had had to defend his countrymen against attacks that they were degenerate. In 1900, the Germans still assumed it. A Jena medical student reviewed the literature of the day to summarize contemporary notions about the etiology of hysteria. One generally held German opinion he found was that "among the French . . . there are just more hereditarily tainted individuals than among the German races . . ." (Enke, 1900, p. 5) (see below, p. 80).

Moreover, the type of hysterical symptoms seen in France also proved "Latin decadence" (Bromberg, 1954, p. 183; 1937, p. 170). The grand hysterical convulsions reported by Charcot were not only bizarre, they never occurred in German clinics. The son of a leading Berlin neurologist, himself a neurologist, "regretted" Freud's visit to the Salpêtrière because it had focused Freud's attention on a "fruitless and unreliable theme" (Jones, 1953, p. 189). The examples of French psychiatry and neurology could not be applied to German science.

Most German physicians and psychiatrists regarded hypnotism "as hocus-pocus or something worse. Denunciations were frequent and did not lack vigor" (Jones, 1953, p. 235). There were some rare, relatively isolated attempts among German physicians to learn about hypnosis or to use it in their work. A few even joined the thousands of European physicians who journeyed to the two centers of hypnotism at Paris and Nancy. These men returned with the notion that many emotional and physical ailments could be cured through "psychotherapy," a word much in vogue in Europe around 1890 (Ellenberger, 1967, p. 175; Zilboorg, 1941, pp. 361, 363, 371). Georg Wanke, a Thuringian neurologist who later became a psychoanalyst, followed the work in France with great interest, and was influenced by the articles that appeared in the *Revue de l'Hypnotisme* (Wanke, 1926, p. 106). Among others who used hypnosis were Eugen Bleuler, the famous Zurich psychiatrist whose work on schizophrenia was highly influential in Germany (and who was psychoanalytically oriented); P. J. Möbius, an independent-minded Leipzig psychiatrist who was known for his "pathographies" of historical personalities; Albert Moll, recognized for his studies and journals on sexual matters; Rudolf Heidenhain, a Breslau physiologist whose 1880 article was the first serious German recognition of hypnotism in the late nineteenth century; William Preyer, who lectured at the University of Berlin in 1880-1890 on the "physiology of hypnotism"; and Alfred von Schrenck-Notzing, who wrote prolifically on hypnotism. Two neuropathologists of stature, Korbinian Brodmann and Oskar Vogt (the latter the exponent of an intellectual therapy for emotional illness which he called "causal analysis") also employed hypnosis.[23]

Some of these men were so well established in their fields that they could afford to suffer whatever criticism came their

[23] Ackerknecht (1959, p. 77); Ellenberger (1967, p. 175); Jones (1953, p. 235); Kirchhoff (1924, pp. 274-280, 308-313); Kolle (1956, pp. 7-16; 1959, pp. 39-64; 1963, pp. 109-120); Schultz (1952, pp. 41-44).

For a vivid impression of the amount of and types of German literature on hypnotism and suggestion compared to that in French and English see *The Psychological Index* (1895-1909).

way as a result of their practice of hypnosis. But others risked compromising their careers, losing their practices, and being called quacks and fools. In addition there were a few practitioners of hypnosis who carefully concealed their activity because of the opprobrium attached to it (Ellenberger, 1967, pp. 171-172).

For a while there was enough interest in hypnosis in Germany for a journal to be founded in 1892: *Zeitschrift für Hypnotismus, Psychotherapie sowie andere psychophysiologische und psychopathologische Forschungen*. It languished for ten years before being incorporated in another journal in 1902. It is true that the decline of German interest in hypnosis was also a part of the generally decreased attention paid to hypnosis after Charcot's death in 1893 (Bromberg, 1937, p. 185; Ellenberger, 1967, p. 174; Veith, 1965, pp. 241, 244). But the French *Revue de l'Hypnotisme*, founded in 1886, continues to this day, though under another title. German medical contempt for hypnosis was reinforced by the existence of a number of hypnotists who became self-proclaimed apostles of a new faith. These "teachers" traveled extensively, organized stage performances, and at times caused riots and psychic epidemics. Since most German doctors knew nothing about hypnosis, they were as ready believers in popular myths as any ignorant layman. They wrote of the complete subjugation of the will through hypnosis and believed that crimes could be committed by unwilling innocents who were hypnotized by malicious characters. Psychiatrists who read the German translation of George du Maurier's bestseller *Trilby* accepted the portrayal of the sinister figure of Svengali, with his piercing black eyes, lean fingers, and cadaverous frame. The hypnotist was a sort of demon who could look into people's minds and fill them with strange desires and moods.

There was a large group of German psychiatrists, the most prominent of whom was Meynert, who emphasized the erotic nature and danger of hypnosis (Ellenberger, 1967, pp. 172, 175). "The unscrupulous hypnotizer could stir the mind of a girl or child, arousing new passions and demanding allegiance for his nefarious activities. . . . hypnotism [was] a sort of clandestine sexual experience and the hypnotist a libertine." The few German clergymen who took notice of hypnotism raised a hue and cry over the threatened indiscriminate use of this immoral French import (Bromberg, 1937, pp. 172-174).

Distrust of hypnosis extended to other forms of psychotherapy that were popular at the turn of the century: Hippolyte Bernheim's (1840-1919) suggestion therapy; Ottomar Rosenbach's (1851-1902) persuasion and moral appeal known as *Psychagogik*; Paul Dubois's (1848-1918) "rational therapeutics" and "moral orthopedics," also based on persuasion; the psychotherapy of Jules Joseph Déjerine (1849-1917), and the autosuggestion of Émile Coué (1857-1926).[24]

Thus German distaste for hypnosis and psychotherapies based on either hypnosis or suggestion was caused by many factors. It was a reaction against the mesmerizers' ties with Romanticism. Growing out of this reaction and linked with the somatic interests of German psychiatrists was their dislike for the intangible and unquantitative aspects of hypnotic phenomena. This dislike was bolstered by the air of quackery that had been attached to hypnotism ever since its discovery in the eighteenth century. Moreover, the anxieties aroused in German doctors by the sexual nature of the relationship between the hypnotist and his female subject were especially strong in the sexually repressive setting that was characteristic of Wilhelmine Germany.

Quite important also were German opinions that their science was superior to that of the French. The comparative French neglect of the basic sciences was considered a serious fault. The poorer medical care received by the French army in the Franco-Prussian War, though not the fault of French physicians, still served to cast discredit on French medicine. The Prussian army had almost four times as many physicians as did the French. The German wounded, therefore, were properly and efficiently handled, and infectious diseases were relatively few. Because the German troops had been quite thoroughly vaccinated against smallpox, there were only 483

[24] Ackerknecht (1959, pp. 76-77), Alexander and Selesnick (1966, pp. 176-177), Bromberg (1937, pp. 185-189), Ellenberger (1967, p. 174), von Gruenewaldt (1927, pp. 106-147), Kolle (1959, pp. 217-224; 1963, pp. 133-142), Schultz (1952, pp. 43-67, 180).

cases of the disease. But in the only partly vaccinated French armies there were 4,178 cases of smallpox, and almost 2,000 of the afflicted died (Castiglione, 1958, pp. 900-901).

The Germans' belief in the higher level of their scientific interests was being confirmed by the large numbers of foreigners who came to study at their universities. The main focus of Western medical attention had shifted from Paris to various German cities. And in fact, many German psychiatrists and neurologists had little use for the French concentration on the neuroses. The Germans, both in their laboratory investigations of the brain and in their asylum building, were investing their energies in studying the psychoses and providing modern custodial care for psychotic persons. Hypnotism and psychotherapy seemed to offer minimal contributions toward the understanding and care of the mad and the insane.

GERMAN PSYCHIATRY IN 1900: HEGEMONY AND IMPOTENCE

In the course of the nineteenth century, German psychiatry became a fully recognized medical specialty. By the time Freud began his psychoanalytic work in the 1890's, its accomplishments were numerous: the building, administration, and reform of hospitals and the training of supervisory staff; the systematic teaching of psychiatry to medical students; meticulous anatomical, physiological, and neurological researches; the classification of mental diseases; the organization of local and national psychiatric societies; the foundation of flourishing psychiatric journals; the organization of the aftercare of mental patients; and the introduction of psychiatry into the courtroom. And soon after Kraepelin's Munich clinic was founded in 1904 it became a prototype for similar facilities the world over (Braceland, 1956, p. 875).

The obvious, swift, and energetic progress of German psychiatry took place at a time when Germany as a whole made giant steps to reach a commanding place among Western nations. The economic and industrial growth of the German states was already advanced before the unification of the German states into the German Empire; the unification, mainly by military means, accelerated this process. Accompanying the political, economic, and military expansions, and partly responsible for them, was the vigorous growth in scientific education. The German universities were reorganized and curricula were set up that took cognizance of the continual stream of new scientific developments. In this way, German science and medicine not only wrested supremacy from France, but enjoyed exceptional scientific renown throughout the Western world. Universities, industrial concerns, and governments sent various delegations to study German laboratories, universities, and industries (see, e.g., Rose, 1901). The findings of these committees were then often used in the West as the basis for the design of new facilities, the reform of old ones, and the institution of new methods and practices.[25] The leaders of German industry, commerce, politics, science, and medicine basked in the fame that accrued from German contributions especially to pure chemistry, the chemical industries, and physiology; they gloried in the respect shown for the brilliance of German teachers and for the outstanding quality of the many journals and learned works published.

Thus the leaders and the rank and file of German psychiatry drew confidence from living in an era and in a country where events and opinion seemed to prove the superiority of their psychiatric contributions as well as the achievements of Germany in other fields.[26] Challengers to the established preoccupations of German psychiatry—organic laboratory research, clinical description of mental diseases, and engrossment with psychotic illnesses—would not find that such confidence bred a tolerant spirit. For this confidence was based not

[25] The desire to emulate German research training in scientific education led to the foundation of Johns Hopkins in 1876. Various Englishmen who had studied in Germany wrote papers urging the British government to subsidize scientific activities, as the Germans were doing (Cardwell, 1963, pp. 668-669). Cardwell discusses the achievements and reputation of German science in the nineteenth century and theorizes intelligently on the possible bases for German scientific success as well as its impact on the industry and economy of Germany and, ultimately, other nations.

[26] The historian Hughes (1958) and the sociologist Ben-David (1968) believe, however, that by the turn of the century Germany had already passed her peak, though this fact was not evident for some time.

on a secure, embedded tradition, but on the work of less than fifty years. German psychiatry came into being as a special branch of clinical medicine only very late, at a time when medicine at large had a long history. Not until 1904 did the German government begin to administer special examinations to doctors who intended to practice psychiatry (Kraepelin, 1917, p. 113). The leaders of German psychiatry—pleased by their new status, determined to preserve it, treasuring the recognition that newly won success brings, and desiring ever greater appreciation of their brilliant entry into world medicine—guarded their scientific reputation closely. They were aware that for more than half of the century they had been ignored by physicians in France, England, and the United States. Pliny Earle, the well-known nineteenth-century American psychiatrist, described the Germans at mid-century as "idle metaphysicians, verging on infidelity" of whom "little notice was taken" (Sanborn, 1898, p. 164). German concern for the opinions of foreigners directly affected the reception of psychoanalysis. Theodor Ziehen, Chief of Psychiatry at the Charite, prevented any discussion of the psychoanalytic paper of Karl Abraham at a meeting of the Berlin Psychiatric Society because some foreign psychiatrists were guests at that meeting.

German psychiatrists would take no step, acknowledge no theory, that might destroy their freshly won gains. And before 1900 no challenger of stature crossed their path—Freud's *Interpretation of Dreams* having appeared in November, 1899. So they continued to work hard in their laboratories and clinics and vigorously expound their results in their journals and at their scientific meetings. Kraepelin's (1917, pp. 9,113) boast exemplified a widely shared attitude:

> We have moved forward in spite of all impediments and have overcome difficulties once considered insuperable. . . . psychiatry can look back with pride on the ground already covered and be assured that nothing in the future will impede its progress. Within the span of one century we have made advances comparable in every respect to those scored in other fields of medical science. . . . Today German medical schools have regular chairs for psychiatry and exemplary instructional facilities. We are in this respect superior to all other nations of the world.

Perhaps there were broader influences on the ambitious sentiments of some German psychiatrists. Did they share the feelings of certain fellow countrymen that it was now the historical time of Germany to be predominant in world affairs and, in the words of the Emperor, to have a "place in the sun"?

Yet, incongruously, in spite of their many achievements, German psychiatrists were almost powerless.

> The position of a psychiatrist about 1900 was not a particularly happy one. Although he was better able to classify the psychoses and predict their outcome than his predecessors a century before, he still suffered from the same ignorance of the causes of mental illness, and he still had to be content with the same miserable methods of treatment. If he worked in an institution or a clinic, he saw only severe and hopeless psychoses, and although anatomy and physiology had been so helpful to his medical colleagues, they had failed to teach him anything about the nature of these illnesses, except in the case of general paresis. His patients were prisoners, and in a way he himself was a prisoner caught up in the difficulties of the field in which he had chosen to work [Ackerknecht, 1959, p. 72].

Methods of treatment were few and not particularly helpful: making inpatient care more humane; drugs; baths; small doses of electrical shocks (not the modern electroshock therapy); and S. Weir Mitchell's famous "rest cure" — temporary, complete isolation of the patient and utter silence.

Some doctors were content with these obviously inadequate therapies because of their strong theoretical convictions. Certain groups assumed that every mental disease was caused by a cortical irritation and that the answer to mental illness lay in the future discoveries of the brain psychiatrists. At present there was no way of curing the disease, so the patient should simply be made as comfortable as possible. Other psychiatrists let their scientific energies be absorbed by ever closer observations, descriptions, and classifications of the patients they saw. This activity was an end in itself. The psychiatrist's legitimate concern was to study the natural, predetermined course of mental disease and note the inevitable deterioration here, the inevitable recovery there.

But the failure of organic psychiatry and the complacency of Kraepelinian psychiatry took its toll among a great many German psychiatrists. An atmosphere of therapeutic pessimism, even nihilism, was inextricably mixed with the proud and confident air that blanketed German psychiatry at the turn of the century. Karl Jaspers, who was then a practicing psychiatrist, wrote much later:

> The realization that scientific investigation and therapy were in a state of stagnation was widespread in German psychiatric clinics at that time. The large institutions for the mentally ill were built constantly more hygienic and more magnificent. The lives of the unfortunate inmates, which could not be changed essentially, were controlled. The best that was possible consisted in shaping their lives as naturally as possible as, for example, by successful work therapy. . . . In view of the exceedingly small amount of knowledge and technical knowhow, intelligent yet unproductive psychiatrists, such as [Alfred E.] Hoche [1865-1943, Chief of Psychiatry at Freiburg/Breisgau from 1902 to 1934] took recourse to a skeptical attitude and to elegant sounding phrases of gentlemanly superiority. In Nissl's hospital [Heidelberg] too, therapeutic resignation was dominant. In therapeutics we were basically without hope . . . [Schilpp, 1957, p. 16].

Möbius, a first-rate neurologist, also felt defeated by the "hopelessness of all psychology," the title of a small book he wrote in 1907. Kraepelin's (1917, pp. 117, 150) own words are appropriately dreary:

> Along with our knowledge·has come a lack of confidence in the efficacy of our medical practices. We know now that the fate of our patient is determined mainly by the development of the disease . . . we can rarely alter the course of the disease . . . our ability frequently to predict what will happen keeps us from falsely assuming . . . that our treatment will appreciably influence the outcome of the disease. . . . We must openly admit that the vast majority of the patients placed in our institutions . . . are forever lost.

It is within this all-embracing atmosphere of brilliance and impotence, of energy and ennui, that one must view the specific organization, activities, and beliefs of the German psychiatric discipline.

Structurally, German psychiatry at the turn of the century was university-oriented. To become a full-time professor was to reach the pinnacle of professional success. The academic leaders of psychiatry were greatly respected, and their opinions on medical issues of the day often had the force of a ukase. The immense authority of the university professors served to intensify the rivalry that existed among the various schools of psychiatric thought. Fierce theoretical quarrels in journals and at meetings characterized the simultaneous existence of the brain researchers, the strict clinical psychiatrists, and the investigators of hereditary factors. The schisms were so great that they linger to this very day. The editor of a modern book surveying European psychiatry had to get two Austrian psychiatrists to write the chapter on Germany because "no one [German] representative could have been expected to have the necessary detachment to give a balanced view of each [school]" (Bellak, 1961, p. xx).

Each leader of these schools, or a close associate, had his own journal. So if a young psychiatrist aspired to academic success, he allied himself with one of the established professors, rose in the ranks of that man's university department, and published in the affiliated journal. Eclecticism was hardly ever the order of the day, and a fertile ground for new theories, unallied with any pre-existing school, certainly did not exist (Bellak, 1961, pp. xvi, xx). In such a competitive, academic setting, theoretical differences were emphasized, and an obsession with theory, detached from practice, was rampant. Jaspers, commenting on the psychiatric lectures, conferences, and journals, recalled that "frequently, the same things were being discussed in different terms, in most cases in a very obscure manner. Several schools each had its own terminology. It seems as if several languages were being spoken, with deviations to the extent of special jargons at the individual hospitals. There seemed to be no such thing as a common scientific psychiatry uniting all those engaged in psychiatric research" (Schilpp, 1957, p. 17). There was, however, one unifying goal: the desire that psychiatry be an integral part of medicine. Thus German psychiatrists, on the whole, believed mental disease was physical disease. Mental illness was due to a defective organ, or to heredity, or to improper body economy, or to metabolic changes.

"Organic" psychiatry meant not only that the causes of mental disease were physical but that in studying disease, the psychiatrist dealt with a particular body organ. There was scant awareness of the ill person as a whole being, made up of highly complex, interacting physical and psychological systems. Anatomical and experimental investigators assumed that they could study a particular structure or function isolated from the rest of the body and that the accuracy of their findings was not affected by such isolation.

Correspondingly, German psychiatrists believed that laboratory research was the only valid form of scientific investigation. Scientific method had to include seeing, touching, and measuring.

German psychiatrists' suspicion of or hostility to anything that was unmaterialistic partly explains their repugnance for the psychotherapies and hypnotic techniques in style in much of Europe. Freud, in his prepsychoanalytic days, was already very much aware of the different beliefs in France and Germany regarding the validity of psychotherapeutic phenomena. He remarked in 1892 that this difference "may be explained by the historical development of German clinical medicine: namely, the tendency to offer a physiological interpretation of disease states and of the connections between symptoms. The clinical observations of the French surely gain in independence through their subordinating the physiological points of view to a secondary place" (quoted in Jones, 1953, p. 370).

Late nineteenth-century psychiatrists were determined that psychiatry should not reforge its broken links with philosophy. Kraepelin (1917, pp. 27-41), for example, objected to the phrase "philosophical essay" in the titles of works on mental disorders by two well-known French psychiatrists, Joseph Daquin (1733-1815) and Philippe Pinel (1745-1826). Disregarding obvious changes in literary style and linguistic usage, he cited this phrase as proof that Daquin and Pinel had been philosophers, not psychiatrists. He condemned the "naïve" and "extravagant" psychological views of the Romantic psychiatrists, lashing out particularly against the famous J. C.

Reil, whom he judged (quite incorrectly) to have "little or no experience in psychiatry and whose incompetence was clearly reflected in his writing."

Puschmann (1889, pp. 441-442) attacked Romantic philosophy for its "baneful" effect on German science and medicine, which made them "lose touch completely with practical life" and forced them "into the mystico-transcendental realms of speculation." *Naturphilosophie*, because of its contact with "religious mysticism [had] assumed a hostile attitude toward experimental inquiry." Now that "positivism" was the order of the day, German science had "rediscovered the lost path." The "positive knowledge of scientific facts must be presupposed as a self-evident requisite for any intellectual activity [which might] prove fruitful or could hope to win any serious regard." The "subtle hypotheses" of Fichte, Schelling, Hegel, and Schopenhauer "might have for a time captivated [but] the development of modern civilization [depended on] a scientific view of nature." German medicine would err to return to "the question of the essential nature and ultimate foundation of things."

The field of human psychology, of explaining the basic motives of people's actions, was considered a part of philosophy, from which psychiatry had so recently escaped. It was a widely held view that psychology was not a fit subject for medicine. The rising prominence of experimental psychology did nothing to modify this opinion since the Wundtian psychologists were also determined to differentiate themselves from the philosophers (see Chapter 7). The "new" psychology and psychiatry actually joined hands in Kraepelin's monograph series, *Psychologische Arbeiten*, which was devoted to applied psychology and borderline problems between physiological psychology and psychiatry.

Even after Freud had developed psychoanalysis, he denigrated psychology and referred to modern psychologists as philosophers. In 1896, Freud (1887-1902, p. 169) wrote in a letter: "I am in a rather gloomy state . . . perhaps you may supply me with solid ground on which I shall be able to give up explaining things psychologically and start finding a firm basis in physiology!" Though two years later he did accept the psychological nature of his work, he still wrote: "I have set myself the task of making a bridge between my germinating metapsychology and what is in the books, and I have plunged into the study of [Theodor] Lipps [1851-1914, Professor of Psychology in Munich], whom I suspect to be the best mind among the present-day *philosophical* writers" (Freud, 1887-1902, pp. 260-261; italics mine).

The late nineteenth-century psychiatrist's bias against "philosophic" medicine was as deep as his reverence for "scientific" medicine was great. For a critic to label a colleague's work "unscientific" was considered among the harshest of judgments — and this in a professional society where *ad hominem* arguments were frequent. The psychiatrist's commitment to a nonrelativistic, positivistic science was reflected in his materialistic and sometimes mechanistic outlook. This commitment was also mirrored in the way he treated patients. For as German psychiatry gained scientific accuracy and clinical knowledge, it unwittingly lost humaneness.

The scientist was supposed to be concerned with diseased organs, symptoms and syndromes, and the courses of diseases — not with individual patients. This was true whether the psychiatrist worked in a laboratory or in a clinic. Famous academicians like Meynert and Kraepelin provided the example. Moreover, the scientific theories for the treatment of the mentally ill dictated the immediate separation of patients from their families and prompt hospitalization in large institutions. The "moral treatment" of the "institutional" era, which was based on personal contact between the superintendent of the hospital and an economically and ethnically quite homogeneous group of patients was discarded (Mora, 1967, p. 29).[27] Long-term care in mental hospitals became increasingly impersonal as it was influenced by the organic and sometimes fatalistic view of illness. If mental disease was physiological and perhaps hereditary in origin, "personal" and social factors need not be heeded.

---

[27] The removal of the mentally ill from the community and their long-term incarceration in a large institution was a Western phenomenon that lasted a century and has only recently begun to alter.

To what specific extent the growing impersonality of German psychiatrists toward their patients was a part of the milieu fostered by Germany's industrial development and Bismarckian socialism is impossible to document. But in an age where factories already employed hundreds of workers, the new, ever-larger state mental institutions were not anomalous. And at a time when it was not uncommon for a factory hand to be unknown to his employer, Kraepelin's composite portrait of a nonexisting "typical" case of manic-depressive psychosis was not incongruous.

The work done in Kraepelin's Munich clinic offered no cure for mental illness, but it proffered a schematic understanding. Although it is inaccurate to speak of a "genetic" psychiatry before World War I, there did arise a group of psychiatrists who preached a fatalistic, hereditary causation of psychiatric disease. This was based on Kraepelin's division of psychoses into two groups: those caused by external conditions, which would therefore improve with a change of environment, and those caused by inherent constitutional factors, which were incurable.

The inferences of "genetic" psychiatry (as it came to be called) were reassuring. There was a large group of mental patients with which the psychiatrist did not have to be actively concerned; nor did he need to berate himself for his failure to cure them. If he made the diagnosis and saw that they received good custodial care, he had competently acquitted his professional duties.

Genetic psychiatry encouraged another comfortable attitude. It made very clear the line between sickness and health. Mental disease and mental health were not relative states nor was there a continuum between the two (see, e.g., Kraepelin, 1904, pp. 7, 19). If mental illness was hereditary, the sick person was sick and the healthy was healthy. Basically, the sick person would not get better and the healthy person, without the inborn trait, would not get sick. For the physician, there was thus a reassuring gulf between the mad patient and the sane doctor. Most German psychiatrists at the turn of the century saw no correspondence between the thoughts and actions of psychotic persons and their own. It was almost as if there were two different species, physically alike but mentally different.

The belief in a sharp distinction between health and disease both produced the system of isolating mentally ill patients from the rest of the population and received continual reinforcement from this state of affairs. The conviction that health and disease were polar entities also found a ready-made niche in the Victorian morality of the German middle-class psychiatrist. Like others of his social group, the psychiatrist accepted as equitable vast discrepancies in the physical and mental states of the population. There were "us" and there were "them."

The theory of "degenerative stigmata," introduced by Morel in 1857, was popular not only among psychiatrists but among writers. Thomas Mann's *Buddenbrooks,* which appeared in 1900, was illustrative of a widespread belief that mental disease was evidence of a degenerative hereditary strain which would become progressively severe in successive generations, eventually causing the family's extinction. Möbius became preoccupied with the relationship between genius and insanity and wrote a number of "pathographies."

Perhaps the most convincing evidence of the belief that there was no place at which disease and health met is seen in the vast interest in the study of sexual perversions, of which Richard von Krafft-Ebing's *Psychopathia Sexualis,* first published in 1886, is the outstanding example. The number of German journals and congresses devoted to the study of sexuality was awesome, if one considers that they flourished in a society where sexual activities, most body parts, and many bodily functions could not be openly discussed. They were not, however, concerned with normal sexuality, but with the abnormal (Alexander and Selesnick, 1966, p. 174). The first German bibliography of pornographic works had been published in 1875 (Marcus, 1966, p. 38). Perversions were what was practiced by those "sick" people who were driven to tell their tales to their physicians. "Healthy" people were those who—as far as public knowledge went—did not practice perversions. The matter defined itself.

Thus, unlike doctors in other specialities, the Kraepelinian psychiatrist did not first study healthy processes. It was assumed that normal mental behavior bore no relationship to the abnormal. The psychiatrist was concerned only with the diseased. What health was was so fully evident that it was not subject to doubt, still less to discussion. The Kraepelinian system had been gradually and methodically derived from 100 years of somatic theories.

> There was an age-long scientific attitude which assumed as an established fact that mental disease is physical disease. There was also an assumption . . . that everyone knows what a mental disease is and that it is something definite. . . .
>
> For each period of history the question of mental disease seems to have been settled in a manner corresponding to the spirit of the age. The nineteenth century took it for granted that it *was* a disease like any physical disease and it was the express belief of the clinician that his only duty was to proceed in an attempt to prove . . . that the assumption of the age was correct. . . .
>
> The Kraepelinian system was a true triumph of a settled question [Zilboorg, 1941, pp. 459-460].

The German psychiatrists who read (or heard about) Sigmund Freud's early papers and books were physicians who took great pride in the nineteenth and early twentieth-century achievements of their profession and their country. Although confident in their success, these men did not readily welcome any new theories because psychiatry had a very short history as an accepted speciality of medicine, and they feared endangering their newly won status. Moreover, they were already bitterly fighting among themselves about what future direction their organically oriented work should take. A new approach not only had to face severe competition, but, because German psychiatry was university-oriented, it had to find an authoritative academic backer if it hoped for any trial at all. In *Weltanschauung*, German psychiatry was hostile to any ideas that were reminiscent of the psychiatry of the first half of the nineteenth century. The psychiatry of the Wilhelmine era was materialistic and often mechanistic and on guard against contamination by "philosophy." It was firmly committed to "Science" and the "scientific method," knowing exactly what these were and what they were not. The psychiatrist was not primarily interested in treating individual patients, but in dealing with their diseases. More than any other psychiatrist Kraepelin dominated German medicine. His concentration on observation and classification, on diagnosis and prognosis, his pessimism and fatalism, his detachment from his patients, his inclination to explain mental illness by heredity—these characteristics were emulated by hundreds of psychiatrists. And the Kraepelinian system, as well as self-righteous class mores, powerfully abetted a belief in the vast, unbridgeable gulf between normal and abnormal. All these factors played their part in the reception of psychoanalysis in Germany.

2

HYSTERIA

> *The theory of the psychogenic origin of [hysterical] symptoms still lacks confirmation. How, for instance, can an idea cause unusual nervous symptoms in children?*
> —Fürstner, *Die Deutsche Klinik am Eingange des Zwanzigsten Jahrhunderts*

Below we will consider in some detail German medical views of hysteria. There are two reasons for such scrutiny. First, Freud's attempt to treat hysteria was the basis for early psychoanalytic theories. The medical reception of psychoanalysis can never be studied apart from the opinions German doctors held about hysteria at the turn of the century. Second, the physicians' views about the etiology and mechanism of hysteria introduce us to the whole spectrum of medical opinions of Freud's day on the roles played by organic and psychic factors in the production of emotional disorders.

BREUER AND FREUD'S "PRELIMINARY COMMUNICATION"

In January, 1893, Josef Breuer and Sigmund Freud, two Viennese neurologists, published an eleven-page article in two parts: "On the Psychical Mechanism of Hysterical Phenomena: Preliminary Communication" (Breuer and Freud, 1893, pp. 3-17). The article appeared in the widely read *Neurologisches Centralblatt*, founded in 1882 by a Berlin professor of neurology, Emanuel Mendel. This journal was a likely place for the appearance of the "Preliminary Communication." Freud knew Mendel's son, Kurt, also a neurologist, and since 1886 Freud had been abstracting the Viennese neurological literature for the *Centralblatt* (Jones, 1953, p. 189).

In their communication, Breuer and Freud postulated that normally, if an experience is accompanied by a great deal of "affect," that affect is either "discharged" (*entladen*) in a variety of conscious acts or becomes gradually worn away by association with other conscious material. But in the life history of hysterical patients there are certain experiences in which this process does not occur. For each of these "psychic traumas," the affect is not discharged but remains "strangulated"; memory of the experience is cut off from access to consciousness.

The authors believed that their explanation of the mechanism responsible for the "repression" of the memory was "the basis and *sine qua non* of hysteria": the affect-laden experience took place while the subject was in an abnormal, "dissociated" state of mind described as "hypnoid," and he was therefore unable to discharge the affect.[1] Thereafter, the affective memory was manifested in physical (hysterical) symptoms, which were to be regarded as symbols of the suppressed memory. ("Hysterics suffer mainly from reminiscences.")

On the basis of this theory, Breuer and Freud offered a psychotherapeutic "cathartic" procedure for the relief and cure of hysterical attacks. The memory of the original experience, along with its affect, must be verbally expressed. In that way, the affect is discharged or "abreacted." The force that has maintained the physical symptom ceases to operate, and the symptom disappears. The method Breuer and Freud relied on both for bringing back memory of the trauma and for ridding

---

[1] This explanation was Breuer's, and never again appeared in Freud's writings. In the 1893 paper, there was only a brief suggestion (p. 11) of the theory Freud was soon to develop: the hysteric's "ego" regarded the trauma as "incompatible," and the mental "censor" therefore rendered the memory of the event unconscious. Over the next thirty years, Freud further refined and clarified this concept.

the patient of his symptoms was hypnosis. To effect a cure, either they subjected the repressed memory "to associative correction by introducing the memory into normal consciousness (under light hypnosis)" or they removed the memory through suggestion, under deep hypnosis, the patient remaining amnesic for the entire incident.

The authors declared that as far as cures of lingering hysterical symptoms were concerned, their method was "a radical one; in this respect it seems to us far superior in its efficacy to removal [of chronic attacks] through direct suggestion, as it is practiced today by psychotherapists." Nevertheless, they stressed that they had dealt only with "the mechanism of hysterical symptoms and not [with] the internal causes of hysteria . . ." (Breuer and Freud, 1893, p. 17).

HYSTERIA IN THE LATE NINETEENTH CENTURY

The language and presentation of the 1893 paper were circumspect; the conclusions were carefully and modestly stated. For if a German worker in the field of hysteria wished to be seriously regarded, he did well to step cautiously. The word "hysteria" comes from the Greek *hystera*, meaning uterus. Until about 100 years ago, it was almost always believed to be a disorder of women, caused by various changes in or alterations of the womb. But at the time of the "Preliminary Communication" the entire subject of hysteria—what caused it, whether it occurred in men, even what constituted its symptoms—was a highly controversial one. And that the recommended cures were legion showed that physicians of the day were baffled and kept at bay by the disease. Hysteria was mysterious, irksome, and ubiquitous.

A disease called hysteria, putatively affecting only women, had been described and taken seriously by European medical men for centuries. But after the early years of the nineteenth century the manifestations of the disease and the ability of doctors to deal with it had altered somewhat. Traditional hysterical symptoms of paralysis, aphasia, aphonia, blindness, and pain had become modified by the prevailing feminine ideal. Women and girls were expected to be delicate and vulnerable, both physically and emotionally. Because this delicacy was considered to be enhanced by illness, the incidence of hysteria increased. After all, hysteria, as opposed to many other diseases, not only had the advantage of being thought specifically feminine; it also was never fatal. Simultaneously there was a striking rise in the literature about hysteria during the later decades of the nineteenth century. Even superficial examination of the *Index-Catalogue of the Library of the Surgeon-General's Office* (1880-1932) and the *Index Medicus* (1879-1899, 1903-1908) attests to this fact.

Concurrent with its proliferation, which reached almost epidemic proportions, the malady in many women was of diminished severity, and truly disabling symptoms often gave way to faintings, whims, and tempers—the oft-described Victorian "vapors." These less dramatic phenomena made up in chronicity for what they lacked in severity.

> In the earlier centuries the physician of a hysterical patient had the frequent and highly satisfying experience of returning his patient to normalcy with almost miraculous speed. The later literature gave evidence of a great variety of persistent physical ailments of lesser form. [These attentuated symptoms] not only lacked the element of gravity, but also made much greater demands on the diagnostic and therapeutic astuteness of the physician [Veith, 1965, p. 210].

Hysterical sufferers, especially of the middle and upper classes, now had a vested interest in the permanence of their disease; it was evidence of their femininity. And in a society where sexuality was not openly acknowledged, a disease that usually had a psychosexual etiology would naturally be tenacious and on the rise. One can also speculate about the unconscious use of hysterical symptoms by many educated women, deprived of real power by a male-dominated society. Illness can be an effective weapon for the gaining of one's ends—what is today called "secondary gain."

The nineteenth-century physician was already committed to the primacy of the physical etiology of disease. Yet hysteria was an illness which had no demonstrable cause. Moreover, whereas in previous centuries hysteria had usually been characterized by acute attacks, it was now in many women, nothing more than a chronic enumeration of petty complaints. But trifling as the phenomena were, they yielded not one whit to the new scientific armamentarium of the highly educated physician. The altered profile of hysteria, the prevailing interest in organic disease, and the inability of the physician to cope with hysteria not illogically engendered contempt and disdain in many physicians toward their hysterical patients.

This late nineteenth-century attitude had been forshadowed in Griesinger's 1845 textbook. Griesinger censured his hysterical patients for what he considered their unattractive traits and willful misdemeanors. As for etiology, since none was provable, he disregarded the subject entirely (Veith, 1965, pp. 195, 198). In the decades immediately following, hysteria was commonly regarded as a matter of "stimulation" or "imagination" on which no reputable physician would waste his time. Or if some explanation was sought, the doctor fell back on the centuries-old belief in the "wandering womb," which might be driven back into its place by valerian, the smell of which it disliked. The "nervous" patients who thronged the clinics and consulting rooms of German physicians were usually given large doses of contempt, thinly disguised by treatments of electrical stimulation and prescriptions for vile-tasting medicines like asafetida. If a neurotic patient persisted in her attempts to find medical succor, she might then meet either an angry physician, lecturing on the virtues of will power, or an indifferent one who shrugged his shoulders and recommended a nearby spa or two (Bromberg, 1937, p. 222; Jones, 1953, p. 226). Some German doctors reacted drastically, their ire resolving itself in treatments which had a large punitive component. The famous gynecologist Alfred Hegar (1830-1914) and his pupils (at a time when the connection between the womb and hysteria had already been seriously challenged) performed ovariectomies in cases of "intractable" hysteria. The renowned neurologist Nikolaus Friedreich (1825-1882) led a group of men who cauterized the clitorises of those patients who responded to no other treatment (Garrison, 1929, pp. 512, 603; Veith, 1965, p. 210).

In France, however, Jean Charcot (1825-1893) was making

the study of hysteria legitimate (Ackerknecht, 1959, pp. 72-74; Ellenberger, 1970, pp. 89-101; Veith, 1965, pp. 235, 238-239). Because of its association with the name of one of the world's foremost neuropsychiatrists, "hysteria" became scientifically respectable. Charcot's own view was that hysteria was a disease of the nervous system, one due to congenital degeneration of the brain. Charcot also recognized the role of emotions in the production of hysteria, and though he was not the first to do so, his name lent this view considerable prestige. Still, his serious concern with the disease was startling to most German neurologists, who only very slowly—and some never—began to give hysteria critical thought. The German psychiatrist Willy Hugo Hellpach lamented the backward state of research on and treatment of hysteria in Germany, especially as compared with developments in France. The work of Paul Julius Möbius (1853-1907), Oskar Vogt (1870-1959), and Freud, wrote Hellpach, had not penetrated into the consulting room, sanatorium, or polyclinic. Perhaps the only exception was Otto Binswanger (1852-1929) of Jena (see below), but even his work could not be compared with that done in the Salpêtrière. And only Hermann Oppenheim (1858-1918) of Berlin paid any attention to the traumatic neuroses (Hellpach, 1904, pp. 489-490). When Freud stopped in Berlin on his way home from Charcot's lectures, Kurt Mendel told him that he "regretted that Charcot had turned [Freud's] attention to such a difficult, fruitless, and unreliable theme as hysteria" (Jones, 1953, p. 189).

But there was a significant minority of German psychiatrists and neurologists who, because of Charcot's work and because of the large number of hysterical sufferers who filled their waiting rooms, were dealing seriously with hysteria at the same time Freud was doing so in Vienna.[2] An examination of the German literature on hysterical disorders reveals a wide range of opinion on this subject. The foremost controversy hovered on that most basic of questions: occurrence. Was hysteria a female disease? Could a man have hysteria? It is obvious that

[2] Freud began the clinical treatment of psychiatric patients in 1883. In 1885 he journeyed to Paris to study under Charcot, and in 1889 he went to Nancy to watch Bernheim at work. His first paper on hysteria (1886b) concerned hysteria in men.

since these questions were being asked, many physicians were not even sure what hysterical symptoms consisted of; this the literature proves. A reading of the entries under "Hysteria" in the United States Surgeon-General's *Index*, Volume VII (second series), covering the years 1885-1902, reveals countless papers merely describing a case of hysteria. Similar titles recur continually. The listings show that in Germany knowledge about hysteria was in a state of considerable flux, many physicians constantly discovering new forms the illness might take. This preoccupation was especially strong after 1890. At a time when Breuer and Freud had already accepted that hysteria could have multifarious symptoms and were concerned with the mechanism of the disease, most German physicians were not in agreement on the definition of a hysterical symptom.

Breuer and Freud also knew, along with more knowledgeable German psychiatrists and neurologists, that hysteria existed in men. But the existence of male hysteria was not accepted generally in German medical circles, although Griesinger had recognized it in his text. German research workers of the day interested in male hysteria commented on their countrymen's neglect of it, even though it had now been proved by the French (Mendel, 1884; Enke, 1900). A study of the Surgeon-General's *Index*, Volume VI, 1885 (first series) and Volume VII, 1902 (second series) confirms these investigators' subjective impressions. Between 1885 and 1902 only ten articles on male hysteria appeared in the German literature, all in a five-year period, 1895-1900.

When Emanuel Mendel gave a paper on "Hysteria in the Male Sex" before the Berlin Medical Society in 1884, he aroused such controversy that the discussion of the paper had to be carried over to a second meeting. Many doctors disagreed that "hysteria has as little to do with the uterus as with any other organ." Though four discussants rose to say that they had seen hysterical symptoms in their male patients, there were others who stated that hysterical pain is connected with disease of the ovaries and that they had never observed in men the classic Charcotian symptoms of hysterical women (Mendel, 1884, pp. 315, 331, 347).

By the turn of the century, the question had still not been

settled. A medical student working under the well-known psy-chiatrist Binswanger at Jena received his degree with a disser-tation that, by reviewing the literature of the day, tried to prove that there was male hysteria. His short book is notable for the explanation it gives as to why other peoples had so many more cases of hysteria than did the Germans:

> Among the French—natural born and not naturalized—there are just more hereditarily tainted individuals than among the German races. . . . As concerns other races, there is much more hysteria among Jews and Slavs, especially Poles. Concerning Jews, Oppenheim is of the opinion that here above all the nerve-destroying influence of psychic trauma is influential . . . such as the frequency of intermarriage, lack of physical education, the emotionally wearing search for profits, etc. [Enke, 1900, pp. 5-6].

From the comments of Mendel's discussant and of Bins-wanger's pupil, it is clear that German doctors believed that even if men did have hysteria there were fewer such men in Germany than in France. Hysterical disease was basically un-Germanic.

The second great medical debate concerning hysteria was the specific mechanism of its various symptoms. That hysteria was physically caused was rarely doubted, though this was variously interpreted. Basically, the view prevailed that hys-teria was hereditary. The volume on emotional illnesses in the textbook series of the medical publisher Johann Barth stated the position forthrightly: "Hysteria is an abnormal psychotic condition, based on hereditary endowment . . ." (Fuhrmann, 1903, p. 225). Mendel also believed that in both male and female hysteria, heredity played a large role. The medical student, Enke, concluded on the basis of his review of the literature that 40-45 percent of all cases of hysteria were hereditary, though he could not account for the other 55-60 percent. Kraepelin considered hysteria an "inborn psycho-pathic peculiarity" and thus placed the disease on a "degen-erative" basis. The Germans were reinforced in their opinions by the views of two leading French neurologists, Charcot and Pierre Janet (1859-1947). Charcot believed that hysteria was always a hereditary disease and that all other factors that might be considered etiological were merely "*agents provocateurs* . . . that only awake the slumbering illness." Janet thought that hysteria was the result of a "constitutional" weakness of the mind and nervous system; the disease was an inevitable manifestation of "*dégénérescence*" (Mendel, 1884, p. 316; Enke, 1900, p. 6; Eschle, 1907, pp. 181-182; Zilboorg, 1941, p. 376).

Under the umbrella of heredity, then, the controversies blew around mechanical details. Mendel's paper and the resulting discussions richly illustrate the concerns of knowledgeable physicians in Berlin. Four discussants violently disagreed with Mendel's view that pain in hysterics is muscular. A Dr. Landau said pain in female hysterics came from a "visceral neuralgia of their reproductive glands" and that this held true for males also. He cited the literature on the "irritable testis" which he found to have a "surprising similarity" to ovaries. He concluded that hysteria has to do with the "ganglia and nerves of the genitals." A Dr. Ewald also challenged Mendel; perhaps hysterical pain was caused by "nervous dyspepsia." A Dr. Remak said he would not be surprised to find that the hemianesthesia that corresponds to a defective ovary on the affected side in women should in men correspond with a defective testicle on the anesthetic side. Finally, Remak and Landau got into a bitter fight with a Dr. Nathanson over the mechanism of hysteria in women. Nathanson held the view that hysterical pain stems directly from ovarian disease and, therefore, castration or removal of the ovaries should be performed. Because Remak and Landau believed that hysteria was a "neurological" disease they were against these operations (Mendel, 1884, pp. 330-331, 347-348).

These late nineteenth-century preoccupations continued well into the twentieth century. Yet simultaneous with them there was a limited appreciation of other factors in hysterical illness. After all, there was the persistent and overwhelming clinical evidence of the role emotional events seemed to play in the production of hysterical phenomena. These factors were not ignored by all. A sizable minority of German physicians (who again could look to Charcot and Janet for support) were able to combine their belief in an organic *etiology* of hysterical disease with a psychic *mechanism* of hysterical symptoms. As early as 1884, Mendel (pp. 316-317) cited the important role of imitation in childhood hysteria and said that sometimes emotional upset could bring on a hysterical attack. He was critical of the physical treatments of the disease. He advised against using the latest "antineurosis" drug (Bromkalium); in his experience it did absolutely nothing. None of the other means of treatment worked either, including the dynamite pills being used in Frankfurt. The best thing to do was to remove the patient from his normal surroundings. Above all, the treatment of hysteria should be a psychical one and excessive strictness or intimidation were "misguided efforts."

Nineteen years later, Manfred Fuhrmann (1903, p. 226), the author of the Barth Verlag textbook, continued to combine these views with ease. Fuhrmann was the assistant physician at a state mental hospital in northern Germany, near Hannover. After announcing that hysteria was "based on hereditary endowment," he went on to say that "recently the name 'psychogeny' has been proposed as a replacement for the old, completely useless expression 'hysteria'; 'psychogeny' best reproduces the core of the hysterical condition, namely that all hysterical symptoms, psychic as well physical, can be called forth, influenced, and eliminated essentially as a result of abnormally strong ideas." The joining of organic etiology with psychic mechanisms also figured in the thought of Oskar Vogt, the prominent neuropathologist who underwrote a method of psychotherapy known as "causal analysis" (1898-1899). Theodor Ziehen (1862-1950), who was to hold the prestigious chair of psychiatry at the Charité from 1904 to 1912, likewise propounded these views in his textbook (1902). His relationship with psychoanalysis figures eventfully in German psychiatric history (see below, pp. 160-163).

There was even a small group of German physicians who discarded the notion of an underlying organic etiology of hysteria. They received their French support from Bernheim, who postulated that hysteria was not actually a disease at all and that everyone was potentially more or less hysterical (Veith, 1965, p. 240). The leader of the German rebels was the Leipzig neuropsychiatrist and "pathographer" Möbius.

Möbius was also the editor of the respected *Schmidts Jahrbücher der in- und ausländischen gesammten Medizin* and a clinician of note: mótor paralysis was formerly referred to as "Möbius' Syndrome." It is possible that he arrived at his views on hysteria independently of Bernheim. Möbius wrote in 1888 that hysteria was a mental condition in which "ideas" (*Vorstellungen*) produce physical symptoms. He explained this rather fuzzily by saying that a void occurs in consciousness as the result of a certain affect. This void is then filled by the first free idea to occur. The idea thereupon produces a symptom by operating like a suggestion made during hypnosis. Möbius questioned the belief that hysteria was a disease. Perhaps hysteria was just attacks occurring in persons whose psychological reaction to emotional trauma was exaggerated or distorted. The tendency toward hysteria could then be corrected through education or guidance, i.e., suggestion (Möbius, 1888; 1895). Möbius was supported in his contentions by Adolf von Strümpell (1892), director of the medical clinic at Erlangen and one of the editors (along with the famous Wilhelm Erb) of the *Deutsche Zeitschrift für Nervenheilkunde*. Strümpell (1853-1925) had written a textbook of medicine that went into twenty-eight editions and was translated into French, English, Russian, and Turkish. The book was sometimes refered to as the "Bible of German medicine" (Garrison, 1929, p. 430). "Strümpell's disease" was the dreaded poliomyelitis.

But the broadest statement of a psychogenic etiology of hysteria came from the fringes of German psychiatry. Franz Eschle was a follower of Ottomar Rosenbach and the director of a mental hospital near Heidelberg. Eschle (1907, p. 182) dismissed Charcot's and Kraepelin's theories of degeneration as too extreme and concluded "that emotional upheavals, mental excitations, fright, accidents, weakening, and above all toxic influences are *only provocative. Much more decisive among the factors that one can hold responsible for the appearance of hysteria, I consider the influence of the social and familial milieus, i.e., 'upbringing' [Erziehung] in its widest sense*" (Eschle's italics). But as late as 1907 Eschle did not cite Freud's views.

These forays into the psychogenesis of hysteria continued to be ignored or resisted by most German physicians. Typical of this group was Robert Sommer, professor at the University of Giessen, who displayed the usual irritation at hysterics. In his textbook on diagnosis of mental diseases he was totally unsympathetic to "hysterical" (the word is always in quotation marks) patients because they produce their symptoms quite "arbitrarily." "Cramps and contractures . . . show the characteristic of *arbitrary imitation*." The fact that these symptoms could be gotten rid of through command and suggestion made Sommer contemptuous of his patients. He consistently put the name of the symptom in quotation marks ("cramps") or prefaced it by "so-called." Furthermore, Sommer was completely dissatisfied with the medical nomenclature for the hysterical condition. On the one hand, the word "hysteria" was no good because it lent weight to the general lay belief that hysteria had a sexual cause. He advocated that the doctor eliminate the use of the word hysteria in order to do away with this "nonsensical idea." On the other hand, there was also a need for a better word than "psychogeny," which was "abstract" and "lacked meaning." Sommer felt that the way Möbius and Konrad Rieger (1855-1939), who held the chair of psychiatry at Würzburg from 1887 to 1925, had used the word "psychogenic" in Germany had "grave consequences for science" (Sommer, 1901, pp. 281-287).

Five years later the psychogenesis of hysteria still lacked general acceptance. The common reaction to this theory was one of skepticism. This is seen in the article on hysteria in the multivolumed *German Clinical Practice at the Start of the Twentieth Century as Seen in Academic Lectures*. There, the well-known psychiatrist Carl Fürstner (1848-1906) wrote: "The theory of the psychogenic origin of various symptoms still lacks confirmation. How, for instance, can an idea cause unusual nervous symptoms in children?" (1906, p. 157).[3]

[3] Fürstner, of Strassburg, had preceded Kraepelin as head of the University Psychiatric Clinic at Heidelberg. The roster of contributors to the volume was a *Wer Ist's* of German psychiatry: Sommer, Binswanger, Krafft-Ebbing, Fürstner, Pelman, Hoche, Baer, Moeli, Mendel, Siemerling, Jastrowitz, Seiffer, Wollenberg, Bonhoeffer, and Liepmann. There was no mention of Freud by any of them.

GERMAN REACTION TO THE "PRELIMINARY COMMUNICATION"

The survey of late nineteenth- and early twentieth-century German medical thought on hysteria has shown that the subject was a provocative one. Although most German doctors were firm in their belief that its etiology had to be organic, they agreed on nothing else: neither the extent of its symptoms, nor whether it occurred in men, nor how to treat it. The disease was ubiquitous and almost all physicians considered themselves competent to deal with it: general practitioners, internists, psychiatrists, neurologists, neuropathologists, surgeons, and gynecologists. These men also commented on it, and there was a burgeoning literature in the field.

Breuer and Freud's 1893 communication was one more paper about a difficult and disagreeable subject which challenged German medicine. Although the short paper received more than passing mention in one authoritative textbook, the attention paid to it was not exceptional. The briefest reference to it occurred the following year in the same journal in which it was originally published. A Dr. Weil of Strassburg reviewed in some detail a comparative study of organic and hysterical paralyses that Freud had published in a French journal in 1893. Dr. Weil (1894) concluded that in a review it was not possible for him to give the details of Freud's explanation of how hysterical paralyses came into being. Instead he referred the reader to the original work, giving the full citation for Breuer and Freud's "Preliminary Communication."

There was a detailed summary in Leopold Löwenfeld's *Pathologie und Therapie der Neurasthenie und Hysterie*, (1894). This was to be expected. Löwenfeld (1847-1924), a *Nervenarzt* in Munich, now a forgotten man, was at the turn of the century one of Germany's foremost clinical experts on neurasthenia and hysteria, and continually cited as an authority by his colleagues. He was known for his constant examination and evaluation of new theories and methods for their practical significance. He published prolifically, books and articles, and all of his books were widely reviewed. He was the coeditor of a successful and esteemed monograph series, *Grenzfragen des Nerven- und Seelenlebens*. In recognition of his professional status, the Bavarian government awarded him the honorary title of Privy Councilor (*Hofrat*). Löwenfeld was also an expert hypnotist and advocate of hypnosis as a curative method. He was later to publish Freud's (1901a) *On Dreams* in his journal, and to request that Freud write a chapter in two of his books: on the psychoanalytic method (Freud, 1904) and on Freud's views on sexuality in the etiology of neurosis (1906a).

Breuer's and Freud's 1893 paper immediately engaged Löwenfeld's attention. (The foreword to Löwenfeld's 1894 book was dated September, 1893.) As a hypnotist, Löwenfeld (1894, p. 563) was attracted by the talk of abnormal "hypnoid" states, and he was quick to report on how the existence of these altered states of consciousness in hysterics could be used to explain why hysterical sufferers were usually quite "normal," even "mentally clear" and "critical" in their thinking.

As a hypnotherapist, Löwenfeld was also interested in the Viennese authors' new treatment and gave an accurate account of how it worked. He concluded judiciously (p. 688) that "only extensive practical experience can determine how far this treatment surpasses in effectiveness Liébault's method, previously described."[4] Then in his bibliography under "Etiology of Hysteria" he listed Breuer and Freud's paper.

The most surprising reference to the "Preliminary Communication" was in a textbook on *Diseases of the Nervous System* by a famed Berlin neurologist, Hermann Oppenheim. If Oppenheim had not been Jewish he might have held a chair at the Charité; but in the circumstances he was given the next best thing, an Extraordinary Professorship at the university. Oppenheim was head of his own neurological clinic and was a specialist in traumatic neurosis (i.e., emotional sequelae to accidents or great frights). Oppenheim's text was very popular; it reached its seventh edition in 1923 and was translated into Russian and English. In the section on hypnotism Oppenheim (1894, p. 676) reported that Breuer and Freud had found "another use for hypnotism" and he briefly gave the essence of their theory.

---

[4] A. A. Liébault (1823-1904) was Bernheim's teacher and co-worker at Nancy.

Obviously, no one who paid attention to Freud's first psychoanalytic paper saw in it the seeds of a psychological revolution. It had not been presented in such a way as to invite extraordinary scrutiny or reflection. Yet Breuer and Freud had published a paper on hysteria in which they had advanced only psychological explanations and advocated only psychological treatment. The German medical reaction was limited, but it was interested and appreciative. Two of the three commentaries were by well-known authorities. There was no hostile reaction.

3

PSYCHOANALYTIC PSYCHOLOGY

> *... the first text-book of psychiatry to refer to psycho-analysis was written in Norwegian [in 1907].*
> —Freud, *On the History of the Psycho-Analytic Movement*

By 1895, Breuer and Freud had expanded their 1893 "Preliminary Communication" into a book, *Studies on Hysteria* (1893-1895). With the reception of this book, German medical reaction to psychoanalysis began in earnest. By 1907, the first stage of this reaction had ended; in December of that year, Karl Abraham (1877-1925), Freud's Berlin disciple, opened his psychiatric practice. In reminiscing about the early years, Freud himself expressed the view that the first phase of the history of psychoanalysis had extended from c. 1895-1896 to 1907.

By 1907, Freud's main beliefs about mental operation and personality development had been published. Freud posited the existence of an unconscious[1] and a mental mechanism known as repression, which consigned once conscious thoughts, wishes, and fantasies to the unconscious. He gave vast importance to early childhood personality development, which he showed to be under the dominance of a changing

[1] The terminology used here reflects Freud's view of the mind before 1923. A modern psychoanalyst would speak of "the existence of unconscious *mental processes.*"

88

pattern of sexual impulses. A person's psychosexual development could result in sexual conflicts, personality fixations,
and sublimation of sexual drive in the service of other activities. Freud amassed numerous examples in great detail in an
attempt to prove that the interpretation of dreams was an
invaluable technique for gathering information about unconscious thoughts and processes. And one of his main contentions was that the mechanisms he described operated in all
human beings.

THE UNCONSCIOUS AND REPRESSION

The existence of an unconscious is basic to all psychoanalytic
thought. It was natural, therefore, that those physicians who
were fundamentally in agreement with Freud did not dwell at
length on this aspect of analytic theory. In most of their
writings they took the unconscious and the mechanism of
repression for granted, only occasionally embarking on any
prolonged discussion of them. This total acceptance characterized the work of Eugen Bleuler, Carl Gustav Jung, and Iwan
Bloch. The strict rule of dealing only with German psychiatrists must be broken in the cases of the two Swiss, Bleuler and
Jung. They were vitally important to the propagation of psychoanalysis in Germany in the very early years, writing books
that were widely reviewed in German periodicals and
contributing liberally to the periodical literature themselves.
Moreover, they soon acquired international reputations as
psychiatrists. Bleuler's ability to make psychoanalysis academ-
ically respectable was of vital concern to Freud.

Bleuler (1857-1939) was Professor of Psychiatry at the University of Zurich and a director of a mental hospital, Burghölzli. In a 1908 paper he formulated the concept of "schizophrenia," which gradually replaced the older "dementia praecox." In an earlier monograph that relied heavily on the new
Freudian insights, Bleuler (1906c, pp. 16-17, 21, 114-115)
usually saw no need to justify his use of such terms as "unconscious acts" or to explain how in a certain patient "her unconscious transferred this guilt [about the death of a sister] to her
husband." Only once did he recognize that some readers
might not clearly understand his meaning. In discussing the

cases of patients whose hysterical symptoms were really the fulfillment of their wishes, he emphasized: *"All these 'wishes' here referred to are naturally not clearly conscious to the individual. The mechanism of their realization is wholly outside of his knowledge. His acts are bona fide"* (Bleuler's italics).[2]

The writings of Jung (1876-1961) also took for granted his readers' familiarity with concepts of the unconscious and repression. Jung was for many years Bleuler's assistant at Burghölzli and then established a private practice. While still at Burghölzli he became well-known for his word-association experiments and his use of the term "complex," although the word had originated with Ziehen. Before Jung and Freud fell out in 1912, Freud regarded him as the heir to the leadership of the psychoanalytic movement (McGuire, 1974). In Jung's (1902, pp. 76, 106) doctoral dissertation he casually tossed off the word "repressed" in referring to certain affects, without ever explaining the mechanism of repression. He discussed the "unconscious personalities" of certain patients and how they reminded him of the repressed thoughts Freud described in his investigations of dreams. The only justification for his discussion was the reference to Freud's *Interpretation of Dreams* and Breuer and Freud's *Studies on Hysteria* (see also Jung and Riklin, 1904, p. 142).

Iwan Bloch (1872-1922) easily used phrases like "[the patient] missed the first unconscious natural sexual stimulations" with merely the mention of Freud's name by way of explanation (Bloch, 1907b, p. 641). Bloch was a Berlin sexologist and sexual reformer and for a time a member of Abraham's embryonic Berlin Psychoanalytic Society. His *Sexual Life of Our Time in Its Relation to Modern Civilization*, which included ample references to Freud's theories, was a best seller.

Only one of Freud's detractors, though admittedly not one of the most hostile ones, was as casual about the unconscious

---

[2] See also Bleuler's (1905, p. 231), essay "Bewusstsein und Assoziationen," in Jung's (1906a) *Diagnostische Assoziationsstudien*. All the papers in this book were originally published in Vols. 3-7 of the *Journal für Psychologie und Neurologie*, 1904-1905, in spite of the facts that (1) the editors of the *Journal*, August Forel and Oskar Vogt, were openly anti-Freudian, and (2) the various authors of the articles liberally acknowledged their indebtedness to Freud.

and repression. In the fourth edition of his textbook, the neurologist Oppenheim (1905, p. 1158) concluded that Freud's concept of the etiology of obsessions "in no way has general validity." But he raised no questions (nor assumed his readers had any) in his precise and accurate summary of Freud's views that a person can separate an idea from its affect by "repression" or that an "unconscious" does indeed exist.

Other German physicians were more concerned to investigate the existence of the unconscious and the repressive mechanism. These men were either struggling to come to terms with psychoanalysis or, on the whole, had come down against it. One of the former was the psychiatrist Ludwig Binswanger (1881-1966), Otto Binswanger's nephew, who was grappling with "unconscious complexes in the Freudian sense" as opposed to "*repressed* complexes." Binswanger was one of the first doctors to carry out a psychoanalysis on an inpatient in a German hospital; he did this in 1909 in his uncle's clinic at Jena. Later he became famous as an existential psychiatrist, although maintaining a friendship with Freud. In a 1906 word-association study, Binswanger sought to clarify the difference between thoughts temporarily out of consciousness but which could be recalled at any time ("repressed complexes"), and unconscious thoughts not amenable to voluntary recall ("unconscious complexes"). Binswanger, wrestling with Freudian terminology, was trying to differentiate Freud's concepts of the preconscious and the unconscious respectively.

Of great interest in studying the reception of Freud's ideas in Germany is a 1902 talk given before the medical society of Greifswald by a well-known internist and pathologist, Ludolf von Krehl (1861-1937), whose textbook on pathology went into fourteen editions. Krehl had read *Studies on Hysteria* and his thought had been deeply influenced by it. He accepted the concept of the unconscious completely, but never used the word "unconscious." He believed that

> mental experiences . . . exerted the greatest influence on the physical condition of . . . patients . . . because the experiences kept themselves alive with towering strength inside the patients' psyche — but outside consciousness.

Psychic events, lying in a great world that exists outside our consciousness, overflow their boundaries (inside of which the balanced condition of healthy persons keeps those events) and play an independent, unhealthy role. This is the splitting of the psyche . . . [Krehl, 1902, pp. 736-738, 744].

Krehl's dealing with the reality of an unconscious and his endeavor to convince his audience was a cautious and sophisticated effort. His precise and thoughtful remarks have received no mention anywhere in the psychoanalytic literature. Yet they are an example of the sober assessment of and attempts to come to grips with Freudian theories that existed contemporaneously with the flamboyant and well-publicized rejections of psychoanalysis. Krehl's talk was published in the *Sammlung Klinischer Vorträge*, a "well-known" series, which "contains some of the most valuable monographs of recent times" (Garrison, 1929, p. 594).

The Bavarian clinician Löwenfeld was another who did not use the word "unconscious" but accepted the concept. He agreed that one could hold certain ideas but not be aware of them because these ideas were "inadmissible to consciousness." Rather than "unconscious," Löwenfeld (1897a, p. 22) used the word "subconscious." But he never spent much time on theoretical issues, being more concerned with treatment.

The idea of repression and the existence of the unconscious were dealt with at great length by Willy Hugo Hellpach (1877-1955), a Karlsruhe *Nervenarzt* who also held a doctorate in experimental psychology. Hellpach was a prolific (and wordy) writer on the psychological aspects of social problems. He was well acquainted with all of Freud's works, acknowledged Freud's "cleverness" and "capability," minutely noted his indebtedness to Freud, and then proceeded to reject a large part of psychoanalytic theory. Influenced by his training under the physiological psychologist Wilhelm Wundt, Hellpach was particularly concerned to refute the existence of an unconscious. "The unconscious, when used in scientific psychology, is merely a helpful hypothetical concept, a stopgap. Because it is inaccessible to psychological experimentation, the idea of an unconscious is best used as little as

possible. With just such scanty utilization I credit Lipps'
theory. . . . The opposite of scanty utilization I find just as
clearly in the efforts of the ingenious inventor [*Konstrukteur*]
Freud . . ." (Hellpach, 1906c, pp. 115-116).

According to Hellpach, Freud should

> have kept us from the headlong fall into the unconscious . . . I
> draw a line between his *idea* of repression and his *theory* of
> repression. . . . I would . . . be able to value Freud's fruitful
> service to psychopathology still more if his theory had turned out
> differently, if he had just uncovered, developed, and brought to
> ripeness out of the hidden germ in the idea of repression the
> apparent unconscious only as a conscious that had taken a
> detour. . . . For my train of thought, the theory of repression is
> as useless as the idea of repression is significant [1904, pp.
> 364-365].

Hellpach's understanding and acceptance of repression,
after reading all of Freud's works, was limited to the popular
idea that it is possible to "hold in" an idea on a conscious level.
He thought Freud's contribution lay in giving scientific bles-
sing to the "beneficent, freeing effect of letting off one's
emotions . . . a woman can often weather a difficult experience better than can a man because she 'cries out' . . . while
the man is inclined to 'shut it up inside himself' " (Hellpach,
1904, p. 366). This is an example of a type of reaction Freud
faced continually: misunderstanding and trivializing of his
views and a selective discovery in them of only what the reader
wanted to find.

Freud was not the only physician whom Hellpach condemned for a belief in the unconscious. He criticized equally
Möbius, Janet, and Vogt: "It is completely incomprehensible
to me how thinking men who are precise investigators can give
themselves up to the simplicity of this argument." The unconscious was superfluous, and the processes of repression and
conversion (of repressed ideas into physical symptoms) could
be shown to operate without it once being necessary to leave
the "firm ground" of the conscious. The concept of the unconscious was "unscientific." But Hellpach (1904, pp. 401-406;
453-454) could conclude quite cheerfully: ". . . it is a grati-
fying thing for me to remember . . . how strongly my own

attempted explanation of hysterical abnormality is in accord with that of the Viennese author."

After this improbable statement, we must remind ourselves that illogicalities creep into the work of every serious scholar. For Hellpach was highly regarded, and was asked by Martin Buber to compose a monograph on mass hysteria for Buber's journal, *Society* (*Die Gesellschaft, Sammlung sozialpsychologischer Monographien*); other authors who wrote in this series included Werner Sombart, Georg Simmel, and Eduard Bernstein. Hellpach's works were widely reviewed, and he in turn reviewed significant literature of the day, such as Löwenfeld's *Sexual Life and Nervous Complaints* of 1906.

Hellpach, like others, was unsympathetic to Freud's views on the unconscious and repression because his flexibility and imagination were overcome by his rigid espousal of "science." But he was never malicious. He deplored the "usual multitude of sarcasms against Freud's theories. As strongly as my thoughts—to this day—have remained against various investigative and interpretive details of Freud's method, I know of no achievement in the last few decades in the field of theoretical psychopathology, outside of the experimental researches of the Heidelberg school, that is stimulating and powerful enough to claim a place at the side of Freud's work" (1904, p. 38). The rejection of psychoanalysis in Germany was often just such a mixed phenomenon and not the open-and-shut matter early psychoanalysts (as well as later ones) have claimed.

Unimaginative—though again unmalicious—refusal to consider anything but the obvious was exemplified by the Berlin *Nervenarzt* who wrote that the mental disturbance in a hysteric does not exist "in a mythical subconscious, but in the same mental life that also contains the phenomena of the waking state . . . patients have knowledge of the [etiological] event just as well in waking life as under hypnosis; but they frequently refuse to talk about it while awake because it is painful to them to reveal the secrets of their intimate mental life" (Hirschlaff, 1905, pp. 191-192). Most probably Hirschlaff's antipathy to psychoanalysis was also influenced by his belief that deep hypnosis was therapeutically worthless and superfluous, and useful only for experimentation.

SEXUALITY

Although comments and opinions on the unconscious and repression were quite varied, their tone was never agitated. Their presentation was always scientifically "correct." Comments on Freud's sexual theories, however, were sometimes emotional, though most of them were also expressed in a calm, expository manner.[3]

After returning to Berlin from Vienna, where he had studied with Freud, Felix Gattel (1898) published a small monograph extolling Freud's view of the role played by sexuality in certain nervous diseases. But before the turn of the century, at the very time Freud was making explicit his sexual views, there was only one other work that was uncritically accepting of the role of sexuality. This was a book on the relationship between the nose and female sex organs by Freud's close friend Wilhelm Fliess (1897), a Berlin otolaryngologist. Both Gattel and Fliess publicized a now almost completely discarded psychoanalytic theory, postulating a direct connection between sexual frustration and anxiety. Such adulatory works on Freud's sexual theories were rare and did not occur again for several years. Then another German physician, Arthur Muthmann (1907), applied himself to the cause of propagandizing the sexual etiology of neurotic symptoms, but, like Gattel and Fliess, he was not an important figure in "official" German medicine.

There was wholehearted acceptance of psychoanalytic sexual theory in a review of Freud's *Three Essays on the Theory of Sexuality* (1905d) by Albert Eulenberg (1840-1917), a well-known Berlin neurologist. Eulenberg was the editor of an authoritative, many-volumed medical encyclopedia (*Realencyklopaedia der gesamten Heilkunde*), of which there were four separate series. In 1884 he had been considered for the chair of neurology in Vienna. He was interested in sexology

---

[3] This section deals with the medical reaction to Freud's early theories of universal sexual develoment and his *general* linking of sexuality with the etiology of nervous disease. The reaction to Freud's specific connection of sexual experiences and *particular* mental disorders is described in Chapter 4. Chapter 4 also shows how the controversial subject of the psychogenesis of illness affected the medical reception of psychoanalysis.

and worked for the reform of laws relating to sexual matters. Though Eulenberg's enthusiasm waned in later years, in 1906 he had no reservations.

> The gifted Viennese neuropathologist whose psychoanalytic researches . . . have proved so significant, has recently again presented us with a ripe fruit of his studies—three extremely short contributions, but valuable because of the direction of thought and their ingenious development. . . . This work is also, like Freud's earlier creations . . . the product of an interpretive . . . dialectic acumen. It is a mind which proceeds more constructively and deductively than inductively and synthetically. It throws an abundance of new thoughts and often lightening and dazzling aperçus into the still unenlightened, nocturnal obscurity of sexual life. . . . For the physician, all three essays are equally valuable and instructive; yet the first [on sexual aberrations] must be designated as an especially estimable contribution to the literature of sexual pathology, opening completely new points of view; while the two following [on infantile sexuality and transformations of puberty] are essentially of importance for the recent, careful research into childhood and for pediatrics especially [Eulenberg, 1906, p. 740].

Freud's sexual theories also received unqualified concurrence from Christian von Ehrenfels, whose monograph, *Sexualethik* (1907), was published in Löwenfeld's monograph series (see Chapter 12).

More typical than uncritical acceptance or glowing praise of the sexual theories was the "Yes, but . . ." reaction. This was common in men like Bleuler, Bloch, and Löwenfeld. These men discused the practical uses to which they had put Freud's sexual views, or stated their theoretical concurrence with most of the new information. But each in his own way drew limits. Bleuler reported that "at our hospital the Freudian theories have been confirmed in many thousands of individual symptoms, [and] . . . we daily see sexual roots, in Freud's sense, in the symptoms of dementia praecox, and only exceptionally find other causes, and then only as secondary factors" (1907a, p. 531). Yet, though "sexual matters play a very important part, they perhaps do not so completely dominate the symptomatology as one might believe from reading Freud's works . . ." (1906c, p. 23).

Löwenfeld (1901, p. 367) reported that Freud's writings had given him the idea that one of his own female patients with sexual problems was suffering from "certain existing anxieties." Löwenfeld then cured her frigidity through hypnotic suggestion. But he refused to deal with her "anxieties."

Bloch had written widely on many sexual subjects: the Marquis de Sade and the eighteenth century; sexual life in England; the origin of syphilis and its appearance in Europe; the etiology of sexual psychopathology; perversions. His book on modern sexual life (1907b) was a runaway success. In the first nine months it was necessary to print six editions to meet readers' demands, and the book was in its twelfth edition by 1919 (see Chapter 12). Throughout his comprehensive work, Bloch (pp. 46-47, 413, 456, 641, 653, 686-687, 756) repeatedly buttressed his arguments with a variety of Freudian terms and explanations. He talked about Freud's division of the sexual impulse into two stages—"the stage of '*pre-libido*' (sexual desire) and the stage of the proper sexual '*libido*' (sexual gratification)." He adopted Freud's view that "pre-libido" is governed by a "chemical stimulus," what is today called a hormone. Bloch enumerated the "erogenic zones" described by Freud, and discussed the significance for adult sexual behavior of the "auto-erotic" character of the infant's "ecstatic sucking." He pointed out that heterosexual anal intercourse had become a comprehensible phenomenon because Freud had shown that the anus is an early erogenic zone. He credited Freud with demonstrating the "biologico-physiological derivations of sexual perversions." But he could

not go as far as Freud, who, on account of the now generally recognized wide diffusion of perverse sexual tendencies, was compelled to adopt the view "that the rudiments of perversions are the *primeval* general rudiments of the human sexual impulse, out of which the normal sexual mode of behavior is developed in the course of evolution, in consequence of organic changes and psychical inhibitions" (*Three Essays on the Theory of Sexuality*) [Bloch, 1907b, p. 456].

The "Yes, but . . ." reception was also found in conventional reviews of the *Three Essays*. One reviewer opened with a factual account of the book's contents, expressed an interest in Freud's psychoanalytic terminology, and then concluded:

> We meet with manifold original and stimulating ideas. . . . Even if Freud's claim, that sexual reminiscences form the basis of hysteria, hardly has up to now the prospect of general recognition, and even if the transcending significance that he has allotted to sexuality for general emotional development and formation of character has awakened various doubts, yet this stimulatingly written work will be of great use in the investigation of the normal sexual drives as well as the perversions [E. Meyer, 1906, pp. 92-93].

Paul Näcke (1851-1913), director of an asylum at Colditz in Saxony and a prolific publisher, also was enthusiastic with reservations: *"Few works would seem to be so worth their price as"* the *Three Essays* because of "the enormous wealth of its contents," which Näcke conscientiously described (1906, p. 166). But that did not mean that he could accept Freud's theories of the sexual etiology of all cases of hysteria, obsessional neurosis, and paranoia: ". . . not even the majority arose from repression of sexual content."

The unambivalent critics of Freud's ideas on sexuality can be divided into two groups on the basis of the tone of their comments. By far the majority of those who rejected the sexual views were dispassionate and matter-of-fact in their expression. As usual, Hellpach (1904, pp. 367-371) had an array of original, extended arguments on which he brought to bear his sociological interests. He started out with the ubiquitous complaint that Freud had made infantile sexual experiences "monopolize" the production of pathological symptoms; according to Freud "only sexual experiences" are repressed.

Hellpach strenuously objected to Freud's asserting that sexual experiences are universally repressed (which Freud had actually never claimed). Rather, only children of the middle and lower-middle classes experienced the earliest erotic impressions and desires as something absolutely forbidden — "sinful" — and consequently sought to repress them. But the children of the lowest classes never learned to feel that sexual things ought to be repressed. On the contrary, the acting out of sexual impulses was obvious to them. If Freud was right, and only sexually repressed experiences were the source of illness, the pathological results of repression must be much rarer among the lower classes than among the middle classes. But the facts were otherwise. *"Actually, hysteria is more frequent among the lowest classes; and male hysteria here is enormously rampant, while it presents a decisively much rarer picture in middle-class circles"* (Hellpach's italics). Yet for the proletarian men the "possibility of repression of sexual impressions . . . is completely out of the question. It seems absolutely impossible to accept that the innumerable male hysterics that we meet among the proletariat should be understood as 'defense neuroses' as a result of the repression of sexual experiences."

Hellpach believed his conclusions could be supported by looking at the operation of "disgust, which doubtlessly plays a significant role in sexual repressions and is occasionally clearly described by Freud as a symptom in hysterical conditions." Yet feelings of disgust were aroused in children by many experiences other than sexual ones: they had to eat food that disgusted them, sit next to other children who disgusted them, let themselves be kissed by grownups who disgusted them. Daily, children had to repress their feelings of disgust. Hellpach therefore offered the repression of nonsexual disgust as a possible departure point to explain the genesis of hysterical phenomena.

Hellpach argued that, logically, education should play a prime role in the production of hysteria if repression were the cause of hysteria, since "repression is the main weapon of all education." Hysterical suffering should be the most frequent where there is the most education. Middle-class education perverted natural aggressiveness, implanting and cultivating emotional defenses from the start, imposing "modesty." The proletariat was sexually healthier and less repressed, yet Hellpach found that hysteria was spreading "enormously" among the proletariat and in rural areas. Freud's hypothesis did nothing to explain this proliferation nor the widespread existence of male hysteria among the lowest classes.

Thus, Hellpach offered the theory that repression had a

"natural" relationship to social class. Perhaps there were differences in the nature of hysteria which made it possible that
repression entered the picture only for a "socially localized"
part of hysterical illnesses, while the other part demanded
"other etiological derivation."

To clinch his argument that social milieu was more
important to the nature of sexuality than were any universal
instincts or drives, Hellpach (1904, p. 421) offered evidence
from his clinical practice. He prefaced his case history with the
following observations: "Has not perhaps the gallant Viennese
atmosphere — reminding one of Rococo culture — of which the
extraordinarily erotic refinement of Austrian women is a part,
strongly turned the glance of the authors of *Studies on Hysteria* and especially Freud, in a certain direction? The strong
national differences in hysteria are well-known . . . it is
probable that [these differences] fit in its genesis."

A Viennese married couple had consulted him. Their sexual history "illustrated once more what I had already known
from hundreds of other experiences, but what one often
forgets: what role the erotic, in all its expressions, had played
for these good middle-class people — a role of which the
average north German has not the least concept."

Finally, Hellpach (1904, pp. 362-363) could not accept
Freud's theory of sublimation. He objected to Freud's raising
his ideas "to a psychological system whose intention it is to
reach from the deepest unconscious to the highest thought
process." Freud's views were "completely hypothetical; it must
be decisively denied that the unconscious parts of psychic life
force themselves on the observer as realities or as experiences."
The "creative revelations" of Goethe and Helmholtz did not
stem from unconscious sexual strivings.

Strong resistance to the concept of sublimation continued to
be a prominent feature of German reaction to psychoanalysis.
George Gero, trained in medicine and psychology in Germany
after World War I, emphasized how difficult it was for him,
while in psychoanalytic training, to accept the notion of sublimation (1966, personal interview). For a while, Gero strongly
opposed the psychoanalytic view that man's greatest
achievements and visionary goals were merely products of

sublimated instincts. Because of their idealist philosophical tradition, many German intellectuals thought psychoanalysis demeaned man's positive intellectual, spiritual, and even material attainments. These thinkers, one of whom was Karl Jaspers, were repelled by a *Weltanschauung* that seemed to strip man of what made him so uniquely human. There was also a religious basis to the opposition, seen most clearly in Catholic writers before World War II (Birk, 1970).[4] This response was in sharp contrast to that of many Americans, who welcomed the concept of sublimation as an optimistic sign (Burnham, 1958, pp. 378-379, 381-383). They received from the idea of sublimation the theoretical justification for attempts to make man a "better" person. Sublimation indicated to them that there were magnificent opportunities to convert man's "lower" instincts into "higher" achievements that would benefit both individuals and society.

Other physicians were not as far-ranging and erudite as Hellpach in buttressing their opinions. They contented themselves with less complex refutations. Albert Moll (1907, p. 352), though a sexologist, declared that what Freud said about the sexual etiology of neurosis was one-sided and, he hoped, would not find general recognition. One ought not to regard mankind purely from the standpoint of sexual life. Moll (1862-1939) was a Berlin psychiatrist specializing in criminology and editor of a journal on sexual matters. He also campaigned for sexual reforms. Views similar to Moll's were expressed by Näcke (1901, p. 168) in his review of *The Interpretation of Dreams*. Oppenheim concurred. Even if sexual factors were important, Freud had gone "too far" in considering sexual trauma of early childhood, arising in genital stimulation, to be the specific cause of hysteria (Oppenheim, 1898, p. 728; 1902a, p. 902; 1905, p. 1046).

Literally, Oppenheim was right. Not until 1905-1906 did Freud (1905d, p. 190; 1906a, pp. 274-275) publicly rescind his original view that all his neurotic patients had suffered actual

---

[4] The philosopher von Ehrenfels (1907, p. 88) was one of the few "German" thinkers (he was born near Vienna and taught at the German University in Prague for many years) who immediately accepted Freud's theory of sublimation.

sexual traumatic experiences. In 1897 Freud (1887-1902, letter 69) came to the revised conclusion that most of his patients' sexual remembrances were founded in wish and fantasy. But so shaken was Freud by this discovery that he did not publish it for several years, until he had convinced himself that whether the sexual experience was real or fantasied made little difference in the meaning it held for his patients. Of course, Freud's adamant opponents were no more ready to accept the second view than they had been the first.

Strümpell was most blunt.

> This cathartic procedure demands, as the authors themselves emphasize, a penetrating investigation into the smallest details of the patients' private relationships and experiences. I do not know whether under all circumstances one should permit the most high-principled physician such a penetration into the most intimate private affairs. I find most questionable this penetration when it is a matter of sexual relations, and the authors repeatedly emphasize that it often concerns such things [1895, p. 160].[5]

Kraepelin, in the sixth edition of his textbook, was not only blunt; his sarcasm was cutting. "If . . . our much-plagued soul can lose its equilibrium for all time as a result of long-forgotten unpleasant sexual experiences, that would be the beginning of the end of the human race; nature would have played a gruesome trick on us!" (1899, Vol. 2, p. 511) Nevertheless, Kraepelin's summary of Freud's views was brilliant in its conciseness and obvious grasp of the issues.

Of all early attacks on psychoanalysis, that of Gustav Aschaffenburg (1866-1944) is the most famous because it was an emotional harangue delivered before a large psychiatric congress at Baden-Baden in 1906. Aschaffenburg was professor of neurology and psychiatry, first at Heidelberg and then at Cologne, and an expert in forensic psychiatry. His rebuttals of psychoanalysis had all been made (and less passionately) by others before in book reviews, monographs, and texts. More than anything else, Aschaffenburg objected to

---

[5] Judging by the even-tempered tone of the review from which this quotation comes, I do not think the obvious sexual innuendo and accusation in Strümpell's use of the word "penetrate" three times was conscious.

Freud's method, so only a small part of his talk is relevant to the present discussion. Aschaffenburg found untenable Freud's view that in no case of hysteria is sexual psychic trauma missing. He sharply protested against Freud's discussing sexual matters with his patients for months. The only reason Freud found a sexual trauma in every case was because he put sexual ideas in his patients' heads. Whoever agreed with Aschaffenburg that it was not sexual experiences as such, but rather the associated ideas, which caused nervous difficulties, had to reject every investigation of the sexual life of hysterics and had to put himself to the task of suppressing those ideas in every area (Aschaffenburg, 1906).

Some of the most vivid testimonies to the existence of a repressive sexual atmosphere in Wilhelmine Germany are precisely these thoughts of Moll, Oppenheim, Kraepelin, Aschaffenburg, and Strümpell. The first four not only found it hard to accept the ubiquitous influence of human sexuality, but explicitly or implicitly expressed the wish that pervasive sexuality not even exist. Strümpell said quite openly that even the "high-principled physician" should not inquire into a person's sexual life. He thus (unconsciously?) implied that Freud was getting sexual gratification from analyzing patients, an admission that if *he*, Strümpell, were conducting such analyses, they would afford him sexual gratification. Strümpell believed that talking about sex could have only one result—the sexual arousal of those involved. Strümpell's deduction was quite logical, if not inevitable, in a society where frank, extended, and unemotional discussions of sexual feelings and practices generally did not occur.

It is noteworthy that physicians paid little attention to the connection of Freud's sexual theories with normal personality development. By and large, as the next chapter demonstrates, doctors were only interested in sexuality as it related to illness. Partly, of course, this is to be expected from the nature of a doctor's preoccupations. Partly, also, it was due to the conditions described so graphically by Gattel. Almost all German physicians experienced great difficulty in coming to grips with the basic nature of human sexuality. Moreover, the underlying medical belief that there was a sharp dividing line between sickness and health also prevented most German doctors from unreservedly committing themselves to Freud's discoveries of common psychosexual processes.

DREAMS

Such chary acceptance, however, was not the case with regard to another one of Freud's ground-breaking disclosures: that all dreams had meaning and that the interpretation of dreams was a valuable tool for the understanding of human motivation. Though a number of medical men were unconvinced, there was, in many instances, an unreserved belief that dream interpretation and the elucidation of the mechanisms of dreaming was a scientific discovery of the first order. Bleuler, Jung, Löwenfeld, and Moll were typical of wholehearted partisans. About Freud's *Interpretation of Dreams*, Bleuler wrote that it was "full of sharpsighted observations and explanations. The latter only seem fantastic if one has not himself done research in their direction" (1905, p. 232). Freud had proved that the dream (along with delirium and hysteria) had the quality of wish fulfillment (Bleuler, 1906c, p. 15). Jung (1902, pp. 76, 106) very early guessed that the results of Freud's dream research might be applied to understanding hallucinations. Moreover, Freud's dream investigations had served to confirm the existence of repressed thoughts.

Löwenfeld published Freud's shortened version of his dream work, *On Dreams* (1901a), in his 1901 *Grenzfragen des Nerven- und Seelenlebens*. In the same year, the Munich physician wrote that

> the most important investigator of our day in the field of dream life, Freud, has convincingly shown that absolutely nothing with prophetic meaning is disclosed in a dream. According to his view, popular opinion is, to be sure, right when it says that the dream prophesies the future, but the prophecy has only the meaning of a wish, not of reality. "In truth . . . the future that the dream shows us is not that which will happen, but that which we wish might happen" [Löwenfeld, 1901, p. 278].

Moll (1907, pp. 191, 196) accepted Freud's idea that similar mechanisms operated in dreams as in emotional illness, and that therefore dreams could elucidate emotional disturbances.

C. G. JUNG

EUGEN BLEULER

Iwan Bloch

Karl Abraham

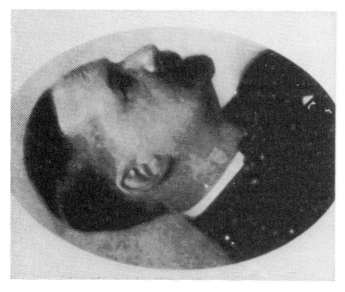

LUDOLF VON KREHL

HERMANN OPPENHEIM

From Haymaker, Webb, *The Founders of Neurology*, 1953. Courtesy of Charles C Thomas, Publisher, Springfield, Ill.

ALBERT MOLL

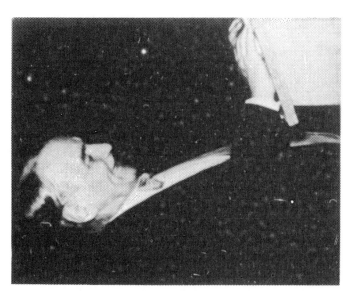

WILLY HELLPACH

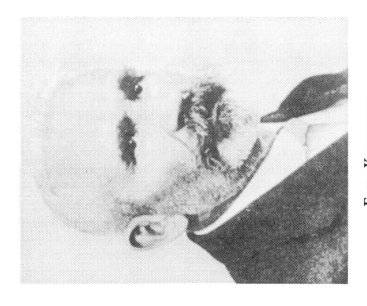

Emil Kraepelin

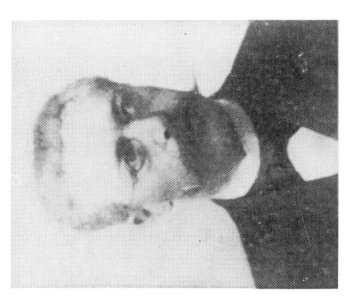

Adolf von Strümpell

P. J. Möbius

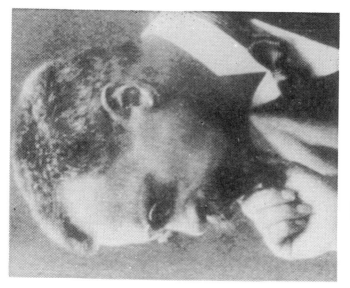

Wilhelm Weygandt

GUSTAV ASCHAFFENBURG

Another large group of physicians were favorably impressed, but held back total endorsement. This reaction typified most of the journal reviews of Freud's two dream books. One review, lengthy by the standards of the periodical in which it appeared, stated:

> Although [Freud] has simply gone too far and appears to have lost himself in sophistries, his new approach and the energy of his penetrating psychological searches deserve decisive recognition and emulation. For only psychological analysis can enter the depths of mental life. . . . It appears to us that Freud has proved with success that the dream is not a dissociated, uncritical emotional work, that it is not an unconnected act determined by physiological stimulation of individual cell groups which are drawn off from a brain sunk in sleep, but that the dream is explainable according to certain rules that also affect waking life, and especially pathological mental life [Kohnstamm, 1902].

In his review, Möbius (1901) summarized with accuracy and care Freud's thesis of dreams as wish fulfillments and the mechanisms of dream operation. He concluded: "Freud presents his new view clearly and supports it by examples from his own and others' experience. As long as it is not claimed that all dreams must be judged according to Freud's schema, one must probably agree with the author unhesitatingly."

Näcke, just as he did with the sexual theories, expressed a slightly more divided opinion. He predicted that "Freud's view that *every* dream, even a painful one, is an open or hidden wish fulfillment . . . will certainly not be generally accepted. . . . His method of dream interpretation . . . is very open to controversy. All notions concerning dreams can be manufactured; where and how, however, is one supposed to prove that in actuality it really happened? Thus the veiled dream interpretations often appear as pure fantasies." On the other hand, this was an "excellent book . . . *psychologically the most profound which dream psychology has produced up to now* [Näcke's italics]. . . . the work is solid and thought through with genius" (1901, p. 168). Like many other critics, Näcke was heavily challenged by the revolutionary nature of Freud's work. He recognized that he was dealing with something unusual, but was hard put to assess its precise worth. Hence, his contradictory judgments.

Hellpach was impressed. He found Freud's "attempt to give a psychological explanation for the emotional life of sleep and to track down its laws . . . extraordinarily noteworthy." Freud was "the most significant of modern dream researchers" (1904, p. 17). Yet Hellpach had "the feeling that the Viennese scholar clouded the view . . . of dream interpretation by his misplacement of work on dreams into the unconscious" (p. 460). Hellpach's rejection of the unconscious colored all his evaluations of Freud's work.

Less impressed was Wilhelm Weygandt of Würzburg, who thought that Freud's *Interpretation of Dreams* was nothing extraordinary—just more evidence of the growing interest in "the change of consciousness during dreams." Before becoming a physician, Weygandt (1870-1939) had studied philosophy and psychology and written a book on the origin of dreams. He later became chief of the Psychiatric Clinic at the newly founded University of Hamburg. Weygandt (1901) found Freud's view of dreams as wish fulfillment "plausible . . . in many examples," and "the detailed analysis of dream mechanisms [condensation, displacement, and composite personalities] worthwhile. . . . The most valuable contributions are always specific observations, e.g., about anxiety dreams, about awakening as a result of dreaming, about repression, etc." Weygandt's faint prasie was outweighed by his criticism. Freud's material was suspect because it came only from his own dreams or from those of "nervous patients." As to specific interpretations, in most cases, Freud had gone "too far." Weygandt could not agree that dreams of flying are a memory of being rocked in childhood, nor that dreams showed one's hostile wishes toward one's father and a desire for sexual relations with one's mother. "Freud goes so far that he wants to place the whole tragedy of Oedipus in reference to marrying one's mother." Freud had followed "the false paths of unfruitful symbolism." Finally, Weygandt labeled Freud's efforts as "*Traumdeuterei*": Freud wanted to explain too much and had fallen prey to sophistry.

Weygandt was typical of those physicians who reacted

negatively to psychoanalytic dream interpretation. They did not condemn Freud's work completely. This or that aspect was actually quite good. Only, Freud had gone "too far." The tone of their reviews was, with minor exceptions, gentlemanly, and quite similar in blandness to most of the reviews that appear in medical journals today. Freud may not have been right, but he was not worth a fuss.

But of course, there were exceptions. An emotional equivalent to Aschaffenburg's outraged speech of 1906 was Hugo Liepmann's lengthy critique of 1901. Liepmann (1863-1925) was a neurologist and brain anatomist at the Charité and chief of the mental hospital at Dalldorf. Abraham studied brain histology under Liepmann before going to Burghölzli to work with Bleuler. Just because Freud was able to present his views in a "captivating and stimulating" way, just because his characterizations were "excellent" and his thoughts "polished," Liepmann warned, Freud posed a danger to psychiatry. After reiterating some of Weygandt's objections, Liepmann (1901) challenged the "scientific value" of Freud's work.

> Does Freud really believe he has given *a foundation* to his ideas by his "analytic" method? In the presentation of the relation between dream content and waking experiences, he proceeds with such violence and caprice that one finds it difficult to remain serious. Freud does not guard enough against those long-recognized and avoided errors of scientific psychology: uncritical self-observation and arbitrary construction; in his work the gifted artist of thoughts triumphs over the scientific investigator. It is to be feared that the example of his fantastic mock-psychology will enchain less acute minds . . . who will throw to the winds the hard-won insights of scientific examination of mental life.

However, Liepmann and others who argued like him, did not go unchallenged. And it was not a Freudian, but Willy Hellpach, who rose to defend Freud. To Liepmann's objections, Hellpach (1904, pp. 38-39) countered: "There are people who ostensibly feel themselvs repelled by a sensation-seeking bent in Freud's publications. [But] that Freud writes well and captivatingly is no disadvantage. It is unavoidable that research which deals essentially with erotic experiences will always offer certain secondary points of attraction to people with deficient objectivity."

UNIVERSAL APPLICABILITY OF PSYCHIC MECHANISMS

Freud, too, of course, did not view his work as "mock psychology." He had analyzed himself and numerous others. After repeatedly observing certain wishes and fantasies, Freud concluded that the information he had gathered had universal validity. People's dreams provided clues to their deeply felt wishes and thoughts. The sex drive was operative in all people, and every human being went through certain psychosexual phases of development. Each person had an unconscious and repressed those thoughts and desires which the ego found incompatible. But the majority of German psychiatrists and neurologists did not acknowledge the general applicability of the psychoanalytic hypotheses. A strong barrier to such acknowledgment was the physicians' fundamental belief that healthy and sick states were two distinct entities.

These were the years that Freud, with a combination of self-pity and grandiosity, designated as his period of "splendid isolation." Yet at this time there were prominent physicians—Bleuler, Bloch, Krehl, and Hellpach—who agreed that certain Freudian theories had general validity. At Burghölzli, not only did the staff attempt to psychoanalyze the patients, at the breakfast table every morning they psychoanalyzed each other's dreams. In his publications, Bleuler (1907a, p. 531; 1906c, pp. 23, 102) consistently maintained that "we find confirmation of the Freudian principles in both healthy and sick individuals." He believed that a knowledge of the psychic mechanisms used by hysterics to get rid of disagreeable affects "will make the symptoms of the abnormal as well as of the normal mind more comprehensible." Furthermore, the same processes that elicit paranoia in some patients "are very frequent with healthy individuals."

In sexual matters, Bloch had long believed that no hard and fast line could be drawn between what was commonly regarded as sick and healthy. He praised Freud's *Three Essays* as "recognizing the justice of my view" and quoted Freud's words as his own opinion.

Daily experience has shown that the majority of [perversions] constitute a seldom lacking constituent of the sexual life of healthy persons. In favourable conditions *the normal individual may exhibit such a perversion for a considerable length of time in the place of his normal sexual activity. Probably there is no healthy person in whom there does not exist, at some time or other, some kind of supplement to his normal sexual activity, to which we should be justified in giving the name of "perversity"* [1907b, p. 464; Bloch's italics].

Before reading Freud, Krehl (1902, pp. 736-737) had already come to the conclusion that "all our ideas are preserved partly as memory images and partly in a form that is separated from consciousness . . . a very thorough and careful observation of healthy individuals . . . shows a protracted aftereffect of ideas as well as their residues." He therefore welcomed the *Studies on Hysteria* for "having proved this for hysteria itself and thereby having also discovered important facts for the inner lives of healthy people." In these discoveries, the "untiring persistence" of the Viennese neurologists through "intricate paths" were to be commended.

Hellpach (1904, p. 459) argued that "dissociation is not something so completely strange and extraordinary that it does not have its analogues in normal lives or in nonhysterical abnormal lives. The most common form of it is the dream." Then he explained the similarities of dream life to dissociated mental states in an awake person. Dissociation occurred in all people while they were asleep. Löwenfeld (1894, p. 563) too had argued this ten years earlier.

Not unnaturally, Freud's *Psychopathology of Everyday Life* (1901b) which appeared in book form in 1904, went furthest in eliciting a recognition that similar mechanisms were at work in healthy and sick people. Freud used the same techniques he used in the analyses of his patients (dream interpretation and free association) to explain common occurrences, like slips of the tongue or pen and forgetting, and to reveal the meanings of commonly held superstitions. Freud's conclusions about everyday occurrences were the same as those about neuroses: in neither were there "internal (psychic) accidents," and the identical unconscious mechanisms were operative in both situations. Though the reviewers balked at swallowing these arguments whole, they generally judged that "the connections Freud had shown should not be considered rarities" (Haenel, 1904).[6]

THE MEDICAL RECEPTION: PRELIMINARY CONCLUSIONS

Although the survey of initial German medical reactions to psychoanalysis continues in the next chapter, the material so far presented suggests some conclusions.

Most obviously, the reception of psychoanalysis was never one-sided, even in the 1890's when Freud first began publishing his psychological papers. Moreover, there was never a period when Freud was completely ignored. As the following chapter will demonstrate, the medical hypnotists in Germany immediately took Freud's and Breuer's work seriously and commented upon it. For Freud,. a neurologist with five months of psychiatric training, to have expected quick recognition from German psychiatrists was unrealistic. In the early years, while Freud's psychological work was associated with the cathartic method, he was given "equal time" with all other hypnotherapists. It is true that after Freud dissociated himself from the cathartic method his name continued to be linked with it, but, as will be seen, there was good reason for that.

After 1900, psychiatric and neurological journals, monographs, and textbooks contained frequent references to Freud. The great degree to which psychiatrists and neurologists were "exposed" to Freud's work does not mean there was a general acceptance of psychoanalysis. But the evidence of extensive exposure refutes a long-standing notion, broadly popularized by Ernest Jones, that for many years almost no one took note of Freud's work. Jones (1955, pp. 107-125) also propagated the notion that most rejection of psychoanalysis was emotionally expressed. There is no question that psychoanalytic theories aroused apprehension or even fear in some of its critics, and that they responded at times with disdain, strong contempt, or bitter hostility. But such responses were only one kind of criticism leveled at Freud.

---

[6] See also Bleuler (1907b), Cimbal (1904-1905), Gross (1905), Möbius (1904), Mönkemöller (1904-1905), Voss (1907), Weygandt (1904), Ziehen (1904).

It should, in addition, be stressed that the leading journals did not reject articles because they contained enthusiastic references to Freud. Furthermore, Bleuler's and Jung's careers never suffered because of their open espousal and defense of Freud. Jung (1906b) and Bleuler (1906a) both published rebuttals of Aschaffenburg's 1906 address and of another scathing attack by Walther Spielmeyer (1906). But the majority of the 1906-1907 reviews of Bleuler's and Jung's books, while mentioning the Swiss involvement with psychoanalysis, were not any the less complimentary as a result. The three exceptions were the reviews of Jung's works by Max Isserlin (1907), Näcke (1906a), and Weygandt (1907). Moreover, it was just about this time that Aschaffenburg asked Bleuler to write the volume on dementia praecox for Aschaffenburg's giant *Handbuch der Psychiatrie*; Bleuler's monograph duly appeared in 1911 and made him famous for his concept of "schizophrenia." And the best testimony to the fact that his psychoanalytic connection did not hurt Jung was his comment to Freud in November, 1908: "Anyway the hullabaloo has not harmed my practice; on the contrary, I am inundated" (McGuire, 1974, p. 181).

Attention must also be drawn to the fact that Freud's earliest work was in hysteria and that his name continued to be associated with that field long after he branched out to the neuroses in general. Considering the knowledge of and feelings about hysteria in Germany at the turn of the century, that fact is vital. Freud's ideas were startling enough in themselves; they acquired an even more upsetting character when persistently linked to the subject of hysteria. First of all, this immediately brought into play the discords between French and German medicine. Second, it played upon the national feelings of many German physicians who viewed hysteria as an un-Germanic disease that appeared mainly in those "races" who were in some way "degenerate." Third, it focused attention on the antagonisms between north and south Germans and served to increase the pre-existing north German disapproval of southern moral deficiencies, as Hellpach's comments vividly illustrate.

Finally, a word is in order about the response to Freud's

sexual theories. In personal interviews and in correspondence, some psychoanalysts have indicated to me that they believe the issue of the unconscious was a greater barrier to the acceptance of psychoanalysis than was the issue of sexuality. Freud himself often emphasized how uninviting was his contention that "a man was not master in his own house." The survey of the early literature partly bears out this belief. Among physicians, it is true, Freud's sexual theories aroused more opposition than did his views about the role of the unconscious. Among the "new" (experimental) psychologists, however, the unconscious was an insurmountable obstacle.

It is impossible that there should ever have been a monolithic "reaction" to psychoanalysis, because nonpsychoanalysts have always viewed psychoanalysis as being made up of several distinct components. In their view, psychoanalysis was not a closed system whose parts were indissolubly wedded to each other. Psychoanalysis did not have to be accepted or rejected as a whole. Workers in other fields have responded in a varying fashion to each component of psychoanalysis, depending on their particular interests and concerns.

4

PSYCHOANALYTIC PSYCHOPATHOLOGY

The varying reactions to Freud's theories on the neuroses must be understood not merely as responses to psychoanalytic hypotheses, but as attempts to grapple with the whole field of neuroses. The psychiatry of neuroses was in a state of confusion at the end of the nineteenth century. No Kraepelin had emerged to rescue it. The main neuroses were considered to be hysteria and neurasthenia, but it was difficult to subsume all neurotic disorders under one or the other. And the number of neuroses was growing, as modern life imposed new conditions. Traumatic or "accident" neuroses proliferated along with industrial growth and workers' insurance. Thus psychiatrists, and especially neurologists, were keenly and impatiently evaluating new classifications, explanations, and therapies for the neuroses. With his theories about hysteria and neurasthenia—but, disappointingly to many, not about traumatic neurosis—Freud strode into the arena.

The Response to Freud's Theories of Hysteria

AFFECTIVE MECHANISMS AND PSYCHOGENESIS

It is significant that German physicians never challenged Breuer and Freud's argument that affect must be discharged in order to prevent psychopathological states. There were several reasons why they did not. First, it was understood by many on the simplest level as merely stating that it was necessary to "let off steam." Hellpach was one of a host who eagerly grabbed at this scientific expression of what everyone knew anyway. On a more sophisticated level, it had an intrinsic appeal because it was based on the "force" and "energy" concepts of Helmholtzian physics and physiology, principles in which every German physician had been schooled, and which he accepted uncritically.[1] The language was comfortable: affect was a "force" that had to be "discharged." Third, it hurt no one to believe it. Basically, normal states were irrelevant matters to German psychiatrists, who occupied themselves almost solely with abnormal states. With his explanation, Freud infringed on no one's vested interests. Little research had been done on normal affective psychology, few books had been written, no one's career was based on an antithetical theory.

These statements, of course, apply only to physicians and to the then newly existent experimental psychologists. For centuries philosophers had concerned themselves with the psychology of emotions, and the nonexperimental psychologists (who were usually considered philosophers) still did. The Wundtian experimental psychologists had still not perfected techniques to enable them to do such sophisticated behavioral research, though Oswald Külpe's Würzburg school tried. At the turn of the century most of the "new" psychologists were still busy with basic work on the sensorium. After World War I, however, a brilliant group of physiologically trained psycholologists, some of whom had worked with Külpe or his assistants, began to consider some of the matters that underlay psychoanalytic explanations of normal affective states and mechanisms (see Chapter 7).

Every time a physician gave an account in a text, monograph, or review of Freud's theories of the mechanism of hysterical and obsessional neuroses, he had implicitly or explicitly to describe what normally happened to affects. If the physician attacked Freud's discussion of affective mechanisms, he attacked only Freud's explanation of what occurred to the affects in neurosis. Hostile doctors never criticized Freud's

[1] Because explaining natural phenomena with electrical and hydraulic concepts is no longer fashionable, several of Freud's explanatory models have been challenged in recent years.

theory of the course affects took under normal conditions. *This is without exception.* These physicians thus seem to have implicitly recognized Freud's explanation of what was normal or never even realized they were doing so. Kraepelin was the only anti-Freudian psychiatrist before 1908 who explicitly acknowledged the psychoanalytic explanation of the normal affective mechanism. That was because he accepted Freud's conversion theory (see below, p. 129). Kraepelin (1904, p 709) was a most careful and precise thinker, and it did not escape his notice that, logically, in order to accept the explanation of an abnormal mechanism, one first had to accept the normal one.

Those physicians who accepted psychoanalytic theory were, of course, very much aware that they were also accepting explanations of normal as well as of abnormal affective mechanisms. Some, like Bleuler (1906c, p. 21), spelled these out for their readers: "Many individuals . . . react quickly and intensely to emotional impressions, but the affect rapidly passes away. When the storm is over they are the same as before. It is as if they exhausted the affect by their outward reactions, by the hurrahing, weeping, scolding, or striking blows." Jung's work on word associations was a more implicit acknowledgment of Freud's theory of normal behavior (see especially 1905b). And Krehl (1902, p. 737) noted that "the affect that has raged and then ceased leaves behind a calm individual . . ."

Having very early (1893-1895) made clear his theory of how affects were normally discharged, Freud then began to deal with abnormal affective mechanisms. He based his theories of both the mechanism and the psychic etiology of hysteria, obsessional neurosis, and anxiety neurosis on the concept that affect took abnormal paths in each of these three emotional disturbances.

The earliest condition dealt with, of course, was hysteria, and the Breuer-Freud mechanism of that neurosis has already been outlined in Chapter 2. Though the explanation was essentially complete in 1893, the word "conversion" to describe the transformation of an undischarged affect into a physical symptom was not used until 1894. In an article on "The Neuro-

Psychoses of Defense," a hysterical symptom was for the first time described as a "conversion symptom" or "reaction," and the terms are still used in modern psychiatry. To recapitulate: The undischarged affect of a memory manifested itself as a hysterical symptom. In other words, the repressed thought, fantasy, or wish was converted into a somatic channel. A conversion symptom was a symbol of a repressed memory. Thus Freud's explanation of the mechanism of hysteria was a psychical one. (Breuer's theory, which Freud first accepted, was not altogether a psychical one.)[2] In espousing a psychic mechanism, Freud had predecessors. Regardless of the etiology of hysteria, a sizable minority of German physicians refuesed to deny what they saw with their eyes: hysterical phenomena obviously had a connection with the emotions.

The psychic *etiology* of hysteria was another matter. Before 1893, this idea had received little consideration among German physicians. Though Möbius and Strümpell were highly regarded, this aspect of their thinking was neglected. As for psychotherapists like Eschle, although they said that they did not think hysteria was a product of heredity, they offered no alternative explanation. Thus when Freud posited the psychic etiology of hysteria, he was championing a type of causality not taken seriously by the vast majority of German physicians and poorly substantiated by those who did consider it.

Freud soon specified that the etiology of hysteria was psycho*sexual* (1894, 1895a, 1895b). This introduced another difficulty. Not only was Freud offering a theory scientifically unpopular. He was now presenting for scientific confirmation a theory based on human sexuality, a matter most Germans

[2] Breuer believed that the reason a person did not discharge his affect was because he was in a "hypnoid state." Breuer never explained why anyone fell into this state. Therefore, the conclusion could be drawn that susceptibility to hypnoid states was a physiological mechanism, thus explaining hysteria once more in terms of a physical etiology. Charcot had argued that hysteria had organic origins, and that only hysterics could be hypnotized. Bernheim had refuted the latter contention, but his work was largely ignored or scorned in Germany. (See Hellpach, 1906a, p. 94.) Basing one's thinking on the Charcotian model, it could be argued that someone who was in a "hypnoid" state was in a "hypnosislike" state and could, therefore, be suffering from a physical disease.

almost invariably regarded with some combination of embar-
rassment, annoyance, and disgust. We have already witnessed
the reception accorded to Freud's conception of normal
psychosexual development. In this chapter discussion of the
reception of Freud's ideas on the etiology and mechanism of
hysteria will pay attention to his theory of the role played by
sexuality in psychopathological states. Freud postulated that
hysterical sufferers had had certain early childhood ("infantile") sexual experiences or fantasies whose affect had been
strangulated; the memories of these experiences or fantasies
had been cut off from access to consciousness. By 1898 Freud
was using the word "sexual" in an extraordinarily wide sense
(1887-1902, pp. 180, 186, 231-234). Sexual did not mean only
the genital sexuality of adulthood, but all the experiences
which were sensually stimulating to an infant: sucking of milk,
cuddling by the mother or mother surrogate, passing of feces
and bowel training, and various masturbatory movements.

The theory of conversion was Breuer and Freud's
contribution to the mechanism of hysteria, and the hypothesis
of psychic and sexual origins was Freud's contribution to the
etiology of hysteria. The early German medical reaction to
both of these ideas was extensive and sometimes contradictory.
For example, some psychiatrists accepted the conversion
reaction, which implied acceptance of the mechanism of
repression and hence of the existence of an unconscious. But
they stopped short with acknowledgment of conversion, and
denied any psychic etiology of hysteria. This dichotomy of
thought was an established nineteenth-century phenomenon
already seen in the views of Mendel, Fuhrmann, Vogt, and
Ziehen, and supported by Charcot and Janet. Hellpach held
the most unusual position of accepting repression (after
redefining it to meet his beliefs), then denying the unconscious, and reversing again to endorse conversion.

As with the reception of Freud's theory of normal affective
discharge, no one challenged the *mechanism* of conversion in
abnormal subjects. And like the discharge theory, conversion
received little explicit attention. Freud's ideas on the
mechanism of hysteria seemed to elicit little response, and
what response there was was all favorable. This subject, then,

will be discussed after the main body of response, which was to Freud's *etiological* ideas, has been considered. These ideas aroused much comment, and physicians responded in one of three ways: either they accepted both the psychic and sexual etiologies, or they accepted the psychic but denied the sexual etiology, or they were against any psychogenetic explanation. The two extremes will be considered first. Then the views of the large middle group will be presented: those who accepted the psychogenesis of hysteria but not its sexual psychogenesis.

FREUD'S SUPPORTERS

Only physicians who enthusiastically supported psychoanalysis championed the cause of the sexual etiology of hysteria. Bleuler (1906c, pp. 23-24) pointed out that

> the foolish restrictions of our culture often require the suppression of the sexual affect itself. It is no wonder that under these circumstances one meets in women patients at every turn converted, repressed, displaced sexual feelings, those feelings which make up at least one half of our natural existence. I say at least one half, for the analogous instinct, hunger, seems to retreat before the sexual and this is true not in the case of civilized man only.

Jung (1905b) opened an essay on the relationship between psychoanalysis and word-association experiments with a lengthy explanation and endorsement of the Freudian etiology of hysteria. Jung believed most physicians were unable to accept Freud's theories because hysterical symptoms were "nothing other than symbolic images of pathogenic complexes [and] most doctors [did not] think in the symbolic way that Freud [did]."

Here it is relevant to note that a significant percentage of the German psychoanalysts interviewed in connection with this study declared that as adolescents they had planned a literary career. Prominent among this group were Hanna Fenichel, S. H. Foulkes, Henry Lowenfeld, Hilda Maas, and Theodor Reik; Reik actually had a degree in literature and was a professional writer. Then, for a variety of reasons, they all decided to enter scientific fields and were later attracted to psychoanalysis because they saw in it a way to combine their original literary interests with their careers. (Except for Hanna Fenichel, who gave up her work as a chemist to become a psychoanalyst.) These were men and women for whom "symbolism" had always been significant.

But Bleuler and Jung aside, only unknown physicians concurred completely with the hypothesis that hysteria has a sexual etiology. Arthur Muthmann (1907) published a monograph presenting psychoanalytic views, liberally sprinkled with quotations from Freud, Jung, and Franz Riklin (1878-1938), Bleuler's and Jung's co-worker. Muthmann's book was also a historical survey of the attacks on and defenses of Freud's sexual ideas. Wilhelm Stekel (1868-1940), Freud's close associate until 1911, published an article on the causes of nervousness, dealing, of course, with sexual etiology. Stekel was Viennese, but much of his work appeared in German publications, including several popular articles that were published in daily German newspapers. Stekel's (1907a) paper on nervousness was reprinted as a separate pamphlet and was reviewed in German medical journals. It is possible that the medical reception of Stekel's writings was aided by his lively prose style.

Another Viennese, Otto Rank (1886-1939), a lay psychoanalyst close to Freud for many years, expounded the sexual basis for hysteria and other neuroses in the opening sections of *Der Kunstler* (*The Artist*) (1907). This contribution by a then unknown author (lacking even a doctorate) is mentioned because it was immediately reviewed in a prominent German psychiatric journal, the *Zentralblatt für Nervenheilkunde und Psychiatrie*. The review of Rank's work illustrates the passive, sometimes sympathetic, effort of the two German psychiatrists who were editors of the *Zentralblatt* to disseminate psychoanalytic information without formally associating themselves with Freud. The two were Hans Kurella, who coedited the *Grenzfragen des Nerven- und Seelenlebens* with Löwenfeld, and Robert Gaupp (1870-1953), who was Professor of Psychiatry and Neurology at Tübingen. Gaupp especially was interested in psychoanalysis. After 1901, not a year of his *Zentralblatt* went by without either reviews of psychoanalytic works or various other reviews in which psychoanalytic theories were discussed. The reviews, though, were not invariably sympathetic (particularly one by Spielmeyer and two by Isserlin of Munich). Rank's work, however, received favorable notice because Gaupp asked another psychoanalyst, Isidor Sadger, to review it. Gaupp stood up for psychoanalysis when it was attacked at the 1906 Congress of South-West German Psychiatrists by the psychiatric nihilist Hoche (McGuire, 1974, p. 9). Moreoever, Gaupp published Abraham's first three psychoanalytic papers. Finally, Gaupp did not discourage (and perhaps encouraged) the investigation of psychoanalysis in his department at Tübingen: one of his assistants—"an emissary," Jung wrote—came to Burghölzli to study with Jung (McGuire, 1974, p. 164).[3]

To complete the survey of physicians who dealt completely favorably with the sexual theory of the etiology of hysteria, we must mention Fliess (1897) and Gattel (1898), as well as three early protoanalysts who published case studies: W. Warda (1900) of Blankenburg, A. Stegmann (1904) of Dresden, and Otto Juliusburger (1907) of Berlin. The latter two first presented their findings at meetings, Stegmann at the tenth congress of mid-German psychiatrists and neurologists at Halle and Juliusburger before the Berlin Psychiatric Society (see Chapter 5).

ORGANICISTS' DISSENT

At the opposite extreme from those committed to ideas of psychosexual etiology stood those psychiatrists who were wedded to the view that hysteria had an organic etiology. Many of these physicians, therefore, never even bothered to mention Freud; psychic causation of hysteria was a view that was theoretically and practically superfluous and could be safely ignored. But several were quite outspoken. Leo Hirschlaff devoted a few pages to Freud in his textbook on hypnotism and suggestive therapy. The Breuer-Freud theory of the etiology of hysteria "stood in contradiction to experiences . . . with practical hypnosis and suggestion as well as with systematic psychotherapy." But even though there was so much

[3] The *Zentralblatt* does not, however, seem to contain an early article about screen memories by A. Storch cited by Grinstein (1956-1966, Vol. 4, No. 32403).

empirical proof against the theory, Hirschlaff (1905, pp. 190-191) explained, "I consider it my duty to take a position on it since this theory has met with great approval [*grossen Anklang gefunden hat*] especially in the literature on hypnosis." Hirschlaff was a firm believer in the existence of the "hysterical constitution," and scoffed both at the "claims . . . that very frequently a psychic etiology is at the basis of hysterical symptoms" and at the idea that "if the etiology is eliminated, not only the accompanying symptom, but the whole hysterical constitution disappears." Actually, mental disturbance "forms in no way the etiology of the hysterical state but is simply a symptom that exists in connection with other symptoms of hysteria and then disappears simultaneously with these; [mental disturbance] can just as well persist isolated, remain, or disappear without the rest of the symptoms of the hysterical syndrome undergoing a change in other respects."

In the sixth edition of his textbook, Kraepelin (1899, Vol. 2, pp. 511-512) had a section on the nature and causes of hysteria, which concluded with two pages about "psychological theories"; in them he sarcastically denigrated Breuer and Freud's "highly remarkable conceptions." Kraepelin's own conclusion was that "to be short and sweet—hysteria is an inborn abnormal mental condition." But then Kraepelin illogically added that he agreed with Möbius's view that "pathological changes of the body [are] called forth 'as a result of strongly felt ideas.' " Kraepelin's uncharacteristic indecisiveness revealed just how inordinately challenging the question of hysteria was to German physicians and how, in spite of a hardened theoretical position, Kraepelin found it difficult to deny the evidence of his vast clinical experience. His acceptance of the conversion reaction shows that what Möbius and Freud were saying tugged hard at his convictions.

Theodor Ziehen, Professor at Jena, Utrecht, and finally at Berlin, very early paid attention to Freud's views on hysteria because of his own great interest in psychotherapy. Ziehen did much work in child psychiatry and the psychology of learning and edited a journal on educational psychology. When Abraham spoke before the Berlin Psychiatric Society in 1908 and

1909, Ziehen, who chaired the meetings, reacted with hostility and contempt. Yet, as editor of the influential *Monatsschrift für Psychiatrie und Neurologie*, Ziehen published four of Freud's early papers (1898, 1899, 1901b, 1905a) as well as five articles by other psychoanalytic authors (Warda, 1900, 1902, 1907; Juliusburger, 1902; Otto Gross, 1904). The relationship of Ziehen to psychoanalysis is quite complex, and I have tried to elucidate it below (see pp. 160-163). In reporting on the 1893 preliminary communication, Ziehen (1898, p. 683) said that Breuer and Freud were

> right in many cases [in supposing] that physical hysterical symptoms . . . are often to be traced back to a certain single event, a trauma in the widest sense. So, for example, a mother strains with all of her will not to waken her child out of sleep, strains to keep herself quiet; as a result of this resolution, she makes a clicking noise with her tongue which, with frequent repetition, develops into an hysterical tic, which as tongue-clicking accompanies every occasion of agitation for years. [Other] examples [of strangulated affect] would be: a paralyzing fright; a suppression of the sexual drive because of social circumstances, etc.

But the importance Ziehen attached to this explanation of hysteria is seen in the title of the section in which the account appears: "Psychotherapy of Physical Symptoms of *Physical Disease*" (italics mine). Ziehen (1902, pp. 519-520) made his view plain in his textbook in which he wrote that the discussion of the physical symptoms of hysteria belonged in textbooks of neuropathology. Of course, he admitted that "these physical symptoms show a common main characteristic which joins them tightly to psychopathology, namely their changeability as a result of ideas. . . . This doubtless correct fact has often lead to the unprovable and not even probable hypothesis that all physical hysterical symptoms are 'psychogenic.'" A reviewer of Stekel's *Causes of Nervousness* (1907a) puts this opinion in yet another way by questioning Stekel's idea that hysteria was a "real" emotional illness (Rosin, 1907).

PARTIAL ACCEPTANCE: DIFFICULTIES WITH SEXUAL THEORY

Although the organically oriented extremists also often took specific issue with Freud's belief in the sexual roots of hysteri-

THEODOR ZIEHEN

ROBERT GAUPP

cal phenomena, what distinguished them was their dogmatic stand against *any* psychogenic explanation of hysteria. At the turn of the century, the majority of German physicians agreed with them. But those who believed hysteria had an organic basis were not the ones who commented most frequently on Freud's ideas.

By far the largest group to take notice of Freud's views on hysteria (greater even than Freud's enthusiastic supporters) were a number of medical men who had prior interests in the emotional aspects of hysteria, in psychotherapy, or in hypnosis. Uniformly, these men welcomed Freud's psychogenetic explanation of hysteria. What dismayed them was the emphasis Freud placed on the role of sexual factors.

A few physicians dealt with the sexual theory of hysteria by disregarding it completely and simply concentrating on the importance of psychic factors. Most psychoanalysts would say that this minority was even more strongly against the idea of sexual causation than those who spoke out against it. Freud's ideas, the analysts say, touched the majority in some way and aroused their feelings. In expressing their hostility, they were struggling to come to grips with a threatening idea whose validity they partly recognized. But the few who never even mentioned the subject of sexuality were so disturbed by it, and so strongly defended against its intrusion into their thinking, that their opposition to it remained completely repressed. Leopold Löwenfeld was the most prominent of this group. In several books on the treatment of neurasthenia and hysteria, in a textbook on psychotherapy, and in a handbook on hypnotism he wrote exhaustively on the hysterical condition without ever discussing Freud's sexual ideas. He had an interesting mechanism for getting around this problem. Three times Löwenfeld asked Freud to summarize his views for Löwenfeld's readers, and these essays were always presented as separate contributions, two of them being signed by Freud (1901a, 1904, 1906a). Although he was not primarily interested in theory and concentrated on technique, nevertheless, Löwenfeld (1894) was one of the earliest to give information about the new theory of hysteria, and each of his books presented Freud's ideas.

Another who managed to give an account of Freud's theory without mentioning sexuality was Alfred von Schrenck-Notzing (1904, p. 75). And this was a physician whom Bloch called "the founder of modern sexual science." Like Löwenfeld, Schrenk-Notzing (1862-1929) was a hypnotist and was concerned mainly with Freud's method. So too was a Wiesbaden psychiatrist who reviewed another one of the innumerable textbooks (this from Poland) on the treatment of neurasthenia and hysteria. The reviewer spoke of "pyschogenic causes of functional neuroses," warmly praised Freud's methodological contribution, and never mentioned sex (Sunnec, 1902).

However, the majority of physicians who accepted the psychogenetic etiology of hysteria felt compelled to comment on the specific sexual cast Freud had placed on it. This reaction varied from Krehl's (1902) mild skepticism ("I cannot be convinced without further proof . . .") to Aschaffenburg's (1906) violent rebuttal ("It is doubtless false to agree with Freud...").

Ludolf von Krehl (1902, pp. 736-738, 744) thoughtfully pondered the difficulties inherent in accepting the psychogenesis of hysteria: "What stands in the way of our understanding [how] physical events derive from ideas is that the causally effective psychic event is, first of all, hidden from the physician, as well as that the form of the symptom is only with difficutly or not even at all understood from the context of a given feeling or idea." Then he answered his own objections:

> But if we now consider that the effective remainder in relation to the correlates of psychic structure are so frequently—indeed in the majority of cases—removed from consciousness, naturally nothing stands in the way of believing that hysterical phenomena ... are causally produced through feelings and ideas. . . . The form of a hysterical symptom is related much more frequently than one might believe through simple observation to the content of the causally effective psychic experience.

Finally, he proclaimed his agreement with the psychoanalytic explanation of the mechanism of hysterical symptoms.

However, as regards the theory that "harmful ideas . . . with sexual content . . . play the decisive role [in] production of psychogenic physical disturbances" Krehl had reservations. His reserve was not based on the frequent fear that the psychoanalytic view of hysteria would put German psychiatry back 100 years. Krehl was perspicacious enough to realize that "there is an extraordinary difference between the type of [sexual] conception held earlier and [Freud's] current one." What troubled Krehl was that " we are dealing with the statements of excitable, fantasy-ridden people, whose desire to fabricate constitutes a part of their emotional condition. . . . I cannot be convinced without further proof that the statements of patients about such often distant and ticklish matters strictly correspond with reality under all circumstances."

Willy Hellpach, as usual, considered the situation in detail and from more than one point of view. In a monograph on mass hysteria (Hellpach, 1906a, p. 57) he summed up the current furor:

> Sexual perversity, nervousness, hysteria . . . the quarrel rages about them all: whether they are the results of material changes like juvenile idiocy and manic-depressive psychosis, or whether they are produced by psychic experiences. One person will say: hysteria arises as a result of repression of painful erotic experiences! Thus it is purely psychic. His opponent answers: nonsense; such repression is already a symptom, a result of a hysterical character; hysteria is there before its symptoms appear. Who is right?

Neither and both, was Hellpach's conclusions. "Mild" hysteria was psychically caused; "severe" hysteria could be "inborn" and "unavoidable." But several pages later, Hellpach (p. 77) decided that, on the whole, "hysteria is still most comprehensible when one pursues the course of experiences in the fantasylike psychic life. Here everything that unwraps itself in hysteria lies folded up like a bud, and a hundred connections unite the two poles." And for the understanding of hysteria, "Freud's scientific work . . . is the latest of significance . . ." (Hellpach, 1904, p. 39).

But Hellpach (1904, pp. 373-374) returned to his pet theme in his final evaluation:

> I reject limiting to infancy the existence of hysteria-producing repression, for there is no proof of the fact that every hysteria

goes back beyond puberty, and, in any case, [the fact of] traumatic neurosis contradicts such a theory. Rather traumatic neurosis proves that repression can cause an hysterical condition at any time of life, providing the psychic experience in question is strong enough. I also reject the limitation of repression to things sexual — in short, the limitation of the sources of hysteria to repression in general. . . . Instead I require . . . an attempt to ascertain a division of the sources of hysteria according to the [group] membership of the stricken individual, be it in familial or according to social groups.

Evaluating Hellpach's reaction to Freud's thought is not easy. One must second Hellpach's insistence that "repression can cause a hysterical condition at any time of life." Yet it seems that he did not understand Freud's theory that what is repressed in later life is determined by infantile conflicts. Moreover, there are gross contradictions in Hellpach's thought. He accepted in theory the psychic etiology of hysteria but denied in theory the psychic mechanism of its occurrence. In practice, however, he accepted the mechanism of repression because he was in agreement with Freud about the conversion reaction. In Hellpach's thought on hysteria, three elements struggled to form themselves into a synthesis: Wundtian psychology, progressive social concerns (Hellpach eventually ran for political office), and the turn-of-the-century psychiatric dilemma over the problem of organic and psychic etiologies of mental disturbance. From this three-sided struggle Hellpach could emerge with insightful single observations, however dubious might be his over-all constructions.

Moll, the Berlin sexologist, reported in a monograph Breuer and Freud's psychogenetic theory of hysteria. Though Moll (1907, pp. 126, 351-352) dutifully added that Freud believed the etiological psychic event to be a sexual one, he made it clear that Freud's views on sexual etiology were "one-sided." Moll's behavior in subsequent years showed a not uncommon ambivalence about psychoanalysis. In 1908 he wrote a book, *The Sexual Life of the Child*, in which he vehemently denied infantile sexuality. But in June of the same year he asked Freud and Abraham to collaborate in a new journal he was founding. So early in 1909, Freud's paper, "Some General Remarks on Hysterical Attacks," appeared in

Moll's *Zeitschrift für Psychotherapie und medizinische Psychologie*. And three months later Abraham gave a paper on "Infantile Fantasies in the Mental Life of the Adult" before a Psychological Society of which Moll was chairman (H. C. Abraham and Freud, 1965, pp. 41, 51, 57, 58, 67, 73-74, 78, 79; Jones, 1955, pp. 46, 104, 114, 244).

As early as 1894, Oppenheim, the specialist in traumatic neurosis, mentioned in his textbook Breuer and Freud's work on hysteria. Four years later, however, Oppenheim was complaining that in making psychic trauma sexual, Freud had gone "too far." Yet Oppenheim considered Freud's work significant, and in 1905 included Freud's name with those of Charcot, Möbius, Janet, Vogt, Löwenfeld, and Binswanger in a list of important investigators in the field of hysteria (Oppenheim, 1894, p. 676; 1898, pp. 728-729, 769-770; 1902a, pp. 902-903, 951; 1905, pp. 1046-1048). Oppenheim, like Moll, showed great ambivalence. Though he made outraged noises at meetings and in print about Freud's theories, he often sent difficult, unresolved cases to Abraham for treatment (H. C. Abraham and Freud, 1965, pp. 16, 25, 42-43, 55-56, 60, 74, 93).

Eventually, Oppenheim passed over into total opposition. This was probably due to two factors, one personal, one professional. Jones (1955, p. 114) claims Oppenheim suffered from anxiety attacks and his wife was a hysteric. Moreover, Freud was no help to Oppenheim in the latter's work on traumatic neurosis. Freud wrote to Abraham (H. C. Abraham and Freud, 1965, p. 72) in 1909 that he believed traumatic neurosis was hard to tackle and that he had no suggestions about linking it with psychoanalytic theories.

Strümpell (1895, pp. 159-161) welcomed *Studies on Hysteria* as "happy proof of the fact that the psychogenic nature of hysterical phenomena is finding more and more dissemination and recognition among physicians. Both authors, with much skill and psychological acuity, have sought to win a deeper insight into the mental state of hysterics and their work presents much that is interesting and stimulating." Strümpell commented that Breuer and Freud's view of the etiology of hysterical phenomena was a "correct and sharp conception of many cases of severe hysteria." But when Strümpell discussed the cathartic method, he was repelled by its reliance on detailed investigation of the sexual lives and fantasies of patients.

Aschaffenburg was a sophisticated psychiatrist who understood the importance and effects of emotions and feelings. While the early psychoanalysts (including Freud and Abraham) were mired in the conventional belief that masturbation itself caused nervous difficulties, Aschaffenburg recognized that it was rather the ideas attached to masturbation, the dread of discovery, the feeling of shame and of doing something considered morally reprehensible, which made someone "neurasthenic." But Aschaffenburg could not tolerate Freud's sexual views about hysteria. At Baden-Baden, Aschaffenburg (1906, pp. 1793-1798) labeled "untenable" such psychoanalytic views. How did Freud account for all the cases in which a certain anxiety is linked with a fright or something similar, e.g., cases of nervous writer's cramp, paralyses from fright, acute agoraphobia which obviously lacked sexual content? And what about all the cases of traumatic hysteria and a large percentage of the cases of single-symptom hysteria?

Aschaffenburg's argument with regard to the various hysterical symptoms he mentioned was pitifully weak and showed the typical inability of Freud's more vituperative opponents to accept even the possibility that Freud was right. Such opponents were not interested in the intricacies of how psychoanalysis worked; just knowing some of the psychoanalytic conclusions was enough to enrage them. And clearly in Aschaffenburg's case, the conclusions about sexuality were especially provocative. Still, about traumatic neurosis Aschaffenburg posed a legitimate question.

THE CONVERSION REACTION

Because there were striking differences in the way German physicians reacted to Freud's theories of hysteria, these men have been grouped as (1) accepting psychosexual etiology, (2) espousing only organic explanations, or (3)—the majority— affirming psychogenicity but denying psychosexual genesis.

The variations among these physicians can be explained by their prior interests and theoretical commitments, cultural pressures, and personal problems. This many-sided reception stands in sharp contrast to the ubiquitous acceptance of Freud's explanation of the mechanism of hysterical symptom formation, the conversion reaction. Here, all who took note of Freud joined hands in agreement, some perhaps unwittingly. For even Hirschlaff and Kraepelin, who did not believe that disease could have a psychic etiology, accepted the idea that a "long forgotten" (Kraepelin's phrase) thought or feeling could be converted into a physical symptom. These men never noticed that they were thereby conceding the existence of a "place" where feelings not being felt and thoughts not being thought about existed, what Hirschlaff (1905, p. 191) derided as the "mythical subconscious."

Fliess (1897, pp. 12, 110, 199) early informed his readers of the specific details they would find in Freud's "pioneering works" about the "conversion" of psychic disturbance into hysterical pains and "the explanation of hysterical dysmenorrhea by the transformation of a repressed idea into a physical symptom." Gattel, Muthmann, Warda, Juliusburger, and Stegmann published case histories of their observations of this reaction. The Austrians, Stekel and Rank, did also, of course.

Bleuler, Jung, and their co-workers mentioned the mechanism more generally, but quite frequently in their many articles and monographs from 1904 onward. Sentences like this of Bleuler's (1906c, pp. 21-22) were common: "If suppression of the affect is wholly successful, so that it exists no longer for consciousness, it is often 'converted'; instead of the affect, some physical symptom appears, a pain, an hallucination."

Krehl (1902, p. 737) told his audience that Breuer and Freud "place very great value on the fact that they are primarily dealing with emotional events which were suppressed [and] that emotion which is held in seeks its outlet in other directions and as a result of inward "conversion" inclines toward the production of psychogenic physical disturbances."

Hellpach (1904, pp. 36-38, 373) discussed the conversion theory at great length, carefully distinguishing between what were Breuer's and Freud's separate contributions to it. He called particular attention to the fact that Breuer had believed that conversion took place only during the "hypnoid" state, but that Freud had shown that such a state was not necessary. Hellpach proclaimed: "I accept repression as a condition from which hysteria can stem and believe that conversion, change in affect, and condensation are concepts that at the very least possess a strong suggestive and stimulating power for gaining further insights into the way manifest hysteria comes from repression."

Though Oppenheim had not mentioned the conversion reaction in early editions of his text, by the fourth edition (1905) he was convinced: "Psychic traumas which do not produce a psychic outburst exert to a certain extent a latent effect, influence the disposition, and cause a *conversion of the excitation of affect into physical phenomena* so that these become independent of the originally experienced feeling" (Oppenheim's italics). This was an "ingenious theory established by the investigators with great exactness" Oppenheim (1905, pp. 1047-1048) pointed out that he and Krehl were in agreement on the conversion reaction.

Kraepelin also valued Krehl's judgment in the matter. In the seventh edition of Kraepelin's *Psychiatrie*, it is hard to tell who has convinced him of the conversion mechanism, Krehl or Freud. First Kraepelin (1904, p. 709) admitted that he had given little thought to explaining the phenomena of hysteria. But, if he had to conclude something, it was

> that *increased abundance of emotional stimulations and a pathological spread of their involuntary accompanying symptoms* probably play an essential role in the occurrence of hysteria. . . . Among hysterics the continuing unconscious action of affects can win a certain independence and, uninfluenced by will or further experiences, can continue to rule particular bodily occurrences. Such "lasting forms" (as Krehl calls them) of unconscious actions are about the same thing, as far as I can see, as the useful core of the experiences reported by Breuer and Freud [Kraepelin's italics].

Some authors had a fuzzy idea of the conversion reaction. Some tried to give it a more exact physiological explanation.

For Schrenck-Notzing (1904, p. 75) it resulted from "continuously harmful excitations of the nervous system." Others took no interest in it at all. Some, like Strümpell, objected to the *word* Freud used to describe the phenomena (see Chapter 6). But no physician ever disputed its existence.

RESPONSE TO THEORIES OF OBSESSIONS AND COMPULSIONS

Very quickly after Freud came to the conclusion that a hysterical symptom was the result of an abnormal attachment of affect to a bodily part, he hypothesized that an obsession or a compulsion was the result of an abnormal attachment of affect to unrelated thoughts and objects (1894, 1895a). A psychosexual etiology was involved, but for a variety of reasons, depending on the individual case, the neurotic "defense" was not the same. Instead of having physical symptoms, like the hysteric, the obsessional patient ruminated on a certain subject (or subjects); the compulsive person performed the same act (or acts) again and again. Freud's remarks on this subject excited nowhere near the number of comments his theories on hysteria aroused. One reason was that the psychoanalytic explanation of obsessions and compulsions was a variation of the earlier explanation of hysteria. Many of the same factors were involved in the mechanism and etiology of both conditions. A second (and weightier) reason was that the subject of hysteria was itself more interesting to German physicians; hysterics posed a more pressing medical problem than did maladapted obsessive and compulsive people. At any rate, until after World War I, Freud's name was more strongly linked with hysteria than with any other mental disturbance.

But those who followed the early Freudian literature were aware that Freud had expanded his theories to cover the field of obsessional neurosis. Several physicians who later became members of psychoanalytic societies quickly attempted to duplicate the experiences Freud reported. Besides Juliusburger (1902), Stegmann (1904), and Warda (1902, 1903, 1907) there was Wilhelm Strohmayer (1874-1936) who, while a lecturer (*Privatdozent*) at Jena, did psychoanalyses at Binswanger's private clinic; later he was a neurologist at Kraepelin's Munich clinic (see Strohmayer, 1903). An article by the Viennese Alfred Adler (1905b) also appeared in a German journal. Bleuler spoke of the Freudian mechanism of obsession as if it were a well-established fact: "It is shown most clearly in pathological cases that affectivity . . . has a certain independence, that affects may separate themselves from some intellectual processes and connect themselves with others. It is well known that they may spread, and that they may invade, as far as time and content are concerned, other mental experiences associated with a decided feeling-tone" (1906c, p. 18). He also explained the difference between hysterics and obsessives with an example:

> Another group of individuals . . . do not take a strong, disagreeable affect into their whole personality. They dissociate the affect together with a large complex from their personality. They are entirely normal when they think of things having nothing to do with the affect and its associated intellectual process. . . . The affect is revealed chiefly in unconscious acts which betray a connection with the experiences [which have gone badly]. A patient whose lover had shot himself forgot the occurrence, but in a casual conversation pressed rose leaves to her temple with a little snap, quite unconsciously. This could be demonstrated to be what Freud calls a symptomatic act [*Symptom-handlung*] [p. 21].

But as happened with the theory of hysteria, much of the reaction was not sympathetic. Quite early, Löwenfeld (1897a, p. 167) questioned the usefulness of the theory of obsessions: "I cannot indulge in any great hopes as regards the results of the treatment for obsessions, and, to be sure, not simply because of my failures up to now but also on the ground that, according to my research, in a great number of cases obsessions can be traced back to completely different circumstances than those Freud hypothesizes." Yet, as was his continual practice, Löwenfeld was reluctant to write off Freud completely. Thus when Löwenfeld (1904b) published a monograph on obsessive phenomena he included in it a specially written chapter by Freud (1904) on the psychoanalytic method. Moll (1907, pp. 267, 351-352) was also aware of

Freud's contributions to the psychic etiology of obsessions and of his claim to be able to treat obsessions. Moll accepted Freud's claim that a frightening experience could give rise to an obsession, but rejected "the view that originally a sexual event effected the psychic trauma and has thus become the origin of the appearance of the . . . obsession."

Oppenheim was a conscientious opponent who kept up with the Freudian literature and did his best for many years to present it objectively. The 1905 edition of his text included a greatly revised and expanded section on obsessions. In it Oppenheim (1905, pp. 1152-1158, 1161) listed the people who were "significant" for their work on obsessions, among them Freud. Oppenheim's account of Freud's "ingenious analysis" of obsessions was the fullest to be found anywhere outside of the writings of the Freudians themselves. Oppenheim also reported on the use of the psychoanalytic method for the cure of obsessions. It is important to note that though, in general, Oppenheim felt that Freud's sexual explanations of hysteria and obsessions went "too far," in the case of many phobias he was willing to accept the Freudian hypothesis. And for an "enemy" who never practiced psychoanalysis, he understood Freud's theory excellently.

Kraepelin (1899, Vol. 2, p. 511) also knew that Freud had extended his theory of hysteria to encompass obsessions and so informed his readers. If, as opposed to the "passive sexual experience [that] lead to a hysterical defense neurosis, [the] sexual experience is not the mere enduring but the actual desire for a sexual act, obsessions arise, according to the same mechanism." Naturally, Kraepelin did not view Freud's psychic explanation of obsessions any more favorably than he had regarded his explanation of hysteria.

NEURASTHENIA AND ANXIETY NEUROSIS

A year after he first dealt with obsessions, Freud turned his attention to that vaguely defined condition, neurasthenia, and specifically, to a syndrome of it which he called "anxiety neurosis" (1895b). Neurasthenia, literally "nerve weakness," is a term coined in 1869 by the American neurologist George M. Beard, who described a syndrome consisting of headaches, neuralgias, hypersensitivities (to certain weather, noise, light, human company, and other diverse stimuli), insomnia, loss of appetite, difficulty in swallowing, and tremors. These symptoms lead to a condition of exhaustion in which the patient is incapable of sustained activity although he suffers from no definite disease (Ellenberger, 1970, pp. 242-245). The term has lingered on among those psychiatrists, especially in Europe, who believe in the organic etiology of emotional disorders and consider that there is a distinct, physically caused illness of nerve weakness. Dynamically oriented psychiatrists have replaced the diagnosis of neurasthenia with that of a particular neurosis, character disorder, or, occasionally, psychosis.

In a quite simple way, Freud postulated that "dammed-up libido" — sexual frustration as a result of sexual abstinence or coitus interruptus — produced the "anxiety neurosis": a condition of chronic diffuse anxiety combined with acute attacks of anxiety. It was a rather naïve mechanical theory, eventually abandoned by most psychoanalysts, that sexual "energy" had to go somewhere. If it was not normally "discharged," it found an outlet as anxiety; anxiety was simply transformed libido. Freud himself eventually gave up the theory in a practical way, reporting to Ernest Jones that he just never saw such cases of "pure" anxiety any more (Jones, 1953, p. 260).[4] In addition to his specific explanation of anxiety neurosis, Freud in general stressed that sexual problems — often "excessive" masturbation — were etiological agents of neurasthenia.

Both of Freud's formulations were enthusiastically taken up only by the dedicated few who before 1908 could be called his followers. Wilhelm Fliess, at that time engaged in an active correspondence with Freud (1887-1902), studded his book with references to these hypotheses (Fliess, 1897, pp. 98-99, 142, 144, 192, 197-199). He told his readers that for enlighten-

---

[4] But theoretically Freud never completely disavowed this idea, though he did evolve a much more sophisticated hypothesis to explain the appearance of anxiety, the theory of anxiety as a "signal" that warned a person of impending internal (psychic) or external danger.

ment on the connection between anxiety and sexual occurrences, he "cannot refer strongly enough to Freud's fundamental [1895b] communication." Freud "had shown new and
completely unsuspected elucidations of sexual conditions and
their effects on the nervous system." He had also demonstrated
that the frequent frustration of sexual excitement during the
engagement period and marital frigidity both resulted in an
"accumulation of anxiety." Anxiety was the inevitable outcome if sexual needs were not satisfied. Even after Fliess and
Freud had broken relations in 1902, Fliess (1906, p. 509) gave
an account of how anxiety arose as a result of repression of
sexual feeling, as in coitus reservatus and interruptus, according to "Freud's investigations."

In 1898 Gattel addressed himself to the questions of anxiety
neurosis and neurasthenia. Gattel had spent six months at the
outpatient psychiatric clinic of the famous Krafft-Ebing and
studied 100 cases to see if Freud was right, i.e., "that anxiety
neurosis has a specific sexual cause." Gattel found that in
every case there was a history of sexual aberrations or
problems. In the course of several analyses he had carried out,
he had come to agree with Freud on the importance of
"looking back into childhood in order to discover the perni-
cious, slumbering germ." Gattel's (1898, pp. 2-5, 9-11, 42-52,
63) conclusions were a caricature of Freud's: ". . . anxiety
neurosis can always be found where a retention of libido
occurs, while pure neurasthenia can only result from masturbation." A few years later, Muthmann (1907, pp. 62, 113)
pointed out that anxiety neurosis was distinctly different
from hysteria. "Freud has designated anxiety neurosis as the
somatic counterpart of hysteria." In the same year, the Viennese Stekel (1907b) published an article on anxiety states in a
German journal.

Bleuler and especially Jung never evinced much interest in
this aspect of psychoanalysis. They were more concerned to see
how Freud's theories could be applied to areas in which they
had prior interests, such as dementia praecox (schizophrenia),
paranoia, hallucinations, dreams, and word associations.
Moreover, from the very start Jung sought to play down the
sexual emphasis of psychoanalysis.

Most physicians were skeptical about Freud's theories on anxiety neurosis and neurasthenia, and expressed various kinds of reservations. In Löwenfeld's own case he also demonstrated open-mindedness and flexibility, while giving considerable publicity to Freud's views among German physicians.

Löwenfeld's response to Freud's (1895b) paper was that Freud had misinterpreted the clinical evidence on the basis of which he had argued for the separate category of "anxiety neurosis." Löwenfeld (1895) challenged the accuracy of Freud's observations two months later in an article in Munich's leading medical weekly. In contradistinction to Freud's interpretation, Löwenfeld held to the conventional view that Beard's conception of neurasthenia was accurate, that there was no basic etiological distinction to be made between hysteria and neurasthenia, and that "hereditary taint" was the major factor in the two disorders.[5]

But two years later, Löwenfeld (1897b) admitted in a long lead article in the Munich weekly that "my personal experiences recently have necessitated a change in my earlier views in several respects. . . . Beard's conception of phobias as symptoms of neurasthenia can no longer be maintained for all cases." Löwenfeld presented the history of the dispute between him and Freud and said that since 1895 he had begun to examine more closely the sexual life of new patients as well as to look back on the sexual histories of earlier ones. As a result, Löwenfeld had altered his views, and was now publishing a new scheme of the etiology of neurotic anxiety states. Now he believed that, in the majority of cases, heredity was "only very rarely" the exclusive cause of anxiety states. In general the role of constitution was limited to the fact that "it increased the pathological effect of other etiological events, the essential causes." With this view, Löwenfeld had moved much closer to Freud's. The "essential causes" were etiological factors which are "usually necessary to the production of anxiety states and according to the corresponding intensity are sufficient to cause such states. . . . On the other hand [as opposed to Freud]

[5] On one of the rare occasions he ever publicly did so, Freud defended his method as scientifically sound (1895c).

we are not in the position to ascertain a specific cause, i.e., a constantly recurring, ubiquitous homogeneous etiological event." Eight years later, Löwenfeld (1905, p. 46) still maintained this opinion but unpolemically presented his readers with a choice of his or of Freud's view that "anxiety has a sexual mechanism."

Similarly, Bloch (1907b, pp. 702-703) fought Freud's all-embracing statement on anxiety neurosis, though he accepted it in certain circumstances:

> It cannot be denied — and has, in fact, been maintained by other physicians such as [here Bloch gives thirteen names, including Freud's] — that ... *coitus interruptus* ... may have a transient harmful influence upon the nervous system; but according to recent researches, it is only in those who are *already* neuropathic that permanent troubles result in the form of "anxiety neurosis" (which, as Freud has proved, is actually dependent upon *coitus interruptus*), or in the form of other neurasthenic and hysterical troubles ... but it has not been proved that in healthy individuals *coitus interruptus* ... gives rise to serious and permanent injuries to health.

Otto Binswanger (1896) in his textbook on neurasthenia also stressed that one must have a "neuropathic predisposition" for the development of neurasthenia; he did not mention Freud's opinion at all.

Oppenheim (1898, p. 794) was straightforward in his disagreement with Freud. "Some authors (Hecker, Freud) wish to regard 'anxiety neurosis' as an independent form of disease," he wrote. But "only in rare cases does anxiety constitute the only symptom of disease . . . as a rule it is accompanied by neurasthenia or hysterical phenomena. . . . The view of Freud, that these phenomena are always due to abnormalities of the sex life, does not agree with my observations." In later years Oppenheim was proved right in his contention that there were no pure anxiety neuroses, unaccompanied by other symptoms.

Aschaffenburg (1906, pp. 1793-1795), more sophisticated than his contemporaries, took exception to the belief of Freud and others that masturbation caused neurasthenia. In its physical effects, masturbation was no different from normal coitus. Rather it was the masturbator's feelings about his masturbation that evoked nervous difficulties. Aschaffenburg was also against Freud's libido theory of anxiety. Sexual abstinence in itself was not harmful. What was harmful was the idea that it was sinful to give up abstinence, or the doubt one had in one's determination to abstain.

Aschaffenburg was obviously more than just the obnoxious screamer of expletives, which is the standard portrayal of him as an enemy of psychoanalysis. He was perceptive, and his intuitive judgment on the causes of neurasthenia and anxiety was sound. But he was severely limited as Freud's critic. First, he did not possess the psychological knowledge (which no one, including Freud, had at the time) to counter Freud on psychological grounds, which, nevertheless, he tried to do. Second, he was, even more than most men, a victim of the cultural pressures of his society. His fear of hypnosis and his sexual prejudices destroyed his good judgment. Freud was immediately aware of the impossible situation Aschaffenburg found himself in, when he wrote to Jung after Aschaffenburg's attack: "What moves him is his tendency to repress everything sexual, that unwelcome factor so unpopular in good society. Two worlds fight with each other there . . ." (Jones, 1955, p. 399). Aschaffenburg was one of a group of opponents of psychoanalysis who fought it so hard precisely because its truths touched sensitive areas of their unconscious. It is likely that Aschaffenburg unconsciously realized the validity of Freud's sexual theories, but they were untenable to his ego. At an international congress on psychiatry and neurology, held in Amsterdam in 1907, Aschaffenburg made a revealing slip: "As is well known, Breuer and I [instead of Breuer and Freud] published a book some years ago" (Jones, 1955, p. 112).

Ziehen (1902, pp. 488-489) recognized Freud's nosological creation of "anxiety neurosis." But in his text he did not mention that Freud believed anxiety and neurasthenia had sexual causes, although he discussed vividly the sexual symptoms and preoccupations of "neurasthenics" (p. 499).

Ziehen was an excellent phenomenologist. His text was comprehensive, well organized, and well written. Ziehen was also a dedicated psychotherapist. He clearly had no qualms about discussing sex with his patients; he was not another Aschaffenburg. Moreover, he published early psychoanalytic papers in his journal. What is relevant about his reaction to Freud's theories on anxiety neurosis is that: (1) he was a staunch believer in the organic etiology of mental diseases; (2) he objected to Freud's universal application of his sexual discoveries; (3) he had a philosophical commitment to the importance of the conscious.

Ziehen's (1902, pp. 505-507) list of the causes of neurasthenia are an instructive illustration of the confused state of psychiatric understanding of mental illness at the turn of the century:

1. Heredity is not as important as in most other "psychoses."

2. An unfavorable nutritive condition often provides the predisposition for neurasthenia. In addition, anemia, obesity, gout, and diabetes play an etiological role. Dieting can bring on depression.

3. Excessive smoking and drinking cause neurasthenia.

4. Sexual excesses do not play an important role. Impotence and coitus interruptus are not without influence.

5. Intellectual overexertion is very often an essential etiological event.

6. Chronic stomach and intestinal catarrh play an essential role.

7. "Of greatest significance are *accidents*."

The internal contradictions in Ziehen's thought and the desperation of his contemporaries for an explanation of neurasthenia are obvious.

Nature versus Nurture

In his writings on hysteria, obsessions, and anxiety, Freud plunged unhesitatingly into one of the most heated medical controversies of his day: Did mental disturbance occur as the result of a tendency toward "degeneracy," biologically passed on from parent to child? Was a person doomed by "hereditary taint," as some of the most famous psychiatrists of the day insisted? Both by implication and by overt statement, Freud strenuously fought the popular notion that hereditary predisposition was one of the main (if not the only) causes of affective disorders. What Freud did was to give a new meaning to the word "predisposition." He did not rule out the influence of what he called "heredity and constitution." In particular, since syphilis was so rife, Freud was greatly inclined to take this disease into account when discussing the emotional afflictions of his patients. Inborn factors played an important part in every person's development. But they were overshadowed by "the accidential influences brought to bear upon sexuality in the course of the subject's life" (Freud, 1906a). Thus "predisposition" to mental illness meant to Freud a person's innate sexual constitution combined with very early sexual experiences — not at all the same as the "hereditary neuropathic predisposition" favored as an etiological explanation by Janet, Otto Binswanger, Möbius, Moll, Kraepelin, Schrenck-Notzing, and others. According to psychoanalytic theory, hysteria, obsessional neurosis, and anxiety neurosis could all be acquired without hereditary predisposition. Early experiences, with or without heredity combined, constituted the predisposition. The predisposition became operative if a person reacted to a later event according to early associations evoked by the event. This was "regression." Although Freud always insisted on the importance of hereditary and constitutional factors, the practical result of his theories was to emphasize an almost completely psychological explanation of emotional pathology.

But the belief of Freud's contemporaries in the organic etiology of all human malfunctioning was very strong. Even those psychiatrists who professed basic agreement with Freud on the issue of degeneracy usually lapsed into talk of "inborn" hysteria or "neuropathic" individuals a few pages later. The only psychiatrist who showed a complete understanding of Freud's meaning was Bleuler. After refuting the physiological explanations of paranoid delusions that had been proposed by the famous neurologist Wernicke, Bleuler emphasized that

> *we are, on the contrary, convinced that in the majority of cases*
> *further investigations will show a constitutional predisposition*

and a chain of Freud's predisposing occurrences. The constitutional predisposition will explain why these people and not others suffer from paranoia, and Freud's complexes will tell us why the critical events have brought out the paranoia, and eventually, why the developed paranoia immediately connects itself with these events [1906c, pp. 102-103; Bleuler's italics].

He was aware that he was battling popular medical opinion.

For the majority of psychiatrists the question of disposition in paranoia is already settled. For them it is a matter of an innate, generally a family disposition. At present, however, neither the personal nor the family disposition is proven. . . . Many speak of "degeneracy," yet this again is not definite. . . . Among the paranoics which I have seen there are very few who could be called bodily or mentally degenerate [p. 106].

All other psychiatrists whose experiences or theoretical reasoning led them to refute prevalent ideas about degeneracy found themselves in a serious bind. Their education and the consensus of the majority weighed heavily on them, making it difficult for their opinions to be as unequivocal as Bleuler's. Löwenfeld succumbed most easily to the pull of preconceptions. His conclusion about the etiology of hysteria was that "purely somatic noxious factors are incomparably rarer than occasional [i.e., environmental] causes . . . in the sense of the theories advocated by Freud" (1904, pp. 13-14). But he prefaced this judgment with a strong statement that "for the development of hysteria a certain disposition — the so-called hysterical constitution — is demanded." A vital part of the predisposition was "the irritable weakness of the nervous system" (p. 7). Moreover, mental overexertion produced anxiety in those patients with "hereditary neuropathic dispositions" (1905, p. 46). In spite of these views, Hirschlaff (1905, p. 190) listed Löwenfeld as among those who believed "that hysterical and mental character changes are not inborn abnormalities."

Hellpach (1904, p. 373) was somewhat clearer in his concordance with Freud on this issue. He astutely rejected Breuer's "hypnoid state" as a necessary condition for the appearance of hysteria, "for there is no causal relationship. If a hypnoid state can produce hysteria, that means we must accept the existence of a primary hereditary predisposition toward dissociation, and with such acceptance we are thrown back on just that hypothesis which we would like to do away with, because it is only a very deficient name for superficially observed phenomena." Yet in distinguishing between mild and severe cases of hysteria, Hellpach (1906a, p. 58) decided that only the former were a result of "life's experiences — of the environment. . . . Severe hysteria may be inborn, it may be unavoidable. . . . And so it is with the majority of psychopathies and neuroses."

Bloch (1907b, pp. 463, 465) came closest to siding wholeheartedly with Freud:

> Degeneration or diseases play only a subordinate part [in the cause of all sexual perversions] and can be invoked for the explanation of only a small number of sexual aberrations. . . . Freud draws attention to the psychological fact that impressions of childhood, which apparently have been forgotten, may, not withstanding, have left the most profound marks upon our psychical life, and may have determined our entire subsequent development. The impressions of childhood are often incorporated fate. For this reason, for example, the children of criminals become criminals themselves, not because they are "born" criminals, but because, as *children*, they grow up in the atmosphere of crime, and the impressions they have received become firmly and deeply rooted in their natures.

But in spite of Bloch's commitment to the Freudian predisposition, when he had to explain how coitus interruptus caused anxiety neurosis, neurasthenia, and hysteria, he decided that these troubles would arise "only in those who are *already* neuropathic" (p. 702).

Clearly, notions of degeneracy were firmly fixed in the minds of most German physicians, and they reacted with either skepticism or disbelief to attempts, like Freud's, to prove otherwise. Even most psychiatrists who professed agreement with Freud succumbed to the easy explanation of "hereditary taint" when they felt it vital to shore up an opinion.

PSYCHOPATHOLOGY EXTENDED

Toward the end of the "prepsychoanalytic" period in German medicine, attempts to apply analysis to psychopathological conditions other than hysteria, obsessional neurosis, anxiety neurosis, and paranoia began to be made. Freud himself made the first contribution with his *Psychopathology of Everyday Life* (1901). The book did not completely convince its medical reviewers that psychoanalytic principles could be used to understand everyday "mistakes"; but the reviewers did acknowledge to a lesser or greater extent the analogies Freud had made between common experiences and dreams and certain neurotic behavior. Ziehen's (1904) judgment was typical: The work "deserved many, but critical, readers."

In 1905 and 1906 Jung began to link inextricably his word-association studies with psychoanalysis. On the one hand, Jung (1905b, p. 281) believed his association tests were a worthwhile aid to the discovery of pathogenic complexes and therefore "illuminated and shortened" psychoanalysis. On the other hand, he stressed that one could not use the word-association technique unless one were completely at home with psychoanalysis (Jung, 1906c, p. 18).

Since Burghölzli was a hospital where the staff usually saw more severely ill patients than those seen by Freud in his private practice, Bleuler, Jung, and Abraham (who worked in Zurich from 1904 to 1907) sought to apply Freud's ideas to more grossly psychotic persons. Bleuler (1906c, pp. 17, 83) unequivocally reported that in dementia praecox "the demonstration of Freud's mechanism is very easy." Jung (1907b) published a ground-breaking monograph which explained in psychoanalytic terms why dementia praecox rather than hysteria occurs in certain people. This book was widely and generally favorably reviewed. Wilhelm Seiffer (1907), a Berlin psychiatrist who wrote frequently on various psychiatric subjects, described Jung as someone who "has made himself very well known" among his professional colleagues. Jung's treatise was an "ingenious [*geistreich*] attempt . . . which favors the Freudian hypothesis of repression. . . . The defense of Freudian theory is a prominent side of Jung's work; another is the acuteness and consistency with which the work is communicated." Workers in the field "will have to come to terms with his conclusions." Isserlin's (1907) and Weygandt's (1907) attacks were in the minority.

In the same year, Abraham (1907) also applied Freud's work to the etiology of dementia praecox. In a talk delivered in Frankfurt before the German Psychiatric Association, he explained the significance of sexual trauma in childhood for the later symptoms of dementia praecox. Two Austrian applications of psychoanalytic theory that were reviewed in Germany also appeared. One was a book by Gross (1907) which stemmed from his experiences as an assistant at Kraepelin's clinic and was an attempt at a synthesis of Freud's and Wernicke's thought. "What interests me most about Gross' book," Freud wrote, "is that it comes from the clinic of the Super-Pope, or at least was published with his permission" (McGuire, 1974, p. 69). The second was Rank's (1907) *Der Künstler*.

In applying psychoanalytic theories of neurosis to schizophrenia, Jung and Abraham drew psychoanalysis deeply into one of the most modern aspects of the heredity versus environment controversy. In this century a staggering amount of research has been devoted to studying the genesis of schizophrenia, and it has not yet been explained to everyone's satisfaction. Biochemical and hereditary theories vie with psychological ones. Psychiatrists are still disputing the extent to which the etiology of schizophrenia can be explained in Freudian terms.

5

TECHNIQUES, TREATMENT, AND THE FREUDIAN RESPONSE

PSYCHOANALYTIC TECHNIQUES AND TREATMENT

Thus far we have studied the reception of Freud's ideas on psychology and psychopathology, i.e., how the mind operates, how personality develops, and how morbid psychic states are formed. These theories were the strongest and most easily defensible parts of Freud's work, and there was a wide range of responses to them. The weakest area of Freud's work, and the one hardest to defend, was that of treatment, and this was the contribution which critics most often attacked. But here, too, reception was never one-sided.

It will be noticed that most physicians before 1908 almost consistently lumped together the cathartic method and psychoanalysis. The two could be distinguished mainly by the reliance of the cathartic method on hypnosis, both to discover the cause of the symptom and to effect a cure. Psychoanalysis dispensed with hypnosis; therapy was conducted with the patient in a normal state of consciousness. Freud no longer pressed the patient's forehead or instructed him to close his eyes. But even Freud, as late as 1905, did not make a careful distinction between the two, implying a certain interchangeability: ". . . psycho-analytic investigation . . . is employed in the therapeutic procedure introduced by Josef Breuer and myself in 1893 and known at that time as 'catharsis' " (1905d, p. 163). The continued association of the cathartic method with psychoanalysis was a natural outgrowth of the piecemeal way Freud published his findings and of the changes he made in theory and technique as he went along. Thus a commentator's reference to the cathartic method does not at all invalidate his remarks.

The responses to the cathartic method and psychoanalysis, and to the specific techniques of abreaction, free association, and dream interpretation, were of three types. The most representative reaction was an objective (or, rarely, pseudo-objective) presentation of Freud's new treatment and then an evaluation of it. The other two types of responses were either angry or sarcastic outbursts, on the one hand, or replies to the most vicious or repetitious attacks, on the other.

ABREACTION

On the whole, the newly coined *word* "abreaction," to define the specific type of discharge demanded by both the cathartic method and psychoanalysis, was readily adopted. The *concept* of abreaction also received widespread acceptance. That was to be expected, since most physicians had not argued against the occurrence of the equivalent of abreaction: conversion. (Though there was protest against the use of the "foreign" *word* "conversion.") Conversion and abreaction were two sides of the same coin: in both cases, affect was discharged. In abreaction it occurred nonpathologically; in conversion, pathologically and indirectly, through symptom formation. Only infrequently was the operation of abreaction minimized. Kraepelin (1899, Vol. 2, p. 511), who was not in favor of hypnotism or psychotherapy, made light of abreaction: "I admit, of course, that all those [sexual] memories are supposed to be rendered innocuous when the skillful physician succeeds in bringing them to light and making them conscious." Löwenfeld (1901, p.358) quoted Krafft-Ebing wondering whether abreaction could be achieved if the physician were unable to put the patient into a state of deep hypnosis. Moll (1907, p. 352) believed that "Freud unintentionally suggested some of the alleged pathogenic experiences to his patients," and that was how they found out about their repressions, not through abreaction alone, as Freud claimed. Hirschlaff (1905, p. 192) maintained that although abreaction usually did eliminate the strangulated affect and the conversion symptom, occasionally it did not. That was also Schrenck-Notzing's (1904, p. 75) conclusion. But these objections to abreaction were sporadic, and the concept and its importance received general acknowledgment.

FREE ASSOCIATION AND DREAM INTERPRETATION

On the other hand, the techniques of free association and dream interpretation — Freud called dreams "the royal road to the unconscious" — tended to be ignored by most commentators. Only the relatively few who had successfully carried out psychoanalyses were impressed by the value of these techniques in uncovering unconscious thoughts and their overwhelming significance for successful therapy. Bleuler (1906c, p. 25), rather than giving the details of a case, which was the common way for partisans to demonstrate how psychoanalysis worked, illustrated free association by allowing his readers to watch undirected thinking at work in his own mind.

When, Bleuler said, he stopped the purposeful directing of his thoughts at this point in his book, i.e., where he is writing about associations, this is what happened: he thought of the work of Jung and Riklin on associations, and then of the work of Aschaffenburg (who also studied associations), and then of the cathedral at Cologne. (Aschaffenburg lived in Cologne.) Such normal "free association," Bleuler pointed out, was intimately related to the abnormal "flight of ideas" (which is often so difficult to follow in a psychotic patient).

JUDGMENTS

Numerous case histories of patients treated with the psychoanalytic or cathartic method (or some combination of the two) were published in Germany by early followers of Freud, starting in 1898 with Gattel's reports. And beginning with 1902, not a year went by without the publication of favorable results with Freud's method, either by a German physician or by Bleuler or Jung. These laudatory descriptions of psychoanalytic treatment techniques have already been cited in other contexts. Muthmann's book was the last of these favorable pieces to appear in the "prepsychoanalytic" years, that is, the years before Abraham established a practice in Berlin in December, 1907. Freud characterized Muthmann's work as "good, fine case histories, excellent cures, dignified and modest; I have hopes," Freud added, in an optimism rarely directed toward unknown self-proclaimed disciples, that "the man will become a staunch collaborator" (McGuire, 1974, p. 64). Muthmann (1907, pp. iii, 5-56) had written that although there existed a substantial psychoanalytic literature, there was still a *raison d'être* for his work because "the question of the worth of the method occupies the foreground of discussion." Muthmann's aim was to show that the method has "priceless worth in the treatment of nervous patients, regardless how one may judge it theoretically." He was making public the details of the analyses he had done so that novices might learn from them.

At the very end (December 14) of this early period, the Berlin Psychiatric Society was treated to its first psychoanalytic paper by Otto Juliusburger (1867-1952), characterized by Jung as "well-known," and as "one of those people who do not hide their light under a bushel" (McGuire, 1974, p. 93). Juliusburger had become acquainted with psychoanalysis through a Hungarian psychiatrist who had spent a year at Burghölzli, and in 1908 became one of the founding members of the Berlin Psychoanalytic Society.

Juliusburger reported on two cases he had treated with the psychoanalytic method. Because it was presented at a meeting of the Berlin Psychiatric Society, Juliusburger's (1907) paper and the discussion of it were immediately published in two psychiatric journals. Gaupp also published the paper in his *Zentralblatt* in 1908. One case was that of a twenty-two-year-old girl who was a compulsive jewelry thief. Juliusburger traced the etiology of her kleptomania to a seduction at five years of age and to a sensual arousal at six years connected with gold and precious jewels. Juliusburger pointed out that through the use of psychoanalysis one could see that the girl was reliving her past by her stealing.

In the discussion immediately following, Ziehen and Liepmann were unimpressed and mildly critical. They both regarded the case as an example of fetishism, "interesting, but not so rare," as Ziehen said. Ziehen acknowledged that in such cases, both conscious and unconscious associations apply. Liepmann, however, could not understand why the Freudian method was at all necessary in this case. The etiological childhood incidents were both conscious. No repressed sexual experience lying in the unconscious was involved. Liepmann sought to diminish Freud's contribution by pointing out that the "formative" role of youthful sexual experiences was commonly recognized in certain circumstances. This "formative" role, however, was not the same as Freud's "original, sensational" theory in which these experiences are supposed to be the "cause" of illness. Certainly, Liepmann admitted, sexuality plays just as enormous a role in pathological persons as in normal ones. But that was known before Freud. On the other hand, "it should be recognized that as a result of his work, in spite of its many exaggerations, insight into the more sensitive and secret connections between the pathological and the erotic has been sharpened."

Two other physicians were eager to point out the similarity of their experiences and Juliusburger's, even though they said the situations were not identical. A Dr. Schuster reported a case like Juliusburger's, but said that it had not even been necessary for him to use the method Juliusburger had described. The patient had spontaneously explained that she believed her symptoms could be traced back to a sexually arousing childhood experience of watching other girls being physically punished at school.

Dr. Paul Bernhardt, who worked under Liepmann at Dalldorf, reported that he had tried to get to the unconscious roots of mental illness through the use of Freud's theories. He had not yet succeeded but he still did not think it "wholly improbable" that one could do so. What he wished to make known that night, however, was that "a few years ago" he had observed "proof for one of Freud's basic ideas, i.e., for the conversion of sexual excitation into anxiety." Bernhardt had been unable to discover the unconscious childhood origins of his patient's hysterical symptoms (roaring in the ears, weakness, inability to work). But the patient herself had told Bernhardt that she experienced her symptoms when she could not satisfy her sexual feelings which were aroused when she was angry. The patient traced her hysteria back to the time when she had to hold back the anger she wished to express against her relatives when they excluded her on account of her fiancé. "The woman herself told me," concluded Bernhardt, "that since she didn't let out the anger then, it was still stuck in her."

The response of these Berlin psychiatrists to Juliusburger's paper offers some valuable insights into the medical reception of psychoanalytic methods as well as psychoanalysis in general. First, Freud's method was obviously more difficult to accept than his theories. Physicians did recognize the sexual significance of early childhood events. But they questioned whether psychoanalytic techniques were necessary to uncover them.

Second, opposition was rarely total. Liepmann's comments illustrate that he did not understand Freud's theories very well. But though he was critical of what he considered their too broad application, he still praised Freud for having sharpened the insight of his colleagues into the connection between pathology and sexuality.

Third, physicians were not always afraid to state their agreement with aspects of psychoanalysis, and such agreement did not necessarily result in damage to one's career. Paul Bernhardt was Liepmann's assistant at Dalldorf but publicly disagreed with his superior. Juliusburger, an open Freudian, continued a profitable professional association with the famous Swiss psychiatrist Forel, whose enmity to psychoanalysis is well-known. The year after the Berlin meeting, Juliusburger and Forel collaborated on a paper for the *Zeitschrift für Sexualwissenschaft* on germ cell degeneration. Perhaps their common great interest in alcoholism overrode their divergent views about psychoanalysis. Forel was a leader in the temperance movement, and in 1904 he had written the introduction to a short book on alcoholism by Juliusburger.

Fourth, as is common, the psychoanalytic literature has misleadingly labeled Juliusburger's reception. Obviously Juliusburger's paper did not encounter the "unanimous opposition" Ernest Jones (1955, p. 113) unaccountably reported.

Freud's followers were not the only ones to pay tribute to his suggestions for treatment. Book reviews often gave German psychiatrists the opportunity to comment favorably. Sunnec (1902) from Wiesbaden reported that Freud's and Möbius's psychotherapeutic approach to "functional" neuroses was the only valid one. He downgraded the common physical and dietetic treatments of nervous diseases and concluded that "the only rational therapy for hysteria . . . is the method of Janet and Freud (raising of the primary causes of hysteria through hypnosis and nullifying them through countersuggestion)." The first appearance of Freud's collected papers in 1906 offered a suitable occasion for admirers to comment. After describing the contents and subject matters of the book, Julius Grober (1907) of Jena, who specialized in mental hospital administration, concluded that "Freud deserves special merit, particularly in the area of the treatment of hysteria. His method will earn lasting notice." A lead review in Berlin's foremost medical weekly was also complimentary. It was written by Siegfried Placzek of Berlin, who wrote widely on sexual and legal problems. Placzek (1907) identified Freud as "an original thinker" and his works as "well-known to the neurological world . . . works in which Freud thought out the ingenious [geistreiche] abreaction method and then transformed it into a valuable therapeutic factor." Placzek described how Freud had given up hypnosis and developed his "unique and pioneering" psychoanalytic method. The reviewer said that even if he "has still not decided on the worth or worthlessness of this method, I may in any case wish that its plan of practical treatment would be more the common property of doctors than has happened up to now. Therefore, the study of the collected writings, from the point of view of the valuable enrichment that the reader will receive about the host of neuroses, ought to be most helpful." This review is all the more significant when one considers that Placzek had been a student of Binswanger and Ziehen and an assistant to Oppenheim.

In lengthier works psychoanalysis also received a favorable appraisal, although with various accompanying reservations. Like Placzek, Krehl had still not made up his mind whether

Breuer and Freud's "special therapeutic treatment" merited wholehearted allegiance. He was waiting for "further proof" since the statements of hysterical patients on sexual matters might not always correspond with reality. And indeed, their statements did not always correspond to reality—a fact that Freud, much to his consternation, had discovered in 1897 but had not yet published by the time Krehl wrote his paper. But Krehl was sure that the cathartic method and psychoanalysis had enormous value as research techniques and that the arduous work demanded of the physician by the methods was fully justified. He emphasized to his audience that the relationship between the precise form of a hysterical symptom and its causal psychic experience could be made clear

> only when there is in each individual case complete under-standing of *all* circumstances, which often intrude themselves as numerous and remarkable intermediates between the start and the end of the [conversion] process. What then comes to light is that there is a connection among all sorts of things which seem to have nothing at all to do with one another. . . . This means that all those who wish to become acquainted in detail with the cause of a hysterical symptom must occupy themselves exhaustively with the emotional states of patients. How far that is therapeu-tically good or correct is not discussed here. Here we are con-cerned with the investigation of the causes of illness. I am con-vinced of the fact that the more the patient knows of his own psychological development, the more he can and wants to say about it—be it in the usual mental state or under hypnosis. And the more thoroughly the physician can probe, the more fre-quently will harmful psychic events cease to be the cause of the development of hysterical phenomena. Certainly it seems at first glance that the relationship between the form of the symptom and the content of the idea would become clear more often [1902, pp. 737-738].

In all this, Krehl revealed a remarkable appreciation of Freud's goals as well as perspicacity in distinguishing between the aims of research and those of therapy.

Hellpach showed greater doubts than did Krehl about fully endorsing the new psychic treatment. Krehl, after all, believed there was an unconscious. Moreover, besides being a psychia-trist, Hellpach was also a social scientist and thus had a greater interest in the role prevention could play in the elimination of mental disturbance. As far as "a systematic psychological control of hysteria" was concerned, Hellpach (1904, p. 492) believed only sex education could do the job. Of course, psychoanalysis was "without doubt palliative—as, in the long run, is every advance against a once existing reactive abnormality." But Hellpach preferred not to prophesy what "significance" psychoanalytic treatment held for the future; perhaps only its inventor was capable of using it satisfactorily. In addition, Hellpach (1906a, p. 58) astutely remarked, while psychoanalysis was fine for "the milder psychopathies, [it] ricocheted ineffectively off the endogenous psychoses . . . and severe emotional illnesses." Yet Freud's treatment techniques impressed Hellpach. He was "frankly pleased . . . finally to find an investigator who honestly admits the difficulties of light hypnosis [and] the pain of the refraction for the hypnotizer, and who finally abandons hypnosis for the majority of the majority of his cases in order to come to the conclusion with closed eyes achieves well-nigh the same thing—psychodiagnostically as well as psychotherapeutically" (1904, pp. 39, 436-437). Furthermore, Freud had done psychotherapy a great service by pointing out the limitations of the role of autosuggestion and suggestion. Clearly, in his evaluation of psychoanalysis, Hellpach was eclectic, and he could be judicious.

Eclectism also characterized Löwenfeld, though he did Freud the great and important service of popularizing the details of his method more than did any other psychiatrist outside of Freud's close followers. Beginning as early as 1894 and in five other publications between 1897 and 1906, Löwenfeld either described the psychoanalytic procedure in great detail or invited Freud to contribute a chapter to a book. Löwenfeld (1894, p. 688) was the first German physician to print the particulars of the cathartic method in a section on various hypnotherapeutic treatments. His initial judgment of it was that it was too soon to tell whether it was any better than the suggestive treatment used at Nancy. This was a fair estimate, since both techniques relied at times on the use of suggestion during hypnosis to effect cures.

Löwenfeld's books of 1897 and 1901 presented more extensive information. As the acknowledged German expert on neurasthenia and hysteria, Löwenfeld lived up to his reputation by keeping abreast of the literature in these fields and by publishing all points of view. His books were really encyclopedic compilations of the available information on "nervous weakness." But his own predilection was for psychotherapy and especially for hypnotic treatment, and that is why he allotted so much space to psychoanalysis, even though he was never in the Freudian camp. In 1897, Löwenfeld was the first German physician to write about Freud's "analysis," although still usually referring to Freud's contribution as the "cathartic method." Freud himself had only begun to use the term "psychoanalysis" the year before. Löwenfeld (1897a, p. 165) stressed that "the treatment is difficult and time consuming for the doctor and . . . is not feasible without a great personal interest in the patient. The treatment also makes great demands on the patient. It requires a certain degree of intelligence, complete trust in the doctor, extreme attentiveness, and a continual willingness to reveal frankly to the doctor the most intimate and closely kept emotional events." Psychoanalysis could also arouse much anxiety in the patient.

In his 1897 and 1901 volumes, Löwenfeld closely examined the results of the new treatment. He gave credit to Breuer and Freud for being the first to show the value of hypnosis for uncovering psychopathogenic factors and decided that hypnosis had proved "very fruitful for diagnosis and therapy." But in abandoning hypnosis and advocating psychotherapy in the waking state "the hopes which the Viennese authors [sic] falsely aroused in themselves and probably also in others . . . have not been fulfilled." Löwenfeld (1901, pp. 356-358; 1897a, p. 166) reported that he had tried to treat three cases with the cathartic method and had failed with all three. In one case, he then put the patient under light hypnosis and "had a dramatic reduction of symptoms." Löwenfeld declared that other prominent psychotherapists such as Krafft-Ebing, Vogt, and Leonhard Seif had also had unsatisfactory or transient results. We should note, though, that Seif (1866-1949), unlike the others, was not deterred. He became a psychoanalyst and in 1911 founded the Munich Psychoanalytic

Society. Seif broke with Freud before World War I and after the war became an adherent of Adler's individual psychology.

At any rate, Löwenfeld readily admitted that Freud had obtained "very remarkable" symptomatic results with his treatment. But even Freud had said some of these results were not long-lasting. Considering Freud's own results plus the minimal successes that he, Löwenfeld, and others had achieved, Löwenfeld, unlike Krehl, thought psychoanalysis was "out of proportion to the time and efforts expended by doctor and patient." After all, with patients who could be hypnotized, Löwenfeld went on, hypnotic suggestion was a much easier — and for the patient much less demanding — treatment, "with whose therapeutic results, as we have seen, we can be quite satisfied." It could not be claimed that psychoanalysis had rendered hypnosis "superfluous" (1897a, pp. 165, 167; 1901, p. 363). It is likely that Löwenfeld, committed to hypnotism, was worried: Might psychoanalysis supplant hypnosis?

Yet Löwenfeld still kept an open mind. "From the above it should be clear that at present we are still not in the position to give a final judgment on the usefulness which the cathartic method affords us in the treatment of hysterical conditions. The relevant data are still too scanty" (1897a, p. 166).

In 1904 Löwenfeld published the fourth edition of his widely read treatise on the treatment of neurasthenia. Here he showed he understood that Freud's psychoanalytic method was no longer what was described in *Studies on Hysteria*. Löwenfeld explained how psychoanalysis had arisen out of the cathartic method and how it differed. The analytic treatment depended on free associations, on the therapist's dealing with the patient's "resistances," and on discovering the repressed events through the patient's associations to dreams and through the elucidation of slips of the tongue and other like errors. Löwenfeld explained Freud's goals as:

1. Doing away with amnesias (memory gaps).
2. Nullifying all repressions (making the unconscious conscious).
3. Aiming for the practical recovery of his patients, i.e., the return of the patient's ability to achieve and enjoy. In an in-

complete cure, a significant alleviation of the general condition was achieved.

Löwenfeld added to the requirements for analysis that he had first publicized seven years earlier. The patient should be under fifty and capable of returning to a normal psychic state. The duration of the analysis could be anywhere from six months to three years. The analyst first had to be analyzed himself. As to the efficacy of the treatment, Löwenfeld (1904a, pp. 145-157) continued to sit on the fence: "With the still very incomplete insight that we, at this time, possess about the details and difficulties of the technique, we are not in the position to say whether a wide utilization of the method will be possible until the author has fully published his experiences in the field of psychoanalysis." Löwenfeld's complaint about "incomplete" knowledge of the technique was justified, as we shall see.

Löwenfeld was a prolific writer of both articles and books. All his monographs and texts were widely reviewed in the medical press. He was consistently quoted as an authority by other physicians. Through Löwenfeld's books, almost every German doctor interested in hysteria and neurasthenia, which covered a wide range of emotional illnesses and physical symptoms, became acquainted with Freud's theories and methods. But because of Löwenfeld's persistent reservations, the physician was only rarely encouraged to test Freud's hypotheses.

Physicians who regarded the cathartic/psychoanalytic method with a mixture of favor and doubt were not the only ones who provided their readers with adequate descriptions of the method. Many German psychiatrists and neurologists who viewed Freud's treatment harshly also published informative accounts of it. Like Freud's more sympathetic discussants, they too based their judgments on a wide variety of factors, usually being influenced by their previous commitment to a certain form of treatment and their individual ideas on hypnosis.

Hirschlaff (1905, pp. 33, 68, 190-192), who used light hypnosis but was against the use of deep hypnosis, discussed the theory and practice of the cathartic method quite adequately. But he had an axe to grind on the subject of the strangulated affect. He acknowledged that there did appear under hypnosis what he called "spontaneous excitement," which he said was the same as the expression of strangulated affect. But he said that "the excitation appears only if one physically touches the patient . . . never merely through verbal suggestion. The patient's excitation disappears after a few minutes, as soon as the physical contact ceases" (p. 68). Moreover, the significance of the evocation and ending of the strangulated affect was not clear (i.e., Hirschlaff did not wholly accept Freud's elucidation of this mechanism) since evoking the affect did not always remove it and its "allied physical symptom." And even when abreaction did "frequently enough occur (as we have already seen in the analysis of single hysterical phenomena), only an existing symptom of hysteria is removed, but not the hysterical constitution of the patient" (pp. 191-192).

Hirschlaff concluded that experiences with practical hypnosis and suggestion, as well as with systematic psychotherapy, had shown that an etiological treatment of hysteria was impossible (p. 190). Freud's theory of the sexual etiology of hysteria and the therapy based on this explanation were

> pertinent in only one instance: namely in demonstrating the existence of certain mental disturbances that are seen in hysterics and that very frequently used to escape the observation of physicians. But the mental disturbance is neither infantile nor sexual. . . . The therapeutic achievements of Freud's and Breuer's "cathartic method" are on the whole no different from the usual symptomatic treatment of hysteria, the technique for which we have presented above [pp. 191-192].

Moll (1907), though no more complimentary than Hirschlaff, did think the cathartic method was "unique" (p. 23) and "special" (p. 351). And he thought that Freud had made a contribution by extending the list of conditions, such as hysterical vomiting, that could be cured through hypnosis (p. 319). But that was the extent of positive acknowledgment. Moll then described the cathartic method, completely, but in a doubting tone. His description of psychoanalysis, which he recognized as distinct from Breuer's cathartic method, was caustic. "Utilizing all kinds of tricks which have been handed over to him, the awake patient is supposed to remember what was the cause of his present difficulty. He is commanded to re-call, he must concentrate, he must close his eyes; then his fore-head is touched, briefly and hard, in order to increase his re-membering capability." Of course, Moll was a bit out of date with his details about the closed eyes and the pressed forehead.

Moll reported that "the experiences of most authors have not been able to fulfill the hopes that had been placed on the Breuer-Freud procedure." Cures had not resulted even though the original psychic trauma had been brought to conscious-ness. Moll here darkly suggested that that was because "some of the alleged pathogenic experiences were suggested unin-tentionally by Freud to his patients." Somewhat conde-scendingly, Moll (p. 352) concluded that this source of error could hardly be avoided.

The year after the "Preliminary Communication" Oppen-heim (1894, p. 676) was already discussing in his widely read text "another use for hypnotism to which Breuer and Freud have called attention." This remained briefly and factually stated in the second and third editions of the book (Oppen-heim, 1898, pp. 769-770; 1902a, p. 951). By the fourth edition (1905), however, Oppenheim was moving toward enmity to Freud ("weighty doubts have been raised against this method" [p. 1107]). He was also aware that the cathartic method was not the latest word from Vienna. In the section on obsessions, Oppenheim gave a short historical description of Freud's move from the cathartic method—because it was "inadequate"—to the *psychoanalytic* (Oppenheim's italics) method. Oppenheim was at home with analytic terminology, and he painted an unusually accurate picture of what went on in Freud's consulting room: how the patient never sees Freud because Freud sits behind him; how the patient's fantasies and associations are used; about Freud's method of *interpretation* (Oppenheim's italics) based on these and on the patient's dreams; how Freud and his patient strove to abolish the amnesias which had resulted from repression.

Oppenheim was obviously abreast of Freud's writings and not unappreciative of what was involved. His final comments, though negative, were temperate and not at all like some of his subsequent emotional charges.

I have described the method . . . because it is, in spite of everything, a very interesting attempt presented by a gifted [*geistvolle*] physician to grasp a stubborn disease by its roots. But apart from the fact that it rests on assumptions that have no or certainly no general validity, I frankly consider this kind of procedure questionable for many patients and base this judgment not only on theoretical considerations, but especially, among others, on a case which came under my observation, after having been treated by this method for three years [1905, p. 1161].

Oppenheim did not say who treated the patient, in 1905 a very important piece of information because of the paucity of qualified psychoanalysts in Germany.

Unlike Oppenheim, Schrenck-Notzing (1904, p. 75) showed that he was not conversant with the latest Freudian literature. His remarks (and his interests) were limited to Breuer and Freud's technique of abreaction through hypnosis. And the noted hypnotist remained skeptical even of this: "The delayed release of the storm of feeling—the air-clearing storm—through suggestion in the hypnotic state is completely uncertain in result."

Strümpell's (1895) review of *Studies on Hysteria* was an important basis for the future reception of psychoanalysis in Germany because it was the first lengthy, serious review of Freud's work by a respected medical figure. His remarks were often quoted by other doctors, and his arguments cropped up repeatedly. Strümpell's description of the cathartic method was a fair statement. But his evaluation, though not entirely negative, chipped away at Breuer's and Freud's personal integrity. First, Strümpell stated that the Viennese physicians had a "correct and sharp conception of *many* cases of severe hysteria and that under some conditions" their method could produce "a certain therapeutic success." But, he went on, he "cannot suppress a few doubts about its general application as a specific medical procedure." Strümpell doubted whether hypnotism could be used as a curative procedure. Moreover, he questioned the propriety of Breuer and Freud's "penetrating investigation" into the sexual lives of their patients. Finally, he wondered "whether what is learned from patients under hypnosis corresponds precisely to reality. I fear that many hysterics under hypnosis let their fantasies roam free and *invent* stories. Then the doctor can fall only too easily into a quite false position." Strümpell recognized the successes of the method in the "capable hands" of Breuer and Freud, but he could not recommend the method for imitation. He did not have the "least doubt that one can achieve the same results with a judicious direct psychic treatment without hypnosis and without a too detailed investigation of the 'strangulated affect.' "

ZIEHEN: FROM BENEVOLENCE TO HOSTILITY

The presentation of Freud's ideas by Theodor Ziehen merits special attention because of Ziehen's frequent use of psychotherapy. When he was only forty-two, Ziehen received the highest academic position in German psychiatry—the chair at the Charité in Berlin. Since the creation of the position in 1840, only the brilliant Carl Westphal held the professorship at an earlier age—thirty-six. Ziehen's descriptions of how psychotherapy should be conducted could still be used in a modern text, to such a great extent are his ideas of seventy-five years ago like present-day ones. In caring for the hysterical patient, Ziehen (1902, p. 529) taught,

> treatment of single symptoms can only be made easier when the doctor listens to the patient. Above all, this is the only way the physician wins the patient's trust, and this trust is indispensable. As for the rest, one should preserve a certain objective demeanor. One should not become too friendly with the patient. The doctor should not get involved with the patient's small sufferings, changes in mood, etc. One should recognize his progress without overreacting to it; his backslidings should be endured without impatience and without sentimentality; toward his intrigues and calumnies, one should respond with unshakable calm and strict objectivity; one should unmask possible simulation without preaching about it; one tries to prevent disobedience through frequent personal controls. Discussions are to be avoided entirely. One must speak briefly, with certitude, and clearly. Persuasion, dissuasion, etc., almost never work.

Psychoanalytic historians have emphasized the difficulties Ziehen placed in the way of Abraham when the latter sought to introduce psychoanalysis in Berlin psychiatric circles in

1908 and 1909. Ziehen's works of 1898 and 1902, however, give no hint of his later intransigence. Moreover, in his influential *Monatsschrift für Psychiatrie und Neurologie*, Ziehen published four of Freud's papers as well as seven articles by other psychoanalytic authors. He appeared at the turn of the century as a thoughtful and moderate physician who was dedicated to the organic etiology of mental disease, but who had an equally firm commitment to the use of psychotherapy.

> Even if one disregards all previous arguments, there is one main justification for psychotherapy: every case of sickness involves psychotherapy. One can mend shoes or graft plants without psychotherapy, but one cannot heal the feeling and thinking organism which is man [without it]. Indeed, every doctor practices some kind of psychotherapy, to be sure, mostly instinctively. Psychotherapeutically we win and keep the allegiance of the patient. Finally, as concerns psychic illnesses and their much-mentioned psychic overlay of pure physical symptoms, psychotherapeutic methods far excel all others in effectiveness and significance. Psychology and psychotherapy must stop being the stepchildren of practical medicine [Ziehen, 1898, p. 696].

Ziehen's descriptions of the Breuer-Freud hypotheses were sympathetic in tone and replete with examples. He agreed that "while they are in a waking state, the patients themselves are often unable to report the event which gave rise to the [hysterical] symptom. Only through hypnosis does one receive the information (psychodiagnosis)." As for the usefulness of the entire cathartic method, Ziehen (1898, p. 683) reported that he had tried the method only once "up to now," and that he had had "little success." On the basis of his experience he did not condemn the procedure. "The method still needs more intensive testing" was his conclusion. That he might use it again himself was implicit in his phrase "up to now."

Four years later, in instructions on the conduct of psychotherapy, Ziehen (1902, p. 529) advised that "one should above all listen to the patient with patience. Especially one should allow him to tell in detail the first development of his illness, including all apparently inconsequential particulars. He must abreact, as the idea has recently been expressed." These words appeared in Ziehen's text in the section on treatment of hysterical patients. There, Ziehen seems to have adopted much of Freud's method; the paragraph implies that the idea of abreaction was common knowledge and commonly accepted.

Ziehen's ultimately hostile attitude toward psychoanalysis can be traced to the fact that Ziehen had never wished to become a doctor. But the only way he could attend a university was to accept a scholarship for medical training (Schmidt, 1923, p. 220). Ziehen's initial interest was and always remained philosophy, and he was particularly interested in studies about the conscious. Finally, in 1912, at the age of fifty, he was — to his great joy and relief — able to quit the practice and teaching of psychiatry and devote himself to philosophy, especially to a psychological subbranch, the theory of learning.

Because of his strong philosophical commitment to the pre-eminence of the conscious, Ziehen could never have become an ardent follower of psychoanalysis and would always have had reservations about Freud's theories. But before 1904 Ziehen exhibited no particular irritation at psychoanalysis. His changed attitude toward psychoanalysis coincided with his assumption of the Berlin chair. The new post was a natural step in the career of a rapidly rising academic psychiatrist but, because of Ziehen's true interests, it proved to be a trying and unhappy experience.

Ziehen wrote that he found the obligations of his chiefship at the Charité a galling yoke that took him away from treating patients and from his beloved philosophical studies (Schmidt, 1923, pp. 228-229). In such circumstances it is logical that Ziehen should not have maintained a benevolent neutrality toward anything that made his post even more burdensome. Unfortunately for its early reception in academic medical circles, psychoanalysis became inextricably linked with Ziehen's attitude about his position. Freud was free to devote his attention to proving the predominance of the unconscious. In sharp contrast, the duties of Ziehen's professorship forbade him from giving any time to promoting the core of his philosophy: the predominance of the conscious.

On of Ziehen's irksome duties was to preside at every meeting of the Berlin Psychiatric Society. Here, as nowhere else, he stood publicly as the official representative of German psychiatry, responsible for its appearance before the outside world. The presence of foreign visitors at one of the Society's meetings in 1909 provoked Ziehen to an unusual, irate outburst. When Abraham presented a paper, Ziehen refused to permit discussion of it so as not to give the impression that psychoanalysis was officially recognized by German psychiatry (H. C. Abraham and Freud, 1965, p. 84).

Ziehen's belief in the organic etiology of mental disease and his doubts about the significance of unconscious processes meant that his regard for psychoanalysis would always be limited. But these important theoretical differences alone had not led him to be an outspoken critic of psychoanalysis. Ziehen's initial reaction to Freud's theories had never reflected any great personal involvement; for many years his attitude toward Freud's work was, at the very least, always correct. Ziehen appreciated Freud's method because he himself was a dedicated and sophisticated psychotherapist. He published eleven psychoanalytic papers in the journal he edited. Ziehen's metamorphosis into one of Freud's emotionally hostile critics was the reaction of a pressured, resentful man. His Berlin post forced him into closer contact with psychoanalysis than he would voluntarily have chosen, and it is clear he believed that as Chief at the Charité he was expected to take a stand on this controversial treatment. Although Ziehen had never had any great desire to attack psychoanalysis, now that he had to speak up about it, he certainly could not defend it. The matter was troublesome, his duties were bothersome. Ziehen vented his wrath at everything together: at the emphasis on the unconscious, at having to spend his time as a psychiatric watchdog, at being kept away from philosophy. For Ziehen, psychoanalysis had become something more personal that the merely "ingenious" theory of a Viennese neurologist toward which he had once been able to be pleasant, noncommittal, and distant.

ATTACK

Kraepelin, on the other hand, never gave any indication that he had adopted any psychoanalytic techniques. Before

1908 he did not even take notice of Freud's abandonment of the cathartic method. From 1899 onward, Kraepelin's textbook explained that, according to Freud, the physician could discover the sexual etiology of hysteria, obsessions, or paranoia "by interrogating the patient while he is under hypnosis." Because of Kraepelin's (1899, Vol. 2, p. 511) long-standing views against hypnotism, he quipped caustically: "We ought not to doubt that in this way one could elicit entirely different things."

Others varied Kraepelin's derogation of psychoanalytic techniques by coining or repeating especially insulting epithets. In 1896, Konrad Rieger, in a general discussion of the treatment of the nervously ill, had occasion to refer to Freud's theory of paranoia. Rieger (1896, p. 196) commented that the new views currently stemming from Vienna aroused in him "a real sense of horror" because of the significance Freud attributed to what were obviously accidental sexual allusions — psychotic babble — of the paranoid patient. Such a theory could take psychiatry out of medicine and throw it back into superstition. Freud's hypothesis was "a simply gruesome old-wives' psychiatry."

This last phrase was picked up ten years later by Oswald Bumke (1877-1950), then a bright young psychiatrist who eventually succeeded Kraepelin in Munich. Bumke (1906) used the words in a review of one of Freud's published analyses, that of an eighteen-year-old girl, Dora. Freud's (1905a) report of the case showed quite clearly how he worked and how he arrived at his conclusions. Today's reader is struck by Freud's creativity and genius, which appear in an immediate and vivid fashion in this short, remarkable analysis. In Dora's case, her hysterical cough was tied to her knowledge of her father's love affair with the wife of an older man to whom she was attracted. Freud reported that he had discussed with Dora, an adolescent girl of "good" family, her belief that her father was impotent and that his mistress performed fellatio on him. Freud's critics saw only disastrous consequences from such conversations between doctor and patient. The publication of the "Dora analysis" did more to arouse enmity against Freud's method than had any other of Freud's writings up to that time. As well as Bumke's attack, it also called forth from Walther Spielmeyer (1879-1935), at twenty-seven a promising neuropathologist, the epithet of "mental masturbation" (Spielmeyer, 1906, p. 322).

Aside from specific reviews of Freud's works, most physicians who attacked psychoanalysis in the early period only commented on Freud's method as part of general psychiatric discussions. But there were a few exceptions to this trend. At the turn of the century, Oskar Vogt (1898-1899, pp. 65-83, 342-355) specifically examined and challenged Freud's method of psychotherapy. Vogt offered as a superior method his own "causal analysis" in which intellectual self-observation rather than reliance on analysis of affective mechanisms was involved. At the end of the prepsychoanalytic period in Germany, A. A. Friedländer (1870-1949) of Frankfurt published a full-scale evaluation of psychoanalysis, objecting to Freud's detailed investigation of sexual perversions, which he considered a dangerous procedure. At this time, Friedländer (1907a, 1907b, 1907c) seems to have made an avocation out of writing papers that were lengthy, critical examinations of psychoanalysis. Friedländer tried repeatedly to arrange a public confrontation between himself and a psychoanalyst but was rebuffed, Freud regarding him as untrustworthy in every respect.

Few critics of psychoanalytic treatment were as blunt as Aschaffenburg. This fact poses a problem of interpretation. Was Aschaffenburg saying in public the things most German physicians were saying in private? Most traditional historians of psychoanalysis would have answered affirmatively. Or did Aschaffenburg represent only a narrow extreme of negative reaction to Freud? His virulent *manner* of expression was *not* representative—that much is obvious both from an examination of printed references to Freud before World War I and from my interviews with psychoanalysts who were acquainted with the reaction to psychoanalysis in the years immediately before and after World War I. These men and women have reported that the typical private reaction to analysis was to take it lightly, shrug it off, or make a joke about it—but not to harangue their listeners.[1]

[1] Based on interviews with Elisabeth Goldner, Martin Grotjahn, Ernst Lewy, Fritz Moellenhoff, and Edith Weigert.

Aschaffenburg (1906, pp. 1796-1798) protested sharply a-gainst Freud's conversing for weeks or even months on sexual subjects with hysterical patients. If, of course, he said, the method had been successful, he would not hestitate for a mo-ment to declare it valuable. But it was not the method, but suggestion that produced results. For months, Freud dangled before hysterics the expectation that their difficulties would disappear as soon as he found the starting point of their prob-lems. Then, when Freud came up with his etiological explana-tion, the symptom vanished. The suggestive effect of Freud's method was "enormous."

Why did Freud find a sexual trauma in every case? Only, replied Aschaffenburg, because Freud himself linked the ideas, words, and dreams of his patients with their sexual lives so that all ideas, etc., led to the area of sex by simple association. Such "mystical" interpretation was unnecessary, and one could achieve the same success without discussing sex in "a thousand details." Exhibiting the common German mistrust of hypnotism, Aschaffenburg expressed worry about Freud's harming hysterics by his "frequent" use of hypnosis and especially the deepest level of hypnosis (though by 1906 Freud had not been using hypnosis in therapy for eight years). In conclusion, Aschaffenburg called on all physicians not to investigate the sexual lives of hysterics and to fight such procedures wherever they appeared, for "Freud's method [was] for most cases incorrect, for many questionable, and for all—superfluous."

The following year, Aschaffenburg (1907) repeated a great many of his remarks at the First International Congress of Psychiatry and Neurology held in Amsterdam, a meeting attended by many German psychiatrists because of its con-venient location. Konrad Alt (1861-1922), a German neuro-logist commenting on Aschaffenburg's paper, voiced Rieger's old worry. Many people looked down at hysterics, declared Alt, because of the popular belief that hysteria was linked with sex. German neurologists had tried hard to destroy this common myth. If Freud's theory gained prominence, what-ever benefit hysterics had won from the changing public atti-tude would be lost. Psychoanalysis was a regressive force and nothing but *"Schweinerei"* — smut (Jones, 1955, p. 113). Jung, who was attending the meeting in Freud's defense, reported that Aschaffenburg and Alt were seconded by Ziehen, Heinrich Sachs of Breslau, and Karl Heilbronner of Utrecht, but that Otto Gross and Ludwig Frank of Zurich "spoke up for [Freud] energetically." The elder Binswanger and Oppenheim were described as "maintain[ing] a position of benevolent neutrality although both show signs of sexual opposition" (McGuire, 1974, pp. 84-85; see also Ellenberger, 1970, pp. 796-798).

Aschaffenburg was the first German psychiatrist to give a paper against the psychoanalytic method at a general psychiatric congress. Binswanger had spoken up against Stegmann's paper at the 1904 Congress of Mid-German Psychiatrists and Neurologists, but this had been an impromptu comment. Aschaffenburg initiated a fashion. For the next four years attacks took place at several large meetings. By 1910, the furor abated.

THE FREUDIANS' RIPOSTE

Freud refused to defend himself publicly against the attacks of these men. He had been, for example, personally invited to address the International Congress in Amsterdam at that very same session at which Aschaffenburg and Jung had spoken. The session was on modern theories of hysteria, and the main paper was given by Janet. Freud wrote Jung that he declined the invitation hastily "for fear that I might talk it over with you and let you persuade me to accept. . . . Apparently a duel was planned between Janet and myself, but I detest gladiatorial fights in front of the noble rabble and cannot easily bring myself to put my findings to the vote of an indifferent crowd" (McGuire, 1974, pp. 32-33). In a transparent attempt to lighten the seriousness of these remarks, Freud added that the "chief reason" he had no wish to go to Amsterdam was that he needed a vacation.

Freud also discouraged his early supporters from rebuttals. If Freud had felt differently on this issue, the journals of psychiatry and neurology would have contained before 1908 an extensive literature supporting and condemning psychoanalysis. Still, Freud was not able to prevent all his followers from engaging in debate. Jung, Gross, and Frank went off to Amsterdam, and in 1906 and 1907 several articles and books were published, answering the charges of the opponents of psychoanalysis.

Most commonly, the advocates of analysis did not try to meet their enemies' particular charges. Instead, Freud's supporters issued a broad counterattack which denied the antagonists' ability to judge psychoanalysis because they had never tried it — or tried it properly. Jung and Bleuler were particularly active in defending psychoanalysis in this manner. Indeed, down to this day such an argument is often the standard answer of psychoanalysts to their disparagers. Jung (1906b) challenged Spielmeyer and Aschaffenburg in a 1906 essay, and in the Foreword to his book on dementia praecox (1907b) emphasized that "Freud can only be contradicted by whoever has himself used the psychoanalytic method many times and actually worked with it in the way Freud works, i.e., observes long and patiently daily life, hysteria, and dreams from *Freud's* standpoint. Whoever does not or can not do that may not judge Freud; otherwise he acts like those famous scientists who refused to look through Galileo's telescope." This argument went back many years and had first been used by Fliess (1897, p. 142).

Bleuler (1906d) wrote to Gaupp, in whose journal Spielmeyer's review of the Dora analysis had appeared, protesting the review because Spielmeyer had never tested the psychoanalytic method. That Gaupp printed this letter was rather unusual, for letters to the editor were not a common feature of German medical journals at that time. The same year Bleuler (1906a) published a short essay in an attempt to minimize the effects of Spielmeyer's words, which Bleuler felt sure had frightened away many from becoming acquainted with Freud's "stimulating" ideas.

In 1907 Gaupp allowed the publication of the strongest indictment yet of Freud's critics: a short article by one of Freud's Viennese disciples, Isidor Sadger (1867-194?). Sadger's (1907) holier-than-thou tone was to become the prevalent one among the defenders of psychoanalysis in German journals, though his rhetoric had an especially intense fervor. Freud sourly identified him as "that congenital fanatic of orthodoxy, who happens by mere accident to believe in psychoanalysis rather than in the law given by God on Sinai-Horeb" (McGuire, 1974, p. 130). There was the familiar reproach that none of Freud's critics had taken the necessary time and effort to learn psychoanalytic technique. These men thought their conclusions that psychoanalysis did not work were justified if after the first or second session of trying Freud's methods the patient was not healed. Sadger, however, wished to point out what was involved in becoming a successful analyst. He had had nine years experience with the method. And even after several semesters of theoretical lectures from Freud, it had still taken him three years of practice before he conquered all difficulties. The technique did not suddenly spring full-blown as did Pallas Athene from the head of Zeus. In his conclusion, Sadger's arrogance was boundless: "It has been my frequent experience that when an otherwise completely intelligent man understands nothing about the human psyche, but literally nothing, then he is always a professional psychologist — or psychiatrist. So, learn, test, and verify — then we will compare our results!" (p. 42). The effects of such continual self-righteous finger-shaking from the analysts only irritated German physicians and added weight to the belief of some that Freud's followers were a group of fanatics blinded by their theories.

Sometimes Freud's supporters did undertake to reply to specific charges. Bleuler (1906a, pp. 338-339) wrote that Aschaffenburg had attacked Freud on his weakest point, therapy. To evaluate its therapy alone was to judge psychoanalysis unfairly. It "showed that one was inclined to throw out the bath as quickly as possible, before one had the time to see whether there was a fine and viable baby in it." It was necessary, rather, to have a balanced critique of all psychoanalysis. Bleuler believed that Freud's contribution formed the starting point for a radically new observation of the psyche. One ought not prematurely to exclude from science such important knowledge.

Muthmann dealt with the often stated objection that psychoanalysis only alleviated the "symptoms" of illness, while the neurosis was and remained constitutional. Muthmann (1907, pp. iii-iv) retorted that when a tubercular process is completely halted in a consumptive, one may still designate the patient's constitution as consumptive, but that in no way denied his new healthy condition. Furthermore, psychoanalysis did not only cure, it had a prophylactic value as well. It gave patients protection against relapse by acquainting them with the origins of their illnesses.

Jung (1907b, Foreword) sought to dispel any notion that subscription to psychoanalysis meant giving up one's intellectual freedom. "Acknowledging Freud," he assured, "does not mean, as many fear, an unconditional subjugation before a dogma; one may very well preserve an independent judgment." Considerations about how much of psychoanalysis to accept "are subsidiary issues which completely disappear before the psychological principles whose discovery is Freud's greatest service."

Perhaps with these words Jung was seeking more to reassure himself than his readers. When Jung and Bleuler eventually broke with Freud, they did so partly over the issue of intellectual freedom. From the earliest days of his correspondence with Freud, Jung had been uneasy. In his second letter Jung had written of feeling "alarmed by the positivism of your presentation." Two months later he was explaining certain passages in his book on dementia praecox by the fact that "we do not see eye to eye on certain points. This may be because I. my material is totally different from yours . . . II. my upbringing, my milieu, and my scientific premises are in any case utterly different from your own." Then after Jung had met Freud for the first time, he wrote of his "uncomfortable feeling that Rank ['swears to the words of the master'—Horace] and lacks empiricism" (McGuire, 1974, pp. 7, 13-14, 26).

Was Jung voicing a personal Oedipal rebellion? Was Freud in fact dogmatic and authoritarian? The extent to which Freud was comfortable with questioning and dissent within the psychoanalytic movement has always been the subject of much controversy.[2]

[2] Paul Roazen (1975) is the latest to tackle this issue.

The most comprehensive and convincingly written defense of psychoanalysis to appear in medical circles in this early period was Bleuler's (1907a) review of Freud's collected essays. It was a spirited plea to the medical profession to familiarize itself with Freud's works.

> Whether Freud's theories are right or not, they are uncommonly stimulating: no one ought to be allowed to call himself a psychologist or a psychopathologist who has not come to terms with Freud. Unfortunately, thorough study is required to assimilate these completely new ideas; but whoever does not look into these matters for himself, cannot be permitted to judge them.

Bleuler urged physicians not to carp endlessly over details but to get to the theoretical core of Freud's theories.

> It is a matter of complete indifference whether Freud's therapeutic results can also be obtained in other ways; also whether it is good or evil to talk to young and old women about their sexuality; or whether there is conversion, repression or abreaction in Freud's sense of the terms; or whether all or only a part of the enormous complex of diseases that we call neuroses are dependent on sexuality, etc. No matter what the definitive answers to these questions turn out to be, the significance of the new discoveries will in no way thereby be reduced. And a great part of Freud's statements are certainly correct. . . . Among others, such an experienced, clear-headed, and objective researcher as Löwenfeld confirms Freud in the essentials.

Bleuler concluded with an account of the enormous extent to which his experiences and those of his staff at Burghölzli had confirmed the Freudian postulates.

From interviews with German analysts about the origins of their psychoanalytic interests, it is possible to conclude that Freud's advice to his followers not to answer critics may at least have been utilitarian. German physicians were not attracted to psychoanalysis (directly, at any rate) because of the exhortations of Freud's early defenders. Indirectly, no doubt, the debates focused more attention on psychoanalysis than would otherwise have been the case. But they did not change the minds of those already committed to opposition. And those who became analysts after 1907 did so for a variety of reasons, but none were specifically influenced by polemics.

6

GERMAN PHYSICIANS AND PSYCHOANALYSIS

It has been commonplace for many years to ascribe resistance to psychoanalysis as originating overwhelmingly in the
sexual revulsion — indeed, nausea — Freud aroused in his
critics. Jones (1955, pp. 107-110) opened his chapter on
"Opposition" with a four-page general and anecdotal account
of the "moral loathing" Freud's sexual theories had aroused.
Because of these theories, Jones stressed, "Freud's name was a
byword of . . . notoriety to German psychiatrists and neurologists." Not until the fifth page in the chapter did Jones mention other objections German doctors had to psychoanalysis.

And it is certainly true that Freud's sexual theories more
consistently stirred up negative comments than did any other
of his contributions. It is also the case that the most frenzied
reactions came in response to those aspects of psychoanalysis
which concerned sexuality. But it is perhaps just because of
this latter occurrence that two myths about the rejection of
Freud have arisen. One is that for about ten years after *Studies
on Hysteria* appeared, Freud was uniformly ignored or
rejected. The second is that all real opposition to psychoanalysis centered on sex.

The study of the medical literature at the turn of the
century shatters these myths. Freud's loud bemoaning of his
splendid isolation was based on the illogical expectation that
the entire medical world would immediately recognize the
truths he had uncovered. Because it did not do so, he felt
"isolated" and wrote about it in all his accounts of psychoanalysis; his version has often been accepted without further inves-

tigation. Freud's official biographer, Ernest Jones, did little to correct Freud's distortion. Jones lived through Freud's trying times with him and felt as keenly the lack of recognition that afflicted all the early, dedicated psychoanalysts. But Jones disparaged the efforts of many Germans who sought to test Freud's findings and then published favorable accounts of their psychoanalytic experiences: Warda, Strohmayer, Juliusburger, Muthmann. According to Jones, these men never practiced the "real thing." Jones never discussed the writings of doctors like Bloch, Krehl, and Löwenfeld. Their less than complete acceptance of psychoanalysis consigned them to oblivion. Nor did Jones give weight to the ambivalence of men like Hellpach, Moll, Oppenheim, and Ziehen; they were always the "enemy." Mixed or shifting reactions were indications of the deepest hostility.

Jones quoted in great detail all the sensational slandering of Freud on the issue of sexuality that occurred before World War I. But he discussed only in the broadest of terms the review articles that dealt with psychoanalysis in a more serious vein. He did not report on monographs and textbooks at all. Moreover, Jones contributed to the psychoanalytic prejudice of regarding all criticisms of psychoanalysis as "resistance." This latter is a neat device for discounting all intellectual questioning as quite beside the point. Yet it is a legitimate scientific concern to be sure that clinical evidence is properly evaluated. When Freud's critics raised this issue, however, they were told to carry out psychoanalysis themselves. How they were to learn, short of a year's visit to Vienna, was not part of the advice. In 1904 Freud declared that "The details of this technique of interpretation . . . have not yet been published" (1904, p. 252). And as late as 1909, Freud wrote to the Swiss minister and psychoanalyst, Oskar Pfister, that "my own technique of free association . . . has not been fully communicated yet" (Meng and Freud, 1963, p. 17). Meanwhile, critics' carping about clinical evidence was indicative of resistance.

There is a great deal of evidence in the medical literature that psychoanalysis was attacked for several reasons and not only because of the sexual sensitivities it irritated. Important as the latter may have been, respectful and intense consideration of psychoanalysis was given by German physicians during the entire time that early psychoanalytic theory and methods were being formulated. It is Jones's (1955) contention that these medical evaluations of psychoanalysis are misleading. He predicted that if one day a student of the history of science probed into the written sources,

> he would get a very imperfect picture of the amount of anger and contempt with which those intellectual circles strove to cover the more panicky emotions that agitated them, since only a small part of the flood seeped through into scientific periodicals, and then only in a relatively civilized form. Most of the invective was to be encountered in unrecorded outbursts at scientific meetings, and still more in the private conversations outside these [p. 107].

While this argument has some validity, it also has some important weaknesses. Jones used it to dismiss whole sections of books whose authors were discussing psychoanalysis dispassionately—sometimes critically, sometimes receptively. The aim of these authors was to carry out a serious inquiry. It is at this point that the historian of ideas has a very specific task. He must evaluate what appears to be the serious thought of a serious thinker and not dismiss it because it has unconscious meaning as well as manifest substance.

More specifically, in the foregoing statement, Jones admitted that he concerned himself with the hostile "flood" in "scientific periodicals." Monographs and texts, which he did not investigate but have been surveyed in this study, do not tell the same story as the periodicals. Jones also dropped tantalizing hints of "unrecorded outbursts" and "private conversations," but he recorded relatively few, especially the conversations. Significantly, these "outbursts" vary greatly in their indictment of Freud; some are quite mild. Moreover, they are matched—in Jones's work itself, in other books, and in my interviews with German psychoanalysts—by other anecdotes that demonstrate that private conversations about Freud were quite varied. They ranged from the (formerly) unprintable, to sarcasm and epithets no worse that Spielmeyer's or Aschaffenburg's or Kraepelin's, to, finally, private repudiation of public attack against Freud. There are anecdotes that prove every-thing, so anecdotes cannot be the base of history.

THE ACCEPTANCE OF PSYCHOANALYSIS BY GERMAN PHYSICIANS

If, then, we take seriously the remarks of the many earnest commentators on psychoanalysis before 1908, it should be possible to discover various reasons for the early rejection of psychoanalysis in German medical circles. Initially, however, let us consider the acceptance of psychoanalysis in order to es-tablish that not all reception was rejection and to spell out precisely the extent of the early acceptance.

First of all, Freud was taken as a serious worker in the fields about which he wrote. This is readily seen from the numerous lists of authorities with which it was the custom of many authors to introduce a subject: "So and so are considered to be the major workers in this area." In these inevitable lists, Freud's name joined those of prominent persons whose place at the time, and often in history as well, was secure. Three ex-amples come to mind, but the literature contains several others. In a monograph on severe neuroses, Oppenheim (1902b, p. 4) enumerated those who had contributed impor-tant information on neurasthenia, hysteria, and psychothera-py: Beard, Weir Mitchell, Bouveret, Levillain, Löwenfeld, Binswanger, Ziehen, O. Vogt, Forel, and Freud. Two years later Hellpach (1904, p. iv) cited as the "classicists" of the psy-chology of hysteria P. Janet, Möbius, Vogt, Breuer, and Freud. Moll (1907, p. 126) listed as prominent hypnothera-pists Moritz Benedikt, Breuer and Freud, Vogt and Brod-mann, and Hirschlaff.

Second, Freud's views about hysteria received early attention from those physicians who were interested in the same treat-ments as Freud—hypnotism and psychotherapy.[1] Hirschlaff made it an issue that he had to refute Freud because his theories had met with "great approval," especially among hypnotists. This aspect of Freud's acceptance has not received

---

[1] There is no justification for the amazement of some historians of psychoanalysis at the relative lack of attention of *most* German physicians to Freud's ideas about hysteria in these early years. Most German psychiatrists and neurologists had an unalterable commitment to the organic basis of all disease.

attention because psychoanalytic historians dismiss Freud's early involvement with hypnosis; Freud abandoned hypnosis about ten years after he took it up, and hypnosis is not a part of the psychoanalytic method. Yet Freud was actively relying on hypnosis at the same time that he was making and publishing some of his fundamental discoveries. Freud's contemporaries therefore, took the fact of his involvement with hypnosis quite seriously. There was an understandable time lag before many discovered that he had abandoned hypnosis. Moreover, even at a time when Freud (1905c, pp. 298-299, 302) had long abandoned hypnosis, he championed its general use and its efficacy in a great number of situations. This was in a 1905 article in which he said *not one word* about psychoanalysis, though he did point out that hypnosis had certain drawbacks and that a better therapeutic technique was needed.

The entire issue of hypnosis is very important in the reception of psychoanalysis. The opinions many physicians had of both the cathartic method and psychoanalysis were heavily influenced by the stand they took on hypnotism. Krehl, an open-minded person, welcomed any research technique that gave promise of a deeper psychological understanding of human actions. When he discussed the hard work the psychoanalytic method entailed, he believed it was justified. But most German physicians were not so liberal. Both Löwenfeld and Moll were committed to the use of hypnotism in psychotherapy. These two men were more acquainted with Freud's work than most and knew that he had repudiated hypnotherapy. Though Löwenfeld was much more sympathetic to Freud than the highly ambivalent Moll, the close similarity of their judgments on psychoanalysis is striking. Both physicians accused Freud of having aroused false hopes in the medical world. They reported that they and others had tried psychoanalysis and that the results had been paltry—certainly, in Löwenfeld's opinion, not justifying the great expenditure of time and effort required from both doctor and patient. Moll ascribed the major part of Freud's successes to suggestion. Both retreated to hypnosis as the treatment of choice. Logically, Moll, Löwenfeld, and other hypnotists might be considered as the potential core of Freud's supporters because of their extensive psychological interests. And indeed, in reality, almost all the hypnotists did provide Freud with his initial audience, and they helped to popularize his ideas. But when it came to acclaiming Freud, their commitment to hypnosis—the method of treatment on which their careers and reputations were based—was stronger than their psychological interests.

Freud's use of hypnosis was also instrumental in making enemies. The majority of prominent German psychiatrists and neurologists were against hypnotism. Hirschlaff, though a hypnotherapist, was against the use of somnambulism (deep hypnosis), which Freud had originally considered necessary in some cases. Strümpell, Ziehen, Kraepelin, and Aschaffenburg, all early or late opponents of Freud, were decidedly against hypnotism in any form, and all except Ziehen specifically criticized Freud for using it. In their eyes the use of hypnosis made him suspect as an ethical physician and his results scientifically doubtful.

As usual, Hellpach occupied a unique position. He was against hypnotism, but, like Löwenfeld and Moll, having more than a cursory interest in psychoanalysis, he knew that Freud had dropped hypnosis. Thus, in Hellpach's extensive cataloguing of Freud's good and bad points, Freud was commended for not using hypnosis.

Freud's employment of hypnosis was an early drawing card of his method. It attracted the interest and comments of the hypnotherapists. When Freud abandoned hypnosis, the hypnotists lost their main reason for supporting him and often joined the ranks of his critics.

There is a third category of evidence which delineates the type of reception accorded Freud in German medical circles. After 1900 hardly a month went by without some major psychiatric or neurological journal containing some reference to Freud: there were reviews of his works, reviews of works of authors who had prominently discussed his ideas, expository articles, critical articles. And references to Freud can be found in a fair number of monographs. Enough of the widely read textbooks reported on Freud's findings for medical students and residents to have the opportunity to become acquainted with his work. None of this is to imply any general acceptance of psychoanalysis. The matter of "impression" and "understanding" is, of course, another one. It is one of the purposes of this study to explain why, in spite of adequate "exposure," Freud made little "impression" and did not receive significant "understanding" in Germany.

The only area where Freud was truly ignored was at large medical congresses. One looks in vain through various proceedings before 1904 for any recognition of Freud's contribution. Of course, if Freud had so wished, he could have given papers at those meetings. His presentations would have generated a great public (medical) debate before the heyday of controversy which began in 1906.

In summing up the matter of acceptance, it is obvious that Freud's theories engendered few noticeable changes in medical theory or practice in these early years. The word "abreaction" was the only one to be assimilated into the German medical vocabulary, the concept of abreaction being widely accepted. As late as 1906 there was still a fight over the use of the word "conversion" (see below, p. 181). The idea of conversion was considered plausible and enjoyed broad, though not unanimous, respect.

Physicians who devoted their energies to the liberalizing movements of the day such as birth control, sex education, women's rights, and penal code reform, sometimes used the discoveries of psychoanalysis on behalf of their causes. This was the case with Bloch, Eulenburg, Hellpach, and Moll, who were prominent members of The League for the Protection of Maternal Rights (*Bund für Mutterschutz*), actually a league for sexual reform, founded in 1905 with branches in Berlin, Munich, and Hamburg. Freud himself became a member of the Committee of the Austrian *Bund* in 1907. Another case is that of Löwenfeld (1908) who, at the end of 1907, spoke to a group of lawyers about changing the criminal codes applying to homesexuals and discussed Freud's views about homosexuality extensively (see Chapter 12). The opening years of this century marked the start of the converging of psychoanalysis and other new socially progressive movements of the day, a convergence that was complete after World War I. The simultaneous beginning and existence of such coinciding trends is a powerful argument for the role of the *Zeitgeist* in history.

Though interpreted in a distorted way, psychoanalysis sometimes prompted a doctor to action he might otherwise not even have contemplated. Löwenfeld (1901, pp. 366-367) reported that he had cured a woman of sexual frigidity by suggesting to her while she was hypnotized that she have "normal feelings" during intercourse. However unpsychoanalytic (even "uncathartic") this approach may have been, it helped the woman, and Löwenfeld confessed that he got the idea for doing so from Freud's theory that "the lack of sexual satisfaction in a woman is connected with certain existing anxieties." The impromptu discussion which followed the paper Juliusburger gave before the Berlin Psychiatric Society in 1907 is further evidence of this kind of impact of psychoanalysis. Though comparatively few physicians understood psychoanalysis before 1908, it nevertheless had an educative and practical value.

THE REJECTION OF PSYCHOANALYSIS BY GERMAN PHYSICIANS

Now for the matter of actual rejection. There is abundant proof that Freud's hypotheses ran counter to two of the major premises of German medicine. One premise was that there was a sharp dividing line between sickness and health. This clashed uncompromisingly with Freud's postulate of a common psychosexual development for all—those who appeared well and those who appeared ill, the upper classes as well as the lower classes, and, perhaps most meaningfully, physicians and their patients. Psychoanalytic theory held that all manifestations of emotional behavior were ranged along a continuum and that every person had his place on that undemarcated line: every aspect of everyone's personality was to a greater or lesser degree normal or abnormal. Like the modern progressive income tax, psychoanalysis held out the prospect of being the great leveler. The second premise was that there was a physical predisposition to mental disease. This received an enormous assist from the theories of racial or familial "degeneracy" in vogue at the turn of the century. But Freud's hypothesis nullified the idea of hereditary degeneracy and placed great stress on the significance of early-life sexual (that is, sexual in the wide Freudian sense) experiences. Freud demanded a medical revolution by asking the German physician to accept the psychic etiology of disease as well as to identify himself with his emotionally disturbed patient. Such demands met all the more resistance because Freud first presented them in connection with the medically difficult and provocative subject of hysteria. And soon Freud was applying his new concepts to the poorly understood field of mental illness in general.

Ziehen's list of the causes of neurasthenia attests to the chaotic state of medical knowledge of emotional disturbance. Löwenfeld's books on treatment offered the physican a staggeringly wide range of cures because no one knew which ones worked when, or why they worked or did not.

Under such conditions and in the light of the development of German psychiatry in the nineteenth century, it is not hard to see why Freud's views were often condemned as unscientific and regressive, and why German psychiatrists feared the loss of status that would inevitably result if Freud's views were accepted and then proved incorrect. In many speeches and books psychiatrists were still demanding that psychiatry stop being the "stepchild" of German medicine (Becker, 1899, p. iii). Liepmann was not only an archenemy of psychoanalysis when he agonized that Freud's theories would "enchain less acute minds . . . who will throw to the winds the hard-won insights of scientific examination of mental life." He was also a pioneer in histopathology who had helped make German psychiatry "modern," as then defined. When Konrad Rieger called Freud's "Further Remarks on the Neuro-Psychoses of Defence" (1896) an "old wives' psychiatry," he was not just mudslinging. He and Alt, who seconded Aschaffenburg in 1907, were also unnerved at the thought of a return to the mysticism and superstition that had characterized German psychiatry only a few decades before. And did not Freud deal copiously with those very same subjects in which the philosophers of nature and their medical friends had become mired: inner hidden conflicts, the "passions," the unconscious?

This is not to excuse the blindness of Freud's enemies to the limits of somatic psychiatry. Nor should one overlook their unquestioning passive response to the grossly imperfect understanding of mental disturbance which characterized early twentieth-century medicine. But critics who attacked psychoanalysis as "unscientific" were just as much concerned with defending psychiatric progress as they were with attacking Freud's particular postulates (see also Bry and Rifkin, 1962, p. 14). Of course, the epithet "unscientific" was not always thrown at Freud out of great concern for scientific method. This concern was at times a mask behind which detractors could hide. They could say Freud was not being scientific — the ultimate condemnation of men who had sanctified the word "science" — when they really objected on other grounds, but grounds which they did not care to commit to paper (Theodor Adorno, personal communication, Sept. 5, 1963).

One objection the critics of psychoanalysis took no trouble to hide was their displeasure at Freud's use of the French word *conversion* instead of the German *Umformung* or *Umwandlung*. (Freud did not Germanize its spelling by writing it with a "K"; he always spelled it *Conversion*.) The word *Konversion* has never entered everyday normal German usage the way "conversion" has in English. Even today, *Konversion* is normally used only as a commercial or religious term. Kraepelin and Aschaffenburg both refused to accept Freud's new term, Kraepelin (1899, Vol. 2, p. 511) sticking to *Umformung* and Aschaffenburg (1906, p. 1795) to *Umwandlung*. Strümpell (1895, p. 159) was annoyed at what he called Breuer and Freud's "peculiar manner of expression." Strümpell admitted that psychological subjects must be dealt with in psychological language, but "this language gains nothing in clarity when it employs a number of unnecessarily strange words, e.g., 'conversion into a somatic phenomenon'; it perhaps gives the appearance of evoking scientific depth, but in reality it only impedes and obscures." Freud's Jewishness and his consorting with Charcot and Bernheim conspired to cast him in the light of being somewhat un-Germanic. Perhaps his unconventional use of a foreign expression brought to mind thoughts of Viennese *Schlamperei*. All this coupled with his objectionable theories was partly responsible for his German critics' resistance to a new term of French derivation.

Perhaps even if Freud had not been Freud, national feelings of the day alone would have sufficed to raise objections to "unnecessary" imported words. But Freud's dealing with hysteria may also have touched on national differences. These were not a major determinant of reception but were definitely influential in some cases. The subject of hysteria inevitably reminded some physicians of Charcot's "theatrics" and the different emphases of French and German medicine. It also touched the national biases of many German physicians who regarded hysteria as an "un-Germanic" disease, existing primarily in "degenerate races." Furthermore, as Hellpach's remarks illustrate, it stimulated German doctors to express once again long-standing north German disapproval of south German morality.

It is helpful to call attention to some of the new components of scientific controversies in the late nineteenth century. The period from 1880 to 1914 was one which saw nationalistic passions reaching a new height. The aura of competition that overlay so much of Europe's military, economic, and colonial exploits extended to science as well. Ellenberger has pointed out that from the beginning of the nineteenth century there were growing rivalries involving German, French, and English science. The Franco-Prussian War provided an additional basis for acrimony between the former two. Celebrated disputes between Fustel de Coulanges and Mommsen and between Pasteur and Koch contributed to hostile feelings (Ellenberger, 1970, pp. 268-269). In the nineteenth century, science lost much of the international character that had previously characterized it. Latin as a common language had disappeared. Scientific activities expanded and the reporting of new results accelerated. Whereas in previous generations a scientist often had dedicated himself to producing a life work, now, with so many more scientists, pressures accumulated to report findings quickly. "Firsts" took on a new and important character, and individual competitions imperceptibly metamorphosed into national competitions. Governments subsidized scientific activities. We know from first-hand experience with American and Russian space activities the emotions that result from government involvement with science.

In the 1880's, scientists turned to large international congresses in an attempt to create a new international science, but this new mode of communication faced many difficulties. The attempt at internationalization could lead instead to an emphasis on national differences. The progress of individuals was often viewed as the progress of nations. Delegates boasted of their new, government-supported facilities. Deprived of the use of a common language, congresses operated with three official languages (French, German, English) with no facilities for simultaneous or even daily translation. The harmonious dissemination of knowledge sometimes suffered. At the International Congress for Hygiene in 1882, Pasteur used the phrase *recueil allemand* (German collection of papers). Koch thought he had said *orgueil allemand* (German conceit) and interrupted Pasteur's paper (a sensational occurrence at that time) with angry protests (Ellenberger, 1970, p. 269).

For the "official" authorities of a particular scientific field to lend the weight of their support or acceptance to a new theory took on added meaning with nationalistic implications. The reputation of a whole group of people was now at stake rather than just the reputation of one person. There was an awareness that a group of specialists was inevitably ranked vis-à-vis their counterparts in other countries. Ziehen, for example, felt the weight of this pressure when he refused discussion of Abraham's paper because foreign physicians were present. German psychiatrists were most desirous of finally finding an honored place in Western medicine.

German medical resistance to psychoanalysis also stemmed from the stubborn loyalties individual psychotherapists of repute had for their own brands of psychotherapy. To these men Freud was a competitor and interloper. Thus Vogt, author of "causal analysis," bitterly attacked psychoanalysis. The Swiss Dubois, champion of "rational therapeutics" and "moral orthopedics," also entered the fray against Freud. Ottomar Rosenbach, originator of *Psychagogik*, another therapy based on persuasion, studiously ignored psychoanalysis.

At the other extreme, psychoanalysis drew the venom of the psychiatric nihilists. Analysis was a convenient target for the sallies of men like Alfred Hoche, who delighted in criticism of all psychiatric efforts.

Even those few perceptive men who immediately saw that Freud's discoveries were fundamental to psychiatric progress refused to commit themselves completely as disciples. These were brilliant young psychiatrists who had already begun to stake out a future for themselves. Men like Bleuler, Jung, and Bloch had interests prior to psychoanalysis and continued to give primacy to their original concerns. Psychoanalytic theories could play an important role in their work, but there was more to psychiatry than psychoanalysis, and these physicians insisted on an eclectic approach. They were never prepared to devote themselves single-mindedly to psychoanalysis. In spite of their enthusiasm for psychoanalysis, hesitations and doubts appeared in their support of Freud from the very start.[2]

Naturally, most doctors, since they were doctors and performed their jobs by treating individual patients, had no quarrel with Freud's individual approach to the treatment of human malfunction. Critics who believed mental disease could be cured only by changing society tended to be laymen and, later, Marxists. Even in this early period, however, Hellpach considered the individual treatment of hysteria only "palliative." This criticism reflected Hellpach's sociological orientation. In a sense, it foreshadowed the determined but futile attempts of psychoanalysts who were also socialists to reconcile psychoanalysis and Marxism. Hellpach's criticism was also a harbinger of some modern critiques of psychoanaly-

---

[2] The story of the Jung-Freud break and Jung's founding of his own school of psychoanalysis is, of course, vastly complicated. (See Stepansky [1976] for a recent interpretation.) But, temporally, it occurred several years after the period under discussion, and topically has no real place in this book. Through 1907, Jung's position on psychoanalysis was pretty much as described. Though Bleuler never founded a separate school, he and Freud performed a complex *pas de deux* until Bleuler bowed out in 1911. Bleuler's defection can be traced in part to the pressures from Freud and the Swiss psychoanalysts that he accept all of psychoanalysis, which Bleuler was most reluctant to do. Bloch had strong sociological and anthropological interests that were in heavy competition with his medical work.

sis which condemn the essentially conservative nature of analysis, i.e., its attempt to make the individual fit into society as it is currently constructed.

THE PROVOCATIVE BEHAVIOR OF THE PSYCHOANALYSTS

Rejection of psychoanalysis for whatever reason did not always initiate with the critic. Sometimes it was created or intensified by the manner in which the early analysts replied to attack. This became grossly apparent in the years immediately before World War I when a psychoanalytic *movement* sprang into being, replete with international congresses and its own journals and yearbooks. These gave the analysts a greater feeling of beleaguered brotherhood as well as sympathetic platforms from which to declaim and publish statements of fervent faith in their new science and its expected triumph.[3]

Freud (1914, pp. 23-24; 1925, pp. 49-50) himself had a typical response to criticism, which was to regard all of it as identical to the "emotional resistances" psychoanalysts encountered in their patients. This led him to view his critics as somewhat recalcitrant patients rather than as professional equals (Jones, 1955, p. 124). It is difficult to assess precisely the effect this view had on his opponents. Undeniably, however, Freud's attitude was provocative, especially since he manifested it by refusing to engage in debate with his critics, even though at times they asked him directly to answer their objections.[4]

---

[3] The editorial board of the *Zentralblatt für Psychoanalyse* (1911, pp. 531-534) published greetings (presumably written by Stekel) to the Third International Psychoanalytic Congress: For the third time the followers of psychoanalysis were gathering "to strengthen themselves in the conviction that they are on the right path. . . . Every one of us stands against a world of antagonists; each must hold his ground against the scorn and mockery of the enemy and must support his conviction with difficult idealistic and sometimes even material sacrifice. *We know that the future belongs to us.*

"We can exclaim: 'La verité est en march!' We feel on this festival day like brothers of an order which demands from each individual sacrifice in the service of all."

[4] Moreover, Freud seemed unaware that in dismissing criticism as invalid because it was "emotional resistance," he was being logically inconsistent. When his theories were attacked, he comfortably rejected the attacks as "neurotic." He thereby used the hypotheses under dispute to prove his opponents were wrong, i.e.,

The appropriateness of Freud's response is a complex matter. Obviously, it was not usual scientific behavior, and his silence was an ill-concealed sign of disrespect toward his medical colleagues. Yet in many cases it was entirely justified. Undoubtedly a large number of attacks on psychoanalysis were rationalizations of unconscious conflicts aroused in the attackers by psychoanalytic theories. Thus trying to convince critics with papers at meetings and articles in journals would have had little or no effect. (There is, of course, the entirely separate issue of what refusal to debate meant for the dissemination of psychoanalytic ideas.) Strictly from the viewpoint of the reception of psychoanalysis, however, it must be noted that Freud's attitude, where known, may have been extremely irritating, and that his obdurate silence may have increased the hostility of his opponents.

Some supporters of Freud, like Sadger, went as far as to say that no one could call himself a psychologist or psychiatrist unless he practiced psychoanalysis. Sometimes a religious fervor crept into the Freudians' statements: they had discovered the Truth and someday the world would believe as they. Meanwhile, all who did not recognize psychoanalysis completely were misguided—if not worse. This defensive posture of the early analysts is quite understandable, and their besieged position even calls forth our sympathy. Nevertheless, under the stress of attack, Freud's supporters responded with arguments that only elicited even greater antagonism.

They heightened that antagonism by rejecting the interest and support of physicians who were willing to accept only part of the psychoanalytic corpus. Leonhard Seif (1911), the Munich analyst, reported in 1910 to the International Society for Medical Psychology and Psychotherapy that the psychoanalytic method was a unified, "closed" whole, out of which one could not tear out parts without essentially changing that whole. Anyone was free to accept or reject this whole. Seif's view stemmed from Freud's belief that any temporary com-

the opponents did not see the virtues of psychoanalysis because they were "ill"—suffering from the very neuroses psychoanalysis was elucidating. Yet obviously one cannot invalidate a criticism of a theory by using that theory as part of the invalidation.

promises would lead to eventual dilution of his thought. Freud was also against popularization on these grounds. He wrote to Abraham in 1908:

> The Charlottenburg endemic is priceless. [Abraham had written to Freud about "a strange endemic cluster of Freudians" at a secondary school in Charlottenburg.] There seems to be a similar centre of infection in Munich [in the suburb of Schwabing, involving the analyst and social revolutionary Otto Gross], and it seems to have affected the craziest artists and people of that kind. No doubt one day there will be a great deal of noise, if the appropriate impulse is given. But that is nothing to look forward to. Every theory sacrifices something valuable when it becomes popular [H. C. Abraham and Freud, 1965, p. 64].

This meant that, in whatever direction they moved, the early Freudians lost. Concessions would bring friends but would lead to a corruption of theory and a break in the momentum of their mission to give psychoanalysis to the world. When Abraham was preparing to open his practice in Berlin, Freud cautioned him: "I hope you will make no attempt whatever to win the favour of your new colleagues who are primarily like those everywhere else and then a whole lot more brutal on top of it, but will instead turn directly to the public" (H. C. Abraham and Freud, 1965, pp. 9-10). Rebuffing all but "true believers" would keep support at a minimum, but would preserve psychoanalysis intact and in the end make it an even more impressive body of knowledge that would eventually win converts because the strength of its evidence would be overpowering. The Freudians chose the latter course of action. At the 1911 International Psychoanalytic Congress, Jung in his presidential address reminded his colleagues that the goal of the International Psychoanalytic Association was to disavow "wild" psychoanalysis "and not to bear with it." Psychoanalysts should not worry about appearing dogmatic, "even though our enemies say it of us" (*Zentralblatt für Psychoanalyse,* 1912, p. 234). Thus, psychoanalysts lost potential supporters, made more enemies, and increased the already great atmosphere of ill will with which they were surrounded. Freud's personal idiosyncrasies about attracting pupils did not help matters either.

The medical rejection of two of Freud's early hypotheses ultimately proved to have been justified. Freud (1905d, p. 190; 1906a) amended his original belief, that an actual sexual experience had occurred in the childhood of his patients, to the more discerning conclusion that in many cases the sexual experience had been only fantasied or wished. Of course, the significance for the etiology of neurosis was the same. Still, the distinction is an important one, and Freud's error justified those of his critics who had reproached him for taking at face value the statements of severely neurotic patients.

Freud also abandoned his explanation of anxiety neurosis as the direct outcome of sexual frustration. Instead, he developed in the twenties the much more plausible and sophisticated hypothesis of anxiety as a signal. In addition, most modern pyschoanalysts have dismissed Freud's theory of dammed-up libido as simplistic, and view it as a relic of nineteenth-century mechanistic science. The clinical judgment of Löwenfeld, Bloch, Oppenheim, and Aschaffenburg, who seventy years ago expressed reservations about the theory of anxiety neurosis, has been proved correct in this instance.

SEXUAL PREJUDICES AND PERSONAL RESISTANCES

The last several chapters have shown that psychoanalysis was rebuffed by German physicians for a wide variety of reasons. And deeply embedded in the medical rejection of psychoanalysis there was always the issue of sexuality. Although psychoanalysis was not always attacked with vituperation, the worst attacks were usually against Freud's sexual views. For a minority of German psychiatrists and neurologists the challenge posed by the issue of sexuality was absolutely and completely insuperable. It was the frightening chasm they could not even approach. This fear issued forth as emotional and violent attacks on all aspects of psychoanalysis: its theory of normal psychic development, its explanation of psychopathology, and its method.

But for most German physicians, Freud's sexual theories were not so much unbridgeable abysses as giant stumbling blocks. The most consistent complaint of the majority was that Freud had gone "too far." Sex *was* important, they agreed, but Freud had definitely overreached himself about the significance of sexual matters. Having denounced Freud for this error, psychiatrists felt free to accept other teachings of psychoanalysis: the significance of dreams and of the unconscious, the mechanism of conversion, or the psychic etiology of hysteria, obsessional neurosis, and anxiety neurosis. Traditionally, psychoanalysts have insisted that those who take out of psychoanalysis for their use only certain elements are really wholly antianalytic, since all parts of psychoanalysis are inseparably interrelated. This is an untenable view. Rejection of the sexual hypothesis of psychoanalysis played a large and important role in the way German physicians reacted to psychoanalysis. but because it was so pervasive, the historian cannot ignore in what ways psychoanalysis was accepted or conclude that partial rejection was identical with total rejection.

It is also self-defeating, for the purposes of reconstructing the past, to assume that all conventional historical or sociological explanations of hostility toward psychoanalysis are merely rationalized manifestations of inner, personal resistances. Not that the reception of Freudian theory lacked intellectual "cover-ups" for unconsciously felt opposition! How else to explain the strange criticisms by Hellpach, Löwenfeld, and Strümpell that maybe Freud could do psychoanalysis, but no one else could? Or the continual charge that Freud's cures could not be due to any validity of his method but merely to the power of suggestion? The frequent vacillations and ambivalence of supporters as well as attackers demand more than conventional historical explanations. The tortuous and involved arguments indulged in by men like Hellpach are testaments to the fact that German psychiatrists did not always react to psychoanalysis on the grounds of cold logic. There are innumerable examples of such "resistances." But "resistances" cannot ultimately be the entire explanation for whole episodes of human history. Neither can it be accurate to conclude that only one *real* cause—in this instance Victorian sexual morality—underlay the medical rejection of psychoanalysis in Germany at the turn of the century. The interplay of professional burdens and philosophical convictions that prompted Ziehen's change from benevolent neutrality to outspoken hostility is a telling reminder of the complexities of motivation.

PART II

THE NEW PSYCHOLOGISTS
AND PSYCHOANALYSIS

7

THE "NEW" PSYCHOLOGY
AND THE CONSCIOUS

> *We look upon . . . psychology as
> the study of the contents of con-
> sciousness. Indeed it seems to us
> so much a matter of course to
> equate them in this way that any
> contradiction of the idea strikes
> us as obvious nonsense.*
> —Freud, *Introductory Lec-
> tures on Psycho-Analysis*

Physicians' responses to psychoanalysis corresponded to their exposure to psychoanalytic ideas. Moreover, the medical reaction to psychoanalysis was not limited to reviews, but was expressed in monographs, texts, and to a lesser extent at medical meetings and congresses. This was not so in the case of the German experimental psychologists. A great imbalance existed between the psychologists' early exposure to psychoanalysis and their reaction to it. Freud's works were consistently reviewed in the leading experimental psychology journal, but—with only a few exceptions—his ideas were not discussed in the texts, monographs, or at meetings. Psychoanalytic ideas were not accorded any extensive consideration, in spite of the psychologists' awareness of their existence, because of the great difference in the theoretical concerns and dominant interests of the psychologists and the early psychoanalysts. In this chapter I describe these differences and indicate their extent. In so doing, I raise the question: "What is science?" In Chapter 8 I then evaluate the actual response of psychologists to psychoanalysis.

THE RISE OF SCIENTIFIC PSYCHOLOGY

The same positivistic and materialistic influences which affected German psychiatry in the second half of the nineteenth century also affected German psychology. As psychiatry allied itself with neurology, psychology associated itself with physiology. The "new" psychology after 1850 was "*experimentelle Psychologie*," the phrase coined by Wilhelm Wundt (1832-1920) to indicate the dissociation of psychology from philosophy. In his Heidelberg lectures of 1862, Wundt told his students he was going to teach them about psychology "from the standpoint of natural science."

Like the late nineteenth-century psychiatrists who depreciated the work of their predecessors, the new psychologists dismissed earlier conceptions of psychology. Freud's teacher, the psychiatrist Meynert, had declared that psychiatry could no longer be defined as "treatment of the soul." So Gustav Störring (1860-1946), an early experimental psychopathologist, rejected the definition of psychology as "the science of the soul" (Störring, 1907, p. 1).

The psychologists went even further than the physicians in dismissing their past. Even psychologists who had prepared the way for psychology to become "scientific" were denounced because some of their writings were "theoretical" and not in accord with "experience." Significantly, it was often just those ideas of the older psychologists-philosophers which the psychoanalysts had come to share that the new psychologists found "metaphysical." Thus Oswald Külpe (1862-1915), one of Wundt's followers, did not recognize the psychologist F. E. Beneke (1798-1854) for his empiricism and antinativism. Rather, Külpe (1893, p. 25) chided Beneke for his "theoretical" discussions of the unconscious, which eschewed "exactness and logical coherence."

J. F. Herbart (1776-1841) was the first to have a dynamic conception of the mind and to believe in the "repression" of ideas. Not only could one idea drive another out of consciousness, but the repressed idea could then influence conscious thought. We know that Freud, while a high school student, read a textbook of Herbartian psychology published by G. A. Lindner in 1858 (Jones, 1953, p. 374). Herbart, who had been an associationist, a critic of traditional faculty psychology, and had attempted to express certain observations in mathematical formulas, received little appreciation from Wundt.

Wundt related that Herbart had gone "so far as to declare that the idea, when once it has arisen, is imperishable, [and that] all the other elements of mind—feelings, emotions, impulses—are merely the resultants of the momentary interactions of ideas." Clearly, Herbart's "opinions . . . rest[ed] upon no better foundation than hypothesis, and [were] at every point, in conflict with an exact analysis of experience" (1902, p. 26). Wundt further criticized Herbart for saying that the reproduction of earlier, pre-existing ideas proves the existence of unconscious psychic contents. To Wundt it was evident that "the assumption that ideas reappear *unchanged* is completely contradictory to experience . . . ideas cannot endure unchanged . . . every seeming reappearance is really a *new* ideational process" (1903, p. 327). Külpe (1893, pp. 24-25) criticized Herbart's conception of ideas as forces which reinforce or inhibit each other, and summed up Herbart's contribution with the same double-edged word that came to be by far the most often used to evaluate Freud's theories: "ingenious."

The rejection of the psychology of the past was one aspect of the positivistic strivings of the psychologists. The other was their desire to turn psychology into an experimental science and relate the mind to the brain by means of the concept of cerebral localization (Young, 1970, p. 3). The ontological and epistemological speculations of prenineteenth century psychologists were discarded. Separate chairs of psychology were created. Laboratories with instruments for measuring and quantifying information about the senses were set up wherever space could be found; the first laboratory was the one Wundt opened in Leipzig in 1879. The methods of the already acknowledged scientific disciplines were applied to the study of the mind and behavior. Wundt thus evolved a physiological psychology which he and his pupils described as being based on an indissoluble combination of "introspection" and "experimentation." The new method was the grafting of the experimental methods of physiology onto the centuries-old observational and logical methods of the philosophical psychologists. Wundt—soon followed by dozens of other psychologists—decreed that introspection could never be scientific if it was not linked with experimentation.

In introspection the investigator has an experience and describes how he perceived it, felt about it, reacted to it. It is a self-observation of one's mind or mental capacities. Reflecting on his mental experiences, a person forms a notion of what his mind can do. He then compares notes with other observers, learns that they have similar experiences upon similar occasions, and on these bases makes some generalizations about human minds. But this kind of describing and classifying by itself, said Wundt, could not make psychology a truly empirical science. One was still faced with the subjective nature of one's own observations, as well as with the obstacles of studying any mind other than one's own. Introspection had been conscientiously carried out for hundreds of years, and psychology had remained part of philosophy.

What psychology needed, said Wundt (1901, pp. 23-28), was "exact" observation, and this physiological psychology could supply through its method of "*experimental*" observation. "*Pure observation*" was "impossible" in studying the psychology of the individual. The only time pure observation could be used was in social psychology, which field Wundt did not believe was accessible to any kind of experimentation. Wundt (1902, p. 8) condemned the unscientific quality of all psychologies, past and present, that did not rely on physiology. Physiology and psychology were "interdependent"; that is why Wundt had entitled his work a "physiological psychology." He took issue "with every treatment of psychology that is based on simple self-observation or on philosophical presuppositions. . . . The supreme advantage of the experimental method lies in the fact that it and it alone renders a reliable introspection possible."

According to such definitions, psychoanalysis was not scientific. Wundt was most blunt:

> Sometimes—as in the great majority of books of the kind emanating from the Herbartian School—certain hypotheses of metaphysical origin are put forward as results of self-observation. It has been said that if a prize were offered for the discovery by this whole introspective school of one single indisputable fact, it would be offered in vain. Nevertheless, the assurance of the Herbartians is incredible. Their compendia appear, one after another, and the memory of the students who use them [of whom Freud was one] is burdened with a mixed medley of purely imaginary processes [Wundt, 1902, p. 8].

What the method of experimental observation meant in practice was the application of the new psychologists' talents and energies to learning about sensation and perception with the use of precise measuring instruments. The workers at the Leipzig laboratory, for example, were overwhelmingly concerned with the quantitative relations between stimulus and sensation. At first, as a direct offshoot of Helmholtz's work in optics, the sense of vision claimed the greatest attention. Then they dealt with hearing and later with touch. Their work with touch and vision led them to investigate space perception. Eventually they carried out experiments on time, word association, and attention. The results of the Leipzig experiments appeared from 1881 to 1903 in Wundt's journal, *Philosophische Studien*. In 1893, the year of Breuer and Freud's "Preliminary Communication," the first one-volume systematic presentation of the experimental work was published by Külpe in text form.

The psychologists became scientific—and with great success, too—in studying human functions by controlled experiments, the results of which were expressed in mathematical equations. In the tradition of basic science, and impelled by the enthusiasm of being the "new" psychology, the experimentalists longed to test every aspect of human perception. Külpe (1893, p. 2) joyfully proclaimed: "There is no single fact of experience which cannot be made the subject of psychological investigation." To accumulate information, to formulate relationships, to know more—these were goals in themselves. The pure scientist need not question to what end he labors. Human curiosity and the future are his justifications.

Yet the physiological psychologists were ensnared by their method. Every new discipline must begin by devising methods to solve pertinent questions. The new psychologists chose the methods of physiology but did not frame the overriding questions for which they desired answers. The object of their investigations became subordinated to their methods. They did not first pose a vital problem in human behavior and then seek suitable methods to answer it. In the gathering of quantities of data by exact introspection, the experimental psychologists were analogous to the contemporary brain anatomists. The psychologist followed the Pied Piper of "scientific progress" and ignored the pleas of any "philosophy." For to consider to what purpose information was being collected was to court metaphysics and be open to the damning charge of speculation. Not only was the interrelationship of various sensory perceptions not considered, but the age-old psychological questions were no longer the subject matter of psychology: What motivates a human being? Why does one person act differently from another? Why do people make the choices they do? In short, why does a person act as he does? The psychologists lost a conception of the human being as a highly intricate organism and found one in which he could be reduced to the study of his isolated parts. William James was one contemporary who recognized this characteristic of German laboratory experimental psychology by calling it the "brass-instrument" psychology. He believed that the laboratory method tended to become the dissection of dead minds (Murphy, 1949, p. 193).[1]

---

[1] This was not the first time in the history of psychology that subject matter and goals had taken second place to what Peters (1953, pp. 325-336) has called "dogmatic methodism — the view that success in science is the result of following a definite method." Both Francis Bacon and René Descartes succumbed to "the [misguided] belief in the magic of technique . . . of the physical sciences" because they had just broken with "traditional ways of thought and action. . . . The infiltration of other sciences into psychology is healthy in so far as it shows that the separation between the sciences is quite arbitrary but dangerous in so far as it derives from dogmatic methodism."

The tenacity with which psychology clung to its belief in the experimental method as the only acceptable one was not solely a function of the *Zeitgeist*. It can also be attributed to the longevity and personality of Wundt, a man whose influence carried the scientific ideas of the mid-nineteenth century into the first two decades of the twentieth. Wundt brooked no oppostion and overwhelmed dissenters "with a horde of facts, arguments and dicta" (Boring, 1950, p. 390). Wundt did not originate the experimental movement with which his name is inextricably linked. The empirical spirit predated his career, having come to flower in the work of Helmholtz. But Wundt had immense prestige, and his experimentalism embodied the powerful culmination of a vital scientific trend of more than half a century (Murphy, 1949, p. 159, p. 160 fn.).

Part of the scientific value of the use of experimental technique lay in the fact that the work of the new psychologist could be verified by others. Replication of results is, of course, crucial to the progress of a laboratory science, which the new psychology had defined itself as being. The intuitive conclusions of the psychological "loner" were therefore mistrusted. In his book on German experimental psychology, Ribot (1885) admitted that "internal observation is, without doubt, the first step"; but, he went on, "it cannot be a method. [Moreover] subtilty [*sic*] of spirit is also too fragile an instrument to penetrate the compact and serrated line of the facts of consciousness." Relying only on his own observation and sensitivity,

> the psychologist becomes a romancer, a poet of an especial kind. . . . Psychology becomes a kind of literary criticism, very penetrating and acute, but nothing more. . . . In this refinement of subtleties, always increasing, we reach at last symbols only; all reality has disappeared. . . . This abuse of the subjective method and the reasoning powers paralyze the best minds. . . . Too much reasoning: this is the impression that the old psychology makes upon the disciples of the new [pp. 3,5].

Ribot scorned the very phenomena psychoanalysis relied upon: the analyst's intuition, his attention to subtleties and to symbolism, and his reasoning based upon them.

The new psychology strove to join the scientific movement of the day in other ways besides the use of experimental technique. One way was the creation of an exact terminology. This was especially significant for the psychologists' receptiveness to the psychological writing of those who were not in the profession. Wundt developed a precise vocabulary for the use by the new psychology. He showed consciousness to be an extremely complicated subject. The process of becoming conscious of an object was different from the actual appearance of the pictorial image of an object; this needed to be accurately described. Wundt also sought to show that there were many states of consciousness, and he distinguished an increasingly large number of types which were in turn broken up into special, subordinate groups. The loose or incorrect use of words like *Empfindung* (sensation), *Wahrnehmung* (perception), *Vorstellung* (idea or image), *Begriff* (concept), *einfache Gefühle* (feelings), *Gemütsbewegungen* or *Affekte* (emotions), and *Willensvorgänge* (will) was no slight matter to the experimental psychologist. It is therefore significant to note that Freud himself was not well acquainted with the works and concerns of the experimental psychologists. He seems to have derived only from hearsay the knowledge he had of them and freely admitted his ignorance in this regard. He was careless and imprecise in his use of terms; for example, he used "perception" and "idea" interchangeably (Jones, 1953, p. 371).

To this should be added that Freud was both publicly and privately critical of the academic psychology of his day. In a talk (1906b, p. 104) on the problems involved in arriving at the truth in courtroom proceedings, he declared that the Wundtian word-association experiments had not been fruitful until they were picked up by Bleuler and Jung. In a 1907 letter to Abraham, Freud condemned current psychology as "surface psychology" (H. C. Abraham and Freud, 1965, p. 12).

For many years there was a great gulf between the academic psychologists and Freud's followers, based in part on the Freudian's lack of knowledge of and respect for contemporaneous psychological developments. "Freud's followers were partly defensive [about psychoanalysis] and partly disdainful toward 'scholarship,' and certainly unfamiliar with its canons and prejudices" (Shakow and Rapaport, 1964, p. 82).

The psychologists were quickly irked by the analysts' loose

terminology, and their disdain was obvious. Or perhaps the analysts' imprecision was only a convenient excuse for the psychologists to dismiss psychoanalysis. At any rate, in his review of Jung and Riklin's work on word associations, the psychologist Messmer made no comments about the authors' praise of Freud or their discussion of the unconscious. Instead he focused on the sloppy phraseology in Bleuler's introduction to the *Diagnostische Assoziationsstudien*. Sometimes, Messmer (1904) pointed out, Bleuler correctly defined association as "a basic phenomenon of psychic activity. . . . But sometimes its nature is falsely identified with thinking." Messner wished to inform Bleuler that there is a sharp distinction between "associative and logical events." The reviewer concluded loftily: "One ought to view the psychological attempts of psychiatrists with interest. The usefulness of psychological experimentation is best demonstrated in light of such attempts."

PSYCHOPHYSICAL PARALLELISM AND CEREBRAL LOCALIZATION

The new psychology sought not only a methodological identification with the natural sciences but a theoretical orientation as well. By far the most significant theoretical influences on psychology from 1860 to 1910 were neurology and neurophysiology. The psychological theories of learning and the theory of associations were greatly revised as a result of the enunciation of the neuron theory: nerve cells are anatomically independent but physiologically interconnected at points of junction (synapses). Neurological explanations of how reflexes were facilitated or inhibited proved very useful to psychologists. The preoccupation of physiology (among other scientific disciplines) with formulating universal laws as opposed to studying individual differences was also taken over by psychology. And especially important for the reception of psychoanalysis was the particular cast Wundt placed on the theory of psychophysical parallelism in which he was influenced by theories of cerebral localization.

Like all psychologists (and philosophers) before him, Wundt was faced with the problem of defining the relationship between mind and body. His solution, and that of many contemporaries, including Freud, was to adopt the seventeenth-century theory of psychophysical parallelism, which was a response to some of the difficulties of Descartes's dualism. Psychophysical parallelism is itself a dualism, one in which the body and mind exist as separate entities without ever interacting. This theory holds that there is not a causal but a "parallel" relationship between physical and mental phenomena. Wundt thought of matter as having a closed system of causality "which cannot affect the mind or be affected by it. One may get . . . the appearance of interaction, as in the case of sensation where nervous stimulation seems to give rise to sensory experience, but it is only an appearance." What happens is that "identical conditions give rise to both physical and psychical processes," but the processes are only concurrent; they are "neither identical nor causally related to each other" (Boring, 1950, p. 333).

About such psychophysical parallelism, Külpe (1893, p. 4) wrote bravely in his text: "This regulative principle is based upon experience, and we may expect that it will receive further confirmation from experience in the future." Külpe (pp. 6-7) concluded that one day psychologists expect to discover a causal connection between experiences and certain bodily processes, and the not yet exactly known excitations in the cerebral cortex.

A theory like psychophysical parallelism, is , of course, good for most men and most seasons: by not committing its adherents to a definitive statement on the mind-body relationship, it gives each parallelist the freedom to interpret it in a way that is suitable to his scientific proclivities. Freud was a parallelist. Yet he was the proponent of the conversion theory of hysteria, seemingly an interactionist theory—though Freud did admit that how it worked was "a mystery." He also held monistic conceptions of disease and knowledge.

But the theory of psychophysical parallelism is compatible with entirely different theoretical positions which contradict psychoanalytic hypotheses. For one thing, strict parallelism is philosophically opposed to psychoanalysis because it sees no possibility of real interaction between mind and body, an interaction Freud worked with in a practical way even though he eschewed it theoretically. Freud strove continually for a synthetic explanation of the human "mind." As far as Wundt (1902, p. 17) was concerned, however, "there is here involved a metaphysical presupposition, which psychology may possibly be led to honour at the conclusion of her work, but which she cannot on any account accept, untested before she has entered upon it." What Freud was attempting was something that for Wundt lay far in the future and for which at the present only the building blocks existed.

Moreover, parallelism had the effect of encouraging a practical, if not theoretical, belief in the importance of physical centers for psychic acts. *Theoretically*, there was no belief that physical events cause mental ones. That was merely an appearance. Strictly speaking, what happened was that the identical conditions gave rise to *both* physical and psychical processes. The processes were only concurrent; they were not causally related. Practically, it was very hard to maintain this view under the pressures of the physiological discoveries of cerebral localization, beginning especially with the demonstration in 1870 by two young German physicians, Fritsch and Hitzig, that one part of the cerebral hemisphere of a dog's brain controls motor function. The Fritsch-Hitzig experiment established that the cerebral cortex could be stimulated electrically, showed that the cortex plays a role in the mechanism of movements, and established cerebral localization. The two physicians discovered five cortical "centers" which, when stimulated, affected certain neck and leg muscles and the facial nerve. Portentously, Fritsch and Hitzig closed their paper by saying that "some psychological functions and perhaps all of them, in order to enter matter or originate from it need certain circumscribed centers of the cortex." Fritsch and Hitzig "were prepared to localize at least some of the functions of the soul" (Young, 1970, p. 232).

The "epoch-making" experiment was soon replicated, and physiologists reported favorably. Excitement grew in the physiological articles and texts of the 1870's, '80's, and '90's (Young, 1970, p. 234). The principle of cerebral localization provided a paradigm for the searching for centers and, with more precise techniques, researchers were able to discover cerebral areas related to sensation.

The new psychologists leaped to a belief in the cerebral localization of particular states of consciousness as a result of their and the physiologists' ascertaining the localization of sensations in the cerebral cortex. Large amounts of specific information were gathered about the localization of color vision, sound, smell, taste, heat, cold, touch, pain, sense of motion and sense of balance, and visceral sensations. These successful accomplishments of sensory physiology and psychology, which determined the physiological correlates of sensation, encouraged the search for specific centers of "higher" psychic experiences. The parts of the brain were supposed to have their separate functions and their specific energies to which isolated elements of consciousness were supposed to correspond. "The ideal aim was to prove the existence of a single brain cell for every image or idea" (Müller-Freienfehls, 1935, p. 164). The psychologists tried to find separate areas in the brain for various images, feelings, and acts of thought and will. Even single ideas were ascribed to their own cells, in which they were supposed to be "deposited." Many psychologists computed from the number of existent brain cells the possible number of ideas that a normal person could form. In accordance with the principle of localization, Wundt tried to localize apperception and discovered a "center of apperception" in the frontal brain, though he did recognize that his physiological theory of apperception was hypothetical (Müller-Freienfehls, 1935, pp. 163-177).[2]

Külpe (1893, pp. 216-217) admitted that there were "spontaneous" ideas whose appearance he was unable to explain, since they were "distinguished from other reproductions by the absence of a conscious incentive to their arousal." Moreover, the psychological literature of the last decades had been "overwhelmed . . . with cases of pathological derangement of memory, association and reproduction." Yet the only possible interpretation of these events was "physiological." If not, "we shall be compelled either to give up the facts as enigmatical,

---

[2] Though correctly condemning the experimentalists' flights of fancy, Müller-Freienfehls heaped too much scorn on their activities, failing to recognize the nature of their professional aspirations.

or to take refuge in metaphysics or mysticism. In neither event is justice done to the scientific problem."

Although Wundt and Freud were both psychophysical parallelists, physiological psychology had in practice come to champion the primacy of physical causation of psychic events and was incompatible with psychoanalysis, which in practice stressed the primacy of psychic etiology.

THE HEGEMONY OF CONSCIOUS PROCESSES

The psychologists had several basic commitments which were fundamentally at odds with those of psychoanalysts. The most important was their preoccupation with consciousness and their hostility toward the concept of an unconscious. Ziehen, who eventually abandoned medicine for philosophy and psychology, wrote that "the attributes of our consciousness and *only* these, have psychological significance." (Müller-Freienfehls, 1935, p. 35). By this he meant two things. One was the renunciation of all research that probes behind consciousness either for a material soul or for a psychic force. The other was the assertion that it was just this consciousness which could be the only firm foundation for the erection of a scientific psychology. These two assumptions, one negative, the other positive, were explicitly stated over and over again, either alone or in combination with the belief in the *primacy* of laboratory work in psychological investigation.

Wundt (1901, pp. 223, 227-228) dismissed the views of psychologists who believed in the existence of an unconscious. He would go no further than acknowledging the obvious fact that psychic contents could disappear from consciousness. This was

> continually taking place in the flow of mental processes. Complex ideas and feelings and even single elements of these compounds may disappear,[3] and new ones take their places. Any psychical element that has disappeared from consciousness is to be called *unconscious* in the sense that we assume the possibility of its renewal, that is, its reappearance in the actual interconnection of psychical processes.

[3] Wundt meant this literally; he never said where they disappeared to or why they went.

But once out of the conscious, a psychic element lost all significance.

> Our knowledge about an element that has become unconscious does not extend beyond this possibility of its renewal. For psychology, therefore, it has no meaning. . . . Assumptions as to the state of the "unconscious" or as to "unconscious processes" of any kind which are thought of as existing along with the conscious processes of experience, are entirely unproductive for psychology.

In accord with these principles, Wundt criticized the famous Munich psychologist Theodor Lipps (1851-1914), who believed that unconsciousness mental processes exist side by side with conscious ones, and that these unconscious processes underlie and accompany all conscious ones (Lipps, 1903, p. 39).[4] Wundt (1903, p. 237) countered that, in reality, it is not a matter of unconscious but only of *dimly perceived conscious* (Wundt's italics) psychic elements. Wundt, as was noted earlier, also attacked Herbart's belief in an unconscious. Wundt concluded that a psychologist could not accept that ideas operate out of an unconscious background of psychic phenomena, from which memories of earlier impressions reenter the consciousness, or that memories could affect consciousness without crossing over the threshold of consciousness. But, he said, "this is, in general, the popular conception of the matter, and is still rather widespread in psychology" (Wundt, 1903, p. 117).

---

[4] Lipps was primarily an esthetician and not an experimental psychologist. In 1896, at the Third International Congress of Psychology, he read a paper in which he said that our conscious life is largely dominated by unconscious representations (Ellenberger, 1970, p. 774). Yet even Lipps did not believe that the study of the unconscious was a job for psychology. He defined psychology as the science of the contents of consciousness or conscious experiences as such (1903, p. 1). From the other side, Lipps was criticized by Ernst Kris (Freud, 1887-1902, pp. 260-261 fn.) for holding a "romantic" view of the unconscious, not at all in accord with Freud's. Freud (1887-1902, pp. 261, 262, 267), however, did not dismiss Lipps as lightly as Kris later did. A great deal of attention has been paid to what Lipps said or did not say about the unconscious (Hellpach — who did not believe in an unconscious — also quoted him approvingly), but nobody seems to have noticed his basically ambiguous position: "The concept of unconscious feelings and ideas is only a supplementary — albeit a necessary — one; this concept is the establishment of a qualitative phenomenon, in itself completely uncertain, in order to plug the causal gaps in explaining psychic phenomena" (Lipps, 1903, p. 39).

Külpe (1893, pp. 1, 3), the first of Wundt's pupils to write a readable scientific text, agreed with his teacher in all the essentials. Psychology deals only with the "facts of experience," not with "reflection on experience." The latter is a subject for philosophy. "Consciousness" or "mind" means only the experiencing that an individual does. "We shall nowhere discuss anything like a 'transcendental consciousness,' a 'substantial soul,' or an 'immaterial spirit.' " Sometimes, Külpe (p. 450) admitted, a case comes along in which an unconscious state seems to exert "a perceptible influence on consciousness. But here we really have a conscious process, whose sole difference from the other conscious processes of the time is its impossibility of separate perception."

Emphasis on the conscious and rejection of the unconscious not only formed the backbone of work on normal psychology but extended to books on abnormal psychology. Psychologists who were also physicians not unnaturally had an interest in psychopathology, and brought to this field their psychological orientation. Hellpach had investigated peripheral vision at Wundt's laboratory in Leipzig, and the dissertation which qualified him to become a university lecturer in psychology was on psychopathology. His theme in the eighty-six-page *Habilitationsschrift* was that "psychopathology is the science of the events of the diseased conscious." The method of psychopathology was the psychological method: psychological observation and psychological experimentation. He believed it "profitable to remove the quarrel about the unconscious completely out of the foundation of psychology..." (Hellpach, 1906b, pp. 10-11, 33-34).

Gustav Störring was another psychologist-physician who had worked with Wundt and later dealt with psychopathology. He gave a well-known series of lectures on psychopathology in the Faculty of Philosophy at the University of Leipzig. When the lectures were published, he dedicated the book to Wundt. Störring (1900, pp. 1-2) defined psychology as *"the science of conscious processes.* Everyone knows what is meant by conscious processes — our thoughts, our feelings, our passions, wishes, desires, and decisions." In his first lecture Störring told his students that "objection has been taken to this definition of psychology on the ground that the science must deal, not only with conscious processes, but also with certain unconscious processes." By definition these latter were not the subject matter of psychology. But certain persons have maintained that " the causal chain of connexion between our conscious processes includes links which are not conscious. . . . Therefore in the attempt to discover the causal relations of the conscious processes with which we have to deal we shall be forced to investigate the connected unconscious processes. The latter are, of course, on this view not subject-matter of psychology in the same sense as conscious processes."

Several lectures later, Störring (pp. 155-161) devoted himself to the issue: Do "unconscious ideas" exist? Or rather, as he believed was a more correct way of phrasing the question: Are there *"unconscious and purely psychological* links in the train of ideas?" (italics mine). Störring thought no. He cited many case reports (including some by well-known figures like Alfred Binet [1857-1911], Janet, and Vogt) that sought to prove the existence of unconscious ideas.[5] On the one hand, Störring told his classes, he was unconvinced because

> I assume that there are present in these cases dimly-conscious ideas [as Wundt had stated in his reply to Lipps] and sensations [rather than] unconscious phenomena . . . it is better to assume such and such dim ideas and not such and such unconscious phenomena because there is no doubt that phenomena of the former kind do *sometimes* occur, whereas it remains to be proved that the latter ever do.

On the other hand, he remained vaguely troubled since

> no one can deny that there sometimes occurs in our minds ideas which do not depend on any clear and distinct contents of consciousness, and at the same time we feel that there is something else there, though we cannot tell what; and now and then this something else afterwards becomes clear and distinct, and confirms our conjecture that it had led to the reproduction of those ideas.

But he brushed away these nagging thoughts because

> there is not a single fact of normal mental life to make us believe that unconscious phenomena can have this reproductive action.

[5] Störring was also very familiar with *Studies on Hysteria* (see Chapter 8).

People are apt to raise the question of the reality of unconscious phenomena in the abstract, instead of asking whether they are real factors or a particular result. For these reasons, then, the hypothesis of dimly conscious psychical states is preferable to that of unconscious links in cases like those we have been discussing, unless and until facts can be indicated which force us to adopt the other view.

In some psychological circles, even Störring's acceptance of dimly conscious ideas was questioned. Reviewing Störring's book in a neo-Kantian philosophical quarterly which was sympathetic to "the interests of the new psychology" (Ribot, 1885, pp. 301-302), a Leipzig colleague maintained: "Of course, the assumption of half-conscious or dimly conscious ideas is likewise very controversial; actually their existence is necessary only if demanded by logical deduction" (Schumann, 1901, p. 128).

THEORIES OF ASSOCIATION, FORCE, DREAMING, AND HYPNOSIS

The experimental psychologists also disagreed with other Freudian theories. Külpe (1893, p. 3) believed there were no inner laws governing the order of ideas. Ideas were not dependent on each other. They came and went "at random; their interconnections are . . . not due to mutual influence, but obviously follow a law imposed upon them from without." The possibility of an infinite number of connected associations could not even be conceived of by Wundt (1901, pp. 260-261). He advised psychology students that "in the great majority of cases [an] association . . . is limited to *two* successive ideational or affective processes. . . . New sense impressions . . . then connect themselves with the second member of the association." Sometimes the original process might lead to a second or third member of an associational series. But when this happened it was usually a pathological sign. It could be seen, for example, in the "so-called 'flight of ideas' of the insane. In normal cases and under ordinary conditions of life, serial associations hardly ever appear." Wundt had read Freud's *On Dreams* by the time he wrote this in 1901, and he reiterated it in 1905 in the seventh edition of his *Outlines* (see Chapter 8). Wundt's and Külpe's conception of associations was diametrically opposed to Freud's and to the analytic method based on it. Wundt's description of association also serves as a reminder of the belief in the dichotomy between sickness and health that pervaded turn-of-the-century thought.

The idea of "energy" also figured largely in Freud's early explanations of psychological mechanisms. The concept of "discharge of affect" is one well-known example of Freud's reliance on ideas of force. But to Wundt (1901, p. 19), this was unscientific thinking at its worst—"a legacy which has come down to modern science from a mythopoeic age." Unfortunately, Wundt wrote, concepts like "sensibility," "feeling," "reason," and "understanding" "have retained a trace of the mythological concept of *force*; they are not regarded simply as—what they really are—class-designations of certain departments of the inner experience, but are often times taken to be forces, by whose means the various phenomena are produced." One example of such "mythopoeic" thinking was to describe memory as a force which stores up ideas for future use.[6] The year after Wundt published this, Freud set forth in "The Neuro-Psychoses of Defence" (1894) how the "memory trace" of a psychic trauma could remain isolated from the rest of the mind and might form the nucleus of a secondary system.

The subsequent development of ideas of energy ("drive theory") in psychoanalytic thought is interesting because it has veered away from Freud's original position, though it has not come around to Wundt's description of "feeling." Freud himself later stopped describing feeling *as a force*, in favor of saying that feeling results from a force, i.e., force being discharged leads to a feeling. This is a slight de-emphasis of the role of energy, though hardly a great step. Some post-Freudian ego psychologists have said that feelings are not forces. but "ego states." In general, in (orthodox) psychoanalysis, there has been a tendency to diminish (though not to drop) the explanatory importance of drive theory and to accentuate the

[6] These remarks on "mind" and "force" are in the fourth edition (1893) of the *Physiologischen Psychologie*, but Wundt dropped them from the fifth edition of 1902-1903. For some reason, however, when E. B. Titchener (1867-1927), Wundt's famous American disciple, translated the fifth edition (1904), he retained these remarks from the fourth edition.

importance of ego factors. To Wundt must be given the credit of caution in the face of limited knowledge; to some extent, time has borne out his criticism.

Freud's explanation of neurotic malfunction depended upon a belief that ideas have emotional equivalents. When ideas are separated from their affects, hysteria or obsessional neurosis can occur. Wundt (1903, p. 514) was emphatically against this conception. Those who believed in the "emotional equivalents of ideas" had "lent support to the mythological concept of the 'unconscious.'" Unhappily, "many psychologists and nonpsychologists" held the latter concept. Although Wundt did not list the names of these persons, by 1903 he had read *On Dreams* and must have been acquainted with *Studies on Hysteria* through Störring and Hellpach, if not directly.

Their belief that there was no unconscious also influenced the new psychologists' discussions of dreams and hypnosis. They saw "conscious processes" as ubiquitous. Külpe (1893, p. 452) pointed out that they even appear in sleep in the form of dreams; he called the state of dreaming "dream consciousness." Contemporary science now understood how dreams arose: "The older theories looked upon [dreams] as the result of a spontaneous ideational activity and attempted to wring some deep meaning from them by all manner of symbolical explanations. The more sober methods of modern inquiry have traced the origin of dreams to the intensive action of external or internal stimuli upon definite sensory centres."

Wundt (1901, pp. 303-307) was, of course, at one with his pupil in his explanation of dreams. Since the ideas in dreams come from sensations, they were "mostly illusions of fancy." Therefore, it was "a *physiological* problem to formulate a theory of sleep, dreams, and hypnosis." That it was a physiological problem was an assumption, but it was one "based on psychological symptoms of an inhibition of activity in certain parts of the cerebral cortex, and increase in the activity of other parts." This presumption seemed the most likely scientific one. Yet often "mystical and fanciful hypotheses" were applied to dreams and hypnoses. One such was that there was increased mental activity in dreams. "In reality all that can stand the light of thorough examination in these phenomena is in general readily explicable on psychological and physiological grounds; what is not applicable in this way has always proved on closer examination to be superstitious self-deception or intentional fraud."

In the minds of most observers, Freud's method was linked with hypnotism because of the many years Freud had actively used hypnosis. Freud's earliest publications told of his use of hypnosis to unearth the etiology of neurotic symptoms. Even after Freud had abandoned reliance on hypnosis, all but those intimately knowledgeable about his work continued to think he was still a hypnotherapist. But the experimental psychologists had only scorn for hypnotism. Wundt (1902, p. 11) commented that "the great majority of what are called 'hypnotic experiments' either possess no scientific value at all, or lead to the observation of interesting but isolated facts, whose place in the psychological system is still unknown."

An American psychologist ran into great problems in his attempt to conduct psychological experiments based on hypnosis in a German laboratory (Martin, 1907). He finally found a place in Külpe's Institute and wrote that "anyone who goes to Europe in order to find a laboratory in which hypnotic experiments are allowed and in which conditions for them are favorable will understand how greatly I am indebted to [Külpe]." But even at Würzburg, the path was not smooth. One of the subjects, an assistant in one of the scientific laboratories at the university, had to be disguised as "Dr. X."

> This experimental subject wished that his name not be mentioned. One can easily understand why someone who works in an exact science makes such a condition. Hypnotism is so little understood and has recently fallen into such great miscredit, especially in Germany, that the fact that someone has allowed himself to be hypnotized, even for scientific reasons, is not calculated to increase his colleagues' esteem of his work.

The American was advised by "a very well-known psychologist" that "there is still enough to do in normal psychology without having to drag in hypnotism" (Martin, 1907, pp. 322, 297).

PROFESSIONAL INSECURITIES

In its theoretical bases, probably in most instances without having Freud specifically in mind, physiological psychology showed itself to be incompatible with psychoanalysis. To this incompatibility can be added the new psychologists' general mistrust of data coming from outside their own field. Külpe admitted that "in certain cases" it was possible to supplement the knowledge derived from psychological methods by "assistance from without." The latter phrase in itself is indicative of a belief that there was little common ground to be shared with "outsiders." But Külpe (1893, pp. 15-16) unambiguously enunciated this feeling. "For the beginnings and foundation of our knowledge of the facts and relations of consciousness we must always have recourse to [psychological] methods, and in particular to a trained and adequately checked introspection. It is but very rarely either necessary or practicable to obtain from any . . . secondary sources information which we could not have acquired in a more direct way."

First of all, Külpe ruled out of bounds a great deal of psychiatry and neurology. As far as "mental diseases" were concerned, "it seems more likely . . . that general psychology may be able to throw some light upon their rise, development, and causes, than that their study will afford any material aid to the student of psychology. The insane are usually incapable of introspection in the scientific sense" (pp. 16-17). Like so many contemporaries, Külpe, too, embraced the creed of the polarity between health and sickness. Furthermore, it was "useless" to examine pathological states whose conditions and symptoms were not "clear and unmistakable" (p. 16). The best illustration of this was the experiments in hypnotism. First of all, hypnosis was dangerous to the subject. Second, psychologists could draw no reliable conclusions from hypnotic experiments because of "the scantiness of our knowledge of the state of consciousness in hypnosis." Rather, hypnotic states and "similar conditions . . . are . . . themselves problems demanding explanation, [and not] the source of any increased knowledge of general psychology" (p. 17).

Second, the science of "psychogenesis" could sometimes be of value in teaching psychologists about the origin of language, the development of memory, and the formation of associations. "But here again, we are met by the difficulty that there is no guarantee of trustworthy and properly directed introspection. This makes inquiry into the psychology of childhood as uncertain as is the psychological study of animals" (Külpe, 1893, p. 17). Hellpach (1902, p. 194), in a *Festschrift* for Wundt's seventieth birthday, did say that psychology played a role in the treatment of nervous disease, but he added that it was a "rather peculiar kind of psychology."

The new psychologists' entrapment by their method is shown not only by Külpe's disparagement of psychogensis for the study of childhood, but by his depreciation of what he called "mental productions." His objections call to mind Alfred North Whitehead's pithy observation that "some of the major disasters of mankind have been produced by the narrowness of men with a good methodology. . . . To set limits to speculation is treason to the future" (Peters, 1953, p. 725). Külpe gave the examples of the study of art, law, and language as being basically unamenable to "the illustration of certain mental connections or relations." By 1907, Freud, of course, had drawn from all three fields in order to support his theories.

The psychologists' desire not to depend upon "assistance from without" was partly a defensive reaction prompted by their very new position in German scientific circles. Though convinced of their own scientific advances and triumphs, the experimentalists did not gain immediate acceptance. Ribot (1885, pp. 8-9, 18, 19, 287) pointed out that, first of all, fellow academicians did not acknowledge the intent of the psychologists to break with philosophy. Try as he might to gain the title of scientist, the psychologist continued to be thought of as a philosopher. Though "metaphysics had lost its crown . . . men continued to treat [psychology] as an illegitimate child of metaphysic [sic]. . . ." (p. 287). "A tradition thus formed is difficult to break" (p. 19). Second, there was the problem of getting trained adherents. Ribot complained that the physiologists knew too little psychology and the psychologists too little physiology. "We live in a period of transition," he explained, "and its difficulties are sufficient to tax the greatest courage" (p. 18). Third, opposition came from within the ranks. Many psychologists who were primarily logicians, estheticians, and moralists argued against the new psychology, saying it was surrendering psychology into the hands of the physiologists (pp. 8-9).

Thus the early experimental psychologists had their problems. When Külpe first came to Würzburg as a full professor in 1894, he had no laboratory. After two years he was given the use of a few rooms in the library. He and a lecturer, Karl Marbe, began to experiment without assistants, staff, or funds. It was only after the government knew that Külpe had declined appointments at Münster and Stanford that he was given state monies for his laboratory. Külpe did not hire his first assistant until 1904 (Revers, 1968, p. 467). It was also hard for the psychologists to find subjects who would put up with what seemed like humiliating and absurd procedures, especially when, as a new science, experimental psychology had little prestige. The experimenters tended to use each other as subjects, and as a result they become a closely knit, somewhat beleaguered group, looked down upon by the philosophers in their department (Flugel, 1933, pp. 153-154).

Indeed, a beleaguered feeling was common to both the psychologists and psychoanalysts at this point in the development of their disciplines. Only as time wore away some of the hypersensitivities of each group did a dialogue between them become possible.

Even more than the contemporary psychiatrists, the new psycholologists were very much concerned with establishing themselves professionally. The resulting situation (as German psychiatry) did not foster great tolerance for new ideas and approaches. The experimentalists were simultaneously defensive and aggressive, a condition implicit in Hermann Ebbinghaus's (1850-1909) remark that "psychology has a long past but only a short history" (1907, p. 173). Indeed, the extent of Ebbinghaus's concern to prove the revolutionary nature of the new psychology and to justify the scientific contribution an "independent" psychology would make is well illustrated in the very article which opens with that oft-quoted statement.[7]

Ebbinghaus's stress on the superiority of a "pure" psychology complemented Külpe's emphasis on the desirability of avoiding "assistance from without." Both positions guarded against any linking of psychology with the "metaphysics" of the past and at the same time sought to proclaim to the world the introduction of a new science, based on a unique method and on a preoccupation with consciousness. Even more than the psychiatry which was its contemporary, the new psychology was on shaky historical ground, eager to prove itself, proud of its achievements, and in no mood to welcome or even acknowledge the contributions of competitors with rival themes.

THE WÜRZBURG SCHOOL

Nowhere is the impossibility of an accord between experimental psychology and psychoanalysis seen more clearly than in the work of the "Würzburg School" of the new psychology. The Würzburg School (c. 1894-1909) was both the logical and extreme extension of the Wundtian philosophy. Its members boldly sought to apply introspection to the psychology of thought. In the Würzburg School experimental psychology reached both its peak and its downfall. The major schools of psychology that followed it — the Gestaltists and the behaviorists — came into existence partly as a reaction to what seemed to them to be the sterility of the Würzburg approach. Yet the Würzburgers came very close to infusing academic psycholosy with a dynamic psychology. But bound by their links to Wundt, the introspective method, and a slavish devotion to consciousness, they were unable to make the necessary theoretical leap. Ultimately they fell out with Wundt and were rejected by the second generation of scientific psychology. Not

[7] The article was Ebbinghaus's contribution to the highly regarded series *Die Kultur der Gegenwart, Ihre Entwicklung und ihre Ziele*, edited by Paul Hinneberg. The sixth volume, *Systematic Philosophy* (1907), contained, besides Ebbinghaus's piece, essays by Dilthey, Riehl, Wundt, Ostwald, Eucken, Paulsen, Münch, and Lipps. The very thorough index to this volume contains no entry for the word "unconscious."

until the flowering of Gestalt psychology in the twenties and thirties did the real possibility arise of a linkage between academic psychology and psychoanalysis.

Psychologists at the Würzburg Institute worked under the leadership of Külpe, the man who had written the first Wundtian textbook in 1893. Beginning in 1901, the Würzburgers began to publish monographs and articles describing their experiments and showing that "mind was . . . an irrational associative train of mental contents that nevertheless reaches a rational conclusion" (Boring, 1950, p. 503). The Würzburg investigators upset centuries-old assumptions of associationist psychology by demonstrating in careful detail that a conscious thought, judgment, or decision need not be arrived at "rationally," i.e., in a certain orderly way in which all factors necessary for a decision were kept in the mind constantly.

Though the researchers recognized the "insufficiency of consciousness" (Watt, 1905, pp. 423-431) to explain all human thought, they were at a loss to name what they had discovered. Clearly, the "images," "sensations," and "feelings" so precisely defined by Wundt were not involved. The Würzburgers puzzled over the irrational mental contents they kept discovering in their subjects. Every couple of years, Külpe's coworkers gave the phenomena new names. In 1901 and 1903 Karl Marbe and J. Orth called them "conscious attitudes." Orth included William James's "fringes of consciousness" under this heading. In 1905 H. J. Watt discovered the "set," which Narciss Ach soon called the "determining tendency." Ach also recognized another determinant which he called an "awareness." Like a conscious attitude, it was "a vague, intangible, conscious content that is not image or sensation." Ach said all consciousness was filled with these "impalpable" (*unanschaulich*) moments (Boring, 1950, p. 405). Two years later Karl Bühler (1907, pp. 297-305) showed there were actual thought processes that were nonsensory and labeled them "imageless thoughts." Yet whatever their designations, the psychologists kept thinking of them solely as conscious phenomena.

In their work, the Würzburgers had actually "produced the knowledge that consciousness cannot be understood by means of consciousness alone" (Müller-Freienfehls, 1935, p. 113). Their experiments pointed to the existence of an active unconscious mental structure at work behind many conscious states. Boring (1950, p. 405) has generously written that through its recognition of determining tendencies, "the Würzburg school has taken its place in . . . the history of dynamic psychology." It might be more accurate to say that with this recognition the Würzburg school brushed against and recoiled from dynamic psychology. For though the Würzburgers very accurately recognized and described what was going on, they did not really deal with the implications of their discoveries.

Before 1908, the Würzburg psychologists never spoke of Freud's or Jung's work in their articles or books, although it is difficult to imagine that they had not heard of psychoanalytic theories. Freud's and Jung's publications were fully reviewed in Ebbinghaus's *Zeitschrift für Psychologie* as early as 1895 and occasionally mentioned in the Würzburgers' own *Archiv für die gesamte Psychologie* which had been founded in 1903. Two factors were at work here. One was the advice of their teacher, Külpe, to avoid wherever possible "assistance from without." The second was the primacy of consciousness in their theoretical and practical concerns. When the unconscious intruded itself, it was given a vague name which indicated merely that the researchers had come across something whose existence they recognized but whose significance they only dimly understood.

As little as psychoanalysis affected the Würzburgers did the Würzburg school affect the new German psychology of its day. Psychologists attached to experimentalism saw only that, in experimental terms, the Würzburg Institute had failed to achieve what it had set out to do: explain scientifically the psychology of thought. The Würzburgers' contribution was thus seen in negative terms. They had shown "that the essential conditions of the course of conscious events were not conscious" (Boring, 1950, p. 407). But psychology was not yet prepared to deal with "attitudes" and "tendencies," i.e., the unconscious, in a positive way. First German psychology had to revolt against Wundtian psychology, which it did not really do until after World War I, though the beginnings of this revolt — the Gestalt school — can be seen as early as 1912 in the work of Max Wertheimer, in Frankfurt.[8] Gestalt theory was a reaction against Wundt's elementism, against the psychophysiological study of isolated human functions. Instead, the Gestaltists believed the whole to be more than its constituent parts. Emotion, for example, is a response involving the entire living system, rather than the local response of the mid-brain, No separate act of impulse or will can be mapped out and independently studied. Eventually, many Gestaltists combined the Gestalt approach with psychoanalytic concepts in one guise or another.

THE INCOMPATIBILITY OF EXPERIMENTAL PSYCHOLOGY AND
PSYCHOANALYSIS

German psychology, as Ebbinghaus correctly realized in 1907, had "only a short history." As a discipline it was not "ready" for Freud before the 1920's. Before 1908, psychology was too much wrapped up in experimental introspection, with everything that is implied by that term, to admit the validity of the psychoanalytic method and of the evidence gathered by it. This unreadiness is apparent in the ease and swiftness with which many German psychologists accepted Wundt's denunciation (1907, 1908) of Bühler's methods and his "imageless thoughts." The new psychology needed to go through a period of internal intellectual development before it was prepared to accept ideas "from without" (most specifically and importantly, ideas about the unconscious), and to regard man, as did Freud, as a complex, integrated organism rather than as a collection of unimpinging elements. Independently of

[8] There are links, as might be imagined, between the Würzburg and Gestalt Schools. When Külpe went to Bonn in 1909, Marbe (who had done the original work on conscious attitudes) succeeded him as chairman at Würzburg. Marbe's first assistant was Kurt Koffka, who later did pioneering work in Gestalt psychology. Moreover, the man who became the leader of the Gestaltists, Kurt Lewin, worked as a student at Würzburg with Narciss Ach, the psychologist who named determining tendencies (Revers, 1968, p. 467; Shakow and Rapaport, 1964, p. 126).

Freud,[9] Gestalt psychology noted that the individual reacts to a great deal more than the stimulus or situation which the experimentalist wants him to react to. Much that is not explicit in the situation as defined, much that is half-hidden or even completely ignored in the social context, is highly relevant. Freud had come to this conclusion twenty years earlier and was neglected by the psychology of his day.

But Freud was neglected not only because of psychology's "short history" but also because of its "long past." And nothing past was more decisive for German psychology's disregard of psychoanalysis than the Kantian tradition. Kant firmly implanted epistemological dualism in German thought. Seventy-five years after his death, the classical German curriculum still taught future physicians and psychologists Kant's criteria for what constitutes a science of the mind: (1) To know another person's mind is impossible. We can have an innate understanding of our own mind but cannot extend this outside of ourselves. (2) Therefore, only manifest behavior is the basis for scientific knowledge. A science of psychology on any other grounds is unreliable. (3) To be studied in a truly scientific manner, manifest behavior must be quantified. Relying on these criteria, Wundt developed a physiological psychology with a mathematical base. Experimental psychology had the tendency, therefore,

> to explore all methods of obtaining quantifiable "data" often without any fruitful assumptions to test. The combination of observationalism with the Kantian prejudice about mathematics encouraged the view that science progresses by the accumulation of measurements, the noticing of correlations or laws between the sets of measurements, and the final relating of laws under theories. Psychologists, increasingly self-conscious about the status of their studies, thought that respectable scientific theories would emerge if only enough mathematics were used in making the initial observations [Peters, 1953, p. 408].[10]

[9] That is, quite strictly speaking, methodologically. What the influence of the *Zeitgeist* was is hard to determine; the Gestaltists claim not to have been influenced by Freud until after their initial studies were performed. Shakow and Rapaport (1964, pp. 126-128) discuss this issue in some detail.

[10] Peters goes on to claim that "the main function of measurement in science is purely to facilitate the testing of hypotheses by expressing them more exactly." See (1953, pp. 508-509) for a sophisticated development of this thesis.

The obsession to amass only quantifiable data was, of course, an immediate barrier to any recognition of Freud's work, which judged by the psychologists' standards was purely speculative. Freud applied the knowledge he gained from investigating his own mind to other human beings. He relied on "impalpable," unconscious thoughts to gain information. He placed theorizing before measurement. While the experimental work of the new psychologists added substantially to knowledge of human physiology, the concerns which animated it were incompatible with those of psychoanalysis.

8

EXPERIMENTAL PSYCHOLOGY
AND PSYCHOANALYSIS,
1895-1907

The experimental psychologists' reception of Freud's work began in 1895 with a summary of two of Freud's articles (1893, 1894) in the *Zeitschrift für Psychologie*. This early (as well as later) exposure of the psychologists to Freud's ideas was due in large measure to Hermann Ebbinghaus's tolerance of widely diverse opinions, which reflected itself in his policies as editor of the *Zeitschrift* (Shakow, 1968, p. 326). In 1895, the *Zeitschrift* was the only general periodical of the new psychologists. The other experimental journal, Wundt's *Studien*, was strictly devoted to reports of the work of the Leipzig laboratory.

In spite of their early response to the ideas of psychoanalysis, the psychologists rarely considered these ideas as belonging in their own field. Many of the *Zeitschrift's* reviews of Freud's works were written by physicians and not by psychologists. Ebbinghaus obviously felt that medical men were in a more logical position to evaluate psychoanalysis. The psychologists' texts and monographs virtually neglected Freud; a single reference by Wundt was the only exception. Only psychopathologists with training as both physicians and psychologists considered the ideas of psychoanalysis at length. Thus in discussing the psychological reception of psychoanalysis, we must constantly be making a distinction between mere exposure and genuine reaction. I define exposure as the psychologists' reading in their journals physicians' ideas about Freud's work. Reaction is the psychologists' own reports and opinions. This distinction between exposure and reaction is a direct reflection of the psychologists' belief that psychoanalysis could play only a very limited role in their endeavors. Freud's works had no real significance for normal psychology; at best they were merely interesting. Involved here are the issues documented in the previous chapter: (1) the overriding cultural commitment to the sickness-health polarity, (2) Freud's preoccupation with the unconscious, (3) the theoretical positions of physiological psychology, and (4) the effort of psychology to establish itself as an independent scientific discipline. Occasionally, ideas (not necessarily Freud's) on the power of emotions were granted some validity but only as they applied to sick people. It was almost as if only an ill person could be affected by his emotional life.

In discussing the psychological reaction to psychoanalysis, the same basic organization used to discuss the medical reaction will be followed. This procedure accords with the threefold division of psychoanalysis into a normal psychology, an abnormal psychology, and a method of diagnosis and treatment. Such organization will also facilitate a comparison between the medical and the psychological receptions of psychoanalysis.

THE UNCONSCIOUS

Freud's concepts relating to the operation of the mind and the development of personality have already been outlined. These are the existence of an unconscious and a mental mechanism of repression; the vital significance of sexuality; the role of dreams in understanding the unconscious; and the universal applicability of all of these factors.

The previous chapter illustrated the preoccupation of most German psychologists with the conscious and their hostility to the idea of an unconscious. Most of this was expressed without any specific reference to Freud. What we gather from it is the basic incompatibility of experimental psychology and psychoanalysis.

But expositions of views about the conscious and unconscious were not limited to generalities; there were specific presentations of psychoanalytic ideas about the unconscious. A

Bonn physician, Fritz Umpfenbach (1896), introduced the *Zeitschrift*'s readers to the *Studies on Hysteria*, concentrating his review on the authors' portrayal of the power of unconscious ideas and the activities and events which are influenced by these ideas. Umpfenbach recommended the "closer study [of] the details of the book . . . to everyone who is interested in psychological questions." Eleven years later Jung (1907a, p. 150) strove to convince the psychologists that "there are . . . no 'purely intellectual' psychic events," but that all psychic phenomena have an emotional component, whether this is realized at the time or not. It is noteworthy that in the four months from April 16 to August 2, 1907, Ebbinghaus published thirteen reviews by Jung. Only one other person wrote more reviews (fourteen) in this period. This is further evidence that Jung's known close association with Freud did not harm his professional reputation.

The physicians urged that consideration be given to the existence of the unconscious. But only one psychologist, William Stern (1871-1938), thought that this aspect of Freud's theories was commendable. Stern, who eventually became famous for his work in child psychology and educational testing, was not a conventional experimentalist. Though trained by Ebbinghaus, Stern was never at home within the limitations of introspection. He was outspoken in his opinions on psychoanalysis and Adlerian individual psychology, and eventually evolved his own philosophy-psychology of personalism which was at great variance with the experimentalist conception of human psychology.

Stern (1901, p. 131), though writing that *The Interpretation of Dreams* must ultimately be rejected, believed that the "most valuable" aspect of the book was that it did not confine the explanation of dream life to "the sphere of ideas, the play of associations, mere fantasy, or somatic relationships." Instead, Freud had indicated "the manifold and so little known components that underlie the more substantial [*kernhaftere*] world of the affects." Perhaps "in reality" only these components can "render understandable the form and selection of the material of ideas."

Stern also accepted Freud's concept of the preconscious,

which functions as an inhibitor of the unconscious. To Stern, this was not a radical idea. As he saw it, the Freudian preconscious played a somewhat similar role in relation to "latent thought content" as did Wundt's concept of "apperception." Both were responsible for "critical suppression, or at least neutralization of those dark sides of psychic existence whose unleashing would interfere with or disgrace our existence."

But Störring and Otto Lipmann (1880-1933) took the more conventional psychological view. Störring (1900, pp. 132-133) told his classes at Leipzig that there were a number of writers, of whom Freud was one, who "assume that even in normal people there exists, side by side with the normal consciousness we know of, another consciousness of which we ordinarily know nothing." Störring indiscriminately lumped the ideas of Freud with those of Binet, Janet, Max Dessoir, and Moll—it being a common early response to view Freud's work as no different from that of other major figures who believed in an unconscious. All these men, Störring explained, believed that in "abnormal periods" the other consciousness became "dominant." They called it the subconscious (*Unterbewusstsein*) and the normal conscious the upper conscious (*Oberbewusstsein*). In "normal" mental states, the subconscious could leak through in isolated circumstances. But, according to these men, "it does not come into full force, this second personality in us, except in abnormal conditions." Störring emphasized his disagreement with the conception of two states of consciousness.

It is not surprising to find that Störring's misinterpretation of Freud was based on the ubiquitous health-sickness dichotomy. Störring did not grasp that Freud believed the unconscious is operative always, as strong an influence in "normal" as in "abnormal" periods.

The other psychologist, Lipmann, was, like Stern, a pupil of Ebbinghaus. When he reviewed Bleuler's 1905 article on consciousness and association, he had just completed his doctorate. The main point of Bleuler's article was to stress the importance of unconscious psychic factors, and Lipmann (1906, p. 120) accurately presented Bleuler's arguments. But then he sarcastically dismissed Bleuler's point of view: "So, the author believes himself able to show for various still rather obscure phenomena that his theory is suitable for their complete clarification — at least [suitable enough] to make a journal contribution."

SEXUALITY

It is noteworthy that the psychologists paid little attention to Freud's sexual theories. After all, these ideas were central to his thesis and had aroused much comment among physicians. But no psychological journal published a review of Freud's *Three Essays on the Theory of Sexuality*. This was no deliberate attempt to prevent Freud's ideas from being known. The psychological journals published reviews of certain of Freud's articles which the medical journals completely ignored. The indifference to Freud's sexual theories arose mainly from the belief that sexual matters were not in the purview of psychology, which indeed they were not in turn-of-the-century German psychology. This psychology, as we have seen, was not a psychology of personality or of the development of personality. Concern with childhood was only an emerging phenomenon among experimentally trained psychologists. Wundt frowned upon "applied" psychology and probably did much to delay its development. Indeed, William Stern and his wife did pioneering studies in this field in the early 1900's based on diaries Clara Stern kept about their children. The German psychology that was concurrent with the early period of psychoanalysis was, if "scientific," confined to the experimental study of distinct facets of sensation and thought; or if "philosophic," it was concerned with logic, esthetics, and morals, or was a faculty psychology.

The small interest of psychologists in Freud's sexual ideas was the result of three factors: (1) the precise nature of what the field of psychology was, (2) the common "Victorian" response of ignoring sexuality publicly, and (3) the idea that Freud's sexual discoveries applied only to sick people, who, anyway, as Külpe said, were "incapable of introspection in the scientific sense." This last point is illustrated in Stern's (1901, pp. 132-133) explanation of Freud's "tendency . . . to attribute to all possible and impossible contents of dreams a sexual sense

. . . perhaps the predominance of material from hysterical patients is responsible for that."

This remark by Stern is one of only four (!) references to Freud's sexual theories to be found in the psychological literature from 1894 through 1907. And two of the other three references were made by a physician, Gaupp, who, as we have noted, appreciated significant portions of psychoanalysis. Gaupp, in two reviews in the *Zeitschrift*, did not dismiss Freud's sexual discoveries lightly. He gave credit to Freud's "superior idea of the significance of sexual matters." What Gaupp (1900a, p. 234) "deplored" was that Freud had let it get out of hand and "now everywhere and always seeks sexual causes and connections." In the next volume of the *Zeitschrift*, Gaupp (1900b) defended Freud against Konrad Rieger's charge that the sexual etiology of the neuroses was "old wives' gossip." Specifically, Gaupp denounced the "acerbic criticism [with which Rieger] persecutes scientific theories when they appear to him to be dangerous heresies." And, in general, Gaupp disagreed with Rieger's attacking "modern views of the influence of sexual matters on health and sickness."

The fourth reference to Freud's emphasis on the significance of sexual matters was made by Hellpach in the *Festschrift* in honor of Wundt's seventieth birthday. As was not uncommon, Hellpach (1902, p. 210) misunderstood Freud, but the import of his remarks was to defend Freud against Kraepelin. In his textbook, Kraepelin, understanding Freud perfectly, had attacked Freud for the importance he placed on "long-forgotten sexual experiences." Kraepelin knew Freud was referring to infantile experiences. In his *Festschrift* article, Hellpach scolded Kraepelin for his "strong undervaluation of puberty." Hellpach had "often observed that the majority of people gloss over their later love life quite easily, but that the smallest details of their earliest pubertal sexual experience remain with an astonishing tenacity." Any psychologist unfamiliar with the details of Freud's sexual theories would regard Hellpach's comments as a defense of Freud.

The argument can be made that only four references to Freud's ideas on sexuality do not permit any valid conclusions to be drawn about the nature of the psychological reaction.

But one thing is clear. The *Zeitschrift* never gave Freud a bad press in this regard.

DREAMS

Dreams were another matter. Here was something very much within the psychologists' purview, and Freud's ideas elicited a strong negative response from the psychologists'— though not from the *physicians* who reviewed Freud's works for the *Zeitschrift*. In these latter instances, the psychologists were exposed to Umpfenbach's (1906, p. 240) detached, factual account of Freud's theory that dreams are the fulfillment of wishes and that "an ordinary dream stands, as it were, on two legs, one being the current life situation, the other an important event of childhood. The dream establishes a connection . . . between both of these." The psychologists also read C. M. Giessler's (1902) scholarly discussion of Freud's *On Dreams*. In choosing Giessler to review this book, Ebbinghaus picked a physician who had previously, in the *Allgemeine Zeitschrift für Psychiatrie*, expressed his strong belief in the importance of dream research for investigations in related fields of hypnotism, child psychology, and psychiatry, as well as the psychology of normal life. Giessler (1901, p. 182) thought that workers in these fields paid too little attention to dreams. It was his opinion that dreams could give doctors important clues about both physical and mental illnesses.

Giessler (1902) wrote a lengthy review of Freud's monograph. He concluded that *On Dreams* contained much that was correct, above all the confirmation of the processes of condensation, displacement, and working through (*anschaulichen Verarbeitung*), as well as the presentation of the mode of working through. He also accepted Freud's concept of denial. Giessler believed there was a basis for saying that children's dreams are wish dreams, but he "unfortunately" could not concur in the view that most dreams express the uncovering of a repressed wish. He was also opposed to Freud's idea that the dream state is a dissociative state. However, he agreed with Freud that the dream can compensate for external stimulations that might otherwise awaken the sleeper.

The psychologists themselves were less disposed to make the very careful distinctions which Giessler had drawn among various aspects of Freud's dream interpretation. Paul Mentz (1901), who had worked with Wundt in Leipzig, in a review of *The Interpretation of Dreams* broadly criticized Freud's claim of being able to decipher dreams as wishes. There was in such interpretation "something mystical," implying that somewhere there existed a "life [*Ausleben*] of reactively stimulated wishes, inclinations, conscious habits [*bewussten Gewohnheiten*], [and] drives with their psychic connections." There was also "a certain appearance of literal teleology." The discharge of psychic energy, which Freud said had a function, was merely "accidental." Mentz disagreed that dreams with painful content were really concealed wishes. But he concluded that: "In spite of these small theoretical shortcomings . . . this work ought to be counted among the most significant publications in this field because of the abundance of its material in both factual matters and psychological analyses."[1]

Stern (1901), in the *Zeitschrift*, was less appreciative. He did show his respect in the length of his review (three pages was a long review for the *Zeitschrift*). Also, he admitted "that this new way of observing dream life and its proposed analogizing, in many places, to pathological conditions, opens many new perspectives to us . . . the book contains many individual instances of highly stimulating ideas, sensitive observations and theoretical views — above all an extraordinarily rich material of very exactly described dreams — that must be highly welcome to every worker in this field." All the same, the theory must be "rejected" because it was "false," being based on the interpretations of Freud's and his patients' dreams. "To these

---

[1] Mentz's review appeared in the *Vierteljahrsschrift für wissenschaftliche Philosophie* (*Quarterly for Scientific Philosophy*), a journal that devoted half of each issue to reviews (not merely abstracts). Since reviewing was obviously an important function of the journal, I tabulated the publication dates of all the books reviewed to see how quickly Freud's book had been reviewed in comparison with the others. *Die Traumdeutung* had a publication date of 1900 (though actually it appeared in November, 1899). Of thirty-one books reviewed in the March, 1901, issue of the *Vierteljahrsschrift*, sixteen had appeared in 1900, eight in 1899, six in 1898, and one in 1897. At least in this periodical, Freud's book was not reviewed with any less dispatch than others.

interpretations the sober reader shows at first reserve, then doubt, and finally increasingly energetic head-shaking [since] what the waking analysis has accidentally discovered is made into the principal content of the dream synthesis."

Stern opposed "everything" about this method.

> "Introspection" is not such a simple thing when one is being influenced, as is the author by his theories, and his patients by penetrating interrogation and instruction on the wish character of dreams. . . . The inadmissibility of this so-called dream interpretation as scientific method must be emphasized with all possible rigor; for the danger is great that uncritical minds could find this interesting play of ideas comfortable, and we will be pulled down by it into a complete mysticism and chaotic arbitrariness — for one can prove anything with anything.

In the fifth edition of the *Grundzüge der physiologischen Psychologie*, Wundt (1903) listed *On Dreams* as one of a group of recent works on dreams which he considered noteworthy. Without speicifically commenting on Freud's thesis, Wundt presented his own explanation of dreams. This was that external irritants and stimulations are the effective agents of dreaming. For example, lying in an uncomfortable position causes a dream about hard physical labor. Slight intercostal pain is responsible for a dream that one is being stabbed by an enemy. An asthmatic attack turns into the frightful anxiety of a nightmare about an elf dancing on the chest. When the sleeper dreams he is flying, he is reacting to his perception of the rhythm of his own breathing movements. Wundt (p. 653) indirectly criticized Freud's ideas by attacking those of Scherner in *Das Leben des Traumes*, published in 1861. "[Scherner's] effort to give an over-all symbolic quality to the dream is naturally wrong. So, for example, he deduces the flying in a dream not simply from the feeling of breath movements, but he believes: because the lungs themselves have two wings [and] move in air . . . so they represent themselves as two organs of flight."

But Freud (1900, pp. 83-84) had written that

> the most original and far-reaching attempt to explain dreaming as a special activity of the mind, capable of free expansion only during the state of sleep, was that undertaken by Scherner in

> 1861. . . . [Scherner showed how] 'imagination', liberated from the domination of reason and from any moderating control, leaps into a position of unlimited sovereignty. . . . [Dream imagination] has a dislike of representing an object by its proper image, and prefers some extraneous image which will express only that particular one of the object's attributes which it is seeking to represent. Here we have the 'symbolizing activity' of the imagination.

Freud went on to discredit Scherner's *exact* symbolic interpretation, which he found as naïve as did Wundt. But in contradistinction to Wundt, Freud (1900, p. 227) upheld the general correctness of symbolic interpretation: "Scherner's theory [cannot be dismissed] as an idle invention without looking for its kernel of truth. The task, then, that faces us is to find an explanation of another kind for the supposed symbolization . . ." But Wundt did not agree, nor did he believe Freud's explanation was any more convincing than Scherner's. Eight years were to elapse before Wundt gave Freud's theories more extensive consideration in the sixth edition of the *Physiologischen Psychologie.*

UNIVERSAL APPLICABILITY OF PSYCHIC MECHANISMS

Freud's (1905b) book on jokes was a direct offshoot of his work on dreams (Freud, 1925, pp. 65-66). It was another of his attempts to show that the same psychic mechanisms were operative both in the normal course of events and in pathological situations. The two psychologists who reviewed this monograph gave accurate and full summaries of Freud's theses: that all jokes had as their purpose the expression of hostile or sexual feelings; that the exact ways in which jokes are told correspond to the economical "dream work" of condensation, displacement, representation by opposite, etc.; that we derive pleasure from jokes because they are an acceptable way of discharging repressed feelings and gaining pleasure from otherwise suppressed drives.

Richard Baerwald, a traditional philosophic psychologist, attempted to undermine Freud's central concept of the role of economy in wit. Baerwald had written his Jena thesis on the objectification of a subjective idea and was bothered by

Freud's view that the techniques of wit are similar to psychotic breakdowns in communications, like the use of clang associations (four, score, door, more) or words of double meaning. Freud also pointed out the similarities between jokes based on nonsense and the great appeal of nonsense to children; adults under the influence of alcohol also respond hilariously to pure nonsense. The mature person is forced to give up this enjoyment, but he can safely revel in it in a joke. One of the manifestations of wit, therefore, is that it is a return to the infantile. To this Baerwald responded that Freud had failed to show how this is an "economical" process. Rather it seemed to him that the "sense" Freud made out of "nonsense" was "disguised and hard to find." Baerwald was also antagonistic to Freud's connection of jokes and the unconscious. He did not agree that because the characteristics of dreams are all to be found in wit that therefore unconscious influences underlie wit.

Baerwald's (1906) critique was the lead review in the first issue of Max Dessoir's new *Zeitschrift für Ästhetik*. In its first year, this *Zeitschrift* had articles by Theodor Lipps, Konrad Lange, Georg Simmel, Hugo Spitzer, and Karl Groos. Baerwald's unsympathetic review was a lengthy consideration — four closely printed pages — of what he clearly saw as a scholarly monograph. "Even for those who cannot agree with the basic ideas of the book," Baerwald concluded, "it remains very valuable because of its subtle observations and shrewd individual statements. It is obviously not a product of the moment, but has grown organically out of years' long, significant, and thoughtful work."

The other reviewer of Freud's book on wit was Jonas Cohn (1869-1947), the later famous philosopher, psychologist, and educator, who wrote in Ebbinghaus's journal. Professor Cohn had impeccable credentials, having recently published *Allgemeine Aesthetik* (1901), and having done experimental studies on feeling at the Leipzig laboratory. Cohn's (1906) review was entirely complimentary. Freud's work was not only significant," but was "pleasant and stimulating to read." There was "an abundance of the most valuable thoughts. . . . Every psychologist and esthetician will have come to his own terms

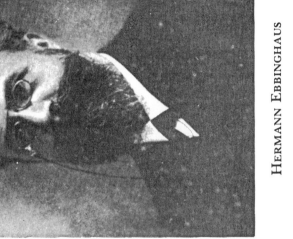

HERMANN EBBINGHAUS

WILHELM WUNDT

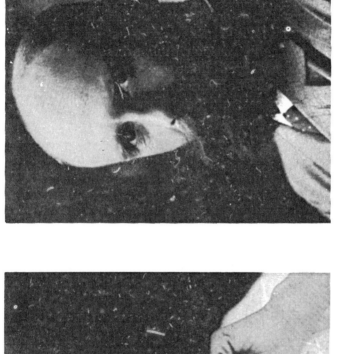

CHRISTIAN VON EHRENFELS

From *The Austrian Philosophy of Values*, by Howard O. Eaton. Copyright 1930 by the University of Oklahoma Press.

WILLIAM STERN

with Freud and — even if he repudiates his theories — will have to learn from him." Cohn predicted that Freud's book would run into obstacles. "The objections against these theories will be directed partly against [Freud's] utilization of the unconscious and partly against [his having] intellectualized the discharge of ideas which are so full of feeling." But Cohn believed these objections would be overcome "by the essence of Freud's theory, at least as far as the interpretation of jokes is concerned."

The next year in the *Zeitschrift*, psychologists were exposed to two further attempts to show the relationship of Freud's psychopathology to normal psychology. Umpfenbach (1907) pointed out that Freud drew a parallel between the use of psychoanalysis to determine the etiology of hysterical symptoms and the investigative methods of judges to ascertain the truth. Jung (1907a, p. 152) stated that psychologists henceforth would have to understand "the enormous importance of the Freudian mechanisms" for normal psychology. He advised "all who are interested in research on the emotions" to read Bleuler's book on affects, which was based on "Freudian principles."

Starting in 1896, then, psychologists were exposed to Freud's ideas on how the mind operates and personality develops. As with the medical reception, the exposure and reaction were never one-sided, but as opposed to the medical reception they were minimal. And although the Würzburgers began publishing their own journal in 1903, they paid absolutely no attention in it to this aspect of psychoanalysis.

On the whole, the experimental psychologists failed to see the significance of psychoanalysis for normal psychology. This was partly because Freud was a doctor and wrote about illness. Psychologists' belief in the sickness-health polarity was as strong as anyone's. Moreover, very few of the new psychologists were as yet interested in theories of personality development. Stern, who subsequently developed his own theory of "personalism," was one of the few who had an early interest in the work of Freud and, later, Adler.

HYSTERIA

Freud's early work on the etiology and mechanism of psychopathological states dealt mainly with hysteria, obsessional neurosis, and anxiety neurosis. German psychologists at the turn of the century lacked any real interest in these states. Mental illness was still a field for physicians. This is seen from a scrutiny of the *Zeitschrift für Psychologie* and the *Archiv für die gesamte Psychologie*. With but one exception, all reviews of and references to Freud's work on hysteria were by doctors.[2]

The *Zeitschrift*'s medical coverage of Freud's work at the time of the appearance of *Studies on Hysteria* was extensive enough so that any psychologist who wished to keep abreast of the newest work in the field was able to do so. In 1895, Josef Peretti accurately summarized two of Freud's recent articles. Peretti (1852-1927) was director of the Grafenberg (Düsseldorf) mental hospital and in 1912 became professor of psychiatry at the Düsseldorfer Akademie für praktische Medizin. Peretti (1895a) described how Freud differentiated between hysterical and organic paralysis. He also presented (1895b) Freud's explanation of hysteria and other neuroses as defensive reactions against occurrences or ideas which the ego finds incompatible. Thus there was a report on the mechanism of conversion as well as Freud's finding that the incompatible ideas had, so far, turned out to be related to his patients' sexual lives.

Peretti (1895b) and Umpfenbach (1896, p. 308) called the psychologists' attention to the difference between Freud's and Janet's views on the nature of the split in consciousness that occurred in hysterical states. Janet believed the cleavage was primary, i.e., that it preceded the hysterical state and occurred as the result of "original mental weakness." Freud, on the other hand, believed the splitting of consciousness in hysterical states was secondary, i.e., that it was acquired and did not oc-

---

[2] Even the exception confirms the general observation. In reviewing *The Interpretation of Dreams*, William Stern (1901, p. 131) explained the connections between Freud's ideas in this book and Freud's theories on the treatment of hysteria. But this was only an aside; Stern's primary topic was not hysteria.

There was also one unsigned review, which may not have been by a physician, but probably was.

cur "because the persons in question are weak-minded. [Rather] they appear weak-minded because their psychic activity is split, and only a part of the capacity for work is at the disposal of conscious thoughts."

The only early attempt to contradict Freud's psychic explanation of hysterical paralyses was in the anonymous review (1896) of an article by a Dr. C. S. Freund. The reviewer quoted Freund: "An essential difference between previous investigations (Charcot, Moebius, Janet, Freud, and others) and ours (Sachs and the author) [is] that, on the basis of the anatomical facts, we are in opposition to the purely psychological explanation."

Aside from Stern's passing reference, no more was heard in the psychological journals about Freud and hysteria until 1904, when again it was discussed by physicians. Jung (1904, p. 350) called to the attention of the *Archiv*'s readers that the analysis of mental pathology in his book on the psychology of so-called occult phenomena was based "on the Freudian investigations into hysteria." Three years later Jung (1907a, p.151) wrote in the *Zeitschrift* that it was Freud who had discovered the mechanisms of "wish-fulfilling hysterias . . . which enable highly repugnant emotional states to be made as undistressful as is possible." Freud had shown that "a conversion phenomenon" occurs when "the affect is more or less dissociated [from consciousness] and repressed."

Umpfenbach (1906) came forward again to review Freud's analysis of the hysterical Dora and recounted the psychoanalytical theories of hysteria, repression, and psychosexual influences. The next year a well-known Munich psychiatrist, Eduard Hirt (1907), published a twenty-six-page review of Hellpach's text on hysteria in which he outlined (pp. 77, 78, 85-88, 95) everything Hellpach had had to say in the book about Breuer and Freud. In his own historical introduction to the subject of hysteria, Hirt said "even" Breuer and Freud had done little to add to the basic ideas about hysteria which Charcot had first elaborated.[3]

---

[3] Hirt's review was published three years after Hellpach's book appeared. All authors—not just Freud— suffered at times from delayed notice.

GUSTAV STÖRRING

Obviously, psychologists were "exposed" to Freud's ideas on hysteria. But at the turn of the century, the subject of mental illness did not kindle professional curiosity. The only psychologists who exhibited more than a passing interest in psychopathology were those who had also received medical training. Theoretically, they were pioneers in a new, nonmedical field. In practice, however, they were physicians whose viewpoint was shaped by their Wundtian training. Thus these early psychologists of abnormal psychology approached the problem of mental malfunction with one aspect of it already irrevocably settled: the answer to the problem was not to be found in unconscious processes. This attitude is vividly illustrated in the psychological writings of Störring and Hellpach.

Störring's lectures on psychopathology in the Faculty of Philosophy at Leipzig were published in 1900. His introduction to the subject of hysteria was quite perceptive. His thoughts echoed Freud's, though, astonishingly enough, he claimed a certain originality, even though he was thoroughly familiar with the *Studies on Hysteria*. Störring focused on "derangement of affectivity" as being characteristic of hysteria. The disorder was accompanied by an "abnormal intensity [of] reproduced affective states," by which he meant "such as are attached to ideas of past experiences that possess strong affective colouring." This point, Störring claimed, had never been emphasized before (1900, pp. 129-130).

But the whole thrust of his discussions on hysteria was to prove the improbability of "unconscious ideas." It had been suggested, he told his students, that unconscious auto-suggestion could cause a hysterical paralysis. This was "most unlikely." In the first place, how could an idea which has "such strong inhibitive effects" be unconscious? After all, the physiological processes of the cortex of which "unconscious ideas" consist were actually of "*slighter* intensity" than the physiological correlates of "ideas proper." In the second place, even if "unconscious ideas" did exist, it was "obviously a dubious proceeding" to use them as an explanation before "every other possible interpretation of the facts had been carefully weighed and eliminated." Besides, what "guarantee" was there that all hysterical paralyses had the same basic etiology? (p. 151).

Nevertheless, Störring claimed to have an open mind. He said he agreed with Freud that in hysteria ideas may be repressed and still continue to exercise an abnormal influence on consciousness. Yet, as will be seen, Störring's conception of "repression" was nothing like Freud's. "Now surely," Störring pondered, "if 'unconscious links' ever occur at all, it is here they should be most easy to detect. But if their presence cannot be established even in these hysterical cases, we may be pretty certain that they do not exist at all" (p. 161). Having set up his straw man, Störring proceeded to knock him down.

First, Störring gave a copious presentation of Freud's ideas on repression and conversion in hysteria. He quoted at length theoretical sections from the *Studies on Hysteria* and described in great detail three of Breuer and Freud's cases. He complimented the authors on their "excellent" description. "Unfortunately," however, the authors had impoverished their work by their belief in two states of consciousness. Freud had said that the repression of an idea was due to an unpleasant feeling, to an incompatibility between the idea and one's self-conception. Störring contradicted this: "Repression" was a simple matter of "diverting attention away" from overwhelming psychic events. Since hysterical persons have "an abnormal power of exclusive concentration . . . they are bound to furnish notable instances of repressed ideas" (pp. 137-140). We see here simultaneously Störring's view of repression as a conscious phenomenon and his attribution of "an abnormal power" to hysterical persons, a power not shared by normal people.

Störring admitted that he was puzzled by "how repressed ideas manage to affect the life of clear consciousness," i.e., what is the mechanism behind a hysterical symptom. But he was sure that Freud's theory of conversion was not the answer.[4]

---

[4] Freud had explained a hysterical symptom of saying that affect ("the sum of excitation") had to be discharged. If it could not take its proper road, "psychical association," it had to take the wrong road, "bodily innervation." "The repressed idea avenges itself by becoming pathogenic." Since the time of Störring's objection over three quarters of a century ago, the exact process of conversion has remained unexplained.

Störring did agree with Freud that the "strong affective states" of the original incident became associated with some sensation which was particularly prominent in consciousness, like the sensation of smell in Freud's first case description or the sensation of pressure on the thigh in the second. The line of connection was "idea→affective state→sensation" (p. 140). But there was no conversion involved in this linkage, since conversion implies a repository for a repressed idea (in Freud's sense), i.e., an unconscious.

Rather, there were other "factors tending constantly to increase the intimacy of this connection [idea →affective state→ sensation] after the idea's partial or complete repression" (Störring's sense). Störring's explanation devolved from a basic assumption of Wundtian psychology, which is that a conscious state, by repetition and under the law of habit, is telescoped and reduced until the given process is largely or entirely unconscious (in the Wundtian sense). In the case of hysterical symptoms, then, what appears as unconscious sensations are really learned associations. They may appear to be inevitable, but they have been learned and they can be unlearned.[5] An idea is "always [reproduced] along the old line: affective state→ reproduced sensation. The result must be to make this connexion more intimate" (pp. 140-141).

Thus, concluded Störring, he was able to explain in other ways the cleavage of consciousness as described in Freud's three cases, "without needing to have recourse to the theory of an upper- and a sub-conscious." The split was actually "due to abnormal intensity of affective (and especially of reproduced affective) states, combined with the abnormal power of exclusive concentration which hysterical persons possess—and in the end this abnormal concentration is itself due to the abnormal intensity of their feelings" (p. 142).

Störring's argument about the abnormal power of a hysteric's concentration displayed poor clinical acumen and exemplified the prejudice and resultant theoretical distortions that the health-sickness polarity produced among

[5] Boring (1950, p. 311) points out, by way of example, that many optical illusions are practically compulsory. But many of them can be corrected, reduced, or even abolished by analyzing exactly how they occur.

most clinicians. Moreover, Störring could not even entertain Freud's brilliant notion of repression as stemming from the unacceptable nature of certain thoughts because for Störring there was no unconscious. But Störring was correct in his insistence that the conversion theory did not provide an entirely satisfactory solution to the problem of hysterical symptoms.

Störring's lectures give the appearance of neat logicality, so it seems safe to assume that a good many of his students came away impressed by his formal refutation of Freud. At the same time, they saw Freud being treated as a serious scientific figure. The arguments were courteous, respectful, and allowed for certain areas of agreement. Störring's rebuttal was "correct" in every way, including generous quotations from his opponent's writings.

WILLY HELLPACH

Freud's views on hysteria were considered by another pioneering psychopathologist: Hellpach. Two years before Hellpach dealt with psychoanalysis as a physician (*Psychologie der Hysterie*, 1904), he examined it from the psychologist's standpoint (1902). The occasion was a *Festschrift* in honor of Wundt's seventieth birthday. Hellpach made a deliberate effort to draw together what were obviously still considered two separate fields: psychology and the treatment of nervous-disorder. Early in the essay he warned his colleagues that what resulted might appear "a rather peculiar kind of psychology" (p. 194). Perhaps the aim was novel, but the ideas for its achievement were only too familiar:

> What psychic event is responsible [for] the physical phenomena? — that question recurs repeatedly in trying to solve the problem [of hysteria]. Unfortunately, it has been dealt with in more verbiage than is good for it. "Unconscious" events in different variations have been brought into play. . . . I am sure we ought never to admit unconscious factors: it is better not to explain hysteria at all, than to explain it with mythical resources. Every type of psychology stops "on the other side of consciousness" [Möbius's phrase for the unconscious]; there, either physiology or metaphysics begins and which of the two offers less for the understanding of psychic relationships, I shall not go into here [pp. 207-208, 210].

With his position clear, Hellpach plunged into what must remain the most ludicrous simultaneous appreciation of and attack on psychoanalysis during its early period.[6] In one essay Hellpach managed to misunderstand Freud's views both on the sexual etiology of hysteria and on the significance of unconscious factors, and to wind up by *praising* Freud for what Hellpach imagined Freud had said. In this venture, Kraepelin emerged as a sort of psychiatric dim-wit, unable to understand the essence of Freud's contribution.

First of all, Hellpach (1902) considered it "great progress" that Breuer and Freud did not work with "unconscious influences in the large sense of the French interpretations, but rather with the obscure contents of the effects of emotions, which Kraepelin . . . himself adduces as the most frequent causes of hysterical phenomena" (p. 211). Therefore, it was "hardly comprehensible" to Hellpach why Kraepelin partly acknowledged the French theories of hysteria while he simultaneously "polemicized with strong irony" against Breuer and Freud's hypotheses. Considered from a purely theoretical standpoint, the Breuer-Freud hypothesis of the importance of the aftereffects of early childhood sexual experience was "a much more possible" one than Janet's "split of consciousness" or Möbius's "effective ideas from the other side of consciousness" (p. 210).

We know, Hellpach declared, that there is a great deal of emotional coloration in the experiences of childhood, which often, quite unexpectedly, affects our inner selves in later life. This can happen without our having any clear memory of the experiences. But if a given memory appears, we find that the particular inner frame of mind fades away. Such an aftereffect is especially connected with the first sexual experience. Kraepelin was strongly undervaluing puberty when he made light of "long forgotten sexual experiences" in his textbook (p. 210). (Kraepelin, of course, knew exactly what Freud was talking about: infantile sexuality.)

---

[6] Hellpach's attack on Freud concerned the psychoanalytic method (discussed separately below). Hellpach kept emphasizing that "theoretically" he agreed with Freud, though he could not accept psychoanalysis as "clinically" and "psychologically" sound.

Hellpach emphasized Kraepelin's shortsightedness by comparing current etiological theories of homosexuality and hysteria. Schrenck-Notzing, Hellpach explained, had successfully contradicted Krafft-Ebing's theory of the inborn nature of homosexuality by stressing the significance of childhood incidents for later homosexuality (p. 211).

> I cannot see why similar influences should not be possible in the etiology of hysteria. Von Schrenck-Notzing's conception of homosexuality is today almost universally recognized and Kraepelin counts himself as one of its most decisive representatives. But as far as hysteria is concerned, [Kraepelin] seems to accept the principle of degeneration, and his opposition to Breuer and Freud's theory revolves almost exclusively around this point: the impossibility that a healthy psyche could be led astray and harmed through lasting memories of sexual events [p. 211].

Along with his obfuscatory bent, Hellpach always had moments of unquestioned lucidity and forward thinking; this was one of them. He pointed out that such an "impossibility" had never been proved. There were many instances, known to all physicians, when healthy and not in the least degenerate people developed the most severe nervous conditions as a result of strong emotional upheavals. In these cases, it depended entirely on subsequent events in their lives whether their sickness was healed or became chronic. The acute nervous breakdowns experienced by students taking examinations, officers on maneuvers, and artists making their debuts were sometimes due to the lasting damage that earlier events could inflict on a person's stability. "One can hardly think of a more fruitful culture-medium for the adverse effect of the earliest sexual experience that the direct connection between puberty and our customary secrecy and dissimulation as regards sexual matters." (This was a theme Hellpach returned to two years later in an article for educators; see Chapter 12). Thus, Hellpach declared that "psychologically" he considered Freud's theory at least as possible as the French neurologists' "fantasies of an unconscious state and cleavage of consciousness" (p. 211). Moreover, Freud's hypothesis had the advantage of being "connected with the well-known fact concerning memories which has also been described by Wundt: that unpleasant moods and their completely unfathomable after-affects disappear as soon as it is possible to apperceive the constellation of ideas [*Vorstellungsgruppe*] which carries them" (pp. 211-212). Unfortunately, though, Hellpach concluded, psychoanalysis had as little to say as any other theory about the connection of emotional memories with psychogenic events. Psychologists should not place their hopes of learning the nature of hysteria on "psychological investigation of the hysterical psychic state, but on knowledge of the physiological substratum which produces it" (p. 239).[7]

It is difficult to categorize Hellpach's essay in the history of the psychological reception of psychoanalysis. Hellpach's opinionated and provocative style, here and elsewhere, served to assure his writings a large audience. But what then? Does the article stand as an example of the way Freud's psychological critics misunderstood his ideas or took from psychoanalysis just those elements that suited them? Or should it be viewed as one of the first pieces that made a positive connection between early sexual events and the etiology of hysteria for dozens of experimental psychologists? Hellpach's article certainly argued for the psychic mechanism (if not quite the etiology) of events and against the theory of inborn hereditary taint. Like Stern, Hellpach pointed out the confluence of psychology and psychoanalysis in the matter of Wundt's theory of apperception and Freud's theory of the lasting effect of undischarged affect. On the other hand, Hellpach emphasized how greatly he disagreed with cathartic and psychoanalytic techniques (see below).

Hellpach's psychological writings introduced a generation of experimental psychologists to some of the major controversies of early twentieth-century psychopathology. Four years after his article in the Wundt *Festschrift*, surely widely read, Hellpach's *Habilitationsschrift* (1906b) on psychopathology was published in the Würzburger's *Archiv*. And the year after

---

[7] It seems that when Hellpach spoke of the role of childhood incidents in the "etiology" of hysteria he really meant the "mechanism" of hysteria. Underneath any psychic mechanism there was the "physiological substratum."

that, Hellpach's text on hysteria was the object of an important review (Hirt, 1907) in the *Archiv*. Yet Hellpach's role must not be overblown: in 1907 psychopathology, and, therefore, Freud's contributions to it, was still a peripheral concern to most physiological psychologists.

Nevertheless, psychologists who regularly read Wundt's *Philosophical Studies* or the Würzburg Institute's *Archives* had seen favorable arguments for Freud's theory of the sexual etiology of hysteria made by a colleague. These arguments, of course, inveighed against unconscious factors, so the psychologists never received from Hellpach an accurate or unbiased appraisal of psychoanalysis. For this they had to rely on short notices from physicians, which probably did not carry equal weight.

OTHER NEUROSES AND PSYCHOSES

Like the physicians, the psychologists paid much less attention to Freud's views on obsessional neurosis than to those on hysteria. In the case of the psychologists, this meant practically no reaction at all. Three references exist. The first is Peretti's review (1895b) of "The Neuro-Psychoses of Defence" which briefly explained that an obsession arises when an incompatible idea is separated from its affect. This was entirely a psychic process, as opposed to the somatic process of the hysterical conversion reaction. The affect then attaches itself to a compatible idea. Obsessive ruminations and repeated compulsive acts are the result.

In his *Festschrift* article, Hellpach (1902, p. 220) dismissed this theory. Hellpach believed there was "nothing psychologically extraordinary" in a compulsive act. Even though he knew that Löwenfeld had welcomed Freud's discovery of this process, Hellpach opposed it because he said that the union of an idea with an unattached affect "constantly happens every day among healthy people, without it producing a single obsession." As in hysteria, "psychological investigation" did not hold the key to the understanding of obsessional neurosis. One day, when the physiological causes of neurasthenic degeneration and nervous exhaustion became known, it might become clear on what basis obsessions form; today nothing was known.

As has been amply documented, Hellpach was not a believer in the theory of degeneration. But its pull was as strong on him as on many others. When faced with the inability to explain something, Hellpach, like Bloch and Löwenfeld, unthinkingly fell back on this almost ubiquitous medical belief with which psychoanalysis so often clashed, implicitly and explicitly.

Finally, Stern's associate in applied psychology, Otto Lipmann (1907a, p. 153), explained with obvious impatience how Jung, that "ardent champion of Freud's theories, tries anew to prove the correctness of these theories, this time as regards a compulsion." There followed a brief discussion of how Jung used word associations to discover "the repressed (sexual) complex of ideas which supposedly underlay the illness," and how then Jung "through the Freudian method brought the 'free associations' of this complex to 'abreaction.' " Lipmann's use of quotation marks shows that he did not feel as comfortable with Freudian terminology as did physicians.

Since the psychologists had virtually ignored Freud's explanations of normal psychosexual development, it is not surprising that they paid no attention at all to his theory of anxiety neurosis, whose etiology Freud found in the current sexual lives of his patients.

Hellpach, however, did discuss something similar in his *Habilitationsschrift*—what he called "reactive abnormality." This was an emotional illness which occurred in a person with a vague past history of abnormality, but a colorless kind, with no specific clinical picture and with a changing symptom picture. The person was often labeled by physicians as "nervous" or "psychopathic." Then a certain experience brought about a particular illness; the latter was the "reactive" abnormality. Hellpach (1906b, p. 75) cited two authorities to support this concept of disease—Kraepelin and Freud—and referred his readers to Freud's *Three Essays on the Theory of Sexuality*. Freud had pointed out that in reactive abnormalities the psychological tie between experience and illness is unmistakable. Erotic difficulties and masturbatory aberrations often lead, for example, to the complex of erythrophobia— the fear of blushing.

At the end of the early period of psychoanalysis, psychologists were informed of Bleuler's and Jung's application of Freud's hypotheses to paranoia and dementia praecox. In accord with its previous policies, the *Zeitschrift* chose two physicians to present these newest developments. Jung (1907a, p. 152) wrote that Bleuler had shown that in paranoia "an *affect-laden complex of ideas is the root of the* [paranoid] *delusion.*" This complex of ideas — "a series of predisposing incidents" — was absolutely necessary for the occurrence of paranoia. Because of Bleuler's work, declared Jung, in the future, any adequate explanation of a case of paranoia would have to take into consideration not only the usual "special disposition" (hereditary factors) but also the *"chain of Freudian predisposing experiences."* The investigation of environmental factors had become "almost obvious and could only create an unfavorable impression on those who did not understand the enormous importance of the Freudian mechanisms for normal and pathological psychology. Over-all in psychology, where affects play a role, the Freudian principles are valuable; it is, therefore, more than probable that the study of paranoia will be no exception."

Erwin Stransky, a promising young medical expert on the psychoses, discussed Jung's work on dementia praecox in a four-page review that was published only a few months after the book. Stransky (1900) began by remarking that the "meritorious" works of Jung and the Bleuler school (by which he mainly meant the association studies) were generally well known and he reminded the psychologists that Jung had made himself Freud's "apologist." Jung had taken Freud's "ingenious conception" of hysteria and had applied it to the study of dementia praecox. "The intent is to introduce the theory of repression into the psychology of dementia praecox." Stransky wished to

> re-emphasize [Jung's] unquestionable service in having introduced the theories of the complex and of conversion into psychiatric clinical practice. If the author has thereby doubtless gone too far, that is only too easily explained: whoever finds or makes practicable a new path, the way the author has done, naturally shows a partiality toward it, while the rest of us keep

moving along in our accustomed ways. But that is of secondary importance and can be dealt with by the critic; the core, however, remains and it will probably acquire the keys to the city of psychopathology [p. 397].

NATURE VERSUS NURTURE

It is understandable that the psychologists did not share the physicians' natural interest in the whole matter of hereditary taint and degeneracy. But a psychologist around 1900 could not but be aware of this controversy, and if he read the *Zeitschrift* or Hellpach's articles he was bound to learn of Freud's position in the debate. A number of instances of this have already been presented: Freud's disagreement with Janet over the latter's belief in the "original mental weakness" of hysterical patients; Freud's divergence with Kraepelin over the etiological role of degeneracy in hysteria; Hellpach's concept of reactive abnormality based on Freud's ideas in the *Three Essays*; Jung's proclamation of the investigative importance of Freud's "predisposing experiences" in paranoia; Hellpach's arguments against the theory of degeneracy as outlined in Hirt's review. In addition, there was Peretti's review (1897) of another of Freud's articles in the *Zeitschrift*, in which Peretti summarized Freud's explicit arguments, marshaled to show that heredity does not play the great role in the etiology of the neuroses which was generally ascribed to it. Also, Hellpach (1906b, pp. 70, 73, 84) continued to fight against the "unbounded vagueness" of the concept of degeneracy and against its use to explain emotional illness and the development of perversions. In each case, he relied on the *Three Essays* as his reference.

EXPOSURE: AN INDIFFERENT REACTION

The psychological reception of Freud's theories of *normal* psychology occurred more as actual "reaction" than as mere "exposure." Psychologists themselves reviewed or wrote about Freud's theories twice as often as they recruited physicians to stand in as middlemen in the exploration of psychoanalysis. But as regards the reception of Freud's theories of *abnormal* psychology, the opposite is true. Here, reception must be defined in terms of "exposure" and very little reaction. Outside of the physician-psychologists, Hellpach and Störring, the only psychologist to concern himself with psychoanalytic psychopathology was Lipmann (1906-1907). And even this was indirect. Actually Lipmann was basically interested in the word-association studies being done at Burghölzli, a quite ordinary concern of experimental psychologists at the turn of the century. Every other review in the psychological journals of Freud's, Bleuler's, or Jung's work on psychopathology was by a physician.

Not only were almost all "new" psychologists fairly indifferent to psychopathology, but the two who were interested showed that there was little room for accommodation between experimental psychology and psychoanalysis. At the outset, the disagreement on the subject of the unconscious was practically enough to dictate a permanent standoff. To this must be added the matter of etiology of emotional illness. An idea, according to Störring, could not cause a hysterical paralysis. It was physiological processes which were responsible for ideas and not the other way around. Hellpach spoke en route of the importance of childhood events in the "etiology" of hysteria and dismissed the importance of degeneration and heredity in emotional disturbance. But when drawing his conclusions he came down solidly for the "physiological substratum of the hysterical psychic state" and "the physiological causes of neurasthenic degeneration." As has already been indicated, the new psychologists had a basic belief in the organic etiology of all human function, in spite of fine talk about psychophysical parallelism. The very vagueness of psychophysical parallelism and the influence of physiology and neurology led the psychologists to the assumption that one day all human behavior would be understood in organic terms. Though Freud himself was a subscriber to the eventuality of a physical-chemical explanation, the thrust of his theories was to advocate, for the present, psychological and psychogenic explanations.

PSYCHOANALYTIC TECHNIQUES AND TREATMENT

Scientific respectability was of great importance to the new psychologists. Their method of introspection and experimentation had won them a place in modern science, and so they equated method with progress (see Chapter 7). Before psychologists would grant approval to a new method that called itself "psychological," they would first have to compare it with their own, undeniably "scientific," introspection. Hellpach took upon himself the task of closely scrutinizing the methods of psychoanalysis to determine theoretically whether they were really psychological. Then Hellpach and others also examined psychoanalysis practically on a variety of issues concerning its nature and techniques.

It was a truism of the new psychology that introspection is not a method suited to the mentally ill. Hellpach saw psychoanalysis as an attempt to overcome the limitations of introspection. The question was, could that be done? "Is it possible," asked Hellpach (1906b, p. 39), "to produce, in an emotional illness, a situation in which the usual inability at introspection or the unreliability of introspection is overcome?" Freud, Hellpach explained, had attempted to create such a favorable situation in two ways. First he had used hypnosis and produced a theory of the sexual etiology of hysteria based on the importance of the aftereffects of early childhood experiences. While theoretically Hellpach (1902, pp. 210-211) agreed with Freud's conclusion, "psychologically, the way in which [he and Breuer had] obtained their proof is completely useless." This was because hypnotism was completely unrelated to the methods of scientific research. Breuer and Freud had proved nothing and Külpe was right about the limits of introspection:

> The elucidation of an illness that reaches its climax in a crass disproportion between emotions and their expression, in which apperception is shifted away from its normal activity of putting feelings and ideas clearly into consciousness, can never be the task of psychology. For psychology depends upon attentive introspection, and where it utilizes physical events to draw conclusions about psychic ones, it must rely on the assumption that there is a proper proportion of the two. Therefore, I am in complete agreement with Wundt that suggestion and hypnosis are tasks for physiology, and I would like to apply this statement to hysteria as well. We will be able to attain maximum psychological knowledge about hysteria when the hysterical patient

least suspects that he is being observed; conscious neglect, which plays a role in the treatment of hysteria, may, as an explorative method, give us proportionately the most certain information. To be sure, those like Freud, who do research into the connections of the hysterical consciousness, so that primarily they can make the hysteric a little less hysterical, i.e., hypnotize him, will, at most, experience the satisfaction of finding their previous hypotheses confirmed to their fullest extent through appropriate questioning. But one can answer to that: the more systematically, the more exactly, in the usual sense, the psychological investigation of hysteria is practiced, the more unreliable it is [as previous] explorations of the most progressive French neurologists have demonstrated [Hellpach, 1902, pp. 238-239].

Freud's second attempt to overcome the limitations of introspection was to abandon hypnosis and try "introspection in a waking state." This too had shown that "painful psychic experiences have far-reaching effects and can lie hidden behind remarkable phenomena." But, concurring with William Stern's earlier verdict, Hellpach (1906b, pp. 40-41) declared the newer psychoanalytic method to be as unpsychological as had been the older cathartic one. In this evaluation Hellpach was joined by three other men, only one of whom demurred at his negative findings.

First of all, Hellpach (1906b, p. 41) objected, Freud had not conclusively proved that associations made in the present were also, at a previous time, the psychically causative train of thoughts. Lipmann (1907b) also attacked the psychoanalytic theory of association. Once the psychoanalyst had uncovered a particular sexual trauma which formed the base of his initial interpretation, he used the same trauma to explain later dreams, even though the patient did not dream about this particular trauma in the very same sense again. In his objection Hellpach displayed a poor understanding of what the method of free association in psychoanalysis was supposed to accomplish. Furthermore, neither Hellpach nor Lipmann had grasped Freud's point that there is no past, present, or future in the unconscious. Also, Wundt's theory of a limited chain of associations seems to have been accepted by both psychologists.

Second, there was the frequently heard criticism that the results of psychoanalysis were merely due to suggestion by the psychoanalyst or the autosuggestion of the patient (Hellpach, 1906b, p. 41; Gaupp, 1900a, p. 234; Lipmann, 1907b).

The matter of cures occasioned a split of opinion. To Hellpach (1906b, p. 41) they were not a justification for acceptance of psychoanalysis. "The only proof of the causal connections claimed by analysis—removal of the diseased condition through analysis—is not a satisfactory proof because hysterical and hysteropathic illnesses have already been cured by all possible fortuitous events, especially through those which have suggestive value; and psychoanalytic treatment is still too young to reveal whether an especially high percentage of therapeutic successes develops on its account." This was a telling criticism. Giessler (1902, p. 228), on the other hand, believed that because Freud's method (i.e., free association) had "given him good service in eliminating phobias, obsessions, and delusions" it was valid in understanding dreams.

A vital scientific aspect of the introspective method was that experiments could be replicated. Thus Hellpach (1906b, pp. 41-42) logically considered whether the psychoanalytic method "as regards its *psychological* procedure, is not self-deceiving; to refute this suspicion requires the observation and practice of psychoanalysis by other psychopathologists who are naturally more objective about it than its creator."

This brought Hellpach and Gaupp to a final consideration of the nature of the psychoanalytic method. Gaupp concluded (1900a) without qualifications that "a very subjective, partly even fantastical interpretation has been brought to us here as psychological analysis, discussions that are quite far removed from the scientific method." Freud was guilty of finding what he was looking for. This was also a frequent medical criticism of analysis and was often stated in much the same bald, unsophisticated manner. Hellpach (1906b, p. 42) was more perceptive and, therefore, more convincing:

> The causal working out of the material gained through the analysis is to a great extent dependent on the *empathy of the analyst for his subject*; for the use of the patient's reports depends on the manner in which these reports ensue, and that means that the treatment, in turn, shares the principal logical limitation of all

disclosures based on observation, in that it is subject to decisions of a subjective nature. Though one may recognize that psychoanalysis in the hands of its creator ingeniously and fruitfully illuminates for us some obscure relationships, the treatment lacks the most important elements needed for it to become a "method" and as such to show itself as better than or even on a par with old-style sympathetic observation. The elements lacking are (1) a *psychodiagnostic* superiority; psychoanalysis perpetuates the unreliability of the old observation. (2) A *logical* superiority; this is only attainable with the elimination of the highly personal, godlike influence (*Divinatorik*) of the analyst. But at this time there have been no corrective steps taken in these two directions, and so long as this is the case, the value of the psychoanalytic treatment as a psychopathological method must be completely denied.

Hellpach further bolstered his argument by quoting Löwenfeld (1904a, p. 147): "It is obvious to those who have been taken in by the promise of psychoanalysis that the use of the method ought, for the time being, to be limited to the discoverer himself."

The thorough exploration of the psychoanalytic method from the experimental psychologists' point of view was Hellpach's special contribution to the psychological reception of psychoanalysis. In the nature of things, it can be assumed that many more psychologists read Hellpach on psychoanalysis than read Freud. So while one cannot say that all psychologists' evaluations of psychoanalytic techniques were identical with Hellpach's, it seems likely that a great many psychologists knew either only what was current gossip about Freud's methods or what Hellpach had to say.

THE PSYCHOLOGICAL RECEPTION

As was the case with physicians, Freud was not ignored by psychologists. This can be said with more assurance than was previously possible because up to now no one has thoroughly investigated the experimental psychological journals in order to document precisely the references to Freud's theories. A comparison of the reviews and articles listed in Grinstein's (1956-1966) *Index to Psychoanalytic Writings* with the citations in this chapter shows the extent to which psychological exposure to psychoanalysis has never been fully appreciated.

On the other hand, it cannot be said that before 1908 any significant number of psychologists ever became temporarily absorbed with psychoanalysis as did some physicians who thought that Freud's theories, to a greater or lesser extent, were useful for their particular concerns. There was more "exposure" than "reaction" in the psychological reception of psychoanalysis. Psychologists had the opportunity to become further acquainted with Freud's hypotheses, but his ideas and the theoretical framework of psychoanalysis barely tempted them.

The psychologists' minimal concern is reflected in their reception of psychoanalysis. Although this reception was not all negative, it was a great deal more negative than the medical reception. And yet, just as in the case of the medical critics, disagreement did not automatically mean unbridled or emotional attack. Baerwald, Mentz, Stern, and Störring all were in basic opposition to Freud. But their discussions were thoughtful, their tone respectful, and they took care to show their appreciation of Freud as a serious worker or to point out the particular aspects of his ideas with which they were in agreement.

The different interests of doctors and psychologists and the historical state of psychiatry and psychology at the turn of the century account for the psychologists' greater hostility. Chapters 1 and 7 have elucidated this in detail, but there are five especially pertinent factors that can be noted here: (1) the physicians' great interest in hysteria and the psychologists' lack of interest in psychopathology; (2) the belief of some physicians in the unconscious and the scientific and professional disavowal of its existence by the new psychologists; (3) the corollary: the concern of some doctors with hypnotism and hypnotherapy and the absolute antipathy of the experimental psychologists for these fields; (4) the physiological psychologists' blind and total enchantment with "exact" introspection. Certain psychiatrists were also trapped by their equation of scientific method with scientific knowledge and progress, but not all; (5) the new psychologists' extremely radical break with and renunciation of their philosophical past. This break occurred in psychiatry, too, with some of the same results. But psychiatry's "history" was longer than psychology's, which meant that the break was not as drastic and that there were some important continuities. All these factors are mirrored in the fact that physicians' reviews of psychoanalytic theories in the psychological journals tended to be more favorable than the psychologists' own reviews.

Freud was not ignored by physicians or psychologists. Freud himself began this myth and it has been raised to a truism by many historians of psychoanalysis. It cannot stand unamended. But psychoanalysis was given a fairly negative and apathetic reception by most psychologists. Seventy-five years ago, vast theoretical gulfs separated psychoanalysis from the dominant field of psychology in Germany.

PART III

THE EDUCATED GERMAN PUBLIC
AND PSYCHOANALYSIS

9

THE UNCONSCIOUS

In recent years, there has been a long-overdue effort on the part of historians of medicine, psychiatry, and intellectual history (Whyte, 1962; Ellenberger, 1970) to remind other scholars that interest in and knowledge of the unconscious did not begin with Freud. This "revisionism" has been necessary because of two factors. One was the tendency of many late nineteenth- and early twentieth-century scientists to accord little significance to the work of their predecessors. The second was the psychoanalysts' own tendency to view Freud's work as completely original: before Freud was darkness, after Freud was light.

Of late, however, scholars have rightly brought Freud's precursors to our attention. They have shown that (as in the development of many other complex concepts) the mature description of the unconscious was long preceded by earlier recognition and appreciation of it, and even by a sophisticated awareness of its operation. They have stressed that at the turn of the century there was a growing awareness in Europe of both the existence and importance of the unconscious among certain physiologists, neurologists, psychiatrists, philosophers, and literary figures (Hughes, 1958, p. 63).

THE IDEA OF THE UNCONSCIOUS

The words *Unbewusstsein* and *bewusstlos*, in meanings close to those now current, had been first used by the physician and philosopher Ernst Platner (1744-1818), who not only asserted that unconscious ideas exist, but that they could be responsible for conscious ideas. Thus conscious and unconscious states followed one another in a ceaseless alternation. And even before Platner, G. W. Leibniz (1646-1716) and Christian von Wolff (1679-1754) had given clear expression to the idea of unconscious mental activity. In 1725 Wolff wrote that he objected to the Cartesian belief that nothing could be in the mind of which it is not aware. Leibniz, Wolff, and Platner were only the first of a long series of German thinkers to give explicit recognition to unconscious psychic life.

This recognition grew to a preoccupation as the Romantic literary and philosophic movements came to dominate German thought from around 1790 to 1840. The Romantics began by using the notion of an "unconscious" primarily to indicate the existence of an inherent bond that linked the individual with the universe. This linkage between man and nature, an imperfect remnant of the *All-Sinn* which man had possessed before the Fall, was not really understood, but it could be sensed. It made its presence known in mystical ecstasies, in poetic inspiration, in hypnotic states, and in dreams. The "unconscious" allowed for an intuitive understanding of man's relationship to the various parts of nature—which included, of course, other human beings as well as the components of an individual's self.

Perceiving the numerous events and relationships not under human control, the Romantics soon decided that "the unconscious is really the largest realm in our minds," and that "in all, even the commonest and most everyday [human] production, there cooperates with the conscious an unconscious activity" (quoted in Whyte, 1960, pp. 124, 116).[1] The most sophisticated Romantic notion of the operation of the unconscious was advanced by Herbart: though other thinkers spoke of the *alternation* of conscious and unconscious ideas,

---

[1] Prominent authors whose works illustrate the significant appreciation of unconscious mental "forces" during the early decades of the nineteenth century are Richter, Schelling, Herder, Fichte, Novalis, Goethe, Schiller, Beneke, Herbart, Schopenhauer, and Carus. the last three discussed in the text. Their writings about the unconscious are summarized in Alexander and Selesnick (1966, pp. 45-56, 165-166, 169-170); Bromberg (1954, pp. 190-191); Ellenberger (1970, pp. 202-210; 1957); Freud (1887-1902, pp. 47, 260-261); Jones (1953, pp. 371-374, 377-378); Margetts (1953, pp. 115-138); Mora (1967, pp. 30-31); Shakow and Rapaport (1964, pp. 7-8, 23, 100-102, 104); Whyte (1960, pp. 60-157, 161, 167-168). For the discussion below I am especially indebted to Ellenberger (1970) and Whyte (1960).

before Freud Herbart was the only one to postulate that there is a continual conflict between conscious and unconscious ideas at the threshold of consciousness.[2]

Two Romantic authors who gave particular attention to the complexities of unconscious psychic activity were the contemporaries Arthur Schopenhauer (1788-1860) and Carl Gustav Carus (1789-1869). As early as 1819, Schopenhauer described the world as being divided into "will" and "representation." By "will," Schopenhauer meant the unconscious, a blind, driving force which ruled the universe, a part of which was man. Man was an irrational being led by internal forces which he did not understand and of which he was hardly aware. These forces consisted of two instincts, the instinct of conservation and the sexual instinct. Schopenhauer was also aware that the mental mechanism of repression was a part of the operation of the unconscious.

In 1846, when recognition of Schopenhauer's thought was just beginning, Carus published his *Psyche*, an attempt to give a complete and objective theory of unconscious psychological life. Carus opened his book by stating that "the key to the knowledge of the nature of the soul's conscious life lies in the realm of the unconscious. . . . the first task of a science of the soul is to state how the spirit of Man is able to descend into these depths of his soul." Carus's description of how he believed the unconscious to be structured and his discussion of the characteristics of the unconscious show that a complex conception of the unconscious had been reached by the end of the Romantic period.

The year Carus died, Eduard von Hartmann (1869) published his *Philosophie des Unbewusstsein*, in which what Schelling and Schopenhauer had called "will" was called the "unconscious." Hartmann's comprehensive volume stands as a link between Romantic notions of the unconscious and modern ones. The book is essentially a compilation, not significant for original philosophical theories, but for large amounts of data about the relation of the unconscious to

---

[2] See Ellenberger (1970, pp. 204-207, 209) for a valuable summation of the links between Romantic philosophy and the new dynamic psychiatry of Freud and Jung.

various phenomena: perception, the association of ideas, wit, emotional life, instinct, personality, and motivation. Hartmann also dealt with the role of the unconscious in language, religion, history, and social life (Ellenberger, 1970, pp. 209-210; Whyte, 1960, pp. 154-157). Though the concern with the unconscious grew less pervasive in the second half of the nineteenth century, it never died out, figuring prominently in the thought of the younger Fichte and Nietzsche, for example, as well as in the writings of influential non-Germans such as Dostoevsky.[3]

Interest in the unconscious suffered under the impact of organically oriented medicine and experimental psychology. In 1845, Griesinger clearly expressed his belief in the "constant activity [of] unconscious life and movement . . . which is much greater and more characteristic for the individual than the relatively small number of impressions which pass into the state of consciousness" (Whyte, 1960, p. 152). But contemporary physicians did not seize on this aspect of Griesinger's work, nor was he remembered for it by succeeding generations. The belief in the unconscious underlay Wundt's 1863 *Vorlesungen über Menschen- und Thierseele*, but Wundt later became an enemy of such thinking. Lipp's belief in the unconscious gradually became less clear and emphatic if one compares his unambiguous statements in the *Grundtatsachen des Seelenlebens* (1883) with those in his *Leitfaden der Psychologie* (1903). And just four years after the appearance of Hartmann's book, Ebbinghaus denounced it in his doctoral dissertation.

But the idea of the unconscious remained popular, so much so that both Wundt and Ziehen were moved to deplore its continued acceptance both by professionals and laymen. Various important scientists such as Ewald Hering (1834-1918) contributed to its sophistication. In a popular novel of the 1890's a salon of the 1870's was depicted where conversation dwelt upon Wagner and Hartmann (Whyte, 1960, p. 155).

---

[3] Though Stefan Zweig (1945, p. 117), recalling his student days at the University of Berlin in 1902, remarks that *The Brothers Karamazov* of 1880 had not as yet been translated into German, but was available to him only though the informal translations of a Russian friend.

And ideas about the unconscious were "in the air." The thought of Bergson, Dilthey, Croce, James, and Freud had common sources.

Yet a full appreciation of the unconscious was circumscribed. The notion had not as yet seriously influenced the thought of the educated nonspecialist or nonprofessional. For this part of the German populace seventy-five years ago, the existence or nonexistence of an unconscious was apparently not a provocative issue. At the turn of the century, interest in the unconscious was small as compared with the rapidly growing interest in sexuality. It is instructive to compare the entries under "sex" and "unconscious" in the compilation of German periodical literature from 1896 through 1907 (*Bibliographie der deutschen Zeitschriften-Literatur,* 1893-1908). The entries under "unconscious" remained fairly static both in amount and subject. The entries under "sex," on the other hand, more than doubled in volume and changed in character. While at the start of the period there had been an almost exclusive concentration on anatomical and physiological topics, at the end at least half of the articles were on sexual education, sexual hygiene, and sexual ethics.

The lack of a wide or growing general interest in the unconscious does not at all betoken the educated public's unfamiliarity with the idea of an unconscious. Whyte (1960, p. 161) is quite right in saying that by "1870-1880, the general concept of the unconscious mind was a European commonplace." The idea of an unconscious was quite congenial to many intellectuals, but more on a historical than on a current basis. The great popularity of Hartmann's massive work, which appeared in 1869, rested primarily on an acquaintanceship with works of the eighteenth and early nineteenth centuries rather than on knowledge of the scientific investigations, philosophical inquiries, and literary productions of the last quarter of the nineteenth century. Not until the 1920's did modern concepts of the existence and influence of unconscious mental life become of significant interest to the nonspecializing educated person in Germany.

The "intellectual's" exposure and reaction to Freud's ideas about unconscious mental activity should be viewed with all this in mind. Around 1900 the concept of the unconscious was popular but not dominating. Its vague definition and historically diverse presentation tended to make it an uncontroversial subject to many educated laymen. It had a long history in German philosophy and literature. Those most excited about it in Germany were those trying to disprove its existence and attempting to deal it the fatal epithet of "unscientific." Most intellectuals lived comfortably with one or another of its philosophic or even scientific expressions. Freud had not yet stated his ideas about the unconscious clearly and unambiguously.[4] It was a simple matter for many authors to discuss psychoanalytic theories pertaining to dreams, sexuality, and even hysteria without extensive considerations of the unconscious, the idea of whose *existence* was in no way revolutionary.

REACTION IN LAY PERIODICALS

The general reception of psychoanalytic views of the unconscious will be presented by focusing on agreement or disagreement with the two pillars of these views: (1) an unconscious exists in every person; (2) this unconscious influences our thoughts and actions every day.[5] In addition, one must be aware of the distinction between exposure and reaction in discussing this "lay" reception. When a doctor reviewed a work of Freud's under the heading "Medicine" in a popular publication, the public was being *exposed* to psychoanalysis. So too when a Freudian presented his views. Actual *reaction* can be gauged only in the articles and reviews of nonphysicians and nondisciples. The reaction was small in the first decade of the century, although it was generally favorable.

Freud's assumption of the existence of an unconscious

---

[4] In Chapter VII of *The Interpretation of Dreams* (1900), Freud elaborated for the first time his ideas of the unconscious. But these ideas remained ambiguous until 1912 (and in German, until 1913) when Freud finally gave "a long and reasoned account of the grounds for his hypothesis of unconscious mental processes and set out the various ways in which he used the term 'unconscious' " (Strachey, 1958, p. 258).

[5] A modern expression of psychoanalytic views would be: (1) unconscious *ideation* exists in every person; (2) unconscious *mental processes* influence all our thoughts and actions.

provoked little argument in the lay literature. In his sympathetic discussion of *The Interpretation of Dreams*, Jakob Julius David (1900, p. 239) easily followed Freud in this matter. David (1859-1906) was one of the last of the Austrian "naturalists," and in 1891 converted to Catholicism. He was well known for his stories, plays, and poetry, which began appearing before 1890. Dreams, wrote David, came out of the "most unconscious, the most forgotten things." Even long-forgotten childhood memories appear in dreams. David did not have to depend on Freud for proof of this, for he reported that he knew from his own experience how such "suppressed and troubled" memories can return. Sigmar Mehring (1906), in an essay on the nature of wit, took the existence of the unconscious for granted. His concern was to evaluate Freud's specific contributions to the idea (see below). A Dr. Oppenheimer (1900) was given the job of reviewing *The Interpretation of Dreams* just because it had been written by a physician, and Dr. Oppenheimer was a reviewer of works on "theoretical medicine" and "physiology." Knowing little about dreams or psychiatry, he refrained from any ultimate judgment. Yet he knew that something may be yearned for "either consciously or unconsciously." Even in a basically critical review of the dream book, "yg," the psychiatrist Wilhelm Weygandt (1901, col. 1495) found that one of the "most worthwhile" features of Freud's work was his "specific observations [on] repression."[6]

The only overt, popular attack against Freud because his views were based on a belief in the unconscious was a semi-anonymous review of *Jokes and Their Relation to the Unconscious*. The reviewer (C. D. P., 1906, col. 566) facetiously concluded that Freud's connection of wit with the unconscious "will only be acceptable to those who have penetrated deeply enough into the mysteries of the psychology of the unconscious or unconscious consciousness or conscious unconsciousness."

Naturally, those of Freud's followers who discussed the unconscious in popular publications wasted little time asserting

---

[6] The same month (September, 1901) a similar review signed by Weygandt appeared in the *Zentralblatt für Nervenheilkunde und Psychiatrie*.

its existence. Not only did they believe in it, but they assumed their readers did too. They conceived of their role as one of educating their readers on how the unconscious operates and on its great significance for the life of every human being (see below, pp. 267-269).

This latter assumption of psychoanalysis regarding the unconscious also evoked almost total agreement, sometimes in a surprising fashion. A Rhineland pastor, Ceslaus Schneider, extracted a theological message from Freud's views. Schneider (1901, p. 476) completely accepted Freud's theories about dreams and observed that "quite certainly man is not his own master; good or evil spirits can have an effect on his material nature."

A lengthy article on the nature of wit in *Die Nation* was more conventional. *Die Nation*, in which David's article on dream interpretation had also appeared, was a well-established Berlin weekly which published articles on politics, economics, literature, and the theater, as well as short book reviews. It advertised itself as being a journal of "decided liberalism." Mehring (1906), the Berlin poet and *feuilletoniste*, was captivated by Freud's (1905b) attempt to link jokes with unconscious mental activity. The poet believed that if investigators could only solve the problem of the origin of wit, they would arrive at the solution to the "great puzzle" of man's whole mental activity. Mehring was pleased to inform his readers that "to help us in this investigation for the first time comes a physician equipped not only with the expert knowledge of his profession, but also with the fortunate talent of a writer who has a sense for wit and probably can lay claim to the adjective 'ingenious.' " Freud had been able to demonstrate the operation of unconscious mechanisms in our mundane affairs. He had proved, for example, that the phenomenon of condensation exists not only in wit and dreams but in the everyday act of forgetting. In so doing, Freud had opened "a very important perspective into the phenomena of thought." Mehring completely agreed that involuntary wit comes out of the humorist's unconscious. This was "further proof of the correctness of Freud's theory," which sought to demonstrate that the same "workshop" creates both dream and wit. Freud had shown "a new path to the secret room of our mental workshop." Mehring was still not sure if Freud had "arrived in the room itself" since he had some misgivings about certain elements of Freud's theoretical constructions. But Freud's book remained "a bright path illuminated by the author's own humor and ingenious extensions [*ausgeliehenen*], and no one can regret having followed it."

Not everyone considered Freud's humor illuminating. Richard Meyer, professor of philology at the University of Berlin, missed Freud's point entirely. Meyer had been publishing and editing learned works on literature, poetry, and literary history since 1886, and so he evaluated Freud's book solely on criteria of diction, style, and precision of scholarship. Perhaps this was a case of a careless editor mismatching book and reviewer. In any case, the resulting review (1905) was a strange affair. Meyer criticized *Jokes* because in the main it dealt only with verbal wit. He also objected to Freud's dividing all wit into either aggressive or obscene because such a division was a "hard-hearted conception." From an esthetic point of view, Freud's analysis of the internal working of wit was "barren." As to Freud's illustrative jokes, the book was a "literary-historical" failure; first because of its selection of anecdotes, "among which the suspiciously large quantity of 'Jewish humor' is distastefully conspicuous" — although, Meyer sneered, "taste is quite varied in such a matter." Second, he condemned Freud's scholarship. Freud had attributed certain sayings to the wrong authors. Professor Meyer, as a learned contributor to the *Neue Jahrbücher für das klassische Altertum*, would have none of it.

Meyer's hostile review is worth a moment's scrutiny because it elucidates some of the emotional reactions Freud invariably faced. Jonas Cohn, who had reviewed *Jokes* for the *Zeitschrift für Psychologie*, had predicted that some would object to Freud's attempt to rationalize such an emotional subject as jokes. Meyer fit in this category, for he admitted he had been prejudiced against Freud's work even before reading it: Meyer said he belonged to the many who have their own definition of wit and who consider their own explanation better than most others. Second, though Meyer did not so much as once allude to the subject of the unconscious, he was very much annoyed that Freud offered "complicated psychological considerations" to explain "exceptionally innocent pleasantries." This is, of course, a masked objection to the existence and influence of the unconscious. Indeed, Meyer's strong objection probably explains the fact that he did not openly discuss the subject. Third, there is the matter of Meyer's distaste for "Jewish humor." This is either one of the rare published examples of Freud's Jewishness being used to discredit his psychoanalytic work, or it could be explainable by the fact that Meyer was Jewish and afraid that the large number of Jewish jokes (in what he considered a dubious book) could become grist for an anti-Semitic mill. Unfortunately, it has thus far been impossible to learn Meyer's religion.[7] Yet here is an instance of anti-Semitism determining popular reaction to psychoanalysis. At any rate, as far as the subject under present scrutiny is concerned—the influence of the unconscious—Meyer's review is one of the two in the early popular literature on Freud to deny its influence.

The readers of Maximilian Harden's prestigious *Zukunft* and of the *Beilage zur Allgemeinen Zeitung* (Munich), on the other hand, were exposed to long and closely argued pieces on the importance of the unconscious. In 1904 Harden had written in his weekly about the case of a drama critic, Siegfried Jacobsohn, who had been accused of plagiarizing. Jacobsohn claimed he had not done so knowingly, and Harden tended to agree. Harden asked both Arthur Schnitzler and Jung to comment. Though Jung (1905a) ostensibly addressed himself to this issue by entitling his article "Cryptomnesia,"[8] he actually commented on it only very briefly at the end of his essay. Instead, he devoted himself to a lengthy discussion of

[7] That he was an "extraodinary" professor raises the possibility that he was Jewish and unable to be a full ("ordinary") professor, but that is only speculation. Many Christian professors never rose above the rank of *Extraordinarius*.

[8] "Literally, [cryptomnesia] means 'hidden memory' and refers to the appearance in consciousness of many traces which are not recognized as such but appear to be original creations. Organized ideas, thoughts, or images from the past which are not perceived as part of the past appear novel. The term originally appeared in the French scientific literature and was described by the Swiss psychologist, Flournoy, in 1900" (Trosman, 1969, p. 234).

the operation of the unconscious, the ubiquity of unconscious psychic elements, the relation between dreams and the unconscious, and the role of unconscious memories in hysteria. Throughout the essay Jung informed the *Zukunft*'s readers of Freud's specific contributions to the understanding of all these matters.

Jung presented many commonplace examples of the working of the unconscious. He explained that there has to be a train of associations leading to every conscious thought or act, even if this train is not immediately or at all apparent. He emphasized that this same process occurs in both healthy and ill persons. Jung (p. 98) proposed that the operation of the unconscious in mentally sick people be regarded as "nothing other than a caricature of normal psychological mechanisms."

> Every day thousands of associations enter the luminous circle of consciousness, and we would question them in vain for a more specific account of their origins. We must always bear in mind that conscious psychic phenomena are only a very small part of our total psyche. By far the greater part of the psychic elements in us is unconscious.
>
> Our consciousness therefore finds itself in a rather precarious position with regard to automatic movements of the unconscious that are independent of our will. The unconscious can perceive and can associate autonomously. . . . Our unconscious must therefore harbor an immense number of psychic complexes which would astonish us by their strangeness.

Thus, slowly approaching his appointed task and avoiding any partisanship in Jacobsohn's cause, Jung attempted to demonstrate by a generally pertinent discussion that it was completely possible that someone who commits plagiarism may not have done it consciously. It was entirely possible that the "plagiarist" may have "forgotten" his knowledge of the original; even verbatim plagiarism could be completely unconscious.

Another elaborate presentation of what Freud had learned about the unconscious was the lead essay of one of the literary supplements to the *Allgemeine Zeitung*. The article was a paean of praise to Freud and to psychoanalysis, and combined a joyful and simple style with a great deal of sophisticated information. The author, Hugo Friedmann—a little-known philosopher—took the view that a wonderful thing had been discovered and now, at last, we can all share in it.[9] The article's combination of enthusiasm and explicit information was bound to commend it to a certain portion of readers.

Friedmann's (1907, p. 65) introductory paragraph is noteworthy for its description of Freud's place in "psychology" in 1907:

> Professor Freud is well-known to many. . . . Freud is as far removed from the old psychology, with its schematic, classificatory activity, as he is from modern psychophysics, which has brought purely physical methods into the psychological domain. . . . He works in an area whose fundamental significance had, indeed, already been suspected by several investigators, but for whose enlightenment nothing noteworthy had been done before him: it is the role of the unconscious in psychic life.

The author pursued an orderly plan. He defined the "unconscious," and he discriminated between what was common knowledge about it and what "more alert observers" now know. He explained why human beings repress certain thoughts and impulses and the intricate mechanism and results of that repression. He discussed how unconscious associations are formed and the significance of this. If the reader were "taken aback" by all this information, Friedmann (pp. 65-66) declared, he could prove it to his own satisfaction by making a scientific investigation of the unconscious. For

> now it is possible, even simple. Only a small knack is necessary: the quintessence of the Freudian method. This consists in the ability to attack the unconscious counterwill, capture it and eradicate it. . . . While in the beginning hypnosis was used to break through to the inhibitions, it is now known that expert procedure [based on] much training and patience . . . and a bit of authority . . . can free ideas from their imposed sleep.
>
> Thus it is possible to reveal the riddle of the unconscious and to take cognizance of things which—though hidden from the individual—still make up a dominant portion of the "ego" and are most intimately entwined with all experiences.

[9] This article is not listed in Grinstein's *Index of Psychoanalytic Writings*, though some of Friedmann's later writings on psychoanalysis are.

To illustrate his theoretical explanations, Friedmann append-
ed a wide variety of everyday situations in the life of a ficti-
tious woman and laid bare their intrapsychic meanings. Freud
might have objected to Freidmann's semihucksterish approach. "Be the first on your block to be psychoanalyzed" was
never Freud's motto. Nevertheless, it is clear that by 1907 the
popularization of psychoanalysis was under way in Germany.

Articles and reviews of Freud's ideas about the unconscious
were not a prominent feature in popular publications during
the formative years of psychoanalysis. But then, the unconscious in general was not a conspicuous subject in popular German periodicals before World War I. When we
evaluate the reception of ideas about the unconscious that
were specifically linked to psychoanalysis, we can conclude
that psychoanalysis did not fare badly. Though notice was
scanty, what interest there was tended to be positive. The
semianonymous "C. D. P" and Meyer raised the only objections.

THREE BLOWS TO HUMAN NARCISSISM

In 1917 Freud wrote that his discovery of psychoanalysis
had been the gravest narcissistic blow mankind had ever suffered, rendered all the more severe because it followed two
already ego-damaging events. The first was the Copernican
revolution, the second the Darwinian revolution. In the first,
man's world had been booted out of the center of the universe;
in the second, man himself had lost his unique position on
earth. And now Freud had delivered the supreme insult: man
was not even "master in [his] own house," but at the mercy of a
capricious, illogical unconscious (Freud, 1916-1917, pp. 284-
285; 1917, pp. 137-144).

Freud's view of this philosophical impact of psychoanalysis
and of its role in the hostile reception of psychoanalysis was
shared and propagated by later psychoanalysts. Heinz Hartmann (1894-1970), in a 1927 paper criticizing Karl Jaspers's
verstehende Psychologie, quoted Freud's words on the subject
and emphasized (p. 384) that "here lies one of the most powerful causes of that emotional rejection of psychoanalysis which

has brought it many enemies." In the same year that Hartmann's paper appeared in an English translation, David Shakow and David Rapaport, discussing Freud and American psychology, wrote that psychoanalytic theory is an immediate and deep threat to man's fundamental narcissism. Shakow and Rapaport (1964, pp. 15-16, 23) also repeated Freud's story of the three blows science had inflicted on man's self-image.

In 1960, Lancelot Whyte challenged the special significance which psychoanalysts had traditionally attached to the part Freud's revelation of unconscious mechanisms played in arousing hostility toward psychoanalysis. After tracing the development of the idea of the unconscious in post-Cartesian Europe, Whyte concluded that the idea was "conceivable" around 1700, "topical" around 1800, and "fashionable" around 1870-1880. He also believed that the nineteenth century had seen "many special applications of the idea . . . systematically developed." In this historical setting, asked Whyte, "why was Freud's work . . . treated with angry professional scorn . . . ? Why were Freud's doctrine and methods found so despicable . . . if the background had been so long prepared and he was [soon] to be recognized as a major figure . . . ?" Whyte attributed the angry reception to Freud's initial "explicit and narrow emphasis on sexuality as the source of neurosis." When Freud and his followers later modified the stress on sexuality, Whyte claimed (1960, p. 159), psychoanalysis gained wider acceptance.

The sides were thus drawn. Disregarding, for the moment, the issue of sexuality, we are confronted by two opposite positions. The analysts' own is that Freud's postulation of the prominent role of the unconscious in everyone's daily life was one of the main causes for the rejection of psychoanalysis. Whyte's is that the idea of the unconscious was so "fashionable" at the time Freud's writings first appeared that it could not have been responsible for the scorn with which so many greeted psychoanalysis.[10]

[10] As we have seen, complete rejection and scorn were not the typical reactions to psychoanalysis. But so many of the issues surrounding the reception of psychoanalysis have for so long been couched in "either/or" terms that to fight this en-

I believe there is error and accuracy in both positions. Basically, the two views are oversimplifications of the actual situation. Neither side has considered that it is impossible to make an unqualified general statement about the extent to which the unconscious was a factor in the rejection of psychoanalysis. Generalization is impossible when one reviews the evidence that has been presented in this study. Even among professional and educated circles in Germany, there was no monolithic (or even majority) position on the existence of an unconscious. The "unconscious" meant different things to different groups.

The physiological psychologists, although equating all psychic activity with consciousness, did use the word "unconscious." But to them it meant the absence of all thought—"zero grade" of consciousness, as Wundt said, meaning a literal "unconsciousness" in a physiological sense. Some experimental psychologists did believe in the existence of "unconscious connecting links," but that was not common.

There were Herbartian psychologists, but their number and influence at the turn of the century did not match those of the experimentalists. They believed in an unconscious, and their concept was to a large extent similar to Freud's. Mental activity involved a rapid and constant alternation of "ideas" going "up" and "down," from the unconscious to the conscious and back again. There was conflict in this process. Unconscious "ideas" battled with each other and with the conscious for admittance into the conscious. The unconscious existed simultaneously with the conscious and was a repository for "repressed" ideas.

After Freud had applied his psychoanalytic method to dozens of patients, his description of the unconscious and its operation contained a vividness that Herbart and his followers—for lack of clinical material and a suitable method—had never achieved. There emerged from Freud's theoretical writings and case descriptions the notion of a

trenched view in every sentence would be tiresome, not to say stylistically awkward. For ease of expression and clarity, then, I will speak here in absolute terms; the reader should keep in mind, however, the actual, mixed nature of the reception of psychoanalysis.

controlling unconscious. This was an unconscious whose existence began in a person's infancy and potentially exercised sway over *all* areas of life, important as well as trivial.

A fourth conception of the unconscious was the intellectuals', who often spoke of the unconscious as "spirit," "force," or "will." Romantic ideas about and descriptions of the unconscious had never disappeared. Hartmann's book had fallen on a well-prepared audience. But it was not, on the whole, a scientific audience. Rather, it was a literary audience with a strong belief in a vague concept or, actually, a number of vague concepts. After 1900, those intellectuals who read Freud were presented with a set of quite specific (though not yet well-organized) notions about the unconscious; these men reacted in one of two ways. Some accepted Freud's views without a full realization of what he really meant. That is, they believed in an "unconscious" and so were agreeable to Freud's belief in one too. The word was congenial. The naturalist writer David and probably the Catholic thinker Schneider belong to this group. Some literati, such as Mehring, the poet, and Friedmann, the philosopher, could go further. They understood and accepted Freud's views in their details. These were men who welcomed the precise elucidation of hitherto vaguely stated mechanisms.[11]

It is clear that the judgments of both Whyte and the analysts are in need of some refinement. Whyte is right in saying that there was a considerable acceptance of the idea of the unconscious before Freud. But Whyte ignores the fact that the pre- and post-Freudian conceptions of the unconscious are not the same. Because Hartmann's book was a frequent subject in the salons of the 1870's does not mean that Freud's *Interpretation of Dreams*, shorn of its sexual emphases, would have been eagerly embraced there. It is true that late nineteenth-century beliefs in the unconscious did prepare the way

---

[11] Judging from the voluminous material in Ellenberger's *Discovery of the Unconscious* (1970), as well as from the large number of disparaging remarks made by Hellpach, Wundt, and Ziehen, it is clear that there was a strong popular belief in some kind of "unconscious." This belief was compounded of a mixture of age-old tales and popularized Romantic ideas. The precise attitudes of the mass of people toward an unconscious have been studied by no one, and neither the psychoanalysts, Whyte, nor I are in any position to make a definitive statement.

for certain physicians, philosophers, nonexperimental psychologists, and intellectuals to be either tolerant of or interested in Freud's ideas. But those beliefs played no role as far as the physiological psychologists were concerned. As a matter of fact, this obvious general belief in some kind of unconscious angered the psychologists. They fought against this "philosophical" and "metaphysical" relic and condemned it as "unscientific" and "popular."

A comment might be made at this point on Whyte's simplistic conclusion that psychoanalysis was rejected because of its sexual theories and not because of its ideas on the unconscious. For one thing, the idea of an unconscious was either intellectually or emotionally abhorrent to a great many people. The present study has demonstrated this fact. Furthermore, there is a strong likelihood that some of those who objected to Freud's ideas about the unconscious hid their objections behind attacks against his sexual theories. As noted earlier, sex was a *very* fashionable topic of debate in Germany, much more so than the unconscious. It was an accepted vehicle of discussion and opinion; people thought they knew a lot about it, either to urge sexual reforms or the retention of the status quo. It was much easier to take a stand on sex and express oneself against its misuse than to formulate into words (much less reasoned arguments) vague and embarrassing thoughts and feelings about how the existence of an unconscious deprived one of self-mastery (personal conversations with Hans Kleinschmidt and Edith Weigert; see also Shakow and Rapaport, 1964, p. 23).

The psychoanalysts are thus close to the truth in their estimation of the impact of the narcissistic blow. But they ascribe to it a far more lethal quality than it ever had. It is at least debatable whether the psychological revolution of the twentieth century aroused more enmity and bitterness than did the biological revolution of the nineteenth and the cosmological revolution of the sixteenth centuries. Each, viewed within the context of its own time and in the light of the sensibilities of the significant people involved, was a major threat to various established orders and ideas, and it is difficult to say that Freud's assault against man's supremacy was the most grievous. It can be said that the twentieth century, being the most "mass" of the eras under consideration, offered greater potential for quicker dissemination and greater self-application of Freud's idea. But that is not the point the psychoanalysts have been making. Shakow and Rapaport (1964, pp. 14-32), in particular, have devoted themselves to a historical comparison of the reception of evolutionary theories and of psychoanalytic theories, in order to show that Darwin did not have as tough a time of it as Freud. While they bring to light some interesting and valuable information, it is questionable whether such a comparison—more in the service of partisanship than of history—proves the theory of the "narcissistic blow."

It is on the side of the analysts that a goodly number of people who seemed to accept Freud's theories of the unconscious probably did not have a precise notion of what Freud meant. But a substantial minority who read Freud did, and were able to withstand the blow to their narcissism. People could accept that man was not his own ruler and welcome the elucidation of to what end and to whom man was a prisoner. In this category can be placed the pastor Schneider, the writers David and Mehring, the philosopher Cohn, and the psychiatrist Weygandt.

Moreover, the experimental psychologists did not *mainly* reject Freud because the analytic concept of the unconscious was a wound to their self-esteem. They rejected Freud because of very strong prior intellectual commitments. Freud himself recognized that the scientific *Zeitgeist* among physicians and psychologists worked so as not to allow the psyche any independent life of its own, but to keep it subservient to the soma.[12] Such a belief was incompatible with any recognition of the significance of the unconscious.

[12] "Anything that might indicate that mental life is in any way independent of demonstrable organic changes or that its manifestations are in any way spontaneous, alarms the modern psychiatrist, as though recognition of such things would inevitably bring back the days of the Philosophy of Nature, and of the metaphysical view of the nature of the mind. The suspicions of the psychiatrists have put the mind, as it were, under tutelage, and they now insist that none of its impulses shall be allowed to suggest that it has any means of its own" (Freud, 1900, p. 41). See also Freud (1905c, p. 284).

When one talks about the reception of Freudian ideas of the unconscious, it is necessary to distinguish among various professional and nonprofessional groups. The material presented in Chapters 3, 4, 5, 8, and in this one is ample evidence that there was no single "reception." One must take into account both the strong Romantic tradition which formed a background for acceptance of the unconscious and the scientific spirit of the late nineteenth century which was a powerful force against its acceptance.

Explanations for "rejection" which rely on one reason are simplistic. Single reasons must take their place within a more complex, and hence more realistic, whole. It is not true to say that if it had not been for its sexual theories psychoanalysis would have been eagerly accepted. Yet, of course, there were those who believed in an unconscious and were undeniably repelled by Freud's sexual hypotheses. The "narcissistic blow" was inoperative in many reactions to Freud's ideas of the unconscious, though it obviously played an important role in a large number of others.

Finally, it is helpful to remember that the "age of the unconscious" was only dawning when the twentieth century began. Truly enough, questions surrounding the significance of the unconscious were soon to become vital to many areas of Western life. But seventy-five years ago these issues—in the precise patterns in which they have become familiar to us— were confined to the avant-garde in literature, art, philosophy, and psychology.

10

DREAMS

Pronouncements [that] dreams are an elevation of mental life to a higher level . . . today . . . are repeated only by mystics and pietists.
—Freud, *The Interpretation of Dreams*

Dreams were a subject of much greater general concern than was the unconscious. Obviously, the existence of dreams was universally recognized, and dream interpretation had figured in some fashion in all known cultures. If the fact of greater popular interest in dreams than in the unconscious needs any documentation, a comparative examination of the entries under "Dreams" and "Unconscious" in the *Bibliographie der deutschen Zeitschriften Literatur* (1893-1908) easily provides it. It is also of note that in the period of this study the articles on dreams in German periodicals reached a high point in 1902. This sudden spate of articles strongly suggests that an interest in dreams was stimulated by Freud's publications of 1900 and 1901. But the interest was not sustained, dropping off very quickly after 1902. The question inevitably occurs: Why, in spite of the adequate and appreciative notice in many general periodicals of Freud's ideas about dreams, was there no continued attention to them afterwards? There does not seem to be any definitive evidence to answer this question, but a guess will be hazarded in my concluding remarks.

SCIENTIFIC AND LAY VIEWS OF DREAMING

On the whole, scientific authorities of Freud's day believed that in dreams human mental activity is in a lower and less efficient state and that the higher intellectual faculties are suspended or gravely impaired. These scientists variously regarded dreams as psychic anarchisms, confusions of ideational life, crazy activity, or degradations of the thinking and reasoning faculty. They used such adjectives as incoherent, absurd, nonsensical, or senseless to describe dreams. A dream was considered by most scientists to be a *somatic* and not a psychic process; it was a bodily reaction to some somatic stimulus that had succeeded in disturbing sleep (Freud, 1900, pp. 48-65).[1]

But these ideas were not always shared by educated laymen. For one thing, laymen were more likely than scientists to have remained influenced by age-old popular ideas which always ascribed meanings to dreams. For generations, dreams had been interpreted through fixed explanations: to dream of losing a tooth always meant the loss of a friend. Dreams of funerals always meant forthcoming marriages (Bromberg, 1937, p. 247). Moreover, nonscientists did not have the same commitment to organic explanations of human functions as did scientists of the day. So laymen did not condemn as harshly as did scientists Romantic ideas connecting the psyche with dreaming.

Consequently Freud's dream theories received, on the whole, a much better reception from laymen than from doctors and psychologists (though there are important exceptions to this generalization as far as physicians are concerned). And it was not only those laymen who had read Freud who agreed with him. A basic agreement with Freud's outlook can be seen in essays on dreams written by laymen who seem to have had no knowledge of Freud's works.

A scholar of ancient religions wrote that in dreams we meet people and things as we really feel about them inwardly. A dream teaches more in a second than does a year-long

---

[1] Freud compiled an excellent annotated bibliography of late nineteenth-century scientific opinions on dreams. Even his critics congratulated him on it.

consideration about how a person inwardly regards his father and mother, brother and sister, how he feels about friends and girlfriends, social relationships, religious life. "How difficult it is, in the confusion of daily life, to reach the goal: 'Know Thyself,' but how effortlessly a dream can lead us along this way if we can correctly understand it" (Fabri, 1905, p. 154).

The senior master of a Berlin secondary school urged serious scientific investigation of dreams. Writing in the venerable *Pädagogisches Archiv,* the *Oberlehrer,* Gruhn (1907), announced that dreams were a very important subject and found it "astonishing in these days of exact science" that the dream problem received little notice. "Long, exact observation" had convinced him that the dream has basic connections with thought and feeling in the waking state. "Questions which we do not know how to answer with our waking sense, ideas that we are not able to express, feelings and wishes that are suppressed or held back—they all reappear in dreams and then become completely released."

Gruhn pleaded for some clarity to be thrown on the causes of dreams. It was common knowledge, he said, that sometimes external stimuli play a role, e.g., changes in light or temperature. But why, he queried, do we see in dreams the precise images we do, and not others? In Gruhn's view, the problem could be solved by undertaking a comprehensive, statistical study of dreams, carried out by scientifically trained persons who were used to performing exact observations.

REACTION IN LAY PERIODICALS

With views like these expressed by those unfamiliar with Freud, it is not surprising that an overwhelming percent of the lay response to Freud's theories about dreams was enthusiastic. The reaction to *The Interpretation of Dreams* (issued in November, 1899, with a title-page date of 1900) and *On Dreams* (1901, published in Löwenfeld's *Grenzfragen* series) is contained in four types of literature. These are short book reviews, discursive articles built on Freud's ideas, long review articles on current scientific work on dreams, and educational articles on basic concepts of psychoanalysis which included information on dreams. As in studying the reception of ideas on the unconscious, we must classify some of the notice given to the dream books as "exposure" rather than "reaction," because such attention was the work of either physicians or Freud's followers. But unlike the case of the unconscious, reaction far outshadowed exposure.

Not surprisingly, the subject that received the most attention was Freud's very basic premise that a dream is a fulfillment of a wish. Only one commentator disagreed with Freud's explanation. In his "Report on the Sciences" for the readers of the *Deutsche Revue*, the psychiatrist C. M. Giessler (1906, pp. 245-246) conceded that children's dreams are often wish dreams since the "feelings and aspirations of children generally push them toward the satisfaction of needs which mainly consist of wishes; but this is not the case with adults." Giessler strove to convince his lay readers that the dream is an "event that in all cases is unnecessary and in many cases is pathological." The dream state signified psychic decay, the retrogression of psychic and physiological elements to earlier epochs of the life of individuals and of the species. Obviously, if the dream demonstrated "psychic decay" it could not be for Giessler the fulfillment of the mature adult's wish.

But Weygandt ("yg," 1901, col. 1495), also considered a medical expert on dreams, wrote that in many dream analyses Freud had made it "plausible" that dreams are the fulfillment of wishes. Dr. Carl Oppenheimer (1900, p. 219) in the weekly *Umschau* refrained from an opinion since he had not conducted his own studies and tests. But he concluded that Freud's views were "very ingenious [*geistvoll*] and the whole book very much worth reading." In the monthly *Türmer*, a public health specialist, Georg Korn (1902, p. 441), presented Freud's theory along with several others in a noncommittal review article.

But not all doctors proffered Freud's views to their lay audiences in such reserved manner. Otto Lubarsch (1901-1902, p. 17), a brilliant pathologist at a young age, reported that "Freud's conception . . . is extraordinarily fruitful for the understanding of dreams." Lubarsch (1860-1933) had become famous at twenty-eight for first recognizing carcinoids, relatively benign abdominal tumors with the microscopic picture of malignancy. He was later honored on his sixtieth and seventieth birthdays with *Festschriften* in *Virchows Archiv*. Lubarsch (1901-1902) wrote a two-part series on sleep and dreams for *Die Woche*, a mass-oriented weekly. In evaluating Freud's theory he believed that "we will have to wait to see if it fits all cases or whether it needs some corrections as to particular cases. But as far as I am concerned, after reading Freud's pamphlet [*On Dreams*] many of my own dreams, which previously had been incompletely understood, became clear."

Professor Lubarsch's enthusiastic acceptance of Freud's wish-fulfillment hypothesis was frequently echoed by lay writers. In rich prose, the poet and dramatist J. J. David (1900, p. 239) explained Freud's theory for the readers of the Berlin weekly *Nation*. Freud had shown "an uncommonly honest search for truth," and *The Interpretation of Dreams* radiated "the great joyousness a discoverer derives from his work." Because Freud had sought "to bring law and unity to the senseless childish images with which dreams try to mock us," concluded David, it was necessary to call attention to his work. It is noteworthy that David's article appeared just two months after *The Interpretation of Dreams*. Freud complained about the lack of immediate notice of his work, but he was frequently unaware of or unduly depreciated the attention paid to it.

A teacher of zoology, botany, and chemistry, Ludwig Karell (1900, p. 4), "happily" greeted Freud's "searching and critical" theory in the daily supplement to the Munich *Allgemeine Zeitung*. In the weekly *Gegenwart* Eduard Sokal (1902), a writer of nontechnical articles on psychological matters, announced the arrival of the "Columbus of dream research . . . the famous Viennese neurologist Sigmund Freud [who] with great acumen demonstates the common roots of dream phenomena in individual cases." An anonymous author (1902, p. 44) in *Gaea*, a long-established, serious journal devoted to science and geography, proclaimed "Freund" [*sic*] the first to have established the laws that governed dreams.[2] Naturally,

---

[2] A review I was unable to locate is reported to have been published in *Die übersinnliche Welt*, 8:115, 1900, a journal devoted to occultist research.

Freud's theory of dreams as fulfillments of wishes was also publicized for lay audiences by his followers (Stekel, 1906; Friedmann, 1907).

As regards specific aspects of the wish-fulfillment theory, the majority of commentators were most impressed with Freud's enunciation of the "dream work." These are the processes of condensation, displacement, etc., used by the dreamer. Recognizing these processes enables the analyst to understand the "latent content" (as opposed to the "manifest content") of dreams and to see how a particular dream, though appearing to be meaningless, is really the fulfillment of a wish. The latent content is uncovered by the dreamer's "associating" to the various elements of the dream.

All the physicians except Giessler called attention to these aspects of Freud's theory. Weygandt ("yg," 1901, col. 1495) thought Freud's detailed analysis of dream work was one of the most noteworthy parts of his book. Lubarsch (1901-1902, p. 17) provided his readers with a full discussion of the relationship between manifest and latent dream content, characterizing Freud's work with the usual sobriquet: "extremely ingenious" (*geistreich*).

Among the lay writers, the science teacher Karell (1900, p. 5) praised Freud for the "rich material" which he had compiled on condensation and displacement, both of which Karell carefully explained and illustrated. The Catholic pastor Schneider (1901, p. 476) also was impressed by the "comprehensive material" Freud had gathered in support of his method of dream interpretation. The anonymous author (1902, pp. 46-47) in *Gaea* completely accepted Freud's "very important studies" of how "dream work produces an imposing condensation of the basic elements. There is no element which, by association, does not lead in several directions, no situation which is not connected with three or more impressions or experiences. . . . That dream work utilizes the ambiguity of words is an important discovery of the Viennese investigator; it will probably be a departure point for further disclosures about certain obscure areas of psychic life."

Mehring (1906, p. 284) appreciated the significance of Freud's discovery that the very same processes that existed in dreams also manifested themselves in wit and in the everyday act of forgetting. These "primary" processes all arose from the same source: the user's unconscious. Freud had thus opened "a very important perspective into the phenomena of thought."

Mehring presents us with the curious case of a poet and humorist who completely accepted the one psychoanalytic book he had read (*Jokes*) and then declared himself unable to agree with an idea that had originated in a book he had not read (*The Interpretation of Dreams*). Mehring (1) adopted the view that dreams and wit both originate in the unconscious, (2) agreed that the phenomenon of condensation existed in wit, dreams, and in everyday slips, (3) favored Freud's ideas on fantasy over those of a rival theorist (Scherner) on the sources of poetic creation, (4) but then declared that a dream "is nothing but a chaotic, goalless game"! It seems probable that if Mehring was so won over by *Jokes*, he would have been equally won over by *The Interpretation of Dreams*—if he had read it. Mehring's case suggests that, at least among poets and writers, psychoanalysis in the early years did not so much face the problem of a hostile audience as of an audience that was, quite simply, tiny. It seems clear that Freud's ability to convince people with literary interests was never in doubt. But for a number of years Freud was not particularly interested in lay reaction; it was medical acceptance that he craved at first.

Whether Freud's work was of a scientific nature was always an urgent question. As has been shown, many psychiatrists and most psychologists attacked psychoanalysis on this ground, since they had very definite criteria for what constituted "science" and "scientific method." Weygandt ("yg," 1901, col. 1495) was typical of this group, taking Freud to task for basing his investigations only on his own dreams and those of documented neurotic patients. The pathologist Lubarsch, on the other hand, whose work and reputation met every definition of turn-of-the-century science, did not consider that Freud's subjects had invalidated his conclusions. Clearly, not every German scientist lost his flexibility of thought and succumbed to rigid methodological definitions of knowledge. As a result of Freud's work, Lubarsch (1901-1902, p. 19) concluded that the dream possessed "great psychological worth so that through its exact analysis, we can obtain insight into the innermost recesses of our heart. And, as Freud emphasizes, it is of priceless significance for the understanding of many symptoms of psychic disturbances and perhaps also for their treatment."

Lubarsch's reaction was shared by most laymen who came into early contact with Freud's discoveries about dreams. David (1900, p. 238) began his review by announcing that he was going to discuss a book that was of "great importance" for psychologists. Several months later, the zoologist and botanist Karell (1900) declared that Freud "easily succeeds" in proving that dreams have the character of a wish "by producing experimental evidence." Naturally, also, the dream work was "of the greatest significance for psychologists." Reverend Schneider (1901) reported that Freud's book "does not lose itself — and that is its excellent quality — in aimless psychological speculation that lacks a goal." Freud had "scientifically assimilated" his material, and his "manner of expression was sober, positive, and clear."

The titles of two articles explicitly summed up their authors' outlook: one, quite simply, "Scientific Dream Interpretation" (Sokal, 1902); the other, for the lay scientific periodical *Gaea*, "The Dream in the Light of Scientific Investigation." The substance of this latter essay (Anonymous, 1902, pp. 45, 46, 48) was about equally divided between precise elucidations of the dream work and the significant difference between previous theories about dreaming and Freud's. The author concluded that earlier hypotheses "must be contradicted" because Freud had discovered that "the world of dreams has its own causality." Freud had arrived at his conclusions only after "deep and basic investigations." The author was moved to "recognize how greatly the result of deep scientific investigation contradicts immediate naïve experience."

Other writers were more concerned with Freud's theory of the sources of dreams. No one contested Freud's conclusion that all dreams are a combination of childhood experiences and impressions, as well as subjects of current interest. It is worth noting how eagerly David and Karell embraced Freud's explanation of dreams of the death of family members. If dreams were wish fulfillments, did one really wish the death of a parent or sibling? Yes — but based on angry feelings one had as a child and resting on a child's conception of death as a temporary separation, i.e., the child's inability truly to understand the word "forever." This was why, explained both authors, dreams of death were often unaccompanied by the painful feelings adults associate with death. An adult dreams about death in the manner a child conceives of it.

But some reviewers found it a challenge to agree completely with Freud on the sources of dreams. This probably accounts for the fact that many of those who greeted psychoanalytic dream theories so enthusiastically breathed no word on the role of sexuality in dreams. If one accepted that early life experiences were a fertile source of dreams, then how else to account for sexual dreams except that children had sexual thoughts and feelings? Most reviewers circumvented the problem by accepting the *general* childhood etiology of dreams but not mentioning the *specific* sexual experiences that Freud himself discussed.

Yet not all shied away from the provocative issue. Weygandt ("yg," 1901, col. 1495), at one extreme, was openly shocked at the "extraordinary" relationships to parents described by Freud: hatred of the father and sexual inclination toward the mother. Freud had gone "so far" as to connect the tragedy of Oedipus with Oedipus's marrying of his mother. The usual response, however, was simply to acknowledge Freud's hypothesis but take no position on it. The undisguised openness of Weygandt's recoil from the notion that childhood sexuality was a source of dreams was a rare reaction; and equally uncommon was David's (1900, p. 239) wholehearted recognition of it. First sexual impulses occurred very early. Sensuality grows between father and daughter, mother and son. It manifests itself very early in a kind of jealousy and in caressing. A little girl gladly takes the place of her mother when the mother is absent. "That may appear harmless, and it probably is, but it nevertheless signifies with great exactness the direction of [the little girl's] wishes." Wishes for the fulfillment of sexual relationships between parents and children "lie in all of us," said David.

Not surprisingly, the two authors who dealt explicitly with sexuality were the same two who took stands on Freud's use of symbolism. Weygandt, the scientist, "confessed that [*The Interpretation of Dreams*] offers well-observed material and goes into the endeavor of analyzing this material farther, or , said better, deeper than anyone up to now has tried to do. But there can be too much of a good thing, and the false paths of an unfruitful symbolism are not avoided." To David the poet, however, it did not seem odd that to understand the nature of dreams "one must peel off several layers, clarify the manifold ramifications, be strong and honest toward oneself, before one can advance to this powerfully masked core. . . . Sometimes [sexuality] appears in the clearest of symbols. At other times it disguises itself in the most remarkable manner. Freud's interpretation is strange but enlightening."

Naturally, when Freud's followers wrote for popular audiences, they were quite informative about the role of symbolism. For example, Jung (1905a, p. 99) explained to the readers of *Die Zukunft* that the inhibitions imposed by waking consciousness protect our minds from invasions by "strange psychic complexes." "But in dreams, when the inhibitions of the conscious mind are lifted, the unconscious can play the maddest games. Anyone who has read Freud's dream analyses . . . will know how the unconscious can bedevil the most innocent and decent-minded people with sexual symbols whose lewdness is positively horrifying." Of course, Jung's puritanical tone was his own contribution, somewhat akin to Adler's dire warnings to parents (discussed in Chapter 12).

There was one author, a Munich philologist and scholar of mythologies and fairy tales, whose interest in *The Interpretation of Dreams* prompted him to write an article whose underlying themes cut across several of the psychoanalytic theories already mentioned: that dreams are meaningful because they are a direct continuation of thoughts, wishes, and fears held during the waking state; that early life wishes, including sexual ones, find a place in dreams; that symbolism plays a vital role in dreaming and waking states.

The scholar, Friedrich von der Leyen (1873-1966), composed an essay (1901) for the short-lived *Lotse* (*The Pilot*), an ambitious, avant-garde cultural weekly published in Hamburg. In the same volume as von der Leyen's article, there appeared pieces by Lou Andreas-Salomé, Max Dessoir, Hugo Münsterberg, Rainer Maria Rilke, Georg Simmel, Ferdinand Tönnies, and an article about Stefan George. Because of the pioneering nature of *Der Lotse*, there is a strong possibility that some of the above authors, as well as other *Lotse* contributors, read von der Leyen's essay, thus coming into early contact with Freud's work.

Von der Leyen (1901) demonstrated that dreams stem from life experiences. Dreams are enlarged and explicit versions of what people wish for and what they worry about. Fairy tales, myths, and legends are also magnified accounts of life, which explains their universal appeal. Many fairy tales actually stem from dreams; they are oft-told dreams which have entered the literature and traditions of a people, first verbally and then in writing.

Von der Leyen pointed out that an earlier, forgotten scholar, Ludwig Laistner, had attempted to prove the connection between dreams and fairy tales in his book, *The Riddle of the Sphinx* (1889). But Laistner's work, in spite of its comprehensiveness, had not been well received by scholars because he was not able to prove his conclusions with the help of a consistent method. The book had not been scientific and lost itself in obscurities. Von der Leyen hoped, however, that in the future the "riddle" would receive more sympathetic consideration. He based his hopes on the fact that "strict science" had already arrived at conclusions similar to Laistner's, i.e., *The Interpretation of Dreams* of the learned Viennese doctor, "Siegmund" [*sic*] Freud.

Von der Leyen demonstrated the similarity between many legends and fairy tales and common dreams: the martyrdom of Sisyphus, the trials of Hercules and Odysseus, the myth of the sword of Damocles, the tales of the Arabian nights, the saga of Oedipus, the tale of the emperor's new clothes. For the latter two, von der Leyen cited Freud in detail to prove his contentions.

Von der Leyen also anticipated some of Freud's opinions in *Jokes*. When one investigates those dim eras that gave birth to fairy tales, one simultaneously comes up against the problem of the origin of poetry. Investigation of fairy tales would undoubtedly solve this problem. The poet's motivation and inspiration appear unfathomable to us. But fundamentally they are not hidden or mysterious. One must seek for them in life, in daily experiences and observations, in nightly sleep, and in dream fantasies.

Von der Leyen's conclusion (1901, p. 390) was that it was time to recognize an old truth: "the fairy tale of fairy tales and the wonder of wonders are always life itself. And whoever seeks the primal, true reality has only to look in fairy tales."

In a letter to Fliess (July 4, 1901), Freud (1887-1902) remarked that von der Leyen had sent him a copy of the *Lotse* article. Ernst Kris (Freud, 1887-1902, p. 332 fn.) has reported that Freud and von der Leyen corresponded for a while and that the philologist seems to have drawn others' attention to Freud's work, but that "Leyen regarded Freud's subsequent works with reserve and scepticism."[3]

Freud not only tried to interpret dreams and explain their sources, he also hypothesized that their function was to preserve the continuity of sleep. The great majority of commentators obviously thought this was a subsidiary issue, and it was little discussed. But the theory aroused no opposition, and those who were won over by it reported it in colorful terms to their readers. Lubarsch (1901-1902, p. 19) pointed out that, in general, one regards the dream as the disturber of one's peace. But "in a very exciting fashion" Freud had proved that dreaming is the "prolonger" if not quite the guardian of sleep. David (1900, p. 239) transformed Freud's "guardians" into the "protecting god of dreams who frees the soul." And Sokal (1902, p. 85) enthusiastically sought to convince by an elaborate analogy in which the dream became a night watchman.

Only two reviewers, Lubarsch and David, publicly applied Freud's dream theories to themselves. Lubarsch (1901-1902, pp. 2246, 17-18) presented two of his own dreams to show that one was the fulfillment of a wish, and that the other, though

---

[3] I have been unable to trace the events or publications on which Kris based his report.

apparently senseless, really had a meaning. David (1900, p. 239) wrote that he knew from his own experience that suppressed and troubled childhood memories, long forgotten, make their appearance in dreams.

ACCEPTANCE OF FREUD'S DREAM THEORIES

In the lay reaction to psychoanalytic dream theories we see illustrated more clearly than in any other type of reception a common early response to psychoanalysis. We have come across this response in the medical reception, but never as definitely expressed as it is here. Indeed, in previous chapters, it has been more sensed than expressed. More than a few of Freud's reviewers and even his outspoken critics revealed a feeling of awe at Freud's conclusions, but indicated their helplessness in not knowing quite what to make of them. These men clearly recognized that they had read something brilliant, something unusual, but they were unable to define and categorize it in terms of their past experience. The recurrent use of the adjectives *geistreich* and *geistvoll* to characterize both Freud and his theories is an example of this reaction. For "ingenious" is not altogether a complimentary word. It has implications of cleverness without a foundation, of some slight-of-hand that the viewer senses, even though he has seen no evidence of it.

Partly, Freud's prose style accounts for this response (see my Introduction). The label "ingenious" was also a reaction to the substance of psychoanalysis. Freud logically, step by step, brought his readers to conclusions that at the outset many of them would never have thought possible. When all was done, they stepped back in wonderment, quite unable to realize how they had arrived where they were, unable to find flaws, yet with a feeling of having been misled. They could do no other than to praise Freud for his conclusions. But these conclusions often left them uncomfortable; thus the frequent use of "ingenious." The word was either an escape hatch or a hiding place of last resort.

Sometimes a commentator put his feelings into more precise language. Thus Mehring (1906, p. 284) noted: "One follows him without strong contradiction, to some extent seduced by pleasure in the numerous, very funny proofs. . . . After the tense expectation comes a startling disclosure." Following a wholly favorable review of *The Interpreation of Dreams*, David's (1900, p. 239) closing words were that he owed to Freud's work "much stimulation, both in agreement and *rejection*" (italics mine). The word "rejection" comes like a bolt out of the blue. Parenthetically, we may note here that "stimulating" was another favorite adjective of Freud's re-viewers, a word by which they consciously praised and uncon-sciously refrained from a total commitment. It was Sokal, in his "*Scientific* Dream Interpretation" (italics mine) who most clearly enunciated the problem. Sokal (1902, p. 84) could not praise Freud enough: "Columbus . . . famous . . . great acumen . . ." Yet in the middle of one of the most appreciative discussions of those "two excellent works" on dreams, Sokal wrote: "In the analysis of such particular examples of dreams, Freud shows himself to be a true master of psychological observation, though just this virtuosity of his interpretive artistry may arouse in some a doubt as to the scientific worth of the theory." In an age where science was measured by the dispassionateness of its facts, "interpretive artistry" was a damning indictment.

Now let us attempt to explain the lack of continued interest in the dream theories. The previous observations provide some clue, and also, of course, help to account for lack of accep-tance of other psychoanalytic theories. More specifically, we can ask who could have served as promulgators of Freud's hypotheses, and then we can examine their actual response.

1. The foremost candidates were the psychologists, the only scientists who, as a group, had mapped out for their province the study of the normal phenomena of the human mind. But it has been amply demonstrated why they either did not or could not further Freud's hypotheses.

2. The next likely candidates were the physicians, who might have been expected to see the significance of Freud's dream theories for mental disturbances. But they fought off dream interpretation as a throwback to the fixed explanations of dreams which were such an integral part of folk medicine. For Freud also offered fixed explanations, declaring, for in-

stance, that in a dream of flying the dreamer was always re-experiencing certain types of movements from childhood—either being lifted, rocked, or tossed by an adult, or a romping game. A dream of being naked or insufficiently dressed was a repetition of a time in childhood when one ordinarily appeared before others inadequately clothed. And to all dreams Freud ascribed the common character of a wish. To many physicians, Freud's interpretations seemed similar to popular superstitions which were the stock-in-trade of folk healers.

Freud himself was well aware that it was not only his sexual interpretations or his Viennese Jewish background or the personal resistance of his critics that would prevent sustained interest in his work. "There can be no doubt," he stated emphatically (1900, pp. 63-64),

> that the psychical achievements of dreams received readier and warmer recognition during the intellectual period which has now been left behind, when the human mind was dominated by philosophy and not by the exact natural sciences. Pronounce-ments such as that by Schubert (1814 . . .) . . . and . . . the younger Fichte (1864 . . .) and others, all of which represent dreams as an elevation of mental life to a higher level, seem to us now to be scarcely intelligible; to-day they are repeated only by mystics and pietists. The introduction of the scientific mode of thought has brought along with it a reaction in the estimation of dreams. Medical writers in especial tend to regard psychical activity in dreams as trivial and valueless; while philosophers and non-professional observers—amateur psychologists—. . . have (in closer alignment with popular feeling) retained a belief in the psychical value of dreams. Anyone who is inclined to take a low view of psychical functioning in dreams will naturally prefer to assign their source to somatic stimulation . . .

3. Who then was left to adopt Freud's ideas? The literati were—and they did, eventually. The years after World War I saw the flowering of psychoanalytic dream interpretation in German intellectual circles. But people of literary interests were also creatures of the age of materialistic science. Though this orientation had already begun to lose its special dominance among the avant-garde before the war, it still provided by far the favorite *Weltanschauung* for those who considered themselves "modern."

4. Moreover, Freud was not eager to court this group; indeed, with only two exceptions during his entire psychoanalytic career, he never entéred into any public debate or defense of his hypotheses. A good example of Freud's idiosyncratic attitudes about publicizing his work occurred four months after the publication of *The Interpretation of Dreams.* Having learned from his friend Fliess that the influential liberal periodical *Neue Rundschau* had decided not to review the book, Freud rebelled against Fliess's suggestion that he write an article about it as an alternative to getting it reviewed. He wrote Fliess that he had five reasons for not submitting such an article. The fifth reason was obviously the emotional reaction of a man hurt by rejection: "I want to avoid anything that savours of advertisement. I know that my work is odious to most people. So long as I behave perfectly correctly, my opponents are at a loss. If I once start doing the same as they do, they will regain their confidence that my work is no better than theirs. . . . So I think the most advisable course is quietly to accept the *Rundschau's* refusal as an incontrovertible sign of public opinion" (1887-1902, pp. 315-316).[4] As we well know, authors are not always so prideful, and their desire to spread their ideas is not usually held against them. But Freud seems to have been more concerned with "correct" behavior before his medical colleagues than with convincing a generally educated audience. "Odious" was certainly not to be the response in lay periodicals to psychoanalytic dream theories. And equally certainly, publication in the *Rundschau* was not seeking a mass audience of the commonest denominator.

At any rate, Freud himself bears a small measure of respon-

---

[4] Just how hurt Freud was by the *Rundschau's* rejection can be seen in a slip he made in 1907 when he wrote to Jung (McGuire, 1974, p. 103) that the *Neue Rundschau* had "acquired" a lecture of his for publication ("Creative Writers and Day-Dreaming," 1908b). But the journal involved was not the *Rundschau,* but the new, less prestigious *Neue Revue.*

The other four reasons Freud gave for not writing an article for the *Rundschau* were that (1) "it would be a difficult and disagreeable task"; (2) the proposed article would be a duplication of the monograph he had promised Löwenfeld; (3) an article by Freud in the *Rundschau* would deprive its readers of "the benefit of criticism"; (4) the *Rundschau* would automatically become "hostile" to him if "forced to carry a review against its will."

sibility for the fact that five years later the *Rundschau* published a laudatory article hailing the significance of Freud's work on dreams, but with nary a mention of his name. Without question, the author, Jentsch (1905), was referring to Freud's work. The clearest proofs of this are Jentsch's acknowledgment that dreams are the fulfillment of wishes (p. 882) and his entitling his article "Traumarbeit" — Freud's very own phrase for the dream mechanisms he had discovered. (Other indications are Jentsch's references to (1) the significance of the trivial because of its connection to some distant subject of importance; (2) dreams only seeming nonsensical because we do not understand their language; (3) the role of symbolism in elucidating the psychological meaning of what appears to be basically senseless; (4) unconscious psychic activity.) Jentsch praised the dream studies and interpretations as being "serious . . . scientific . . . legitimate and rational" and, inevitably, "ingenious." The work had been carried out with "virtuosity and acumen." He envisioned that the studies would probably lead to the "important, practical elucidation of both general and specific psychological theories about people."

It remains to be noted that it was often the nonmedical aspects of psychoanalysis that attracted those men and women who became the second generation of Freudians — those young doctors and smaller number of laymen who became psychoanalysts in Germany in the 1920's. One of the foremost of these nonmedical aspects was the reliance of psychoanalysis on symbolism, which figures so prominently in dream interpretation. Many German psychoanalysts have reported a strong literary interest in their adolescent years, which was immensely gratified by reading Freud at that period in their lives. These men and women savored Freud's style, shared his introspective interests, and appreciated the importance he attached to symbols. Here, of course, were the chief promulgators of Freud's dream theories.

11

PSYCHOPATHOLOGY

In the period under consideration, there was very little opportunity for nonprofessionals to learn about psychoanalysis as a system of diagnosis and treatment of mental illness. The turn of the century was still a time of strict demarcation of subject matter. Medical works got little attention outside medical circles. Indeed, Bry and Rifkin (1962, p. 22) think that Freud's writings were pioneering works in the twentieth-century development of what we today call behavioral science, a field incorporating information from medicine and the social sciences. Implicit in behavioral science is the assumption that its discoveries will be passed on to the nonprofessional educated public. But there were few interdisciplinary journals or semipopular medical works seventy-five years ago in which the psychoanalytic ideas about mental illness were thought properly to belong. Thus the dissemination among laymen of Freud's early notions regarding hysteria, obsessional neurosis, anxiety neurosis, phobias, and hallucinations was severely limited. Aside from von Ehrenfels's article (see Chapter 12), such dissemination consisted entirely of the exposure of educated laymen to psychoanalytic psychopathology; there was no lay reaction other than von Ehrenfels's before 1908. Moreover, even the exposure was relatively late in starting. Ehrenfels's plea for sexual reform appeared in 1903, as did an article by Hellpach on hysteria and nervousness. All other information about Freud's medical ideas appeared in 1905 or later.

FREUD ON PSYCHOTHERAPY AND HYPNOSIS

In 1890, Freud had published in a semipopular medical handbook an article on "Psychical Treatment." Because of its good reception, the handbook went into three editions, so Freud's article (1905c) reappeared in 1900 and again in 1905 (Strachey, 1966, pp. 63-64). Freud attempted to show that "mental treatment" (i.e., treatment by words) is legitimate and scientific. The essay was, then, an argument for the validity of psychotherapy. Although composed in Freud's prepsychoanalytic days, the article was extremely educative on some basic assumptions of psychoanalysis: that mental events have a life of their own and are not just dependent on physical ones; that some people are ill because of the effect of their minds on their bodies; that learning about pathological phenomena provides an insight into normal mental phenomena; and that "all mental states, including those that we usually regard as 'processes of thought', are to some degree 'affective', and not one of them is without its physical manifestations or is incapable of modifying somatic processes" (Freud, 1905c, p. 288).

Freud's article is notable — and in the history of the *reception* of psychoanalysis, important — in that it continued to connect Freud's name quite decisively with hypnosis when he was no longer using it. To a large extent the article was a strong and quite deliberate argument for the use of hypnotherapy.

> Thus hypnotic treatment really implies a great extension of medical power and consequently an advance in therapy. Every sufferer may be advised to entrust himself to it, so long as it is carried out by an experienced and trustworthy physician. . . . The family doctor should himself be familiar with hypnotic procedure and he should make use of it from the first, as soon as he judges the illness and the patient appropriate for it. *Wherever hypnotism can be employed it should be on a par with other therapeutic procedures* and should not be regarded as a last resort or even as a descent from science to quackery [Freud, 1905c, pp. 298-299; italics mine].

When the esssay appeared in 1900 and 1905, there was no way readers could learn that Freud had left hypnotherapy behind for psychoanalysis.

"Psychical Treatment" re-emphasizes a significant factor in the early reception of psychoanalysis. The linking of Freud's name with the generally disreputable subject of hypnotism continued to occur quite late. It proves that the historian should not dismiss the reactions to the cathartic method as not part of the reaction to psychoanalysis. Rather, it was a vital part. Freud's connection with hypnosis continued to exert a baleful influence on the reception of psychoanalysis long after Freud himself had abandoned it. Moreover, this influence was not merely born out of physicians' outdated conceptions of what Freud was up to. As late as 1905, in a book which had wide circulation, Freud seemed to be making no effort to dispel notions about his reliance on hypnosis.

REACTION IN LAY PERIODICALS

Other references to or discussion of psychoanalytic ideas on mental illness appeared in five kinds of literature from 1903 through 1907: "highbrow" general magazines; weekly journals of book reviews; newspapers; journals in specialized fields (other than medicine or psychology); and books. Understandably, the vast majority of these articles and book reviews dealt with Freud's ideas about hysteria.

There are ten references to these ideas. Five are solidly in favor, one is mixed, two are noncommittal, and two are against. These statistics show the erroneousness of Freud's assumption that the *Rundschau*'s refusal to review his book was "an incontrovertible sign of public opinion." The philosopher Ehrenfels (1903), in a popular journal of anthropology, explained Breuer and Freud's ideas on the mechanism and etiology of hysteria and demonstrated their significance for the understanding and resolution of sexual problems which Ehrenfels felt were having an enervating effect on German society. The *Nervenarzt* Löwenfeld (1909) in his marriage manual, and the philosopher Friedmann (1907) in the *Supplement* to the Munich *Allgemeine Zeitung*, both praised Freud for his enunciation of the sexual origin of hysterical symptoms. Jung (1905a, pp. 98, 100) in *Die Zukunft* was quite informative about the role of the unconscious in the production of hysteria. He asked his readers to think of hysteria as "nothing other than a caricature of normal psychological mechanisms." Freud had "a simple explanation" for the "seemingly unaccountable acts" of a hysteric:

> A majority of hysterical persons are ill because they possess a mass of memories, highly charged with affect and therefore deeply rooted in the unconscious, which cannot be controlled and which tyrannize the conscious mind and will of the patient. [Patients] try to repress the affect from their daily lives, and so it torments them with horrid dream symbols at night, plagues them with fits of precordial anxiety by day, saps their energy, drives them into all kinds of crazy sects, and causes headaches that defy all the medicine men and all the magic cures of electricity, sun-baths, and food cures.

As Jung acclaimed Freud's discoveries, so did an institutional psychiatrist, Max Liebers, acclaim Jung's on the role of "complexes" in the etiology of hysteria. Liebers (1907, p. 293) pointed out in his review in the *Allgemeine Zeitung* that Jung had derived his theory from Freud and had then gone on in his own work "to further substantially our knowledge of hysteria."

Hellpach both welcomed and dismissed Freud. Writing for a journal of school hygiene, Hellpach (1905) could not praise enough Freud's revolutionary conception of hysteria. Freud had performed a "historic service" in proving that hysteria was an exogenous rather than endogenous illness. But in the same article, Hellpach declared that he could not share Freud's view of the sexual etiology of hysteria, based on infantile experiences. Hellpach agreed that the causes of hysteria did lie in the past, but in childhood and adolescence. Moreover, sexual experiences were ancillary, not basic.

In a journal of parapsychology, Hellpach (1903, pp. 92-93) explained his rejection of the sexual etiology of hysteria. Freud's view was based on "results obtained from questioning hypnotized hysterics. But the theory that the answers of a hypnotized individual in any way correspond to the full range of reality must be energetically combatted." Hellpach based his belief on the ultimate authority, Wundt, who "in his classical work on hypnotism has once and for all shown that information received from someone in a hypnotic state of consciousness does not have any psychololgical usefulness. That is because every question that we direct toward a hypnotized person is a new suggestion."[1] Anyway, Hellpach concluded, in

---

[1] Ellenberger (1970, pp. 171-175) has shown that in fact such a point of view was justifiable.

trying to connect hysteria with sex, Freud was doing nothing new, merely joining the ranks of "many neurologists" who had sought to prove such a connection because two thirds of hysterics were women.

It is instructive to note that Freud was in good company in Hellpach's article, which was a review of the works and opinions of all major thinkers on hysteria and related conditions: Binswanger, Charcot, Freud and Breuer, Janet, Kraepelin, Möbius, Oppenheim, Strümpel, and Wundt. Hellpach freely expressed his opinions for and against various facets of the experts' studies, leisurely making his way in an article that stretched out over three issues of the journal.

Two noncommittal reactions to Freud's theories on the etiology and treatment of hysteria appeared in the reviewing weeklies, *Literarisches Zentralblatt* and the *Deutsche Literaturzeitung* (Hnl. [Haenel], 1905, cols. 244-245; Gaupp, 1906, col. 184). The *Literarisches Zentralblatt* also published one extraordinarily hostile response. This was completely critical, sarcastic, and uncomprehending review of the *Three Essays on the Theory of Sexuality*. But the attack was not directed only at psychoanalysis. In his first sentence, the anonymous reviewer (1906) sneeringly declared his opposition to all so-called "modern" research on sexuality.

Scattered references to Freud's ideas on other mental conditions began to appear in lay literature in 1906. Max Liebers (1906) informed the readers of the *Allgemeine Zeitung* that Freud, "the well-known Viennese psychiatrist," had just published a new essay on the role of sexuality in the etiology of the neuroses. Liebers thus brought to general public attention the view of those psychiatrists who valued psychoanalysis but thought Freud had overreached himself. "Even if Freud and his school definitely go too far in their utilization of noxious sexual stimuli as the etiological event of psychoneuroses, nevertheless it is absolutely necessary, for the modern standing of science, to investigate Freud's ingenious theory."

Like the reactions to some other twentieth-century developments, the reaction to psychoanalysis was affected by differing views on the desirability of modernity. To the anonymous reviewer of the *Three Essays*, "modern" investigations of sexual behavior were all valueless, and some were even harmful. To

Liebers, on the other hand, if science were to be "modern," it had to consider psychoanalysis seriously, even if some aspects of Freud's conclusions seemed farfetched.

The Berlin *Tageblatt* published Stekel's article (1907c) explaining the psychoanalytic view of obsessions. Bloch's immensely popular *The Sexual Life of Our Time* (1907b) publicized Freud's view that coitus interruptus could produce anxiety neurosis or neurasthenia and hysteria difficulties. Bloch (1907a, p. 261) also promoted this view in an article on birth control that he wrote for a periodical concerned with sexual issues. Additionally, readers of *The Sexual Life of Our Time* learned that Freud shared the common belief that masturbation caused neurasthenia.

Freud's ideas on psychopathology received further exposure because of Jung's psychoanalytic work. Jung's study of dementia praecox was widely reviewed and generally well received. An honorary medical privy councilor (*Geheimer Medizin Rat*), who had published numerous works in medical criminology and jurisprudence, wrote a favorable review in a well-established legal journal. This physician, Hermann Kornfeld (1907) informed lawyers that Jung was "a convinced disciple of Freud [and had] analytically demonstrated [that] dementia praecox must have a causal significance." Interested readers of the *Allgemeine Zeitung's Supplement* learned that Jung's study was of "extraordinarily high scientific interest." The reviewer, Liebers (1907), remarked that it was "well-known" that Jung's theory of complexes is "connected with the name of Freud and his pupils, who in their theory of hysteria first proved its significance." Jung had now shown that Freud's theory of hysteria could be applied to dementia praecox. Therefore, Jung's book was highly recommended.

Psychodynamic theories of mental disease never assumed a dominant place in the thought of German psychiatrists, nor did psychoanalysis (or analytically oriented psychotherapy) become the major method for treating mental illness. This medical state of affairs was bound to have a limiting effect on public interest in and valuation of psychoanalysis in Germany. But the lack of authoritative medical appreciation of psychoanalysis did not prevent an intense interest in psychoanalysis from developing among certain individuals and groups after World War I. And, as the' next chapter demonstrates, even before 1914 psychoanalytic explanations of individual psycho-pathology were being used in an effort to understand and deal with problems affecting large groups in society.

12

SOCIAL REFORM AND PSYCHOANALYSIS

Before 1908, the application of psychoanalysis to social problems remained in the theoretical stage, centering on two concerns: the upbringing and education of children and the resolution of sexual problems in adult society. The first instance of the actual use of psychoanalytic theory to effect social change occurred in 1908 when the headmaster of a Berlin suburban school directed his teachers to apply psychoanalytic principles in the handling of their pupils (H. C. Abraham and Freud, 1965, pp. 60-61).

CHILD REARING

In 1905 there appeared two articles on the value of psychoanalytic ideas for the rearing and schooling of the young. One article was specifically addressed to German socialists, and the other to educators and to those doctors who had a strong professional interest in secondary education. Probably neither article reached a wide audience.

Alfred Adler (1870-1937), at that time a follower of Freud and an ardent socialist, wrote an essay for a Berlin socialist weekly on sexual problems in the raising of children. From a historical point of view, Adler's brief essay is significant as probably the first interpretation (really misinterpretation) of Freud's theories of infantile sexuality as meaning that the satisfaction of the infant's physical wishes for being fed and for physical contact was detrimental to the child's future well-being. This view, when combined with the Watsonian behaviorist approach to child rearing, became in the 1920's and 1930's, a common misunderstanding of Freud's ideas on the danger of sexual precocity. Adler's article was thus a harbinger of the future. But in 1905 his views probably did not receive great popular circulation since they were published in a small weekly which survived only three years.

On the basis, he said, of Freud's *Three Essays on the Theory of Sexuality*, Adler (1905a, p. 360) wished to give parents what he considered an important warning. He explained to his readers that the reason for infantile sexuality and the dissemination of sensuality over the entire body was that "sensuality and the seeking of satisfaction force the individual to enter into a connection with all his organs vis-à-vis the external world in order to gather impressions and nourishment. So the sexual drive serves to confront the child with things of the external world and to initiate cultural intercourse." How and how quickly the child's sensuality was satisfied would have a profound impact on the child's ability to become acculturated. Adler cautioned against "considerable elevation of sensual excitability, by which quick satisfaction of the child becomes a constant end in itself." Such satisfaction would "severely limit [later] capacity for achievement" (*Leistungsfähigkeit*) and hinder the civilizing process.

> There was the danger of "a still further abuse." This was the artificial increase of natural sensuality, which in later life can cause sexual precocity or even perversity. Our whole civilized existence presupposes the ability to bear unfulfilled or momentarily unfulfillable wishes . . . until a satisfactory goal can be reached. The surest sign of cultivability [*Kulturfähigkeit*] is not to shrink back before the efforts and demands of a systematic undertaking. . . . If the childish wishes of infancy and later childhood are lulled through all kinds of sensual pleasure, through swinging, rocking, and tossing instead of through only essential attention, then the control of sensual demands by psychic strength will be subnormal.

This stern and untempered warning against overindulgence was extended to games involving running, hopping, jumping, and fighting, and to the climbing maneuvers of gymnastics. "In all these cases, especially where an erotic end in itself and not a physical demand is evident, the obvious excesses must be suppressed" (Adler, 1905a, p. 361).

This was psychoanalysis in the service of Victorianism. Certainly Freud (1905d, p. 223) himself had been far more sophisticated in the *Three Essays*. He was careful to point out that when the "enlightened" mother found out that "all her marks of affection were rousing her child's sexual instinct and preparing for its later intensity," this should not be a signal for "any self-reproaches." The mother "is only fulfilling her task in teaching the child to love. After all, he is meant to grow up into a strong and capable person with vigorous sexual needs and to accomplish during his life all the things that human beings are urged to do by their instincts." Only after this encouragement of maternal spontaneity and warmth, which never entered into Adler's advice, did Freud go on to warn that "an excess of parental affection does harm by causing precocious sexual maturity and also because, by spoiling the child, it makes him incapable in later life of temporarily doing without love or of being content with a smaller amount of it."

Freud, of course, always insisted on the etiological significance of childhood seduction, masturbation, and sexual precocity for future neurosis. But Adler (1905a, pp. 361-362) magnified Freud's concerns into vigorous moralizing and dire warnings which actually fit in quite neatly with Victorian assumptions about the evils of sexuality. Adler wrote: "With the occurrence of sexual precocity there is connected, in fact, a quite conspicuous deterioration of morality. The reins slip away from the person in charge of the child." One sees "the most violent unruliness . . . inclination to lying, to theft, rapid deterioration at school, noticeable incompetence, loss of sense of shame, inclination to gruesome acts, to arson." Adler warned parents that the common childhood game of "playing doctor" was especially dangerous.

Here is an illustration that Freud's emphasis on sexuality would not, as some critics feared, lead immediately to greater and freer sexual expression. For Freud's ideas to have the influence that they eventually had required more than their mere statement. Social change needed the coalescence, with psychoanalysis, of movements for educational reform, sex education, birth control, and women's rights. This did not truly take place before the First World War and, in some cases, not until after the second.

Moreover, scrutiny of the publications of many individuals and groups whose avowed aim was the liberalizing of sexual attitudes and practices shows that Freud's works were at first completely disregarded, and the potential usefulness of his theories in the fight for sexual reforms went unnoticed for several years. One outstanding example of this disregard was by the publication *Mutterschutz* (1905-1907), the journal of the League for the Protection of Maternal Rights, a feminist and medical organization formed to fight for the rights of illegitimate children and their mothers, for the rights of women in the marital relationship, and for the abolition of prostitution. The League advocated abortion, sexual freedom, and sex education. Only one of the issues of *Mutterschutz* ever breathed a mention of Freud's name. Then, in 1908, *Mutterschutz* lost some of its purely feminist direction and changed its name to *Sexual-Probleme*. It came under the editorship of the medical sexologist Max Marcuse, who was quite interested in Freud's work (Jones, 1957, pp. 110, 127). In 1908, therefore, *Sexual-Probleme* contained two articles by Freud, "'Civilized' Sexual Morality and Modern Nervous Illness" (1908a) and "On the Sexual Theories of Children" (1908c).

The early disregard of Freud by sex reformers can also be seen in the magazines published by Karl Vanselow: *Geschlecht und Gesellschaft* (*Sex and Society*) and *Die Schönheit* (*Beauty*). Vanselow founded an association for sexual reform in Berlin in 1906, but there were no articles or reviews about psychoanalysis in his periodicals before 1908. The annual *Anthropophyteia*—subtitled "Yearbooks for the Promotion and Investigation of the Evolution of Sexual Morality through the Study of Folklore"—was founded in 1904 by Friedrich S. Krauss, an ethnologist and expert on folklore of the South Slavs. But Krauss did not consider the subject of psychoanalysis until 1908 (see Kind, 1908). And although founded in 1899, the *Jahrbuch für sexuelle Zwischenstufen unter besonderer Berücksichtigung der Homosexualität* (*Yearbook for Intermediate Sexual States, Especially Homosexuality*) contained only one review of Freud's work before 1908, a 1906 discussion of the *Three Essays*. The *Jahrbuch*'s editor, Magnus Hirschfeld (1868-1935) was a dedicated lecturer before Berlin audiences on the subjects of his journal and a member of the Berlin Psychoanalytic Society from 1908 to 1911.

SECONDARY EDUCATION

The only early deliberate application of Freud's theories to educational reform was Hellpach's (1905) attack on German secondary schools for causing emotional problems among their students. Hellpach argued strenuously for the culpability of the school and against the belief that a student's problems were the result of an incomprehensible congenital malady that inevitably made its appearance when something in the youth's life situation brought it out. The essay was published in a journal newly founded as an outgrowth of the first International Congress for School Hygiene held at Nürnberg, April 4-9, 1904. This article is notable only for its application of psychoanalytic ideas. Hellpach's suggestions for pedagogical reform had been made by others before.

Hellpach based the validity of his point of view on Freud's discovery that hysteria was an exogenous rather than an endogenous illness. Here Hellpach was being rather imprecise in labeling as "hysteria" students' difficulties and their failures to succeed in later life. But, in a general way, he was crediting Freud for saying that neurotic behavior of adolescents and young graduates should not automatically be considered "inborn" or "inherent." Hellpach (1905, p. 225) hailed Freud for having "broken the backbone of the fatalism of endogenesis." In his *Studies on Hysteria* and *Interpretation of Dreams*, Freud had performed a "historic service [with his] basic revision of our ideas; we can no longer overlook Freud without laying ourselves open to the reproach of thoughtless muddling through."

Hellpach defended Freud against the criticism that he had not "proved" his point. "What in general in psychopathology today has been proved? Psychopathology still consists of a few shabby empirical rules and public musings." Freud had "made plausible to a great extent" the view that hysteria is an exogenous disease "for which one may seek both cause and elimination." Frankly, it was now up to the pathologists to prove Freud wrong "through incontestable means."

Before presenting his indictment of the German secondary school, Hellpach outlined Breuer and Freud's theories of the mechanism and etiology of hysteria and gave them his usual critique. He also explained Freud's ideas on bisexuality which he used in discussing girls' secondary school education.

As opposed to the Freudian theory that hysteria was caused by repression, Hellpach (pp. 230-234) offered his own theory of "docility" as the etiological agent, especially among boys.[1] Highly suggestible — docile — people were especially predisposed to becoming hysterical. And unusual suggestibility led all the more easily to hysteria the more often and more strongly "suggestions" were made to suggestible people. By suggestions, Hellpach (pp. 238-239) explained, he meant demands on a person's beliefs and actions. This was how religion could cause hysteria, and how the school also caused it, by "nourishing suggestibility." The school "combined the army's demand for obedience with the church's demand for belief." The school also caused hysteria by conflicting pedagogical aims. "The highest egoism is taught as an example, but silent subordination under an openly degrading police state is demanded in practical terms."

The school's culpability did not end when the student left. If the school did not produce hysteria during the school years themselves, it established a high potential for hysteria afterwards. How else, Hellpach demanded, could one account for the great number of students who left school with high grades, but in life barely mustered an average output, or were complete disasters, or if they had the money for additional schooling, could achieve success only by changing their profession? "For if there is one factor that accelerates the process of hysteria, indeed . . . permits its release, it is the mood produced by failure in one's profession." The failure to achieve a

---

[1] I have oversimplified Hellpach's views so as not to obscure the main point: how schools are responsible for emotional problems. Actually, Hellpach had a more complicated theory of the existence of two kinds of hysterias, one induced by repression (a *conscious* suppression, not Freud's unconscious repression) and the other by docility. But the latter was much more frequent, according to Hellpach.

long-cherished ambition was due to docility, the guilt for whose implanting is shared by the school. The force of an erotic experience in producing hysteria might be more violent, but it could not have a more certain effect than failure at one's profession.

Hellpach (pp. 244-247) then presented six case histories of patients with career problems. He pointed out that they shared a typical syndrome: great demands had been made on the patient, either at school, or at home and at school. The patients had been forced into a course of study and a career not of their choosing. And the patients themselves complained about heavy school work or blamed the school for their problems; they considered their driving ambition to be one of their problems. Hellpach found that all these factors had resulted in the patients' indecisiveness about choosing a career or in unhappiness at their present job. They thus exhibited the unfulfilled potential of "model scholars."

From the point of view of medical history, it is instructive to note that Hellpach felt impelled to defend the manner in which he presented these cases. He said Freud was "guilty" of producing case reports which read like novels, but that he himself could not duplicate such a feat. His readers should understand, Hellpach declared, that a case on paper could never appear as convincing as the living person, and the immediacy and nuances could not be conveyed. Hellpach was not the only physician to act as if in this regard Freud had betrayed the medical profession. Freud was never accused of fabricating any part of his case descriptions, but his literary presentation aroused uneasy feelings in many doctors.

Hellpach (1905, pp. 241, 243, 248-250) concluded his article with several pleas to educators. They should no longer put up with the old fatalism that a student had been "born to hysteria." Breuer and Freud had demolished the endogenous argument and shed much light on the cause of hysterias. Those interested in school hygiene should promote sex education in the schools so that the schools could correct the damage done at home. More urgently, Hellpach asked for a differently organized school system for adolescent children, one that would give scope for individuality. He pleaded for a modern and relevant curriculum and methods which did not deaden a child's interest in learning. Finally, he urged that schools provide adequate vocational guidance. The school should take a student's inclinations into consideration. It should not force on someone a career choice which could only lead to inner disappointment. In this regard the school was more responsible than the home, because the school was the dominant influence on the child in the upper grades.

Like Adler's article, Hellpach's was a harbinger of the future. It was also a pioneering venture in using psychoanalytic concepts as the bases for independent sociological analysis. Moreover, Hellpach's essay is an example of the way psychoanalysis sometimes crept into popular culture; often a distorted psychoanalytic idea served as the essential core of any number of valid proposals or plans.

Hellpach did not accept all of Freud's ideas. He shared to only a very limited extent Freud's emphasis on the importance of sexual events, and he misunderstood Freud's concept of repression. Furthermore, Hellpach used the word "hysteria" in a catchall way that made the medical part of his argument unconvincing. Yet Hellpach introduced educators to Freud's idea of the exogenous nature of emotional illness and stressed the extreme importance of Freud's contribution. Hellpach was the first to show how the school hygiene movement could use this psychoanalytic principle. He emphasized that change was possible, that school children were usually not the victims of a "predestined illness." Hellpach's article is historically interesting because it is an early linking of "progressive" ideas on education with Freud's name. Nevertheless, the lack of early pedagogical interest in psychoanalysis is borne out by the uniqueness of Hellpach's essay.

SEXUAL INHIBITION AND MODERN SOCIETY

In the earliest years of the century, three physicians and a philosopher applied psychoanalytic principles to individual and societal sexual predicaments. Their suggestions were contained in a sociological plea for sexual reform, some passages in a marriage manual, two debates on the reform of the penal code, and a popular "sex and modern culture" tome.

Like Hellpach's educational essay, the sociological article was quite explicit in its debt to Freud; it, too, was *sui generis*. In it, Christian von Ehrenfels (1859-1932), a philosopher who taught at the University of Prague and was greatly involved in various German organizations for sexual reform, urged a most radical solution to sexual problems. As a philosopher, von Ehrenfels is remembered today for his work in the psychology of perception. But to his contemporaries he was also known for his broad cultural interests. Besides writing on sexual ethics, he wrote on drama, Wagner, the theory of values, and the origin of the universe. His ideas on sexuality do not seem to have antagonized his professional colleagues. When he died, the editors of *Psychologische Forschung* (Vol. 18, 1933) felt that "for him no separate memorial is required, for in most of the psychological work of the present day there live the consequences of his work" (Boring, 1950, p. 453).

Von Ehrenfels's article (1903) was published in a monthly dedicated to the practical application of the theory of natural selection to the "organic, social, and intellectual development of peoples"—what Bloch called "racial hygiene." Even where Ehrenfels did not distinctly acknowledge that his essay had been stimulated by the *Studies on Hysteria*, Breuer and Freud's conceptions were markedly present.

At the outset, Ehrenfels stated that the fundamental theme of his article was to be based on his observation that people's sexual lives were currently in an abnormal state that approximated the type of illness well-known to psychiatrists as "double consciousness."[2] In extreme cases, this illness was that of the "split personality." True, such extremes were rare. Yet, on the other hand, "all people suffer from a dissociation of consciousness" which could potentially lead to a split personality. Indeed, Ehrenfels (pp. 457, 459) believed "such dissociations are so frequent that they cannot at all be considered as illnesses." Moreover, among these "healthy" people, there was no complete loss of memory of the activities of the alternate

---

[2] For some reason, Ehrenfels himself gave the English translation of the term he used ("*doppelten Bewusstseins*") as "double conscience"—a misleading translation in terms of modern usage.

personality as there was in cases of split personality. The "sickness" indeed existed in that "we know as Person B what we have experienced as Person A; but we act as if we did not know it — and we act in this manner not only in our dealings with the outside world but vis-à-vis our inner life." Particularly "in the area of sex, human beings in our culture lead double lives; their psyches are split into upper and lower consciousnesses . . . to an extent which threatens to make them incapable of fulfilling the fundamental functions of self-protection [i.e., avoiding syphilis] and hygiene."

The necessity of concealing sexual drives had led to frequent personality cleavages. One of the commonplace dissociations of the times was a result of the problems faced by women who were trapped between their sexual drives and the mores imposed by a society which did not admit that women had sexual drives. Another was caused by the problems of monogamy: if a man was dissatisfied sexually, his two legitimate recourses were to suffer silently or, more frequently, blame his wife. It was Ehrenfels's (pp. 460-462) belief that the numerous publicly expressed obscenities in plays, literature, and magazines, as well as private allusions, were "symptoms of a general psychosis from which our culture is suffering; we are dealing here with the expression of an illness whose causes must be investigated and which can then be eliminated through a rational therapy."

Recently, Ehrenfels went on to say, the mechanism of a certain psychic process had been discovered by the "excellent investigations" of Breuer and Freud. Their discovery could be used to explain the causes of the split of sexual consciousness which was plaguing modern society. The rest of his article, Ehrenfels announced, would be "completely based on the reasoning of the two authors, whose work offers to psychologists an abundance of important information." First, of course, Ehrenfels presented in some detail Breuer and Freud's theories of the mechanism and etiology of hysteria. What obviously attracted and excited Ehrenfels was the idea that if a person could not discharge his affect along "primary paths" then he would do so along "secondary paths." This secondary discharge was what produced various hysterical symptoms. What

Breuer and Freud had discovered "in so convincing a fashion [was] the mechanism of the psychically acquired abnormality of 'double consciousness.' " Now Ehrenfels would demonstrate "its significance for the sexual life of present-day culture."

Ehrenfels (p. 468) had investigated such matters as the strength of the sexual drive, physical sequelae to abnormally low and high sexual activity, and the relative merits of monogamy and polygamy. What was clear after studying people's sexual lives was that "where sexual affect is prevented from its natural manifestation as a result of the restrictive influence of custom and morality, the indwelling dynamic force is pushed toward discharge along secondary paths." Secondary expressions of sexuality included such phenomena as religious ecstasy, asceticism, the various forms of self-mortification such as flagellation and sadism, and masturbation. The therapeutic abreaction produced by Breuer and Freud was another example of secondary discharge. One of the reasons secondary sexual expressions had come to be so numerous was the monogamous tradition, which prevented the "natural and healthy" primary expression of the sexual drive.

It had not come as a surprise to Ehrenfels (p. 471) that Freud had found sexual traumas to be the most frequent cause of hysteria. In everyday life, too, " 'double consciousness' was generally prevalent, and only the slightest weakness is required in order to turn it into an undoubted pathological case." And within recent years, "particular, aggravating circumstances had been driving the situation to a pronounced crisis."

To begin with, certain secondary sexual discharges were no longer permitted or customary. The cruelties of the Inquisition and of torture were things of the past, as generally were experiences of religious ecstasy and asceticism. Second, the great decline in infant mortality had led to an increase in family size which made free sexual expression within marriage more difficult than ever. Third, moral restrictions against primary and secondary expressions of sexuality were growing increasingly tighter, making ever more pressing the need for the "subconscious discharge of that which is morally taboo." Finally, and most important, customs were becoming not more tolerant, but more rigorous. This was corresponding to the "greater exactness" which was characteristic of the psychic apparatus of the individual in the machine age. Ehrenfels's article was only one of a large number of contemporaneous German essays which bemoaned the debilitating effects of modern life on the individual. "Nervousness and Modernity" was a title that often appeared in magazines and periodicals. Today, Ehrenfels lamented, broad public tolerance of illicit sexual liaisons no longer existed as it still did in Goethe's time. The rigidities of modern life were responsible for the fact that prostitution was more hidden than it had been in the sixteenth century and, at the same time, more frequent. Furthermore, syphilis was on the rise.

The "only solution" to this increasingly intolerable situation was that the primary discharge of natural sexual drives "in a state of upper consciousness"—i.e., openly—should be morally acceptable to society. But, said Ehrenfels, he recognized that such a moral revolution would take many generations. Therefore, the immediate goal was to secure "gradual moral approbation" of primary sexual expression plus the development of new paths of secondary discharge. But again, people must be allowed these expressions openly, so as to eliminate the pathological effects of personality cleavages.

After careful study, Ehrenfels (pp. 474-476) had concluded that mankind was not evolving toward monogamy. He therefore proposed the creation of socially approved institution in which mankind would be allowed to discharge its natural polygamous drive. Ehrenfels thought this would be therapeutic for society since for hysterics Breuer and Freud had been able to remove the split consciousness merely by bringing about the discharge of strangulated affect through conscious expressions of excitement and physical motions. "And how much more than mere 'abreaction through word and expressive movements' will our great sexual reform movement offer to restricted natural drives." The first step toward sexual health lay in sexual enlightenment. "To know the truth about our nature . . . is the first step of reform. . . . Let us follow the spirit of truth." The initial results would soon become obvious in the dying away of obscenity and of syphilis.

Ehrenfels's article was an exceptional adaptation of Freud's theories in the early twentieth-century fight for sexual reform. It was just this sort of reaction which many of Freud's critics predicted would be evoked by Freud's emphasis on sexuality. Yet in the early years of lay response to psychoanalysis, it was the only article which actually urged greater sexual freedom as a result of Freud's discoveries. Individuals who urged drastic reforms in the divorce and abortion laws, or who advocated "free love," or who were in favor of the early and explicit sexual education of children, were not at all rare. But their writings and the publications they edited were at first devoid of reference to Freud.

Freud himself was a social conservative, who never suggested revolutionary social applications of his theories. "It is certainly not a physician's business to come forward with proposals for reform [of sexual morality]," he wrote (1908a, p. 204). He did point out, however, that the demands of society made it necessary for the individual continually to restrict his sexual urges, and he spelled out quite specifically the emotional and physical hardships imposed upon Western men and women by the institution of marriage, by the sexual upbringing of women, and by the problems of contraception. He went as far as to say that he "might support the urgency of such proposals [for reform of sexual morality]." In fact, however, he was never an activist.

Ehrenfels, whose writings were later praised by Freud, accurately interpreted the implications of Freud's remarks, even if he thereby moved out of the theoretical realm in which Freud remained. But Ehrenfels was unambiguously in step with Freud in his wholehearted adoption of the psychoanalytic view that there was no sharp break between "healthy" and "sick" persons. In his article Ehrenfels indicated that medical evaluations and treatments of persons formally designated as emotionally ill could be applied with effectiveness to the less severe problems of all persons. It was probably just this belief of Ehrenfels that distinguished him from the scores of people who advocated broad sexual changes but who did not recognize that Freud's work with neurotic persons could be used to underpin their demands. It seems likely that the decisions of most social crusaders, like most physicians, were influenced by the nineteenth-century view of mental illness as clearly demarcated disease. On this issue, at least, there were few portents of the relativism increasingly characteristic of Western thought after World War I.

OEDIPAL CONFLICTS

Not surprisingly, Leopold Löwenfeld was responsible for two applications of psychoanalysis to sexual relationships. These were in a marriage manual he first published in 1906 and in a talk on homosexuality he delivered before a group of Munich lawyers in 1907. In the manual, Löwenfeld (1909, pp. 154-155) cautioned against "a superfluity in children's affections for their parents—especially the daughter's for her father and the son's for his mother." Löwenfeld explained that it was Freud who had elucidated "this condition." For a marriage to be truly happy, it was necessary that both husband and wife give each other "the maximum of affection of which they are generally capable." But if a daughter, for example, had always had an "excessively rapturous" affection for her father, this "childhood love" would continue in her marriage at the expense of love for her husband. "Her husband will not achieve his appropriate place in her heart." Freud had noted about such women: "They become frigid wives and remain sexually anesthetic." The same situation could arise in reverse, in the case of "those sons who as young men persist in rapturous dependency on their mothers and see their mothers as the embodiment of feminine perfection. . . . The powerful feelings they have for their mothers do not permit their feelings for their wives to reach a similar height. . . . The door is opened to influences that will disturb marital life."

Löwenfeld (1909, p. 269) also discussed the importance of a woman's first sexual intercourse for her future health. "The Viennese neurologist, Professor Freud, rightly says that it is a surprise that the bridal night does not more often initiate hysteria, because the sexual events often terminate in a rape."

Löwenfeld furthermore sought to enlist the support of lawyers for the change of article 175 of the penal code, which punished homosexuality and sodomy by imprisonment. A "Scientific-Humanitarian Committee" led by Dr. Magnus Hirschfeld of Berlin had already presented petitions to this effect to the Reichstag, with no results. Löwenfeld (1908, p. 16) reported to his audience that Freud had "demonstrated various facts which are of the greatest importance for the explanation of homosexuality." One was that the homosexual instinct was probably independent of its sexual object and probably did not owe its origin to stimulation from the object. According to Freud, homosexuality could be explained by a combination of the sexual constitution, sexual precocity, and "the heightened fixedness of memories of infantile sexual experiences." Homosexuals were not always unmanly, and feminine-appearing men were not always homosexuals. "Many homosexuals, as concerns their sexual objects, consider themselves men and prefer as a sexual object an individual with feminine habits. Freud has pointed out that among the Greeks, inverts included the most manly men. . . . On the other hand, men with exquisite feminine emotional habits, just like women with a pronounced masculine character, can manifest completely normal sexual relationships" (Löwenfeld, 1908, p. 20).

Homosexuals, Löwenfeld emphasized, were not always "degenerates." "With reference to the theory of degeneration, I am fully in accord with Freud's view that one should not speak of degeneration '(1) where several deviations from the norm do not coincide, and (2) where the ability to live and to achieve appears, in general, not to be badly damaged.' " Löwenfeld accepted Freud's view that part of the etiology of homosexuality lay in universal sexual development. Therefore, he (pp. 22-23) concluded, "homosexuality is an abnormality that in physical and emotional domains is, to be sure, united with sickness and degeneration, but which in the majority of cases constitutes an isolated psychic deviation from the norm which cannot be considered as indicative of a sick or degenerate nature, and which is not capable of reducing the worth of the individual as a member of responsible society."

Bleuler (1906b), on the other hand, in *Mutterschutz*, invoked Freud's name in order to argue *against* liberalization of a particular section of the penal code. Bleuler rebutted a suggestion for the repeal of ¶176,3, which prescribed punishment for sexual assault against children. He agreed with the faction for repeal that the law in question was not sufficient protection against the crime. But, Bleuler argued, it was all society had, it was better than nothing, and it must be used until the passage of a more satisfactory law could be assured.

Moreover, Bleuler continued, those who argued for repeal on the grounds that an assault rarely harms children, since most of them masturbate anyway, were uninformed. Masturbation was "an entirely different matter" from seduction by an adult. In the latter, "the feelings aroused and the psychic results are completely different." Bleuler (pp. 503-504) "strongly recommended that [those for repeal] read the studies of Freud and Breuer on hysteria [which show that] *a large number of hysterias, even if not all, result from such assaults.* The child will therefore be psychically harmed, if not as regards his morals, certainly as far as his psychic health is concerned." Bleuler's contention was based on Freud's original view that patients' memories of infantile seductions were of events that had actually happened. Eventually Freud realized that a large number of these memories were of wishes or fantasies. But Freud did not spell out his changed position until 1906, the same year as Bleuler's comments. Therefore Bleuler had no way of knowing of Freud's new views.

Bleuler's essay provides additional proof that initially Freud's theories were used to buttress all manner of positions, ranging from conservative to progressive.

BLOCH'S UTOPIA: SEXUALITY, HAPPINESS, AND CIVILIZATION

Freud's ideas also made their way into Bloch's best seller of 1907 and 1908. Bloch was already well-known for previous sexual studies when he published *The Sexual Life of Our Time in Its Relation to Modern Civilization*, a staggering compendium of all aspects of sexuality, its problems, and related fields.[3]

But Bloch also had a mission in publishing the *Sexual Life*. He wished to preach the unity of physical and spiritual love as an undivided, "organic" entity. If people could "perfectly and completely infuse the sexual impulse with a spiritual content," love would promote their happiness as well as be an "inalienable gain for civilization."

Bloch's (1907b, pp. 1, 4) outlook was a return to certain Romantic conceptions. These conceptions had never really died out in the nineteenth century, but had undergone a period of suppression. Bloch's world view was a monistic one, denying any duality of body and soul.

> He who has scientifically investigated love, who has based his conception of it philosophically, and has personally experienced it, will become a convinced monist in relation to life, at least, and to the organic world, and will be compelled to regard every dualistic division into a physical and a spiritual sphere as something quite artificial. In love above all is manifest this mystery of the life force, as for centuries the poets, the artists, and the metaphysicians have declared, and more especially as the great natural philosophers of the eighteenth and nineteenth centuries have proved — above all Charles Darwin and Ernst Haeckel.

By affixing the names of Darwin and Haeckel to a basically Romantic belief in metaphysics and a life force, Bloch sought to bestow on his views the necessary authority of modern science.

---

[3] The contents, in summary form, were: (1) sexual customs throughout history and at the present day; (2) what well-known philosophers in the past said about "love"; (3) complete biological and physiological descriptions of sexual anatomy, function, states, etc.; (4) the destruction of old wives' tales, e.g., women are sexually anesthetic; (5) numerous case histories to illustrate points; (6) opinions of all well-known workers in the field, e.g., Ellis, Eulenburg, Edward Carpenter, Freud, Magnus Hirschfield, Krafft-Ebing, Friedrich Krauss, Paul Näcke; (7) sexual reform and social changes, e.g., divorce, free love; (8) prostitution and venereal disease as social problems, with plans for their suppression and treatment; (9) sexual problems, aberrations, and perversions of the individual: description and treatment; (10) sex and the law; (11) advice on the frequency of intercourse and sexual abstinence; (12) sex education; (13) birth control; (14) role of eugenics ("racial hygiene") in choosing a mate; (15) pornography; (16) "love" in literature (belles-lettres); (17) scientific literature on sex.

Bloch's neo-Romanticism also showed in his teleological conceptions. "In the case of man the purely animal feelings have acquired an *importance* far greater than that of subserving the purposes of mere reproduction and aim at a *goal* transcending that of the preservation of the species." The goal of sexuality was not just to preserve the species, but also to promote the happiness of the individual. This was the root of the "sexual problem." Previously, human love was mainly concerned with procreation. But today, modern man conceived of history "as progress in the consciousness of freedom." He was therefore interested in sexuality for what it could mean "for his own inward growth, for the proper development of his free manhood." Without genuine "love" modern man could not be free or achieve his fullest self-expression.

Bloch did not refer to Freud in his introductory philosophical remarks. But throughout his book, Bloch used Freud's writings as an authority for the sexual information he provided as well as for his advice on individual conduct and suggestions for social reform. In this indirect way, Bloch linked Freud with Romantic and teleological views. At the very same time, Freud's critics were seeking to discredit Freud by pointing out the Romantic and teleological elements in his work.

Bloch (p. 6) took it upon himself to "forecast the future development" of those "elements of civilization" which are "influential" in love. Modern society stood at an important turning point in the history of love. People could gain ever more happiness by a more complete connection of the sexual impulse with spiritual content. Man's spiritual nature meant he could transform "the primeval and ever-active sexual impulse" into human love. More perfect love would mirror the advance of mankind to a higher level of civilization.

One of the concrete ways to achieve more perfect love was through sex education for both children and adults, a program to which Bloch (pp. 686-687) was deeply committed. He urged that children from ten on be enlightened in a scientific way about sexual matters at school. Children would suffer no harm from such teaching. Rather, as Freud had pointed out, dangerous sexual knowledge comes from "the intermixture of 'lasciviousness and prudery.'" Bloch (p. 756) also argued against those who believed that ready access to sexual literature would be corrupting. "Scientific authorship—even popular scientific works—dealing with the province of the sexual life cannot therefore be made responsible, in any respect, for the diffusion of sexual perversities. The founder of modern sexual science, A. von Schrenck-Notzing, insisted on this fact and recently it has been once more emphasized by S. Freud, who has probably gone further than any other writer in biologico-physiological derivation of sexual perversions."

Bloch intended his own book to be a vehicle for sex education. He discussed the physiology of sexual excitement; the existence of infantile sexuality as seen in sucking and early masturbation; the causes of sexual perversions; various methods of birth control; the sexual or sex-related origin of various illnesses; the relative roles of heredity and environment in the production of sexual problems. Freud's name or a reference to one of Freud's works always figured prominently in Bloch's discussions. Even Freud's follower, Otto Rank, was cited as an expert on sexual psychology.[4]

Bloch relied on Freud in a work that stressed the supremacy of the individual over society and paid great attention to the importance of sexuality both in the achievement of individual happiness and in the progress of civilization. Bloch strenuously advocated sex education and specifically used Freud's name in this connection. In Bloch's book we see another start of the linking of psychoanalysis with other reform movements that were also in their infancy at the beginning of the twentieth century.

As the past four chapters have shown, the early response of the educated German public to the cathartic method and psychoanalysis was limited. Nevertheless, it was both greater and more favorable than has been heretofore acknowledged. Some of the references cited are unknown to historians of psychoanalysis because their titles do not contain the words "Freud"

---

[4] See pp. 46-47, 413, 428, 456-465, 476, 641, 653, 702-703, 759. Bloch referred most often to the *Three Essays on the Theory of Sexuality*, but also to Freud's collected papers of 1906 and Rank's monograph, *Der Künstler* (1907).

or "psychoanalysis." This is particularly so for the subject of dreams. The articles on dreaming by Giessler, Jentsch, Korn, Lubarsch, Sokal, and by the anonymous author in *Gaea* all fall into this category. Other such references include the essays by Friedmann on the unconscious (1907), Hellpach on hysteria (1903, 1905), and Bleuler on sexual assaults against children (1906b), as well as certain book reviews. And, as it has turned out, many of these rediscovered sources indicate that specific psychoanalytic ideas often received a friendly or, at the very least, impartial, initial reception. This early reaction foreshadowed the later interest in psychoanalysis among many intellectual groups in Weimar Germany.

CONCLUSION

IDEALISM AND POSITIVISM

For several decades, psychoanalytic literature reiterated the story of Sigmund Freud's "splendid isolation" at the start of his psychoanalytic career. The main source of this description of Freud's early reception was Freud himself. But Freud's intellectual biases, emotional reactions, and unrealistic expectations often affected his judgment of the initial response to psychoanalysis.

The myth of how Freud had been utterly rejected, or, at best, ignored reached its apogee in 1955, in the second volume of Ernest Jones's biography of Freud. Shortly thereafter, however, scholars began to gather evidence that sharply modified the Freud-Jones interpretation. The first to do so were Bry and Rifkin (1962) in their study of the early reviews of Freud's writings. Then Ellenberger (1970), in his comprehensive history of depth psychology, attempted to place the reaction to psychoanalysis in a new perspective. I have examined the early German response to Freud's theories and have found that the quite varied reactions to psychoanalysis call for an alteration of the traditional interpretation offered by psychoanalytic historians. Clearly there were a fair number of responses which were not hostile and were even quite appreciative.

I have also stressed that a wide range of circumstances accounted for the negative responses. This position is a modification of the conventional view, which lays heavy weight on a few factors, particularly Victorian sexual attitudes and the critics' neurotic resistances resulting from conscious and unconscious fears aroused by Freud's theories. Without denying the significance of sexual attitudes and of individual neuroses, I think other factors were also fundamentally responsible for

321

the negative reaction to psychoanalysis. The psychoanalysts have been quite correct in believing that ultimately psychoanalysis did not appreciably influence German medicine and psychology. Because of this failure, psychoanalytic ideas also did not become an intimate part of German culture.

There was a brief period in the 1920's when Freud's ideas were quite popular among certain intellectuals, although psychoanalysis had little support from the medical and psychological authorities. If Weimar culture had been allowed a long period of development, it seems likely that psychoanalaysis would have come to have an increasing effect on child-rearing and educational practices. Eventually, therefore, it would have established itself in the personal outlook of educated Germans.

But the fact is that psychoanalysis had less than ten years of popularity among select circles. And it never received significant state or academic support until after World War II. This lack of authoritative approval doomed psychoanalysis to the fringes of German culture.

Interpreters of the history of psychoanalysis have not given sufficient attention to the two nineteenth-century *intellectual* developments that were most responsible for the rejection of psychoanalysis. These were the rebellion against "philosophical speculation" and, its simultaneous contradiction, the continued influence of idealistic philosophy.

By 1840, and probably even earlier, it seemed to the new generation of German scientists that *Naturphilosophie* and Schelling's speculative physics had failed to advance the course of scientific knowledge. They felt little more was known about the world in 1830 than had been known in 1800. Young scientists were disgusted by what appeared to be the intellectual sterility of their teachers and were determined not to repeat their errors. Above all, they told each other, they must avoid seeking to fit facts into a preconceived world view. Henceforth knowledge would consist of precise accumulation of facts. Investigators must also avoid explaining events by the existence of mysterious forces. Only readily observable physical and chemical explanations were scientific. Anything else would be a return to the dark days of *Naturphilosophie*.

Their laboratory and research activities rewarded the new generation of scientists. Their method obviously worked. Every year brought an increase in the store of accurate, replicable information about many areas of life. Here, at last, was the path to knowledge. To mix science and philosophy had clearly been disastrous. The *hubris* of the philosophers was exposed. The aims of late nineteenth-century scientists would be more modest. Meynert, Wundt, and du Bois-Reymond all scoffed at scientific pretensions and embraced limited goals; their byword was *"ignorabimus."*

Freud was regarded by many physicians and psychologists as a throwback to the days of *Naturphilosophie*. He eschewed experimentation and was thus condemned as unscientific by physicians like Liepmann and Weygandt and psychologists like Hellpach and Stern. Freud dared to give universal explanations, so his broad concept of sexuality was attacked (though also for other reasons besides its universality) by Aschaffenburg, Hellpach, Kraepelin, Moll, Oppenheim, and Strümpell. Freud stressed the etiological significance of hidden forces and was denounced for his belief in the unconscious by virtually every experimental psychologist. Physicians who had organic views of hysteria could not accept Freud's psychogenetic explanations. These included the well-known Fuhrmann, Fürstner, Kraepelin, Sommer, Vogt, and Ziehen. Freud's writing style cast discredit upon his conclusions because he did not limit himself to the dispassionate presentation of facts.

The rebellion against "philosophy" was a revolt against concern with final explanations. It was not the scientist's job to give teleological direction to his work nor to expect it to reward him with insights into the origins of the human condition. The rebellion was so effective because paradoxically it continued to propagate certain viewpoints of the very philosophy whose right to existence it had demolished.

The organically oriented scientists of the nineteenth century were, after all, products of an idealistic education. Kant's belief in the limits of human knowledge was taught at all universities. Hegel also frowned on "the vanity of wanting to know everything better." The significance of this view for psychoanalysis can be seen in the writings of Karl Jaspers (1883-1969), who was both a psychiatrist and a philosopher. Jaspers's *verstehende Psychologie* and his criticisms of modern life were deeply rooted in the idealistic tradition. Theodor Adorno (personal communication, 1963) has rightly concluded that Jaspers's criticisms of psychoanalysis were "symptomatic" of the profound repugnance which many German intellectuals felt for psychoanalysis.

Jaspers first began to attack Freud on psychiatric grounds in 1913, though eventually his psychiatric and philosophic critiques merged. The idealistic influence on these was strong. A "science" of human psychology was impossible because no one could really know the mind of another. To make generalizations and on that basis construct a "system" of the mind was therefore impossible. The "soul" was not explainable and reducible and therefore could not be "analyzed." Every psyche was unique, and the best that could be done was to examine its phenomena individually. In his antipsychological and phenomenalist orientations, Jaspers was influenced by Husserl, who had come down strongly against "psychologism"[1] in the first volume of his *Logical Investigations* (1900).

In a critique of modern culture, Jaspers (1931) attacked psychoanalysis, along with technology and Marxism, as an example of what was wrong with modern life. Here too, his idealistic orientation played a part. Philosophically, psychoanalysis was a shallow and base explanation of human nature. It defined man's greatest intellectual, spiritual, artistic, and material achievements in terms of the theory of sublimation. Psychoanalysis robbed men of their dignity not only by "analyzing" creativity but by rooting this ineffable quality in instinctual sexual and aggressive drives.[2]

[1] Adorno described *Psychologismus* as a "curse word" in German thought throughout the nineteenth century.

[2] How much influence Jaspers had on German distaste for psychoanalysis remains a matter of controversy. Psychoanalysts and psychiatrists like Wolfgang Loch (personal communication) of Frankfurt, the late Oskar Pfister (1952) and Hans Kleinschmidt (personal communication) of New York, have tended to stress Jaspers's influence on the outlook of psychiatrists and intellectuals. But Jaspers's pupils, Hannah Arendt (personal communication) and Kurt Rossmann (personal communication), professor of philosophy at the University of Basel, do not entirely

In the tradition of Kant and Hegel, Jaspers and many other educated Germans believed that knowledge had its limits. Freud was criticized because he went beyond its boundaries. Psychoanalysis could not be a science, dealing as it did in essentially unknowable matters. In particular, this philosophical prejudice made it difficult to accept Freud's theories about the unconscious. Many people were willing to accept the *existence* of an unconscious. There obviously could be a "hidden" part of the human personality. But to bring to light this "dark" aspect was attempting the impossible. Some things could never be defined. And Freud added practical insult to theoretical injury by explaining a good part of unconscious activity in terms of sexual wishes and fantasies.

The epistemological dualism of German idealism was complemented and reinforced by its psychophysical dualism — the Cartesian mind-body dichotomy. The mind-body dualism underlay two scientific positions, both incompatible with psychoanalysis.

One of these views was the popular nineteenth-century belief in psychophysical parallelism. Indeed, Freud himself held this view and enunciated it clearly in his famous monograph on aphasia (1891). At its best parallelism simply denied any causal connection between psychic and physical events. All that could be said for sure was that certain psychic and physiological states existed in a temporal relationship. But under the pervasive influence of nineteenth-century neurology and physiology, a belief in parallelism often shifted to a belief in the supremacy of organic processes.

---

agree. They do think that Jaspers probably influenced many psychiatrists against psychoanalysis with his early scientific and methodological criticisms of Freud. But Arendt and Rossmann vehemently deny that Jaspers had any extensive influence in turning German intellectuals in general against psychoanalytic theories.

The camps are neatly divided: Jaspers's pupils depreciate his influence, the psychoanalysts emphasize it. To ascertain it definitively is an important task for future study. But leaving aside the question of *influence* for the present, I concur with Adorno's evaluation that Jaspers's anti-Freudian writings were "symptomatic" of German intellectual thought. The majority of intellectuals may or may not have relied on Jaspers to show them the way, but he was not alien to their *Erbe, Bildung,* and *Weltanschauung.*

Thus the physician or psychologist reached a materialistic conception of human function through two avenues. The indirect path was via psychophysical parallelism. In a more direct way, idealistic mind-body dualism had another impact on nineteenth-century scientists. This occurred in the following way: Because of their great concern with "scientific" method, scientists arrived at the conclusion that they were being "scientific" only when they were investigating something that could be seen, weighed, measured—whether chemical substances, microscopic organisms, human tissues, or the human senses. The effect of this view was to consider the study of "mind" unscientific. After all, there were no physiological or surgical methods of dealing with it.

Thus Wundt (1902, p. 17) concluded that to explain "mind" "involved a metaphysical presupposition, which psychology may possibly be led to honour at the conclusion of her [experimental work], but which she cannot on any account accept, untested before she has entered upon it." In such a frame of reference, psychoanalysis was a collection of "untested . . . metaphysical presuppositions." The Würzburg school of experimental psychology had tried to study higher mental processes and soon found itself dealing in vague "attitudes" about which the Würzburgers requested their subjects' *opinions*. To Wundt, this was treading on dangerous, nonscientific ground, and he lashed out at Bühler and his "imageless thoughts."

Late nineteenth-century scientists received justification for this scientific point of view from their philosophical education, which had stressed the basic duality of mind and body. Thus it was epistemologically legitimate to concentrate on mind or matter and leave the other out of consideration. The German physician or psychologist at the turn of the century generally focused on the body as well as on physical explanations of all human functioning and malfunctioning.

This, of course, had immense significance for the practice of medicine. Man was seen primarily as a physiological organism; his psychic components were ignored. Only the body was considered treatable. Little consideration was given to the possibility that the mind and body might be treated as a unit.

In their practices, most doctors limited their verbal communications with patients solely to the elicitation of information directly relating to physical ailments. It was incomprehensible to many of them that another doctor should question his hysterical patients about their minds. Hysteria was a disease of somatic symptoms; therefore it must have a somatic origin. Though it was obvious that their emotions did greatly affect hysterics, these emotions need not be investigated, for at best they could play only a secondary role in the genesis of hysteria.

A dualistic world view was a convenient prop to physicians and psychologists of Freud's day. It helped them to accept an environment which continually confronted them with all manner of sharp divisions.

The scientists' theory of knowledge had a built-in duality. The study of the human body was scientific. But the study of the human mind as a whole was unscientific. Only separate functions of the mind could be studied scientifically if physiological methods were used.

Influenced by Darwin's discoveries, scientists were preponderantly on the side of nature in the ancient nature-nurture controversy. A person was considered born with a certain "constitution" and was in this way "predisposed" towards certain behavior. Once this behavior became manifest, the physician could do little to affect it. The inevitable "hereditary taint" had made its appearance; it was expected in certain races, nationalities, and families.

The world was further divided into "sick" and "healthy" persons who had little in common with each other. This in turn affected the concerns of psychiatrists and psychologists. We have seen proof of this in the way the two groups reacted to psychoanalysis. The psychiatrist was usually not curious about "ordinary" behavior and its origins because his patients had nothing in common with ordinary people. The psychologist tended to ignore the mentally ill because they were not suited to introspection.

Freud's monism was a sharp intruder in the midst of all this protective dualism. Psychoanalysis proposed that, like the body, the mind was a subject that could be understood scientifically. Furthermore, a person's "predisposition" included not only his heredity but his early life experiences as well. Therefore treatment was possible.[3] Freud said there was no sharp dichotomy between emotionally healthy and emotionally sick persons. All human beings shared a common psychosexual development.

Psychoanalysis represented an integrated world view. Events were "overdetermined" in an intricately meshed and multicausal fashion. Though Freud also at times succumbed to simplistic mechanistic or materialistic views, the essence of psychoanalysis was its departure from the Cartesian dualisms which sanctioned the compartmentalization of knowledge. In the late nineteenth century, a human being was seen simply as the sum of his parts, each of which could be studied separately without reference to the others. When Freudian psychology is juxtaposed with this conception of human function, we must conclude that psychoanalysis was demanding a revolution in the basic scientific *Weltanschauung*.

The idealistic legacies of mind-body dualism and belief in the limits of human knowledge, together with the positivistic rebellion against philosophy, formed a powerful tripartite base in which some of the roots of German resistance to psychoanalysis were embedded. Oswald Külpe demonstrated the influence of this philosopical structure in his *Introduction to Philosophy* (1895) when he warned students that they should not expect of psychology any more that a description of "the elementary processes and their mode of cooperation in the complex whole." If this has been carried out with "scientific accuracy, we have done everything in the way of an 'explanation' of the phenomena that can reasonably be demanded of us" (p. 62). The psychiatrist also had limited goals. A Kraepelinian clinician confined himself to observation, description, diagnosis, and prognosis. Done well—which they were indeed—that too was all that could reasonably be demanded.

---

[3] Today we know that the effects of early life experiences may be as unamenable to change as are genetically determined characteristics. Still, in Freud's day, few persons even suspected that infantile experiences were so important.

Külpe believed that psychology should not resort to "auxiliary concepts" such as the unconscious: "This fantastic extension of the idea of the psychical bars the way completely to any exact formulation of a science of the psychical" (pp. 62, 143). But the way to psychological knowledge did lie through the "fantastic extension of the idea of the psychical." In this century only a minority of Germans have comprehended the remarkable range of the psyche. The majority have been barred from this realization by three powerful circumstances: the combination of idealistic and materialistic intellectual currents; the repressive force of conventional attitudes; and the regressive ravages of National Socialism.

REFERENCES

Abraham, H. C., & Freud, E. L., eds. (1965), *A Psycho-Analytic Dialogue: The Letters of Sigmund Freud and Karl Abraham, 1907-1926*, trans. B. Marsh & H. C. Abraham. New York: Basic Books.

Abraham, K. (1907), Über die Bedeutung sexueller Jugendtraumen für die Symptomatologie der Dementia Praecox. *Zntlbl. f. Nervenh. u. Psychiat.*, 30: 409-415.

Ackerknecht, E. H. (1959), *A Short History of Psychiatry*, trans. S. Wolff. New York & London: Hafner, 1968.

———— (1966), Introduction to T. Puschmann, *A History of Medical Education from the Most Remote to the Most Recent Times*. New York: Hafner.

Adam, H. (1928), *Über Geisteskrankheit in Neuer Zeit*. Regensburg: Rath.

Adler, A. (1905a), Das sexuelle Problem in der Erziehung. *Die neue Gesellschaft Sozialist. Wschr.*. No. 30:360-362.

———— (1905b), Drei Psychoanalysen von Zahleneinfallen und obsedierenden Zahlen. *Psychiat.-Neurol. Wschr.*, 7:263-267.

Alexander, F. G., Eisenstein, S., & Grotjahn, M. (1966), *Psychoanalytic Pioneers*. New York & London: Basic Books.

———— & Selesnick, S. T. (1966), *The History of Psychiatry: An Evaluation of Psychiatric Thought and Practice from Prehistoric Times to the Present*. New York: Harper & Row.

Amdur, M. K. (1943), The Dawn of Psychiatric Journalism. *Amer. J. Psychiat.*, 100:205-216.

Anonymous (1896), Review of C. S. Freund's *Über psychische Lähmungen*. *Ztschr. f. Psychol. u. Physiol. d. Sinnesorg.*, 11:475-476.

———— (1902), Der Traum im Lichte der wissenschaftlichen Untersuchung. *Gaea: Natur und Leben*, 38:44-48.

———— (1906), Review of Freud's *Drei Abhandlungen zur Sexualtheorie*. *Literar. Zntlbl. Dtschland.*, 57:354.

Archiv für die gesamte Psychologie (1903-1907), Vols. 1-10, ed. E. Meumann and later together with W. Wirth. Leipzig.

Aschaffenburg, G. (1906), Die Beziehungen des sexuellen Lebens zur Entstehung der Nerven- und Geisteskrankheiten. *Münch. med. Wschr.*, 53:1793-1798; summarized in *Mschr. f. Psychiat. u. Neurol.* (1906), 20:488-489.

———— (1907), Autoreferat. *Mschr. f Psychiat. u. Neurol.*, 22:565-567.

Baerwald, R. (1906), Review of Freud's *Der Witz und seine Beziehung zum Unbewussten*. *Ztschr. f. Ästhet. u. allg. Kunstwissen.*, 1:435-438.

Barber, B. (1961), Resistance by Scientists to Scientific Discovery. *Science*, 134: 596-602.

Becker, T. (1899), *Einführung in die psychiatrische Klinik*, 2nd ed. Leipzig: Thieme.

331

Bellak, L., ed. (1961), *Contemporary European Psychiatry.* New York: Grove Press.

Ben-David, J. (1960), Roles and Innovations in Medicine. *Amer. J. Sociol.*, 65:557-568.

⸺ (1968), *Fundamental Research and the Universities.* O. E. C. D. Publication Center, March.

⸺ & Collins, R. (1966), Social Factors in the Origin of a New Science: The Case of Psychology. *Amer. Sociol. Rev.*, 31:452-463.

Bernfeld, S. (1944), Freud's Earliest Theories and the School of Helmholtz. *Psychoanal. Quart.*, 13:341-362.

Bibby, H. C. (1959), *T. H. Huxley: Scientist, Humanist, and Educator.* New York: Horizon.

Bibliographie der deutschen Zeitschriften-Literatur (1893-1908), Abteilung A of the Internationale Bibliographie der Zeitschriften-literatur. Leipzig: Dietrich.

Binswanger, L. (1906), Über das Verhalten des psycho-galvanischen Phänomens beim Assoziationsexperiment. *Diagnostische Assoziationsstudien: Beiträge zur experimentellen Psychopathologie*, Vol. 2, ed. C. G. Jung. Leipzig: Barth, pp. 113-195. Also in *J. f. Psychol. u. Neurol.* (1907), 10:1-85.

⸺ (1957), *Sigmund Freud: Reminiscences of a Friendship*, trans. N. Guterman. New York & London: Grune & Stratton.

Binswanger, O. (1896), *Die Pathologie und Therapie der Neurasthenie: Vorlesungen für Studierende und Aerzte.* Jena: Fischer,

⸺ (1904), *Die Hysterie.* Vol. 12 of *Specielle Pathologie und Therapie*, ed. H. Nothnagel. Wien: Hölder.

Birk, K. (1970), *Sigmund Freud und die Religion.* Münsterschwarzach: Vier-Türme-Verlag.

Birnbaum, K. (1928), Geschichte der psychiatrischen Wissenschaft. *Handbuch der Geisteskrankheiten*, Vol. 1, Allg. Teil I, ed. O. Bumke. Berlin: Springer.

Bleuler, E. (1905), Bewusstsein und Assoziationen. *Diagnostische Assoziationsstudien: Beiträge zur experimentellen Psychopathologie*, Vol. 1, ed. C. G. Jung. Leipzig: Barth, 1906, pp. 229-257.

⸺ (1906a), Freudsche Mechanism in der Symptomatologie von Psychosen. *Psychiatr.-Neurol. Wschr.*, 8:323-334, 338-339.

⸺ (1906b), Zur Frage der strafrechtlichen Behandlung von Sittlichkeitsvergehen an Kindern. *Mutterschtz*, 1:502-506.

⸺ (1906c), *Affectivity, Suggestibility, Paranoia*, trans. C. Rickener. Utica, N.Y.: State Hospitals Press, 1912.

⸺ (1906d), Letter to the Editor. *Zntlbl. f. Nervenh. u. Psychiat.*, 29:460-461.

⸺ (1907a), Review of Freud's *Sammlung kleiner Schriften zur Neurosenlehre. Münch. med. Wschr.*, 54:531-532.

⸺ (1907b), Review of Freud's *Zur Psychopathologie des Alltagslebens*, 2. Aufl. *Münch. med. Wschr.*, 54:1947-1948.

⸺ (1908), Die Prognose der Dementia Praecox (Schizophreniegruppe). *Allg. Ztschr. Psychiat.*, 65:436-464.

⸺ (1911), *Dementia Praecox or the Group of Schizophrenias*, trans. J. Zinkin. New York: International Universities Press, 1950.

Bloch, I. (1907a), Neomalthusianismus, sexueller Präventivverkehr, künstliche Sterilität und künstlicher Abort. *Geschlect u. Gesellschaft*, 2:253-267.

⸺ (1907b), *The Sexual Life of Our Time in Its Relation to Modern Civilization*, trans. M. Eden Paul. London: Rebman, 1908.

Bodamer, J. (1953), Zur Entstehung der Psychiatrie als Wissenschaft im 19. Jahrhundert. *Fortschr. d. Neurol. u. Psychiat.*, 21:511-535.

Boring, E. G. (1950), *A History of Experimental Psychology*, 2nd ed. New York: Appleton.

Braceland, F. J. (1956), Kraepelin, His System and His Influence. *Amer. J. Psychiat.*, 113:871-875.

Breuer, J., & Freud, S. (1893), On the Psychical Mechanism of Hysterical Phenomena: Preliminary Communication. *Standard Edition*, 2. London: Hogarth Press, 1955.

———— (1893-1895), Studies on Hysteria. *Standard Edition*, 2. London: Hogarth Press, 1955.

Bromberg, W. (1937), *The Mind of Man: The Story of Man's Conquest of Mental Illness*. New York & London: Harper.

———— (1942), Some Social Aspects of the History of Psychiatry. *Bull. Hist. Med.*, 11:117-132.

———— (1954), *Man Above Humanity: A History of Psychotherapy*. Philadelphia, London, Montreal: Lippincott.

Brome, V. (1968), *Freud and His Early Circle*. New York: Morrow.

Brücke, E. (1874), *Vorlesungen über Physiologie*. Wien: Braumüller.

Bry, I., & Rifkin, A. H. (1962), Freud and the History of Ideas: Primary Sources, 1886-1910. *Science and Psychoanalysis*, 5:6-36. New York: Grune & Stratton.

Bühler, K. (1907), Tatsachen und Probleme zu einer Psychologie der Denkvorgange: I. Ueber Gedanken. *Arch. f. d. ges Psychol.*, 9:297-305.

Bumke, O. (1906), Review of Freud's Bruchstück einer Hysterie-Analyse. *Schmidts Jahrbücher*, 289:168-169.

Burnham, J. C. (1958), Psychoanalysis in American Civilization before 1918. Unpublished doctoral dissertation, Stanford University.

———— (1967), *Psychoanalysis and American Medicine, 1894-1918: Medicine, Science, and Culture, Psychol. Issues*, Monogr. No. 20. New York: International Universities Press.

Cardwell, D. S. L. (1963), The Development of Scientific Research in Modern Universities. *Scientific Change: Historical Studies in the Intellectual, Social and Technical Conditions for Scientific Discovery and Technical Invention, from Antiquity to the Present*, ed. A. C. Crombie. Symposium on the History of Science, University of Oxford, 9-15 July, 1961. New York: Basic Books, pp. 661-667.

Carus, C. G. (1846), *Psyche: Zur Entwicklungsgeschichte der Seele*. Pforzheim: Flammer & Hoffman.

Castiglione, A. (1958), *A History of Medicine*, 2nd ed., rev. & enlarged, trans. & ed. E. B. Krumbhaar. New York: Knopf.

Cimbal [W. J. E.] (1904-1905), Review of Freud's Zur Psychopathologie des Alltagslebens. *J. f. Psychol. u. Neurol.*, 4:70-71.

Cohn, J. (1901), *Allgemeine Aesthetik*, Leipzig: Engelmann.

———— (1906), Review of Freud's Der Witz und seine Beziehung zum Unbewussten. *Ztschr. f. Psychol.*, 43:143-145.

Copleston, F. (1959-1963), *A History of Philosophy*, Vols. 4, 6, 7. Westminster, Md.: Newman Press.

Cranefield, P. F. (1966), Freud and the "School of Helmholtz." *Gesnerus*, 23:35-39.

Crombie, A. C., ed. (1963), *Scientific Change: Historical Studies in the Intellec-*

tual, Social and Technical Invention, from Antiquity to the Present. Symposium on the History of Science, University of Oxford, 9-15 July, 1961. New
York: Basic Books.

David, J. J. (1900), Review of Freud's *Die Traumdeutung. Die Nation: Wschr. f.
Politik, Volkswirth. u. Lit.,* 17:238-239.

De Boor, W. (1954), *Psychiatrische Systematik: Ihre Entwicklung in Deutschland
seit Kahlbaum.* Berlin: Springer.

Demos, J. (1970), *A Little Commonwealth: Family Life in Plymouth Colony.* New
York: Oxford.

Earle, P. (1854), *Institutions for the Insane in Prussia, Austria and Germany.* New
York: Wood.

Ebbinghaus, H. (1902), *Grundzüge der Psychologie,* Vol. 1. Leipzig: Veit.

_____ (1905), *Grundzüge der Psycholgie,* Vol. 1, 2nd ed. Leipzig: Veit.

_____ (1907), Psychologie. *Die Kultur der Gegenwart, Ihre Entwicklung und ihre
Ziele,* Section 6, ed. P. Hinneberg. Berlin & Leipzig: Teubner, pp. 173-244.

Ehrenfels, C. von (1903), Sexuales Ober- und Unterbewusstsein. *Polit.- anthropol.
Revue: Mschr. f. d. soziale u. geistige Leben d. Völker,* 2:456-476.

_____ (1907), *Sexualethik.* Grenzfr. d. Nerv.- u. Seelenleb., No. 56. Wiesbaden:
Bergmann.

Ellenberger, H. F. (1957), The Unconscious before Freud. *Bull. Menninger Clin.*
21:3-15.

_____ (1967), The Evolution of Depth Psychology. In: *Historic Derivations of
Modern Psychiatry,* ed. I. Galdston. New York: McGraw-Hill.

_____ (1970), *The Discovery of the Unconscious: The History and Evolution of
Dynamic Psychiatry.* New York: Basic Books.

Elmer, M. C. (1964), Salomon, Alisa. *Encyclopaedia Britannica,* Vol. 19.

Enke, P. (1900), *Casuistische Beiträge zur männlichen Hysterie.* Inaugural-Disser-
tation der medizinischen Fakultät zu Jena. Jena: Frommannsche Hof-Buch-
druckerei.

Eschle, F. C. R. (1907), *Grundzüge der Psychiatrie.* Berlin & Wien: Urban &
Schwarzenberg.

Eulenberg, A. (1906), Review of Freud's *Drei Abhandlungen zur Sexualtheorie.
Medizin. Klin., Wschr. f. prakt. Ärzte,* 2:740.

Fabri, T. (1905), Das Traumleben—als Erzieher. *Die Woche,* 7:153-155.

Feuchtersleben, E. von (1845), *The Principles of Medical Psychology: Being the
Outlines of a Course of Lectures,* trans. H. E. Lloyd, rev. & ed. B. G.
Babington. London: Sydenham Society, 1847.

Feuer, L. (1974), *Einstein and the Generations of Science.* New York: Basic Books.

Fischer, I. (1932-1933), *Biographisches Lexicon der hervorragenden Ärzte der
letzten fünfzig Jahre,* Vols. 1 & 2. Berlin & Wien: Urban & Schwarzenberg.

Fish, F. (1964), The Historical Development of Modern Psychiatry in Britain and
Germany. *Anglo-German Med. Rev.,* 2:296-307.

Fliess, W. (1897), *Die Beziehungen zwischen Nase und weiblichen Geschlechts-
organen: In ihrer biologischen Bedeutung dargestellt.* Leipzig & Wien:
Deuticke.

_____ (1906), *Der Ablauf des Lebens.* Leipzig, Vienna: Deuticke.

Flugel, J. C. (1933), *A Hundred Years of Psychology, 1833-1933,* rev. ed., with D.
J. West. International Universities Press, 1964.

Freud, S. (1886a), Report on My Studies in Paris and Berlin. *Standard Edition,*
1:5-15. London: Hogarth Press, 1966.

_____ (1886b), Observation of a Severe Case of Hemi-Anaesthesia in a Hysterical Male. *Standard Edition*, 1:25-31. London: Hogarth Press, 1966.

_____ (1887-1902), *The Origins of Psychoanalysis: Letters to Wilhelm Fliess, Drafts and Notes: 1887-1902*, ed. M. Bonaparte, A. Freud, E. Kris. Authorized trans. E. Mosbacher & J. Strachey. Introd. E. Kris. New York: Basic Books, 1954.

_____ (1891), *On Aphasia*. New York: International Universities Press, 1953.

_____ (1893), Some Points for a Comparative Study of Organic and Hysterical Motor Paralyses. *Standard Edition*, 1:160-172. London: Hogarth Press, 1966.

_____ (1894), The Neuro-Psychoses of Defence. *Standard Edition*, 3:45-61. London: Hogarth Press, 1962.

_____ (1895a), Obsessions and Phobias: Their Psychical Mechanism and Their Aetiology. *Standard Edition*, 3:74-82. London: Hogarth Press, 1962.

_____ (1895b), On the Grounds for Detaching a Particular Syndrome from Neurasthenia under the Description "Anxiety Neurosis." *Standard Edition*, 3:90-115. London: Hogarth Press, 1962.

_____ (1895c), A Reply to Criticisms of My Paper on Anxiety Neurosis. *Standard Edition*, 3:123-139. London: Hogarth Press, 1962.

_____ (1896), Further Remarks on the Neuro-Psychoses of Defence. *Standard-Edition*, 3:162-185. London: Hogarth Press, 1962.

_____ (1898), The Psychical Mechanism of Forgetfulness. *Standard Edition*, 3;289-297. London: Hogarth Press, 1962.

_____ (1899), Screen Memories. *Standard Edition*, 3:303-322. London: Hogarth Press, 1962.

_____ (1900), The Interpretation of Dreams. *Standard Edition*, 4 & 5. London: Hogarth Press, 1958.

_____ (1901a), On Dreams. *Standard Edition*, 5:633-686. London: Hogarth Press, 1953.

_____ (1901b), The Psychopathology of Everyday Life. *Standard Edition*, 6. London: Hogarth Press, 1960.

_____ (1904), Freud's Psycho-Analytic Procedure. *Standard Edition*, 7:249-254. London: Hogarth Press, 1953.

_____ (1905a), Fragment of an Analysis of a Case of Hysteria. *Standard Edition*, 7:7-122. London: Hogarth Press, 1953.

_____ (1905b), Jokes and Their Relation to the Unconscious. *Standard Edition*, 8. London: Hogarth Press, 1960.

_____ (1905c[1890]), Psychical (or Mental) Treatment. *Standard Edition*, 7:283-302. London: Hogarth Press, 1953.

_____ (1905d), Three Essays on the Theory of Sexuality. *Standard Edition*, 7:130-243. London: Hogarth Press, 1953.

_____ (1906a), My Views on the Part Played by Sexuality in the Aetiology of the Neurosis. *Standard Edition*, 7:269-279. London: Hogarth Press, 1953.

_____ (1906b), Psycho-Analysis and the Establishment of the Facts in Legal Proceedings. *Standard Edition*, 9:103-114. London: Hogarth Press, 1959.

_____ (1908a), "Civilized" Sexual Morality and Modern Nervous Illness. *Standard Edition*, 9:181-204. London: Hogarth Press, 1959.

_____ (1908b), Creative Writers and Day-Dreaming. *Standard Edition*, 9:143-153. London: Hogarth Press, 1959.

_____ (1908c), On the Sexual Theories of Children. *Standard Edition*, 9:209-226. London: Hogarth Press, 1959.

_____ (1909), Some General Remarks on Hysterical Attacks. *Standard Edition*, 9:229-234. London: Hogarth Press, 1959.

_____ (1912), A Note on the Unconscious in Psycho-Analysis. *Standard Edition*, 12:260-266. London: Hogarth Press, 1958.

_____ (1914), On the History of the Psycho-Analytic Movement. *Standard Edition*, 14:7-66. London: Hogarth Press, 1957.

_____ (1916-1917), Introductory Lectures on Psychoanalysis. *Standard Edition*, 15 & 16. London: Hogarth Press, 1963.

_____ (1917), A Difficulty in the Path of Psycho-Analysis. *Standard Edition*, 17:137-144. London: Hogarth Press, 1955.

_____ (1925), An Autobiographical Study. *Standard Edition*, 20:7-74. London: Hogarth Press, 1959.

Friedell, E. (1954), *A Cultural History of the Modern Age*, Vol. 3, trans. C. F. Atkinson. New York: Knopf.

Friedländer, A. A. (1907a), Kurze Bemerkungen zu der Freud'schen Lehre über die sexuelle Aetiologie der Neurosen. *Neurol. Centralbl.*, 26:953-954.

_____ (1907b), Sammelreferat. S. Freuds neuere Abhandlungen zur Neurosenfrage. *J. f. Psychol. u. Neurol.*, 10:201-213.

_____ (1907c), Über Hysterie und die Freudsche psychoanalytische Behandlung derselben. *Mschr. f. Psychiat. u. Neurol.*, 22: Ergänzungsheft, 45-54.

Friedmann, H. (1907), Die Bedeutung des unbewussten Seelenlebens und eine Methode zu dessen Aufstellung. *Beilage zur Allgemeinen Zeitung*, Munich, Oct. 15, 183:65-68.

Fürstner, C. (1906), Hysterie. *Geistkrankheiten*. 6th Band, 2nd Abtheilung of *Die Deutsche Klinik am Eingange des zwanzigsten Jahrhunderts: In akademischen Vorlesungen*. Berlin & Wien: Urban & Schwarzenberg.

Fuhrmann, M. (1903), *Diagnostik und Prognostik der Geisteskrankheiten: Ein kurzes Lehrbuch*. Leipzig: Barth.

Galdston, I. (1956), Freud and Romantic Medicine. *Bull. Hist. Med.*, 30:489-507.

Garrison, F. H. (1929), *An Introduction to the History of Medicine*, 4th ed. Philadelphia & London: Saunders.

Gattel, F. (1898), *Ueber die sexuellen Ursachen der Neurasthenie und Angstneurose*. Berlin: Hirschwald.

Gaupp, R. (1900a), Review of Freud's Ueber Deckerinnerungen. *Ztschr. f. Psychol. u. Physiol. d. Sinnesorg.*, 23:233-234.

_____ (1900b), Review of Konrad Rieger's *Die Castration in rechtlicher, socialer und vitaler Hinsicht. Ztschr. f. Psychol. u. Physiol. d. Sinnesorg.*, 24:400.

_____ (1906), Review of Leo Hirschlaff's *Hypnotismus und Suggestivtherapie. Dtsch. Literaturztg.*, 27: cols. 184-185.

Giessler, C. M. (1901), Die Grundtatsache des Traumzustandes. *Allg. Ztschr. Psychiat.*, 58:164-182.

_____ (1902), Review of Freud's *Ueber den Traum. Ztschr. f. Psychol. u. Physiol. d. Sinnesorg.*, 29:228-230.

_____ (1906), Die Bedeutung der Träume. *Deutsche Revue*, 31:244-247.

Green, M. (1974), *The von Richthofen Sisters, The Triumphant and the Tragic Modes of Love*. New York: Basic Books.

Griesinger, W. (1845), *Mental Pathology and Therapeutics*. A facsimile of the English edition of 1867, introd. E. H. Ackerknecht. New York: Hafner, 1965.

Grinstein, A., ed. (1956-1966), *The Index to Psychoanalytic Writings*, Vols. 1-9. New York: International Universities Press.

Grober, J. (1907), Review of Freud's *Sammlung kleiner Schriften zur Neurosenlehre. Centralbl. f. inn. Med.*, 28:99.

Gross, O. (1904), Über Bewusstseinszerfall. *Monat. f. Psychiat. u. Neurol.*, 15:45-51.

———(1905), Review of Freud's *Zur Psychopathologie des Alltagslebens. Arch. f. Krim.-Anthropol. u. Kriminal.*, 18:271-272.

———(1907), *Das Freud'sche Ideogenitätsmoment und seine Bedeutung im manisch-depressivem Irresein Kraepelin's.* Leipzig: Vogel.

Gruenewaldt, V. von (1927), *Von Mesmer zu Coué: Ein Beitrag zu den suggestiven Heilmethoden.* München-Planegg: Barth.

Gruhn, A. (1907), Zur Psychologie des Traumes. *Pädagog. Arch. Mschr. f. Erziehung u. Unterricht,* 49:263-265.

Haeckel, E. (1868), *Natürliche Schöpfungsgeschichte.* Berlin: Reimer.

Haenel, H. (1904), Review of Freud's *Zur Psychopathologie des Alltagslebens. Neurol. Centralbl.*, 23:1045-1046.

Hnl. [Haenel], H. (1905), Review of Hellpach's *Grundlinien einer Psychologie der Hysterie. Literar. Zntlbl. Dtschlnd.*, 56:cols. 243-245.

Hale, N. G., Jr. (1971), *Freud and the Americans.* New York: Oxford University Press.

Harden, M. (1904), Der kleine Jacobsohn. *Die Zukunft,* Dec. 10:370-378.

Hartmann, E. von (1869), *Philosophie des Unbewusstsein,* 2nd ed. Berlin: Duncker, 1870.

Hartmann, H. (1927), Understanding and Explanation. *Essays on Ego Psychology: Selected Problems in Psychoanalytic Theory.* New York: International Universities Press, 1964, pp. 369-403.

Havens, L. L. (1965), Emil Kraepelin. *J. Nerv. Ment. Dis.,* 141:16-28.

Hellpach, W. (1902), Psychologie und Nervenheilkunde. *Philosophische Studien,* 19:192-242.

———(1903), Hysterie und Nervosität. *Psychische Studien,* 30:14-21, 89-95, 152-159.

———(1904), *Grundlinien einer Psychologie der Hysterie.* Leipzig: Engelmann.

———(1905), Die Hysterie und die moderne Schule. *Internat. Arch. f. Schulhygiene,* 1:222-251.

———(1906a), *Die geistigen Epidimien.* Vol. 11 of *Die Gesellschaft: Samml. sozial-psychol. Monograph.,* ed. M. Buber. Frankfurt a.M.: Literar. Anstalt, Rütten & Loenig.

———(1906b), *Grundgedanken zur Wissenschaftslehre der Psychopathologie.* Habilitationsschrift zur Erlangung der Venia legendi in der Psychologie an der Grossherzoglich Badischen Technischen Hochschule. Leipzig: Engelmann. Also in *Archiv f. d. ges. Psychol.,* 7:143-266.

———(1906c), *Nervenleben und Weltanschauung: Ihre Wechselbeziehungen im deutschen Leben von Heute.* Grenzfr. d. Nerv. u. Seelenleb., No. 41. Wiesbaden: Bergmann.

———(1906d), Review of Löwenfeld's *Sexualleben und Nervenleiden. Medizin. Klin., Wschr. f. prakt. Ärzte,* 2:1347.

Himes, N. E. (1936), *Medical History of Contraception.* Baltimore: Williams & Wilkins.

Hirschlaff, L. (1905), *Hypnotismus und Suggestivtherapie: Ein kurzes Lehrbuch für Ärzte und Studierende.* Leipzig: Barth.

Hirt, E. (1907), Review of Hellpach's *Grundlinien einer Psychologie der Hysterie. Arch. f. d. ges. Psychol.*, 10:76-101.

Hughes, H. S. (1958), *Consciousness and Society: The Reorientation of European Social Thought*. New York: Knopf.

Husserl, E. (1900), *Logische Untersuchungen*, Vol. 1, Halle a.d.S.: Niemeyer, 1913.

Index-Catalogue of the Library of the Surgeon-General's Office, United States Army (1880-1932), Series 1, 2, & 3, Washington: Government Printing Office.

Index Medicus: A Monthly Classified Record of the Current Medical Literature of the World (1879-1899, 1903-1908), Series 1, Compiled J. S. Billings & R. Fletcher. New York: Leypoldt; Boston & Detroit: Davis; Series 2, ed. Fletcher & Garrison. The Carnegie Institute of Washington.

Isserlin, M. (1907), Über Jungs "Psychologie der Dementia Praecox" und die Anwendung Freud'scher Forschungsmaximen in der Psychopathologie. *Zntlbl. f. Nervenh. u. Psychiat.*, 30:329-343.

Jaspers, K. (1931), *Man in the Modern Age*. New York: Anchor Books, 1957.

———— (1964), *General Psychopathology*, 7th ed, trans. J. Hoenig & M. W. Hamilton. Chicago: University of Chicago Press.

Jentsch, E. (1905), Traumarbeit. *Neue Rundschau*, 16:875-882.

Jones, E. (1953), *The Life and Work of Sigmund Freud*, Vol. 1. New York: Basic Books.

———— (1955), *The Life and Work of Sigmund Freud*, Vol. 2. New York: Basic Books.

———— (1957), *The Life and Work of Sigmund Freud*, Vol. 3. New York: Basic Books.

Juliusburger, O. (1902), Zur Lehre von den Zwangsvorstellungspsychosen. *Mschr. f. Psychiat. u. Neurol.*, 12.

———— (1907), Beitrag zu der Lehre von der Psychoanalyse. *Allg. Ztschr. Psychiat.*, 64:1002-1010; summarized in *Neurol. Centralbl.*, 27:89-91.

Jung, C. G. (1902), *Zur Psychologie und Pathologie sogenannter occulter Phänomene: Eine psychiatrische Studie*. Leipzig: Mutze.

———— (1904), Reply to R. Hahn's review of *Zur Psychologie und Pathologie sogenannte occulter Phänomene*. *Arch. f. d. ges. Psychol.*, 3:347-350.

———— (1905a), Cryptomnesia. *Collected Works*, Vol. 1. New York: Pantheon, 1957.

———— (1905b), Psychoanalyse und Assoziationsexperimente. *Diagnostische Assoziationsstudien: Beiträge zur experimentellen Psychopathologie*, Vol. 1, ed. C. G. Jung. Leipzig: Barth, 1906, pp. 258-281.

———— ed. (1906a) *Diagnostische Assoziationsstudien: Beiträge zur experimentellen Psychopathologie*, Vols. 1 & 2. Leipzig: Barth.

———— (1906b), Die Hysterielehre Freuds. Eine Erwiderung auf die Aschaffenburg'sche Kritik. *Münch. med. Wschr.*, 53:2301.

———— (1906c), *Die psychologische Diagnose des Tatbestandes*, Vol. 4, No. 2 of *Juristisch-psychiatrische Grenzfragen*. Zwanglose Abhandlungen. Halle a.S.: Marhold.

———— (1907a), Review of Bleuler's *Affektivität, Suggestibilität, Paranoia. Ztschr. f. Psychol.* 45:150-152.

———— (1907b), *Über die Psychologie der Dementia Praecox: Ein Versuch*. Halle a.S.: Marhold.

———— & Riklin, F. (1904), Experimentelle Untersuchungen über Assoziationen Gesunder. *Diagnostische Assoziationsstudien: Beiträge zur experimentellen Psychopathologie*, Vol. 1, ed. C. G. Jung. Leipzig: Barth, 1906, pp. 7-145.

Kahn, E. (1956), Emil Kraepelin. *Amer. J. Psychiat.*, 113:289-294.

——— (1959), The Emil Kraepelin Memorial Lecture. *Epidemiology of Mental Disorder*. Washington, D.C., American Association for the Advancement of Science.

Karell, L. (1900), Review of Freud's *Traumdeutungen* [sic]. *Beilage zur Allgemeinen Zeitung*, Munich, Oct. 12, 234:4-5.

Kind, A. (1908), Arbeiten der Freud'schen Schule. *Anthropophyteia*, 5:387-388.

Kirchhoff, T. (1890), *Grundriss einer Geschichte der deutschen Irrenpflege*. Berlin: Hirschwald.

——— (1912), Geschichte der Psychiatrie. *Handbuch der Psychiatrie*. Allgemeiner Teil, Vol. 4, ed. G. Aschaffenburg. Leipzig & Wein: Deuticke.

———, ed. (1921), *Deutsche Irrenärzte: Einzelbilder Ihres Lebens und Wirkens*, Vol. 1. Berlin: Springer.

———, ed. (1924), *Deutsche Irrenärzte: Einzelbilder Ihres Lebens und Wirkens*, Vol. 2. Berlin: Springer.

Kohnstamm, O. (1902), Review of Freud's *Über den Traum*. *Fortschr. d. Med.*, 20:45-46.

Kolle, K., ed. (1956), *Grosse Nervenaertze*, Vol. 1. Stuttgart: Thieme.

——— (1957), *Kraepelin und Freud: Beitrag zur neueren Geschichte der Psychiatrie*. Stuttgart: Thieme.

———, ed. (1959), *Grosse Nervenaerzte*, Vol. 2. Stuttgart: Thieme.

———, ed. (1963), *Grosse Nervenaerzte*, Vol. 3. Stuttgart: Thieme.

Korn, G. (1902), Neuere Forschungen über Schlaf und Traumleben. *Der Türmer: Mschr. f. Gemut u. Geist*, 4:438-443.

Kornfeld, H. (1907), Review of Jung's *Über die Psychologie der Dementia praecox*. *Arch. f. Strafrecht u. Strafprozess*, 54:439.

Kornfeld, S. (1905), Geschichte der Psychiatrie. *Handbuch der Geschichte der Medizin*, Vol. 3, ed. M. Neuburger & J. L. Pagel. Jena: Fischer.

Kossman, R., & Weiss, J. (1905), *Die Gesundheit, ihre Erhaltung, ihre Störung, ihre Wiederherstellung*, 3rd ed. Stuttgart, Berlin, & Leipzig: Union Deutsche Verlagsgesellschaft.

Kraepelin, E. (1896), *Psychiatrie: Ein Lehrbuch für Studirende und Aertze*, 5th ed. Leipzig: Barth.

——— (1899), *Psychiatrie: Ein Lehrbuch für Studirende und Aerzte*, Vol. 2, 6th ed. Leipzig: Barth.

——— (1901), *Lectures on Clinical Psychiatry*. rev. & ed. T. Johnstone. New York: Wood, 1904.

——— (1904), *Psychiatrie: Ein Lehrbuch für Studierende und Ärztze*, Vol. 2, 7th ed. Leipzig: Barth.

——— (1917), *One Hundred Years of Psychiatry*, trans. W. Baskin. New York: Citadel Press, 1962.

Krehl, L. von (1902), Über die Entstehung hysterischer Erscheinungen. *Sammlung klinischer Vorträge*. Neue Folge No. 330. Innere Medicin No. 98. Leipzig: Breitkopf & Härtel.

Kuhn, R. (1957), Griesingers Auffassung der psychischen Krankheiten und seine Bedeutung für die weitere Entwicklung der Psychiatrie. *Beiträge zur Geschichte der Psychiatrie und Hirnanatomie*. Basel & New York: Karger, 1957.

Kuhn, T. (1963), The Function of Dogma in Scientific Research. In *Scientific Change: Historical Studies in the Intellectual, Social and Technical Conditions for Scientific Discovery and Technical Invention, from Antiquity to the Present*, ed. A. C. Crombie. Symposium on the History of Science, University of Oxford 9-15 July, 1961. New York: Basic Books, pp. 347-369.

―――― (1970), *The Structure of Scientific Revolutions*, 2nd ed., enlarged. International Encyclopedia of Unified Science, Vol. 2, No. 2. Chicago: University of Chicago Press.

Külpe, O. (1893), *Outlines of Psychology: Based upon the Results of Experimental Investigation*, trans. E. B. Titchener. London: Sonnenschein; New York: Macmillan, 1909.

―――― (1895), *Introduction to Philosophy*, trans. W. B. Pillsbury & E. B. Titchener. London: Sonnenschein; New York: Macmillan, 1901.

Laistner, L. (1899), *Das Rätsel der Sphinx, Grundzüge einer Mythengeschichte*, Berlin: Hertz.

Leibbrand, W. (1956), *Die spekulative Medizin der Romantik*. Hamburg: Claasen.

―――― & Wettley, A. (1961), *Der Wahnsinn: Geschichte der abendländischen Psychopathologie*. Freiburg-München: Alber.

Letchworth, W. P. (1889), *The Insane in Foreign Countries*. New York & London: Putnam.

Lewis, N. D. C. (1941), *A Short History of Psychiatric Achievement: With a Forecast for the Future*. New York: Norton.

Leyen, F. von der (1901), Traum und Märchen. *Der Lotse. Hamburg. Wschr. f. Dtsch. Kultur*, 1:382-390.

Liebers, M. (1906), Review of Löwenfeld's *Sexualleben und Nervenleiden. Beilage zur Allgemeinen Zeitung*, Munich, Aug. 23, 194:357.

―――― (1907), Review of Jung's *Über die Psychologie der Dementia Praecox. Beilage zur Allgemeinen Zeitung*, Munich, 111:293.

Liepmann, H. (1901), Review of Freud's *Über den Traum. Mschr f. Psychiat. u. Neurol.*, 10:237-239.

Lilge, F. (1948), *The Abuse of Learning: The Failure of the German University*. New York: Macmillan.

Lipmann, O. (1906), Review of Bleuler's Bewusstsein und Assoziation. *Zschr. f. Psychol.*, 43:119-120.

―――― (1906-1907), Reviews of the word-association studies which originally appeared in the *Journal für Psychologie und Neurologie. Zschr. f. Psychol.*, 40:213-215; 41:230-232; 42:69-71; 43:119-120; 44:153, 312-313; 45:299.

―――― (1907a), Review of Jung's Psychoanalyse und Assoziationsexperiment. *Zschr. f. Psychol.*, 44:153.

―――― (1907b), Review of Jung's Assoziation, Traum und hysterisches Symptom. *Zschr. f. Psychol.*, 45:299.

Lipps, T. (1883), *Grundtatsachen des Seelenlebens*. Bonn: Cohen.

―――― (1903), *Leitfaden der Psychologie*. Leipzig: Engelmann.

Löwenfeld, L. (1894), *Pathologie und Therapie der Neurasthenie und Hysterie*. Wiesbaden: Bergmann.

―――― (1895), Über die Verknüpfung neurasthenischer und hysterischer Symptome in Anfallsform nebst Bemerkungen über die Freud'sche Angstneurose. *Münch. med. Wschr.*, 42:282-285.

―――― (1897a), *Lehrbuch der gesammten Psychotherapie: Mit einer einleitenden Darstellung der Hauptthatsachen der medicinischen Psychologie*. Wiesbaden: Bergmann.

―――― (1897b), Zur Lehre von den neurotischen Angstzuständen. *Münch. med. Wschr.*, 44:635-639, 673-677.

―――― (1901), *Der Hypnotismus: Handbuch der Lehre von der Hypnose und der Suggestion mit besonderer Berücksichtigung ihrer Bedeutung für Medicin und Rechtspflege*. Wiesbaden: Bergmann.

———— (1904a), *Die moderne Behandlung der Nervenschwäche (Neurasthenie),* *der Hysterie und verwandter Leiden,* 4th ed. Wiesbaden: Bergmann.

———— (1904b), *Die psychischen Zwangserscheinungen: Auf klinischer Grundlage dargestellt.* Wiesbaden: Bergmann.

———— (1905), *Über die geistige Arbeitskraft und ihre Hygiene.* Grenzfr. d. Nerv.- u. Seelenleb., No. 38. Wiesbaden: Bergmann.

———— (1906), *Sexualleben und Nervenleiden.* Wiesbaden: Bergmann.

———— (1908), *Homosexualität und Strafgesetz.* Grenzfr. d. Nerv.- u. Seelenleb., No. 57. Wiesbaden: Begmann.

———— (1909), *Über das Eheliche Glück: Erfahrungen, Reflexionen und Ratschläge eines Arztes,* 2nd ed. Wiesbaden: Bergmann.

Lubarsch, O. (1901-1902), Schlaf und Traum. *Die Woche,* 3:2243-2246; 4:17-19.

Marcus, S. (1966), *The Other Victorians: A Study of Sexuality and Pornography in Mid-Nineteenth-Century England.* New York: Basic Books.

Margetts, E. L. (1953), Concept of the Unconscious in the History of Medical Psychology. *Psychiat. Quart.,* 28:1-115.

Martin, L. J. (1907), Zur Begründung und Anwendung der Suggestionsmethode in der Normalpsychologie. *Arch. f. d. ges. Psychol.,* 10:321-402.

Marx, O. (1965), A Re-evaluation of the Mentalists in Early 19th Century German Psychiatry. *Amer. J. Psychiat.,* 121:752-760.

McGuire, W., ed. (1974), *The Freud/Jung Letters: The Correspondence between Sigmund Freud and C. G. Jung,* trans. R. Manheim & R. F. C. Hull. Princeton: Princeton University Press.

Mehring, S. (1906), Das Wesen des Witzes. *Die Nation: Wschr. f. Politik, Volkswirth. u. Lit.,* 23:283-285.

Mendel, E. (1884), Über Hysterie beim männlichen Geschlecht. *Berlin. klin. Wschr.,* 21:314-317, 330-331, 347-348.

Meng, H., & Freud, E. L., eds. (1963), *Psychoanalysis and Faith: The Letters of Sigmund Freud and Oskar Pfister,* trans. E. Mosbacher. New York: Basic Books.

Mentz, P. (1901), Review of Freud's *Die Traumdeutung. Vierteljahrsschr. f. wissenschaft. Philos.,* 25:112-113.

Messmer, O. (1904), Literaturbericht. *Arch. f. d. ges. Psychol.,* 4:46-47.

Meyer, E. (1906), Review of Freud's *Drei Abhandlungen zur Sexualtheorie. Mschr. f. Psychiat. u. Neurol.,* 20:92-93.

Meyer, R. M. (1905), Review of Freud's *Der Witz und seine Beziehung zum Unbewussten. Dtsch. Literaturztg.* 26:cols. 2630-2632.

Möbius, P. J. (1888), Über den Begriff der Hysterie. *Zntlbl. f. Nervenh. u. Psychiat.,* 11:66-71.

———— (1895), Über die gegenwärtige Auffassung der Hysterie. *Mschr. f. Geburtsh. u. Gynaekol.,* 1:12-21.

———— (1901), Review of Freud's *Über den Traum. Schmidts Jahrbücher,* 269:271.

———— (1904), Review of Freud's *Zur Psychopathologie des Alltagslebens. Schmidts Jahrbucher,* 282:104.

———— (1907), *Die Hoffnungslosigkeit aller Psychologie.* Halle a.S.: Marhold.

Mönkemöller, [E. O.] (1904-1905), Review of Freud's *Zur Psychopathologie des Alltagslebens. Psychiatr.-Neurol. Wschr.,* 6:288.

Moll, A. (1907), *Der Hypnotismus: Mit Einschluss der Hauptpunkte der Psychotherapie und des Okkultismus,* 4th ed. Berlin: Fischer's Medicin. Buchhandlung.

_____ (1908), *Das Sexualleben des Kindes*. Berlin: Walther, 1909.

Mora, G. (1965), The Historiography of Psychiatry and Its Development: A Re-e-valuation. *J. Hist. Behav. Sci.*, 1:43-52.

_____ (1967), History of Psychiatry. In: *Comprehensive Textbook of Psychiatry*, ed. A. M. Freedman & H. I. Kaplan. Baltimore: Williams & Wilkins.

Müller-Freienfehls, R. (1935), *The Evolution of Modern Psychology*, trans. W. B. Wolfe. New Haven: Yale University Press.

Murchison, C., ed. (1929), *The Psychological Register*. Worcester, Mass.: Clark University Press.

Murphy, G. (1949), *Historical Introduction to Modern Psychology*. New York: Harcourt, Brace.

Muthmann, A. (1907), *Zur Psychologie und Therapie neurotischer Symptome: Eine Studie auf Grunde der Neurosenlehre Freuds*. Halle a.S.: Marhold.

Näcke, P. (1901), Reviews of Freud's *Die Traumdeutung* and *Über den Traum*. *Arch. F. Krim.-Anthropol. u. Kriminal.*, 7:168-169.

_____ (1906), Reviews of Freud's *Drei Abhandlungen zur Sexualtheorie* and Jung's *Die psychologische Diagnose des Tatbestandes*. *Arch. f. Krim.-Anthropol. u. Kriminal.*, 24:166-167.

Nietzsche, F. (1874), "Schopenhauer as Educator," Thoughts out of Season. *Complete Works*, Vol. 5, ed. O. Levy. New York: Russell & Russell, 1964.

_____ (1879), Mixed Opinions and Maxims. *Basic Writings*, trans. & ed. W. Kaufmann. New York: Modern Library, 1968.

_____ (1881), The Dawn of Day. *Complete Works*, Vol. 9, ed. O. Levy. New York: Russell & Russell, 1964.

_____ (1887), On the Genealogy of Morals. *Basic Writings*, trans. & ed. W. Kaufmann. New York: Modern Library, 1968.

Oppenheim, H. (1894), *Lehrbuch der Nervenkrankheiten für Ärzte und Studierende*. Berlin: Karger.

_____ (1898), *Lehrbuch der Nervenkrankheiten für Ärzte und Studierende,* 2nd ed. Berlin: Karger.

_____ (1902a), *Lehrbuch der Nervenkrankheiten für Ärzte und Studierende,* 3rd ed. Berlin: Karger.

_____ (1902b), *Zur Prognose und Therapie der schweren Neurosen*. Sammlung zwangloser Abhandlungen aus dem Gebiete der Nerven- und Geisteskrankheiten, 3rd Band, Heft 8. Halle a.S.: Marhold.

_____ (1905), *Lehrbuch der Nervenkrankheiten für Ärzte und Studierende*, Vol. 2, 4th ed., enlarged and revised. Berlin: Karger.

Oppenheimer, C. (1900), Review of Freud's *Die Traumdeutung. Die Umschau: Übersicht über d. Fortschr. u. Bewegung. a. d. Gesamtgebiet d. Wissensch., Techn., Litt. u. Kunst*, 4:218-219.

C. D. P. (1906), Review of Freud's *Der Witz und seine Beziehung zum Unbewussten. Literar. Zntlbl. Dtschlnd.*, 57:cols. 565-566.

Pagel, J. (1901), *Biographisches Lexicon hervorragender Ärzte des neunzehnten Jahrhunderts*. Berlin & Wien: Urban & Schwarzenberg.

Peretti, J. (1895a), Review of Freud's Quelques considérations pour une étude comparative des paralysies motrices organiques et hystériques. *Ztschr. f. Psychol. u. Physiol. d. Sinnesorg.*, 7:157-158.

_____ (1895b), Review of Freud's *Die Abwehr-Neuro-Psychosen. Ztschr. f. Psychol. u. Physiol. d. Sinnesorg.*, 8:466-467.

_____ (1897), Review of Freud's L'hérédité et l'étiologie des névroses. *Ztschr. f. Psychol. u. Physiol. d. Sinnesorg.*, 13:150-151.

Peters, R. S., ed. (1953), *Brett's History of Psychology.* London: Allen & Unwin.

Pfister, O. (1952), Karl Jaspers als Sigmund Freuds Widersacher. *Psyche,* 6:241-275.

Placzek, S. (1907), Review of Freud's *Sammlung kleiner Schriften zur Neurosenlehre. Berl. klin. Wschr.,* 4:1000.

Psychological Index, The. A Bibliography of the Literature of Psychology and Cognate Subjects. (1895-1909). New York: Macmillan.

Puschmann, T. (1889), *A History of Medical Education from the Most Remote to the Most Recent Times,* trans. & ed. E. H. Hare. London: Lewis, 1891; New York: Hafner, 1966.

Rank, O. (1907), *Der Künstler: Ansätze zu einer Sexualpsychologie.* Vienna: Heller.

Revers, W. J. (1968), Külpe, Oswald. *International Encyclopedia of the Social Sciences,* Vol. 8. New York: Macmillan.

Ribot, T. (1885), *German Psychology of To-Day: The Empirical School,* 2nd ed., trans. J. M. Baldwin. New York: Scribner, 1886.

Rieger, K. (1896), Über die Behandlung "Nervenkranker." *Schmidts Jahrb.,* 251: 193-198, 273-276.

Riese, W. (1958), The Pre-Freudian Origins of Psychoanalysis. *Science and Psychoanalysis,* Vol. 1. New York: Grune & Stratton.

————— (1967), The Neuropsychologic Phase in the History of Psychiatric Thought. In: *Historic Derivations of Modern Psychiatry,* ed. I. Galdston. New York: McGraw-Hill.

————— & Hoff, E. C. (1950), A History of the Doctrine of Cerebral Localization — Part 1: Sources, Anticipations, and Basic Reasoning. *J. Hist. Med. Allied Sci.,* 5:50-71.

Roazen, P. (1975), *Freud and His Followers.* New York: Knopf.

Rose, F. (1901), *Report on Chemical Instruction in Germany and the Growth and Present Condition of the German Chemical Industries.* Miscellaneous Diplomatic and Consular Reports (Cd. 430-416).

Rosen, G. (1951), An American Doctor in Paris in 1828: Selections from the Diary of Peter Solomon Townsend, M.D. *J. Hist. Med. Allied Sci.,* 6:64-115.

————— (1968), *Madness in Society.* Chicago: University of Chicago Press.

Rosenbach, O. (1903), *Nervöse Zustände und ihre psychische Behandlung.* 2nd ed. Berlin: Kornfeld.

Rosin, H. (1907), Review of Stekel's *Die Ursachen der Nervosität. Berl. klin. Wschr.,* 44:727.

Ross, D. (1969), The "Zeitgeist" and American Psychology. *J. Hist. Behav. Sci.,* 5:256-262.

Sadger, I. (1907), Die Bedeutung der psychoanalytischen Methode nach Freud. *Zntlbl. f. Nervenh. u. Psychiat.,* 30:41-52.

Sanborn, F. B., ed. (1898), *Memoirs of Pliny Earle, M.D.* Boston: Damrell & Upham.

Scherner, K. A. (1861), *Das Leben des Traumes.* Berlin: Schindler.

Schilpp, P. A., ed. (1957), *The Philosophy of Karl Jaspers.* New York: Tudor.

Schmidt, R., ed. (1923), *Die Philosophie der Gegenwart in Selbstdarstellungen,* Vol. 4. Leipzig: Meiner.

Schneider, C. M. (1901), Review of Freud's *Die Traumdeutung. Jahrb. f. philosoph. u. spekul. Theol.,* 15:475-476.

Schönau, W. (1968), *Sigmund Freuds Prosa.* Stuttgart: Metzlersche Verlagsbuchhandlung.

Schrenck-Notzing, A. von (1904), *Die Traumtänzerin Magdeleine G.: Eine psychologische Studie über Hypnose und dramatische Kunst.* Stuttgart: Enke.

Schultz, J. H. (1952), *Psychotherapie: Leben und Werk grosser Ärzte.* Stuttgart: Hippokrates-Verlag, Marquardt.

Schumann, P. W. (1901), Review of Störring's *Vorlesungen über Psychopathologie. Vierteljahrsschr. f. wissenschaft. Philos.*, 25:124-130.

Schur, M. (1972), *Freud: Living and Dying.* New York: International Universities Press.

Seif, L. (1911), Autoreferat. *Zentralblatt für Psychoanalyse*, 1:607.

Seiffer, W. (1907), Review of Jung's *Über die Psychologie der Dementia Praecox. Berl. klin. Wschr.*, 44:1460.

Shakow, D. (1968), Ebbinghaus, Hermann. *International Encyclopedia of the Social Sciences*, Vol. 4. New York: Macmillan.

⸺ & Rapaport, D. (1964), *The Influence of Freud on American Psychology. Psychol. Issues, Monogr.* No. 13. New York: International Universities Press.

Sokal, E. (1902), Wissenschaftliche Traumdeutung. *Die Gegenwart. Wschr. f. Lit., Kunst u. öffentl. Leben*, 61:84-85.

Sommer, R. (1901), *Diagnostik der Geisteskrankheiten für praktische Ärzte und Studierende*, 2nd ed. Berlin & Wien: Urban & Schwarzenberg.

Spielmeyer, W. (1906), Review of Freud's Bruchstück einer Hysterie-Analyse. *Zntlbl. f. Nerven. u. Psychiat.*, 29:322-324.

Stegmann, A. (1904), Kasuistischer Beitrag zur Behandlung von Neurosen mittels der kathartischen Methode (nach Freud). *Zntlbl. f. Nervenh. u. Psychiat.*, 27:770.

Stekel, W. (1906), Typische Träume. *Beilage* to the *Berliner Tageblatt*, No. 37.

⸺ (1907a), Die Ursachen der Nervosität. Neue Ansichten über deren Entstehung und Verhütung. *Dtsch. med. Wschr.*, 53:1321-1325, 1372-1375.

⸺ (1907b), Nervöse Angstzustände und deren Behandlung. *Medizin. Klin. Wschr. f. prakt. Ärzte*, 3:1039-1040, 1064-1067.

⸺ (1907c), Zwangsvorstellungen. *Beilage* to the *Berliner Tageblatt*, No. 9.

Stent, G. S. (1972), Prematurity and Uniqueness in Scientific Discovery. *Sci. Amer.*, 227:84-93.

Stepansky, P. (1976), The Empiricist as Rebel: Jung, Freud, and the Burdens of Discipleship. *J. Hist. Behav. Sci.*, 12:216-239.

Stern, W. (1901), Review of Freud's *Die Traumdeutung. Ztschr. f. Psychol. u. Physiol. d. Sinnesorg.*, 26:130-133.

Störring, G. (1900), *Mental Pathology in Its Relation to Normal Psychology*, trans. T. Loveday. London: Sonnenschein, 1907.

Strachey, J. (1958), Editor's Note to A Note on the Unconscious in Psycho-Analysis. *Standard Edition*, 12:257-259. London: Hogarth Press.

⸺ (1966), Editor's Introduction to Papers on Hypnotism and Suggestion. *Standard Edition.* 1:63-69. London: Hogarth Press.

Stransky, E. (1907), Review of Jung's *Über die Psychologie der Dementia Praecox. Ztschr. f. Psychol.*, 45:394-398.

Strohmayer, W. (1903), Zur Charakteristik der Zwangsvorstellungen als 'Abwehrneurose.' *Zntlbl. f. Nerven u. Psychiat.*, 14:317-325.

Strümpell, A. von (1892), *Über die Entstehung und die Heilung von Krankheiten durch Vorstellungen.* Erlangen: Junge.

_____ (1895), Review of Breuer and Freud's *Studien über Hysterie*. *Dtsch. Ztschr. f. Nervenh.*, 8:159-161.

Sunnec, B. (1902), Review of Theodor Dunin's *Die Grundsätze der Behandlung der Neurasthenie und Hysterie. Fortschr. d. Med.*, 20:973-975.

Taton, R., ed. (1961), *The History of Science*, Vol. 3, Pt. 1: *Science in the Nineteenth Century*. trans. A. J. Pomerans. New York: Basic Books, 1965.

Trosman, H. (1969), The Cryptomnesic Fragment in the Discovery of Free Association. In: Freud: The Fusion of Science and Humanism, ed. J. E. Gedo & G. H. Pollock. *Psychol. Issues*, Monogr. Nos. 34/35: 229-253. New York: International Universities Press, 1976.

Umpfenbach, [F.] (1896), Review of Breuer and Freud's *Studien über Hysterie*. *Ztschr. f. Psychol. u. Physiol. d. Sinnesorg.*, 10:308-309.

_____ (1906), Review of Freud's Bruchstück einer Hysterie-Analyse. *Ztschr. f. Psychol. u. Physiol. d. Sinnesorg.*, 43:239-240.

_____ (1907), Review of Freud's Tatbestandsdiagnostik und Psychoanalyse. *Ztschr. f. Psychol.*, 45:298-299.

Veith, I. (1965), *Hysteria: The History of a Disease*. Chicago & London: The University of Chicago Press.

Vereins- und Congressberichte: Wiener Briefe (1895). *Münch. med. Wschr.*, 42:1092-1093.

Vogt, O. (1898-1899), Zur Methodik der ätiologischen Erforschung der Hysterie; Normalpsychologische Einleitung in die Psychopathologie der Hysterie; Zur Kritik der psychogenetischen Erforschung der Hysterie. *Zeitsch. f. Hypnot.*, 8:65-83, 208-277, 342-355.

Voss, [G.] (1907), Review of Freud's Zur Psychopathologie des Alltagslebens. 2. Aufl. *Schmidts Jahrb.*, 296:107-108.

Wanke, G. (1926), *Psychoanalyse: Geschichte, Wesen, Aufgaben und Wirkung. Für Ärzte, Geistliche und Juristen sowie für Eltern, Lehrer und Erzieher*, 2nd ed. Halle a. S.: Marhold.

Warda, W. (1900), Ein Fall von Hysterie, dargestellt nach der kathartischen Methode von Breuer and Freud. *Mschr. F. Psychiat. u. Neurol.*, 7:301, 471.

_____ (1902), Über Zwangsvorstellungspsychosen. *Mschr. f. Psychiat. u. Neurol.*, 12.

_____ (1903), Zur Pathologie der Zwangsneurose. *J. f. Psychol. u. Neurol.*, 2:4-17.

_____ (1907), Zur Pathologie und Therapie der Zwangsneurose. *Mschr. f. Psychiat. u. Neurol.*, 22:Ergänzungsheft, 149-160.

Watt, H. J. (1905), Experimentelle Beiträge zu einer Theorie des Denkens. *Arch. f. d. ges. Psychol.*, 4:289-436.

Wedekind, F. (1891), Spring's Awakening. *Five Tragedies of Sex*, introd. L. Feuchtwanger. London: Vision Press, 1952.

Weil, — (1894), Review of Freud's Quelques considérations pour une étude comparative des paralysies motrices organiques et hystériques. *Neurol. Centralbl.*, 13:226-227.

Weygandt, W. (1901), Review of Freud's *Die Traumdeutung. Zntlbl. f. Nervenh. u. Psychiat.*, 24:548-549.

_____ (1904), Review of Freud's Zur Psychopathologie des Alltagslebens. *Jahresbericht über d. Leistungen . . . d. Neurol. u. Psychiat.*, 8:964.

_____ (1907), Kritische Bemerkungen zur Psychologie der Dementia Praecox. *Mschr. f. Psychiat. u. Neurol.*, 22:289-302.

Whyte, L. L. (1960), *The Unconscious before Freud*. Garden City, N.Y.: Doubleday Anchor Books, 1962.

Wittels, F. (1924), *Sigmund Freud: His Personality, His Teaching, and His School*, trans. E. Paul & C. Paul. London: Allen & Unwin.

―――― (1931), *Freud and His Time*, trans. L. Brink. New York: Liveright.

Wundt, W. (1863), *Vorlesungen über Menschen- und Thierseele*, 2 vols. Leipzig: Voss.

―――― (1893), *Grundzüge der physiologischen Psychologie*, 2 vols., 4th ed. Leipzig: Engelmann.

―――― (1901), *Outlines of Psychology*, 2nd rev. Engl. ed. from 4th rev. German ed., trans. C. H. Judd. Leipzig: Engelmann, 1902.

―――― (1902), *Principles of Physiological Psychology*, Vol. 1, trans. E. B. Titchener. London: Sonnenschein; New York: Macmillan, 1904.

―――― (1903), *Grundzüge der physiologischen Psychologie*, Vol. 3, 5th ed. Leipzig: Engelmann.

―――― (1905), *Outlines of Psychology*, 3rd rev. Eng. ed. from 7th rev. German ed., trans. C. H. Judd. Leipzig: Engelmann, 1907.

―――― (1907), Ueber Ausfrageexperimente und über die Methoden zur Psychologie des Denkens. *Psychol. Stud.*, 3:301-360.

―――― (1908), Kritische Nachlese zur Ausfragemethode. *Arch. f. d. ges. Psychol.*, 11:445-459.

―――― (1908-1911), *Grundzüge der physiologischen Psychologie*, 3 vols., 6th ed. Leipzig: Engelmann.

Wyrsch, J. (1956), Über die Bedeutung von Freud und Kraepelin für die Psychiatrie. *Nervenarzt*, 27:529-535.

yg [Wilhelm Weygandt] (1901), Review of Freud's *Die Traumdeutung*. *Literar. Zntbl. Dtschlnd.*, 52:cols. 1494-1496.

Young, R. M. (1970), *Mind, Brain and Adaptation in the Nineteenth Century: Cerebral Localization and Its Biological Context from Gall to Ferrier*. Oxford: Clarendon Press.

Zeitschrift für Psychologie (1890-1908), I. Abteilung of *Ztschr. f. Psychol. u. Physiol. d. Sinnesorg.*, ed. H. Ebbinghaus. Hamburg & Leipzig.

Zentralblatt für Psychoanalyse: Medizin. Mschr. f. Seelenk. (1911), ed. S. Freud; Managing Editor, W. Stekel. Wiesbaden: Bergmann.

Zentralblatt für Psychoanalyse: Medizin. Mschr. f. Seelenk. (1912), ed. S. Freud; Managing Editor, W. Stekel. Wiesbaden: Bergmann.

Ziehen, T. (1898), *Psychotherapie*. Berlin & Wien: Urban & Schwarzenberg.

―――― (1902), *Psychiatrie für Ärzte und Studirende Bearbeitet*, 2nd ed. Leipzig: Hirzel.

―――― (1904), Review of Freud's *Zur Psychopathologie des Alltagslebens*. *Dtsch. med. Wschr.*, 30:1251-1252.

Zilboorg, G. (1941), *A History of Medical Psychology*. New York: Norton.

Zweig, S. (1945), *The World of Yesterday*. New York: Viking.

INTERVIEWS AND LETTERS

INTERVIEWS

Hilda C. Abraham, July 10, 1968
Mrs. Karl Abraham, July 10, 1968
Therese Benedek, December 27, 1967
Franz S. Cohn, March 14, 1968
Kurt Eissler, February, 1963
Hanna Fenichel, January 6, 1968
S. H. Foulkes, July 9, 1968
Greta Frankley-Gerstenberg, March 13, 1968
Thomas French, December 27, 1967
Erich Fromm (telephone interview), April 4, 1968
George Gero, December 13, 1966
Elisabeth Goldner, March 27, 1968
Martin Grotjahn, January 3, 1968
Joachim A. Haenel, January 2, 1968
Heinz Hartmann, January, 1963
    and December 15, 1966
Max Horkheimer, July 13, 1968
Edith Jacobson, May 2, 1963
Bernard Kamm, December 27, 1967
Hans J. Kleinschmidt, February, 1963
Marianne Kris, December 19, 1966
Eva Landauer, March 27, 1968
Mrs. Karl Landauer, March 27, 1968
Harold D. Lasswell, March 8, 1963
Bertram Lewin, April 3, 1968
Ernst Lewy, January 4, 1968
Henry Lowenfeld, June 14, 1968
Hilda Maas, July 9, 1968
Alexander Mitscherlich, July 12, 1968
Fritz Moellenhoff, December 27, 1967
Sandor Rado, March 11, 1963
Annie Reich, December 14, 1966
Theodor Reik, December 9, 1966
Edith Weigert, March 13, 1968

347

LETTERS

Theodor Adorno, September 5, 1963
Hannah Arendt, May 18, 1966
Renée Gicklhorn, June 10, 1968
Klaus D. Hoppe, September 14, 1966
Werner Kemper, March 13, 1963
Nolan D. C. Lewis, September 9, 1966
Wolfgang Loch, March 20, 1963
Heinrich Meng, February 6, 1967
Kurt Rossmann, July 10, 1966

INDEX

349

ABOUT THE AUTHOR

HANNAH S. DECKER, Ph.D., is a historian of modern Germany. Upon the completion of a Josiah Macy Fellowship in the History of Medicine and the Biological Sciences, she taught in the psychiatry departments of the Albert Einstein College of Medicine and the Cornell University Medical College. Since 1974 she has been an Assistant Professor of History at the University of Houston and an Adjunct Assistant Professor of Psychiatry at the University of Texas Medical Branch in Galveston. Her articles on the histories of European psychiatry and psychoanalysis have appeared in various journals and collections of papers.

PSYCHOLOGICAL ISSUES